Jon Herieff

BEGINNINGS
and BEYOND

Guest Editors
EDITH M. DOWLEY
K. EILEEN ALLEN
JOSEPH H. STEVENS, JR.
THELMA HARMS
DAVID ELKIND
BETTYE M. CALDWELL
ANN PIESTRUP

Contributor
GAY SPITZ
*Teacher, Hartnell College Laboratory
    Training School
Salinas, California*

BEGINNINGS
and BEYOND

Foundations
in Early Childhood
Education

ANN MILES GORDON
Executive Director
National Association of Episcopal Schools
New York, New York

KATHRYN WILLIAMS BROWNE
The Bing School
Stanford University
Stanford, California

DELMAR PUBLISHERS INC.

To my beloved and remarkable children,
Andy and Libby Miles

—AMG

To Julia Andrus Browne, with hope for
a life of discovery, love, and wonder

—KWB

Cover photographic image by Nancy Martin

Delmar Staff
Administrative Editor: Adele Morse O'Connell
Production Editor: Gerry East

For information, address Delmar Publishers Inc.
2 Computer Drive West, Box 15–015
Albany, New York 12212-5015

Printed in the United States of America
Published Simultaneously in Canada
by Nelson Canada
A Division of International Thomson Limited

10 9 8 7 6 5 4 3 2

Library of Congress Cataloging in Publication Data
Gordon, Ann Miles.
  Beginnings and beyond.

  Includes index.
  1. Education, Preschool—Addresses, essays, lectures. 2. Education, Preschool—Curricula—Addresses,
essays, lectures. 3. Child development—Addresses,
essays, lectures. I. Browne, Kathryn Williams.
II. Title.
LB1140.2.G578 1985   372'.21   84–23000
ISBN 0–8273–2282–8
ISBN 0–8273–2283–6 (instructor's guide)

Contents

Beginnings and Beyond was developed to promote the competence and effectiveness of new teachers through a presentation of basic knowledge, skills, attitudes, and philosophies—an understanding of which is essential to delivering quality child care. The text is based on the premise that new teachers must have opportunities to learn fundamental skills as they begin their teaching experience. Once they have mastered these skills, they can address themselves more fully to other areas of the teaching profession.

While the text is geared primarily to the student who will be teaching young children, it has relevance and application as a resource and reference for all teachers who want to reflect on the basic issues that surround early childhood. Parent aides, volunteers, and administrators will find it a valuable resource. The content is also applicable to a variety of settings: day care, nursery school, campus laboratory, parent cooperative center, and Head Start programs.

ORGANIZATION OF THE TEXT

Through a series of six questions (each of which demarcates a section of the text), the student is exposed to some of the root issues of early childhood education. In basic inquiry form, we pose the following questions:

What is the field of early childhood education? Section I sets out the historical framework. Chapter 1 gives an overview of major historical landmarks, from Froebel to Follow-Through. In Chapter 2, pertinent early childhood terms are introduced as are the variety of early childhood programs that have been developed to meet a variety of needs.

Who is the young child? In Section II, the young child is defined through "word pictures," which describe the major characteristics of children from infancy through five years of age. Students will become familiar with expected behaviors in young children as a frame of reference for when they begin teaching. This section also defines several areas of "exceptionality" and prescribes several areas of mainstreaming. In Chapter 4, major developmental theories of Erikson, Piaget, and Freud are discussed with a focus on how they are interrelated and incorporated into most early childhood settings. By adding developmental theory to an early childhood text, we hope the student will come to understand how children learn and will see those learning behaviors reflected in the children with whom they interact in the classroom.

Who are the teachers of young children? In this section, some of the varying teacher roles will be explored. The text will address such issues as how the teacher is—and must be—responsive to children, their parents, each other, and themselves. Before moving into the arena of the classroom, the student will learn what it means to have a teaching philosophy and how important it is to be able to articulate it to others. In the subsequent chapters, the text moves into the classroom setting, focusing on a basic tool: reading the child through observational techniques. Chapter 7 will explore ways of talking to children and effective methods for guiding and directing their behavior. The final chapter of this section concentrates on establishing cooperative and effective home–school relations.

What is the setting? In this section, the student will learn to identify the salient features of the physical space, the temporal environment, and the interpersonal setting. Guidelines for establishing and utilizing physical space (both indoors and out) are set forth in ways that reflect sound child development principles. The last chapter in this section, Chapter 10, speaks to the interpersonal environment, exploring and evaluating the complex relationships between adults in the school, which affect the climate created in each setting. By placing these two chapters in the same section, we imply the linkage between program and environmental goals and how they are met.

What is being taught? Traditionally, educators title this section "curriculum," yet the student must become aware that this entails more than art projects and fingerplays. It is our belief that, to determine what is being taught in the classroom, we must first know how children learn and what happens to them through their play with one another. Therefore, the first chapter of this section, Chapter 11, explores curriculum as it relates to children's play, building heavily on Section II by pulling together the relationships between the child, the theory, and the implementation of the theory within the classroom curriculum.

We believe that the perspective to build curriculum comes from an understanding of the nature of the child, so each of the three subsequent chapters begins with general principles of child growth and development. Exploration of some basic curricular areas follows, with examples of how these childhood processes are best expressed in the early childhood format. The two largest curriculum chapters, Chapters 13 and 14, are divided into separate units: growth and development, skills in the early childhood years, and the teacher's role. This allows for flexibility in teaching the content, yet demonstrates to the student that development, while integrated, can be separated into meaningful components for greater understanding.

How do we teach for tomorrow? This section identifies current major issues in both early childhood and education as a whole. Educational issues (the status of the profession, the use of computers in early childhood, and bilingual education) are explored. Childhood crises and children's programs and services related to social issues confronting today's parents and families are also identified.

FEATURES OF THE TEXT

The six-question approach is one we feel helps beginning teachers make sense of what they are doing in the classroom with children. At the beginning of each chapter, learning objectives, in the form of "questions for thought," are set forth. The content of the chapters reflects these objectives both directly and indirectly. Concrete suggestions are given for implementing the learning experiences suggested within the text of the chapter, and numerous "real-life" classroom examples help reinforce the concepts presented. A brief summary capsulizes the content of the chapter, and review questions and student activities reinforce the material.

A unique feature of *Beginnings and Beyond* is the guest editorials that appear at the beginning of each section of the text. These editorials have been contributed by nationally renowned leaders in the field of early childhood education, and each addresses a relevant and important issue that affects teaching the young child. Each complements the information offered within the text. For history and programs, Edith Dowley fascinates us with her experiences at the Kaiser Child Care Centers during World War II; Eileen Allen helps us struggle with a definition of the young child, while Joe Stevens helps teachers define themselves and their role. Thelma Harms suggests ways to capitalize on the environment as a teaching tool, and David Elkind prompts the reader to think about the content of what we teach. Both Bettye Caldwell and Ann Piestrup discuss pertinent issues that will challenge teachers in the decade to come.

Rather than include separate chapters on multiculturalism and sexual stereotyping in early childhood, we chose to model our concerns in several ways. Photographs show both men and women as teachers, with a crosscultural and multiracial emphasis. The pictures of children represent the broad range of colors and flavors available in all early childhood settings. Girls and boys are depicted in active and passive roles, both in examples cited and in photographs. We believe that weaving a multicultural perspective and consciousness throughout the text will emphasize it as an overriding issue more clearly than treating it separately.

PHILOSOPHY

Beginnings and Beyond is based on the premise that as teachers of young children we are in the business of helping them "get started." We are aware of how important beginnings are. So, too, we are committed to helping new teachers in their beginnings—to make sense of what they are doing without losing the excitement of teaching, yet with an increasing understanding of the underlying relationship between children's behaviors and good teaching techniques. In understanding typical, predictable child growth and behavior, new teachers acquire a foundation for building good programs, for determining good teaching styles, for establishing good physical environments in which optimal growth is fostered, and for promoting good support systems between home and school.

ABOUT THE AUTHORS

Ann Miles Gordon is Executive Director of the National Association of Episcopal Schools. Her early childhood education experiences include six years as Head Teacher at the Bing School, Stanford University; Lecturer at the Department of Psychology, Stanford University; and adjunct faculty member at San Jose City College, Cañada College, West Valley College, and the College of New Rochelle. She is also the mother of two.

Ann has coauthored many articles on children's spiritual development and has served for over 15 years as a consultant in religious education and curriculum. Through her writing she hopes to give back to other teachers and children some of the gifts she has received, and to contribute to better lives for all children.

Kathryn Williams Browne, most recently Head Teacher at the Bing School, Stanford University, has also been a Lecturer in the Stanford Department of Psychology. She chose to become an early childhood educator when she realized that to truly understand children's development, one needs to spend time with children. Kate became involved with this book as an extension of the support and networking she has experienced in the early childhood field. *Beginnings and Beyond* is another professional adventure—part of the stretching and self-challenging integral to her field.

Acknowledgments

The Bing School of Stanford University is a unique place. Long acknowledged as an outstanding setting for young children, "Bing," as we affectionately know it, has had great impact on those of us who have worked there. In the writing of this text, the Bing family of children, parents, and staff has played a pivotal role. We are grateful for the overwhelming support, enthusiasm, and encouragement we received from them. Most of all, we want to thank the four Bing directors—Edith Dowley, D. Michelle Irwin, Aphra Katzev, and Carol Young-Holt—for creating a climate that fostered our own professional growth and development.

Colleagues to whom we have turned time and again, and who gave us the benefit of their collective wisdom, are: K. Eileen Allen of the University of Kansas at Lawrence, Karen McLaughlin of the Bing School, Stanford University, and Gay Spitz of Hartnell Community College, Salinas, California. We also owe a debt of gratitude to former Bing teachers, Joan Ehrenreich and Becky Cooper, who allowed us to use some of their materials on team teaching, and to Susan Wickizer, also formerly of Bing, for her materials on special topics in language and cognition.

We are truly grateful for the important contributions of our guest editors: Edith M. Dowley, K. Eileen Allen, Joseph H. Stevens, Jr., Thelma Harms, David Elkind, Bettye M. Caldwell, and Ann Piestrup. They willingly shared their valuable insights with us, and we appreciate their added perspective to this text.

Photo credits are due the children, parents, and faculty of the Bing School, Stanford, California; to Miriam Kertzman of the Stride Rite Children's Centers in Cambridge, Massachusetts; to Margaret-Ann Brostrom of the Family Service Association of San Mateo County in Burlingame, California; to Stephanie Barry Agnew of Palo Alto, California; to Barbara Milliff of We Care Day Treatment Center in Concord, California; and to the University of Chicago Library. We gratefully acknowledge the extensive contribution their photographs have made to the project. All photographs not otherwise credited were taken by the authors.

To Libby Miles, grateful thanks for editing and research; and to Charles Hanna and Mary Jane Varno, deepest appreciation for manuscript typing. We thank Jeannette Thorp of the School of Education at Stanford University for arrangements of work space, secretarial assistance, and support. We are also indebted to those whose honest critique helped us focus and refine the manuscript, our reviewers: Peggy Teague, Lillian Oxtoby, Margaret Budz, and Robert Doan.

Adele Morse O'Connell redefined and gave new meaning to the word editor. Her perceptive understanding, gentle humor, and sensitivity have guided the direction of this manuscript in ways beyond our greatest imaginings. We extend to her our heartfelt thanks; we would only wish every author the same support, enthusiasm, and respect.

Finally, we appreciate the patience and forebearance throughout this project of our husbands, David Gordon and Martin Browne. Their willingness to put up with a life that included manuscripts and deadlines made a significant contribution.

BEGINNINGS
and BEYOND

SECTION I

EARLY CHILDHOOD EDUCATION IN THE SHIPYARDS

Edith M. Dowley

If you are thinking about working with young children as a career, perhaps you are wondering how early childhood education compares in prestige and importance with elementary or secondary education. Does it have a background of tradition? Is it truly a profession with the potential for growth and change? Can a student preparing to work with young children today look forward to a challenging, intellectually stimulating, and rewarding future in an early childhood profession?

My career with young children began during the Great Depression, a time of arrested economic growth and widespread unemployment. My undergraduate major and minors were in fields where job opportunities were, at the time, apparently hopeless. However, with the help of wise counselors and some very good luck, I spent two years in graduate study with outstanding professors of child development and worked as an assistant with nursery school teachers chosen as models of artistic technique and effective nurturers of young children. I found working with children so challenging and rewarding, I made it my life's work! Forty years later, when I "retired," I could truthfully say I was never disappointed.

All but two of those years were spent in university settings where research and theory questioned, modified, and sometimes changed our attitudes, interpretations, and reactions to child growth and behavior. They were years of growing and learning, of planning, struggling, and some accomplishments. No two years—actually no two days—were ever the same.

But this editorial is about a different, unforgettable experience I had with young children, far removed from a university setting, in a period of national crisis. It occurred during World War II, in an innovative project that not only was a remarkable solution to a problem for those times, but that also has special relevance and appropriateness, I believe, for the 1980s.

What Is the Field of Early Childhood Education?

G U E S T   E D I T O R I A L

In early 1943, the Kaiser Shipbuilding Corporation was faced with the necessity of employing more women to meet the stepped-up schedule for producing warships in their two shipyards in Portland, Oregon. Of the 12,000 women already employed, one third of them were mothers who had no place to leave their preschool children while they worked. Absenteeism among women was running 50 percent higher than among men and was contributing to slow-downs in production that seriously affected the war effort. The reasons most women gave for being late or for missing work were that the baby-sitter did not show up or a child was ill and could not be left at home until seen by a doctor. Henry Kaiser, reportedly in typical fashion, responded to the dilemma by saying that if mothers were worried about leaving their children, he would provide them with nurseries. He resolved to build the finest child care centers in the country.

Within a few weeks, architects were drawing plans for two child service centers to be placed at the entrances to the shipyards—one at Swan Island and the other at Oregon Yard. Paid for by the United States Maritime Commission and absorbed as part of the cost of building ships, these centers turned out to be not only very fine centers, but also the largest child care centers in the world.

Dr. Lois Meek Stolz, a well-known leader in the fields of child development and early childhood education, was chosen by Edgar Kaiser to direct the two child service centers. She planned the entire children's program and made provisions for staffing the centers. She brought James L. Hymes, Jr., former editor of *Progressive Education,* to the program as Manager of the Child Service Centers, and she recruited Dr. Miriam Lowenberg, a well-known nutritionist, to be responsible for the children's nutritional needs.

THE STAFF

Each center had a supervisor who was responsible for the total operation over all three shifts—day, swing, and graveyard. There were group supervisors, head teachers, assistant teachers, dieticians, and nurses under her direction. In addition, each center had a social worker who served as a liaison between the teachers in the centers and the parents in the shipyard. All of the staff members were recruited from nursery school training centers throughout the United States. All of the teachers had college degrees, and the supervisors and most of the head teachers had master's degrees and years of experience with children. They were young, energetic women "chosen for their comfortable qualities as well as for their scientific knowledge." (Jean Muir, from an article she wrote for the *Oregon Journal*, Sunday, December 12, 1943)

THE SETTING

The teaching staff began arriving in late October as the finishing touches were being made on the buildings. They found, to their delight, that the centers, although temporary, were beautifully and functionally designed. Each center was built around a large, octagonally shaped courtyard with four wading pools where children could play away from the hazards of traffic. The courtyard itself was grass-covered, with a hard-surfaced area designed for wheel toys that extended around the perimeter. Because of the long rainy season in Portland, covered porches, equipped with jungle gyms, climbing boxes, slides, and large, hollow blocks, connected the interior rooms to the grassy areas. Children could thus enjoy vigorous outdoor play every day of the year, regardless of the weather.

A cog-wheel plan of architecture provided for 15 rectangular playrooms (26′ by 49′) extending out from a central circular corridor. Between and opposite every two playrooms were smaller rooms for teachers' meetings, special play, or story times. Each of the 15 playrooms had windows on two sides to provide light and interesting views of the outside world. Window seats, low enough for children to sit on, were built so that the children could curl up on them and watch the ships, cars, trucks, and cranes in the busy shipyard below where their parents were working. This proved to be a special delight as darkness came and the yards were lighted, showing the outlines of the ships and their reflections in the water.

The interior colors were soft pastel shades of blue, yellow, and apricot, depending on the exposure of the individual room. Adult-height counterspace covered the expansive shelving where children could readily reach the many unit blocks, toys, games, books, and puzzles that were neatly and meaningfully stored there. Children's lockers, arranged like a dressing room unit, provided hooks for coats and jackets, a shelf for caps, mittens, and art work to take home, and a place for safekeeping of special possessions. Each room had its own toilet room with toilets and wash basins scaled to child size. Wash cloths and towels provided by the center were hung on hooks within the children's reach and marked with individual symbols matching the ones on their lockers.

There was a large room in each center, separated from the playrooms, where children could be cared for when they were ill. Comfortable cribs, like those used in children's hospitals, were placed in glass-sided cubicles that allowed children quiet places to sleep, eat, or sit up and play while recovering from colds, coughs, earaches, or upset tummies. A registered nurse was on duty at all times in the infirmary, and teachers planned and provided the play materials and projects for both the bed patients and those who were up and about.

Each center had a fully equipped, large, modern kitchen that was adequate for serving meals and snacks, over a 24-hour day, to some 400 children and their teachers. Large, heated rolling carts were available to deliver the china, silverware, and food to each room, where children were served at small, low tables. Usually, five children and a teacher dined together each day as a "family."

The architects thoughtfully included one additional feature: several large, square bath tubs raised two steps above the floor. These tubs allowed teachers, when necessary or desirable, to bathe a child without bending over. These tubs also provided safe places for children to "swim" and splash and engage in relaxing water play.

OPENING DAYS

The teaching staff, of which I was a part, arrived in Portland about two weeks before the centers opened. Until we found more permanent places to live, we were housed in a dormitory for female workers at the Swan Island shipyard. Each evening, we met with Dr. Hymes and the supervisors, building a common but shared philosophy about child care and our roles as educators. During the days, we prepared the playrooms in anticipation of the day when the children would arrive.

Oregon Center, where I was a group supervisor, opened its doors on November 8, 1943, to children, age 18 months to six years, of parents working on the day and swing shifts. On that day, a total of 67 children came to the center. We were, of course, very disappointed in this turnout. We realized, however, that the majority of people in the area had never even heard of a nursery school and were not able to imagine a children's center that would stay open twelve months a year, six days a week, and twenty-four hours a day! So we planned "open house" on Sundays and invited the public to tour the centers. We went down into the shipyards to talk to the workers about the child services available. Feature articles with many photographs appeared in the local newspapers. Gradually, more children were enrolled. By Christmas of that year, there were over 100 children being cared for in the center. In January, the graveyard shift was started, as was a Saturday and after-school program for older children. By August 27th, when Oregon Shipyard went on a seven-day work week, the Center was operating seven days a week, with an average daily attendance of 370 children.

Everything possible was done to keep workers on the job of building ships. Parents paid only nominal fees for child service: 75 cents a day for one child in a family and 50 cents for each additional child, paid by the week. If a child came seven days a week, parents were only charged for six days.

THE CHILDREN

The children we worked with in the Center were much the same as the children most of us had worked with before. Each was a unique individual, with distinctive characteristics and special needs. They had strong ties to their parents and families and depended on them for love, approval, and support. Mothers or fathers brought the children to their rooms at the Center each day before their shifts began, and picked them up after the shift ended. Day-shift children often spent nine or more hours in the Center as that was the longest shift. Day-shift parents were always in a hurry, it seemed, and were less able to spend time helping their children make the transition from home to school. Separating from their mothers and fathers was painful for some children at first. It was probably hardest of all for the 18-month-olds and two-year-olds to adjust to being left with strangers in a strange place for such long hours. Some of these little ones, most of whom had not yet begun to talk, cried for long periods and were difficult to comfort. Some refused to let anyone remove their coats, snowsuits, or hats all day, clinging to them as perhaps the last link with home and mother. They would stay on their feet, apart from the others even during snacks or meal times, unwilling to sit or to accept food from a strange table. Eventually, hunger would overcome this reluctance, and when teachers wisely left finger foods within their sight and reach, they devoured them quickly and covertly. Sleep, too, overcame them, even though they steadfastly resisted lying on a nursery school cot when invited to nap. Still in their heavy outdoor clothing, they would drop to the floor, asleep. Then, a teacher would carefully place the child on a cot close to an open window. The child would waken hours later, refreshed and on the way to trusting a smiling, loving teacher and the safety of the nursery school environment.

After working out in the cold and rain for long hours at a stretch, day-shift parents were very tired and in a hurry at the end of the day when they came to pick up their children. Some were cross and impatient as they hurried their preschoolers to avoid missing the bus or car-pool ride. There was no time to talk over their child's day with the teacher. So, teachers communicated with parents about their children by writing brief comments next to a child's name on a chart hung outside the playroom door. These comments had to be worded with great tact, we discovered. Even such comments as "John didn't finish his lunch" or "Betsy didn't take a nap today" could result in angry scolding or slapping of the child. We tried to emphasize the positive behaviors in our messages in order to make each child appear more lovable and interesting to parents.

For the children on the swing shift, life was quite different. They usually arrived early after a leisurely day at home or out shopping with their parents. Mothers and fathers on their way to work often stayed for a while at the center, reading stories or looking at toys or interesting things the children described to them the night before. There was a more relaxed atmosphere in the playrooms during the swing shift than during the day shift. This was evident in the conversations between children, and especially in their dramatic play. In contrast to the day-shift children, who rarely used the doll corner to "keep house," swing-shift children meticulously swept the floor, made the doll beds, set the table, bathed and dressed the dolls, and sat down quietly for pretend tea parties. In contrast, day-shift children, especially the four-year-olds, turned the sink and stove upside down in the doll corner and "launched them" in noisy excitement. They were more aggressive in their play and more destructive of play materials. They probably had fewer occasions to observe their mothers making beds, preparing meals, or enjoying homemaking tasks.

Swing-shift children were served supper as a group, after which they had time to play, listen to stories, enjoy music and play games, paint pictures and, in summertime, play outside until dark. They then undressed and went to bed. The children were then awakened and dressed before their tired parents arrived.

ADDITIONAL SERVICES

The Center also tried to provide time-saving services to parents that might relieve some of the stresses under which they worked. Home Service Foods began in January of 1944. Precooked meals, planned by Dr. Lowenberg, were prepared in the centers' kitchens. Priced at fifty cents each, one order was ample for a working man or woman, and a single portion would serve two preschool children. These ready-packaged meals were ordered two or more days in advance and contained the main course and dessert, the foods that usually required the most preparation time. Directions were included for heating and serving, and suggestions for additional foods to round out the meal were offered.

In time, other services were added, such as mending children's clothes, buying their shoelaces, and haircutting. In February, a program of immunizations was begun. Children whose parents had not been able to arrange for the necessary shots required for nursery school attendance were able to receive their shots at the Center. Teachers, in the absence of parents, brought children in turn to the Center's physician, holding them on their laps to reassure and comfort them while they got their shots.

PARENT–TEACHER INTERACTIONS

Parent–teacher conferences were usually difficult to arrange. We found ways to talk briefly with a mother by walking with her to a waiting bus or car. Teachers invited parents into the playrooms to see the art work of their children or to view special block buildings preserved for their admiration.

Parent meetings took place occasionally when dinner was served to the mothers and fathers in one room while their children had dinner in another. Group supervisors went down into the shipyard to talk to a parent when it seemed necessary. On these occasions, I found myself surrounded by fathers and mothers who eagerly asked "What was my child doing when you left?" As parents realized how much teachers knew and cared about their children, they made time for interviews and shared their problems and pleasures with them.

PROGRAM RESULTS

One of the most gratifying aspects of the Kaiser experience was the steady growth and change we observed in the children. The outdoor play, regular sleep and rest, and especially the excellent nutrition wrought dramatic improvements in the health and appearance of many of the children. Before the centers opened, some of the children had no regular meal times but ate whatever "handouts" (usually bread) were made available to them by neighbors or caretakers. When they first came to the centers, bread was the only food some children would eat. After the children seemed comfortable with the nursery school routines, Dr. Lowenberg omitted bread from the meals entirely. The hungry children began to taste and enjoy a wide variety of unfamiliar flavors and textures. Later on, when bread was again included in the form of small sandwiches, they were accepted as just another food.

Patience and planning reduced aggression and destructive behavior and, as children were convinced that their teachers really liked them and cared what happened to them, they confided in them their fears and worries and sought comfort and assurance from them. An emerging sense of trust freed the children to develop confidence in their bodies. Their motor skills increased, their self-esteem was enhanced, and they grew more friendly, more tolerant of one another, and more giving.

We also saw measurable growth in language development. Opportunities to develop the ability to listen to a teacher's direction, to enjoy longer and more complex stories, and to verbalize shared experiences with pets or on walks was part of the program planning.

Many good things happened in the Child Service Centers in the Kaiser Shipyards—for children, for parents, for the industry, for all of us. We all had a part in winning the war as "champion shipbuilders," as we were told, and for that we were proud. The head of the Maritime Commission told the teachers that, without their help, it would have been impossible to keep the shipyards in production seven days a week. Parents told us that when they were tired and tempted to sleep late on Sunday morning, their children would awaken them, saying "Get up, get up. If you don't go to work, we don't get to go to school." When the centers were closed in 1945 at the end of the war, records showed that "3,811 children were taken care of—a total of 250,000 child care days—which freed almost 2 million working hours for the women." (Stanford University Campus Report, Interview with Lois Stolz, March 30, 1983)

But I think the most remarkable, the best thing that happened was that, in a time of war, when mothers of preschool children worked eight and nine hours a day, six or seven days a week, the lives of almost 4,000 children were made happy, healthy, and in some ways, better than they ever were before. This could only happen as a combination of skillful professional planning, strong professional leadership, and some of the best teachers the nursery school profession has ever prepared. I believe that all children deserve to benefit from that combination, especially in their early years.

You who are beginning the study of early childhood education have many career paths open to you. Ours is a profession that is constantly growing, branching out in many directions and ready to meet emerging challenges in flexible, innovative ways. At present, employment prospects may look discouraging and preschool teachers' salaries substandard, but these conditions must change. In a society where 50 percent of women work for a living, we can no longer function without a nationwide, high-quality program for the care and education of children under six years of age.

When this happens, we must wonder whether there will be enough professionally prepared specialists in the field to provide leadership. Will there be enough teachers who are knowledgeable about the nature and development of infants and young children and sensitive to their individual needs? Will there be enough enlightened and caring personnel to license and monitor (with in-service education) facilities and programs for an entire nation's children? You—and those who follow in your footsteps—hold the answers to these questions.

EDITH M. DOWLEY has been involved in early childhood education for fifty years. She was a group supervisor in the Kaiser Child Service Centers, and later became the first director of Stanford University's Bing Nursery School, a position she retained until 1975. She served as a national consultant to Project Head Start from 1965 to 1968, and from 1971 to 1972 she was a member of the California Task Force on Early Childhood Education.

Dr. Dowley has been a visiting instructor at the University of Victoria (British Columbia, Canada) and the University of Hawaii and has conducted summer workshops in Santa Barbara and Berkeley, California. Dr. Dowley is currently Professor Emerita of Psychology and Education at Stanford University.

1

History of Early Childhood Education

Questions for Thought

- Why is it important to know about the history of early childhood education?
- What other fields have influenced the development of the early childhood philosophy? What has been their impact?
- Why are the roots of psychology and early childhood education so intertwined?
- What have been the basic themes in early education throughout history?
- How do current events—political, social, and economic—affect the direction of education?

Outline

I. Introduction to the Field
  A. Why History?
  B. Defining the Terms

II. European Influences
  A. Through Medieval Times
  B. Comenius
  C. Rousseau
  D. Pestalozzi
  E. Froebel
  F. Montessori

III. American Influences
  A. Colonial Days
  B. John Dewey
  C. Kindergarten
  D. Nursery Schools
    1. Establishment in America
    2. Abagail Eliot
  E. Midcentury Developments
    1. The Depression
    2. Kaiser Child Care Centers
  F. Head Start

IV. Interdisciplinary Influences
  A. Medicine
    1. Sigmund Freud
    2. Arnold Gesell
    3. Benjamin Spock
    4. T. Berry Brazelton
  B. Education
    1. The Macmillan Sisters
    2. The Child Study Movement
    3. The British Infant School
  C. Psychology

V. Themes in Early Childhood Education
  A. Ethic of Social Reform
  B. Importance of Childhood
  C. Transmitting Values

VI. Summary

VII. Review Questions

VIII. Learning Activities

IX. Bibliography

INTRODUCTION TO THE FIELD

Early childhood education has a rich and exciting history. The story of its development is the chronicle of people who took bold steps toward improving children's lives. Critical events have had a hand in shaping the history of early childhood education. Across the globe and through the centuries, the education of children has evolved.

Why History?

Most early childhood students and many educators know little about the origins of their chosen profession. The names of Rousseau, Froebel, Montessori, and Dewey may not have much significance at this time (although many teachers are familiar with some of their techniques), but knowing something about the roots of this profession is important.

First of all, there is a sense of support that comes from knowing that history. It gives one pause to reflect that what is referred to as "education" in the 1980s stems from ancient times. Socrates, Plato, and Aristotle are a part of the philosophical foundation on which this field is built. Even in ancient Greece and Rome, schools were established where literature, the arts, and science were taught.

Knowing that early childhood philosophy has deep roots is inspiring and helps professionals express their ideas today. The past as well as the present and future must be considered when developing sound educational programs for young children. The tenets expressed by past educators help develop better methods of teaching. Looking at history gives an overview of how various ages looked at children and their learning, based on the religious, political, and economic pressures of the time. Reviewing the professional record demonstrates how the needs of society affect education. Perhaps some of the mistakes of the past can be avoided if history is remembered.

Drawing upon knowledge of the past creates an awareness of changes in education. Into the fabric of early childhood education are woven many threads of influence that are responsible for current philosophies. In this chapter, the people, the ideas, and the circumstances that have influenced early childhood are introduced by examining historical forces in both Europe and America that have affected educational trends. Educational changes of a more recent nature follow. The impact of other disciplines, such as medicine and psychology, and the recurrent themes of early childhood education are also explored.

Defining the Terms

The term *early childhood education* refers to group settings deliberately intended to effect developmental changes in children from birth to the age of entering first grade (Katz, 1970). More recent definitions include the elementary years as well (Evans, 1975). For our purposes, we shall define early childhood as from infancy through third grade. That is roughly from birth to eight years of age. It is during these years that the foundation for future learning is set; these are the building block years, during which a child learns to walk, talk, print, and count. In later years, that same child builds on these skills to be able to climb mountains, speak a foreign language, learn cursive writing, and understand multiplication.

EUROPEAN INFLUENCES

Through Medieval Times

The definition of childhood has varied greatly throughout history. For example, before the Renaissance children were considered adults by age seven. A society's definition of childhood influences how it educates its children.

The education of young children was fairly simple before the fifteenth century. There was no educational system, and the way of life was uncomplicated as well. Children learned mostly through their parents or by apprenticeship outside the family. Through medieval times (approximately the fifth through the thirteenth centuries) childhood hardly lasted beyond infancy. The child was expected and encouraged to move into adulthood as fast as possible. Survival was the primary goal in life. Since the common religious belief was that people were naturally evil, children had to be directed, punished, and corrected constantly. Ironically, it was during this time that the concept of equality and brotherhood emerged, a continuing concern to educators today.

With the Renaissance in the fourteenth century and the Reformation in the sixteenth century, society became more enlightened. Several political, social, economic, and religious movements combined. The German school system had its beginnings established at this time and would continue to influence education in all parts of Europe. People changed the way they looked at children and their education. Towns grew and expanded, and there was an opportunity to move to new lands. Living conditions improved and infant mortality waned. Children were living longer. The acquisition of knowledge and skills at an earlier age became important. If educated, children could be expected to help their family improve its situation. Parents found they needed help in teaching their children.

Comenius

John Amos Comenius offered help in teaching children. One of the best educators of the sixteenth century, he wrote the first picture book for children. Called *Orbis Pictus* (*The World of Pictures*), it was a guide for teachers that included training of the senses and the study of nature. Comenius fostered the belief that education should follow the natural order of things. In other words, children's development follows a timetable of its own and their education should reflect that fact. He felt teachers must observe and work with this natural order, the timetable, to ensure successful learning. This idea was later reflected in Montessori's sensitive periods and Piaget's stages of development. Today it is recognized as the issue of *school readiness*.

Comenius also stressed a basic concept that is now taken for granted: learning by doing. He encouraged parents to let their children play with other children of the same age. He also reflected the growing social reform that would educate the poor as well as the rich.

Rousseau

After Comenius, new thoughts were everywhere in Europe. Darwin brought a change to science. The time was ripe for new ideas about childhood. Jean Jacques Rousseau, a writer and philosopher of the middle 1700s, brought forth the idea that children were not inherently evil, but naturally good. He reasoned that education should reflect this goodness and allow spontaneous interests and activities of the children. Soon, children were actively involved in their own education. Each child was considered unique and valuable. While he was not an educator, Rousseau offered insights that were valuable. He suggested that school atmosphere should be less restrained and more flexible to meet the needs of the children. He insisted on using concrete teaching materials, leaving the abstract and symbolism for later years. Rousseau maintained that sense perception was the key to education. His *naturalism* has affected thinking of educators ever since. Pestalozzi, Froebel, and Montessori were greatly influenced by him. In Europe, his ideas had a ripple effect that sent waves across the Atlantic Ocean.

Pestalozzi

Swiss educator Johann Heinrick Pestalozzi helped develop some classic principles of education. Like Rousseau, he used nature study as part of the curriculum and believed that good education meant the development of the senses. Pestalozzi stressed the idea of the *integrated curriculum* which would develop the whole child. He wanted education to be of the hand, the head, and the heart of the child. Along with intellectual content, he proposed that practical skills be taught in the schools. He differed from Rousseau in that he proposed teaching chil-

Cornix cornicatur, à à	A a
The *Crow* crieth.	
Agnus balat, b è è è	B b
The *Lamb* blaiteth.	
Cicàda stridet, cì cì	C c
The *Grasshopper* chirpeth.	
Upupa dicit, du du	D d
The *Whooppoo* saith.	
Infans ejulat, è è è	E e
The *Infant* crieth.	
Ventus flat, fi fi	F f
The *Wind* bloweth.	
Anser gingrit, ga ga	G g
The *Goose* gagleth.	
Os halat, hà'h hà'h	H h
The *Mouth* breatheth out.	
Mus mintrit, ì ì ì	I i
The *Mouse* chirpeth.	
Anas tetrinnit, kha, kha	K k
The *Duck* quaketh.	
Lupus ululat, lu ulu	L
The *Wolf* howleth. [mum	
Ursus murmurat, mum-	M m
The *Bear* grumbleth.	

FIGURE 1.1 *Orbis Pictus*

dren in groups rather than using a tutor with an individual child. Pestalozzi's work detailed some procedures for mothers to use at home with their children. He could well be named the first home trainer.

Froebel

The work of Friedrich Wilhelm Froebel was perhaps the major influence on childhood education of the 1800s. He is known to us as the father of the kindergarten, not only for giving it a name, but for devoting his life to the development of a system of education for young children. The German word *kindergarten* means "children's garden," and that is what Froebel felt best expressed what he wanted for children under six years of age. He advocated the radical thought that children should be able to play, to have toys, and to be with trained teachers. He started the first training school. Over one hundred years ago, Froebel's kindergartens included blocks, pets, and fingerplays. Froebel observed children and came to understand how they learned and what they liked to do. He developed the first educational toys, which he termed "gifts." Some of his theories about children and their education later influenced Montessori and were reflected in the educational materials she developed.

Montessori

At the turn of the century, Maria Montessori became the first female physician in Italy. She worked in the slums of Rome with poor children and with mentally retarded children. Sensing that what they lacked was proper motivation and environment, she opened a preschool, Casa di Bambini, in 1907. Montessori designed materials, classrooms, and a teaching procedure that proved her point to the astonishment of people all over Europe and America.

Before her, no one with "medical and psychiatric training had yet spelled out so clearly" the needs of the growing child (Robison, 1983). Her medical background added credibility to her findings and helped her ideas gain recognition in this country.

Through her enlightenment, child-sized furniture and materials are now used in classrooms. By focusing on the *sequential steps of learning*, Montessori developed a set of learning materials still used widely today. One of her most valuable contributions was a theory of how children learn. She believed that any task could be reduced to a series of small steps. By using this process, children could learn to sweep a floor, dress themselves, or multiply numbers.

Montessori materials are graded in difficulty and emphasize her interest in self-help skills. To foster this, she developed frames with buttons and laces so children could learn to be responsible for themselves when dressing. The layout of the room

---

> When the children are just making friends with the teacher and with each other, it is very interesting and profitable for them to formulate their mite of knowledge into a sentence, each one holding his ball high in the air with the right hand, and saying:
>   My ball is red like a cherry.
>   My ball is yellow like a lemon.
>   My ball is blue like the sky.
>   My ball is orange like a marigold.
>   My ball is green like the grass.
>   My ball is violet like a plum.

FIGURE 1.2 Fingerplays, which are common activities in today's early childhood programs, were also a part of Froebel's kindergarten programs. (Excerpted from Wiggin and Smith, *Froebel's Gifts,* Boston and New York: Houghton Mifflin Co., 1895, p. 22)

FIGURE 1.3 Maria Montessori designed materials, classrooms, and a learning method for young children. (Courtesy of American Montessori Society, New York, N.Y.)

and the distribution and presentation of materials furthered this concept. Montessori placed great emphasis on the environment—the "prepared environment," as she called it. A sense of order, a place for everything, and a clear rationale are hallmarks of the Montessori influence.

Her procedures as well as her materials contain *self-correcting* features. Nesting cylinders, for example, fit together only one way and are to be used that way. Montessori supported earlier educational ideas of sensory development; she felt that cognitive abilities stem from sensory discrimination. Thus, most of her equipment was *tactile* and enhanced the senses as well as the mind.

AMERICAN INFLUENCES
Colonial Days

The American educational system began in the Colonies. When thinking of Colonial America, people often envision the one-room schoolhouse. Indeed, this was the mainstay of education in the New England Colonies. However, children were sent to school primarily for religious reasons. Everyone needed to be able to read the Bible, the Puritan fathers reasoned. All children were sent to study, though historically boys were educated before girls. Not only the Bible was used in school, however; new materials like the New England Primer and the Horn Book were also used.

In the South, it was a different story. Plantation owners imported tutors from England to teach just their sons to read and rule. While the reasons were different, the results were similar: a very high percentage of adult readers. From these came the leaders of the American Revolution and the new nation.

After the Revolutionary War, there were no significant advances in education until the late 1800s. Leaders like Thomas Jefferson felt that knowledge ought to be available to all, but that opinion was not widely shared. Most of the post-Revolutionary period focused on growing crops and pioneering the frontier, not teaching and educating children. Even by the 1820s, education for the common man was not readily available. Industrialization

FIGURE 1.4 One-room New England schoolhouse

in both the North and South did little to encourage reading and writing skills. Manual labor and machine-operating skills were more important. While public schools were accepted in principle, in reality no tax basis was established to support them.

John Dewey

By the end of the 1800s, however, a nationwide reform movement had begun. In education, the *Progressive Movement,* as it was called, got its direction primarily through one individual, John Dewey (1858–1952).

Dewey was the first real American influence on American education. Raised in Vermont, he became a professor of philosophy at both the University of Chicago and Columbia University. In the years that followed, Dewey would be responsible for one of the greatest impacts on American education of all time.

Dewey believed that children were valuable and that childhood was an important part of their lives. At the same time, he felt that education should be integrated with life. As did Pestalozzi and Rousseau, Dewey felt that schools should focus on the nature of the child. Until this time, children were considered of little consequence. Childhood was rushed. Children as young as seven were a regular part of the work force—on the farms, in the mines, and in the factories. Dewey's beliefs about children and learning are summarized in Figure 1.5.

A new kind of school emerged from these ideals. Even the buildings began to take on a different look. Movable furniture replaced rows of benches. Children's projects, some still under construction, were found everywhere. The curriculum of the school began to focus on all of the basics, not just a few of the academics. If a group of six-year-olds decided to make a woodworking table, they would first have to learn to read in order to understand the directions. After calculating the cost, they would purchase the materials. In building the table, geometry, physics, and math were learned along the way. This was a group effort which encouraged children to work together in teams. Thus, children's social skills were developed along with reading, science,

and math. The teacher's role in the process was one of ongoing support, involvement, and encouragement.

Kindergarten

The word *kindergarten*—which is German for "children's garden"—is a delightful term. It brings to mind the image of young seedlings on the verge of blossoming. The similarity between caring for young plants and young children is not accidental. Froebel, the man who coined the word kindergarten, meant for that association to be made. As a flower opens from a bud, so too does a child go through a natural unfolding process. This idea—and ideal—are part of the kindergarten story.

The first kindergarten was a German school started by Froebel in 1837. Over a dozen years later, in 1856, Margaretha Schurz, a student of Froebel, opened the first kindergarten in the United States. It was for German-speaking children and held in her home in Wisconsin. Schurz inspired Elizabeth Peabody of Boston, who opened the first English-speaking kindergarten there in 1860. Peabody, in turn, after studying kindergartens in Germany, influenced William Harris, superintendent of schools in St. Louis, Missouri. In 1873, Harris allowed Susan Blow to open the first kindergarten in the United States that was associated with the public schools.

Froebel's concepts became well-established and are a cornerstone of early childhood philosophy. Froebelian kindergartens emphasized the importance of play and the value of childhood. His curriculum consisted of "gifts"—objects for children to use and manipulate to discover concepts and learning. Some of Froebel's gifts were a ball of yarn, a cube, a cylinder, and a sphere. Activities, songs, and fingerplays were developed that used these gifts as learning tools. Until close to the turn of the century, Froebel's philosophy remained the mainstay of kindergarten education.

By early 1900, however, the voices of dissent were being heard. Froebel's ideas had come under the scrutiny of Hall, Dewey, and others. A classic clash of ideals developed between followers of Froebel (conservatives) and those of Dewey's new educa-

My Pedagogic Creed—John Dewey	What It Means Today
1. ". . . I believe that only true education comes through the stimulation of the child's powers by the demands of the social situations in which he finds himself."	This tells us that children learn to manage themselves in groups, to make and share friendships, to solve problems, and to cooperate.
2. ". . . The child's own instinct and powers furnish the material and give the starting point for all education."	We need to create a place that is child-centered, a place that values the skills and interests of each child and each group.
3. ". . . I believe that education, therefore, is a process of living and not a preparation for future living."	Prepare the child for what is to come by enriching and interpreting the present to him. Find educational implications in everyday experiences.
4. ". . I believe that . . . the school life should grow gradually out of the home life . . . it is the business of the school to deepen and extend . . . the child's sense of the values bound up in his home life."	This sets the rationale for a relationship between teachers and parents. Values established and created in the home should be enhanced by teaching in the schools.
5. ". . . I believe, finally, that the teacher is engaged, not simply in the training of individuals, but in the formation of a proper social life. I believe that every teacher should realize the dignity of his calling."	This says that the work teachers do is important and valuable. They teach more than academic content; they teach how to live.

FIGURE 1.5 John Dewey's Pedagogic Creed. John Dewey expressed his ideas about education in an important document titled, *My Pedagogic Creed* (Washington, D.C.: The Progressive Education Association, 1897).

tional viewpoint (progressives). Support for the latter came from those who saw kindergartens as a social service. Many of the kindergartens started in the late 1800s were established by churches and other agencies that worked with the poor. It was an era of rising social conscience, and the reasons for helping the less fortunate were not unlike the rationale that led to the creation of Head Start and Follow-Through sixty years later.

Critics of Froebel took exception to his seemingly rigid approach. The emphasis in a Froebelian kindergarten was on teacher-directed learning. Dewey's followers preferred a more child-centered approach, with teachers serving as facilitators of children's learning. It is the same tension that exists today between the "back to basics" movement and the supporters of open education. The progressives found fault with the "gifts" of Froebel's curriculum. Those who followed Dewey believed that "real objects and real situations within the child's own social setting" should be used (Read and Patterson, 1980). Froebel was viewed as too structured and too symbolic; Dewey was perceived as child-oriented and child-involved. Even the processes they employed were different. Froebel believed in the unfolding of the child's mind and learning, whereas Dewey stressed the child's "potential developed through social interaction" (Broman, 1978).

The debate raged for another 25 years. The progressives succeeded in influencing the content

CHILD'S DRAWING OF HANDS SPINNING

FIGURE 1.6 School patterned after John Dewey's philosophy involved children in activities of a practical, real-life nature.

of kindergarten programs, retaining some of Froebel's basic concepts. "The reform of kindergarten education continued through the 1920s and 1930s leading to the creation of the modern American kindergarten . . ." (Spodek, 1972). Patty Smith Hill of Teacher's College, Columbia University, was an outstanding innovator of the time and one of the Progressive Movement's most able leaders. She was

> . . . guided by principles of democracy and respect for individuals. She argued for freedom and initiative for children, as well as a curriculum relevant to children's lives. It was she who originated large-muscle equipment and materials suitable for climbing and construction, a departure from the prescribed small-muscle activities of the Froebelians. Patty Hill also urged unification of kindergarten and first grade work, but her objective was not to start 5 year olds on first grade work, we today might readily assume. Rather, emphasis was on giving six year olds the opportunity for independent, creative activities before embarking on the three R's.
>
> (Cohen and Randolph, 1977)

These ideas became the backbone of kindergarten practice. Regardless of controversy within, kindergartens were still on the fringes of the educational establishments as a whole. However, when the 1960s highlighted the problems of the poor and their failure in schools and society, kindergarten and the early years were brought back into the spotlight. Today, the kindergarten remains an important part of the early childhood field.

Nursery Schools

Establishment in America

Early childhood educators took Dewey's philosophy to heart. Their schools reflected the principles of a *child-centered* approach, active learning, and social cooperation. By the 1920s and 1930s, early childhood education had reached a professional status in the United States. Nursery schools and day nurseries went beyond custodial health care. They fostered the child's total development. The children were enrolled from middle- and upper-class homes as well as from working families.

However, until the 1960s, nursery schools served few poor families.

Parent education was acknowledged as a vital function of the school and led to the establishment of *parent cooperative schools.* The first of these parent participation schools was developed in 1915 at the University of Chicago. A group of faculty wives started the Chicago Cooperative Nursery School.

Research centers and child development laboratories were started in many colleges and universities. Among them were:

1919	Bank Street School	1923	Bowling Green Nursery
1921	Columbia Teacher's College Laboratory Nursery School	1923	Cambridge Nursery
		1926	Vassar College Nursery School
1922	Ruggles Street Nursery School and Training Center	1926	Smith College Nursery School
		1927	Mills College Nursery School
1922	Merrill-Palmer Institute Nursery School		

These *laboratory schools* were active in expanding the knowledge of how important a child's early years are.

Abagail Eliot

The nursery school movement was pioneered by Abagail Eliot. A graduate of Radcliffe College and Harvard University, she was the director of the Ruggles Street Nursery School and Training Center, which opened in Boston in 1922. Eliot has made some observations about those early years:

On the "new school": "The big difference—the new idea—was program. I had visited many day nurseries in Boston as a social worker. I can remember them even now: dull green walls, no light colors, nothing pretty—spotlessly clean places, with rows of white-faced, listless little children sitting, doing nothing. There was a drabness, an emptiness, a nothingness. In the new nursery school, the children were active . . . alive . . . choosing . . . gay, busy, happy. That was the difference . . ."

On parents: "Parents chose to send their children to nursery schools. They wanted nursery school for the child's own good . . . I remember telling one of the early graduating classes at the Nursery Training School: 'If the nursery school movement does not result ultimately in better homes, it will be a failure.'"

On learning: "There was a conviction back then, too, that children learn so much from each other . . . I think the early schools were committed to the belief that the physical and mental life of children are inseparable. You cannot educate the mind without the body, and vice versa."

(Hymes, 1978)

Midcentury Developments

The Depression

It was during the Depression, World War II, and the postwar years that the American public focused more sharply than ever before on the needs of young children. These were times when the general public became aware of the importance of early childhood. Government-funded nursery schools later became the Works Progress Administration (WPA) nursery schools, which hired unemployed teachers. Government support from 1941 (Lanham Act War Nurseries) continued until 1946 when the Lanham Act schools were turned over to the states or closed.

Kaiser Child Care Centers

During World War II, funds were provided to deal with the common situation of mothers working in war-related industries. Further support came from industry during World War II. An excellent model for child care operated from 1943 to 1945 in Portland, Oregon. It was the Kaiser Child Care Centers. Kaiser became the world's largest such center and functioned "round the clock" all year long. A number of services were made available on site. An infirmary was located nearby for both mothers and children. Hot meals were made available for mothers to take home when they picked up their children. Lois Meek Stolz was the director of the centers, and James L. Hymes, Jr., the manager. Edith Dowley was one of the teachers. Stolz and Hymes describe the centers this way:

> . . . The centers were to have three distinctive qualities. One, they were to be located not out in the community but right at the entrance to the two shipyards, convenient to mothers on their way to and from work. They were to be industry-based, not neighborhood-centered. Two, the centers were to be operated by the shipyards, not by the public schools and not by community agencies. They were to be industrial child care centers, with the cost borne by the Kaiser company and by parents using the service. Three, they were to be large centers, big enough to meet the need. In the original plan each center was to serve a thousand preschool children on three shifts."
>
> (Hymes, 1978)

These centers served 3,811 different children. As Hymes points out, they provided 249,268 child care days. They had freed 1,931,827 woman work-hours. Once the war ended, though, the workers left. Child care was no longer needed, and the centers closed. The model they provide for child care remains exemplary, especially in light of the numbers of working mothers in the job force today.

Head Start

After the war, few innovations took place until a small piece of metal made its worldwide debut. Sputnik, the Soviet satellite, was successfully launched in 1957 and caused an upheaval in educational circles. Two questions were uppermost in the minds of most Americans: Why weren't we first in space? What is wrong with our schools? The emphasis in education quickly settled on engineering, science, and math in the hope of catching up with Russian technology.

The civil rights struggle in the early 1960s soon followed. In pointing out the plight of the poor, education was highlighted as a major stumbling block toward equality of all people. It was time to act, and Project Head Start was conceived as education's place to fight the "war on poverty." The same goals of Froebel and Montessori formed the basis of Head Start: helping disadvantaged preschool children.

Beginning in 1965, Project Head Start organized summer programs for children four and five years old. All children whose socioeconomic status predicted school failure were eligible. After the first summer, the experiment was expanded to the academic year as well. This was an exciting time—a national recognition of the needs of young children and a hope for a better quality of life. Three major points included in the Head Start program are noteworthy:

- *Compensatory education*—programs that compensate for inadequate early life experiences.
- *Parental involvement*—inclusion of parents in planning, teaching, and decision making.
- *Community control*—local support and participation.

These three objectives combined to reinforce the goals of the program in real and concrete ways. Head Start was an attempt to make amends, to compensate poor children by preparing them for school and educational experiences. Parents, by being required to participate at all levels, were educated along with their children. The purpose of the community-based governing boards was to allow the program to reflect local values and concerns. Concurrently, underprivileged, poor people were being encouraged to take part in solving some of their own problems.

The spirit of Head Start was infectious. As a result of community interest in Head Start, there was a burst of enthusiasm for many programs for the young child. Because of Head Start's publicity, there has been an expanding enrollment in nursery school, kindergarten, and day care programs. Thanks to Head Start, there is national attention to the need for providing good care and educational experiences for young children.

INTERDISCIPLINARY INFLUENCES

Several professions enrich the heritage of early childhood. This diversity was apparent from the beginning; the first nursery schools drew from five different professions: social work, home economics, nursing, psychology, and medicine. Three of the most consistent and influential of those disciplines were medicine, education, and child psychology.

Medicine

The medical field has contributed to the study of child growth through the work of several physicians. These doctors became interested in child development and extended their knowledge to the areas of child rearing and education.

Sigmund Freud

Few can deny that Dr. Freud made important contributions to modern thinking. The father of personality theory, he drastically changed how we look at childhood. Freud reinforced two specific ideas: (1) a person is influenced by his early life in fundamental and dramatic ways, and (2) early experiences shape the way people live and behave as adults. Thus, psychoanalytic theory is mostly about personality development and emotional problems. Although the impact of psychoanalysis on child psychology is not as great as it was 25 years ago, it still contributes significantly to the study of early childhood. Though he was not involved directly in education, Dr. Freud influenced its development.

Arnold Gesell

As a qualified physician, Dr. Gesell was concerned with growth from a medical point of view. Gesell began studying child development when he was a student of G. Stanley Hall, an early advocate of child study. The data collected by Gesell and his colleagues have become the recognized norms of how children grow and develop.

Gesell's greatest contribution was in the area of child growth. He saw maturation as an innate and powerful force in development. "The total plan of growth," he said, "is beyond your control. It is too complex and mysterious to be altogether entrusted to human hands. So nature takes over most of the task, and simply invites your assistance." (Gesell, Ames, and Ilg, 1977) This belief became known in psychological circles as the *maturation theory*.

Through the Gesell Institute, guides were published using this theory. With such experts as Dr. Frances Ilg and Dr. Louise Bates Ames, Gesell authored articles that realistically portrayed the child's growth from birth to adolescence.

Benjamin Spock

Spock's book, *Baby and Child Care*, was a mainstay for parents in the 1940s and 1950s. In a detailed "how-to" format Dr. Spock preached a common-sense approach that helped shape the childhood of many of today's adults. He suggested that mothers use the playpen less and allow children freedom to explore the world first-hand. To that end, he asked parents to "child proof" their homes—a radical thought at the time. The word "permissiveness," as it relates to child rearing, became associated with Dr. Spock's methods.

Dr. Spock has become an outspoken advocate for causes that extend his ideas. He is an active critic of those forces, be they economic, social, or political, that destroy people's healthy development. In his own words:

I'll summarize my thoughts this way: Child care and home care, if well done, can be more creative, make a greater contribution to the world, bring more pleasure to family members, than 9 out of 10 outside jobs. It is only our mixed-up, materialistic values that make so many of us think the other way around.

(Spock, 1976)

T. Berry Brazelton

Dr. Brazelton is a well-known pediatrician who supports and understands development of infant and toddlers. His pediatric guide to parents deals with both physical and emotional growth. His writings speak to the parents' side of child raising, such as setting limits, or listening to what children say and observing what they do. Brazelton (1974) discusses the two-year-old and sharing this way:

> Understanding such concepts as fair and unfair, of giving and receiving and the process of sharing, all demands a kind of self-awareness. If a child is not sure of his own limits and of his own strengths, he cannot afford to allow his toys, equivalent to parts of himself, to be passed out to someone else, trusting that they will come back. At the same time, the ability to do so is evidence of an awareness of behavior in others comparable to his own and denotes the beginning of an awareness of non-self.

Education

Early childhood is one part of the larger professional field known as education. This includes elementary, secondary, and college or postsecondary schools. Along with John Dewey and Abagail Eliot, three other influences from this field bear attention.

The Macmillan Sisters

In the first three decades of this century, these two sisters pioneered in early education. Nursery schools in Britain and America probably were developed because of the drive and dedication of the Macmillan sisters.

Both women had broad international backgrounds. They grew up in North America and Scotland. Margaret studied music and language in Europe. She was well read in philosophy, politics, and medicine. Rachel studied to become a health inspector in England.

Health studies of 1908–1910 showed that 80 percent of children were born in good health, but that by the time they entered school, only 20 percent

could be classified that way. Noticing the deplorable conditions for children under five, the Macmillan sisters began a crusade for the slum children in England. Their concern extended beyond education to medical and dental care for young children. In 1910 they set up a clinic in Deptford, a London slum area, which became an open-air nursery a year later. The Macmillans called it a "nurture school." Later, a training college nearby was named for Rachel. With no private financial resources, these two women faced tremendous hardships in keeping their school open. It is to their credit that Deptford still exists today.

The Macmillan theory of fresh air, sleep, and bathing proved successful. "When over seven hundred children between one and five died of measles, there was not one fatal case at Deptford School." (Deasey, 1978) From the school's inception, a primary function was to research the effects of poverty on children.

Of the two sisters, Margaret had the greatest influence at the school at Deptford. Abagail Eliot writes of her:

> Miss Macmillan invented the name [nursery school]. She paid great attention to health: a daily inspection, the outdoor program, play, good food—what she called "nurture." But she saw that an educational problem was also involved and she set to work to establish her own method of education for young children. This was why she called it a "school."
>
> (Hymes, 1978)

The Child Study Movement

A survey of education influences is incomplete without mentioning the child study movement in America in the 1920s and 1930s. It was through the child study movement that education and psychology began to have a common focus on children. Besides the Gesell Institute, many research centers and child development laboratories were established at colleges and universities around the country. Their inception reflects the interest of several disciplines in the growth of the young child. Schools of psychology looked for children to observe and study; schools of education wanted demonstration schools for their teachers-in-training and for student-teacher placement. Schools of home economics wanted their students to have first-hand experiences with children. These on-campus schools provided a place to gather information about child development and child psychology. This resulted in an impressive collection of normative data by which we still measure ranges of ordinary development. Broman (1978) sums up the influence of the movement this way:

> From the beginning of the child study movement in the 1920s . . . early childhood was not a major emphasis in education until after the War on Poverty and the establishment of Head Start in 1965. The child study movement, however, was the impetus that began the search for the most appropriate means of educating young children.

The British Infant School

In England, the term *infant school* refers to the kindergarten and primary grades. In 1967, the Plowden Report proposed a series of reforms for the schools. These changes paralleled those of American early childhood education. As a result, many American teachers in both the preschool and primary grades adapted the British infant school approach to their own classrooms.

Three aspects of this *open school* style that received the most attention were:

1. *Vertical, or family, groupings.* Children from five to eight years of age are placed in the same classroom. Several teachers may combine their classes and work together in teaching teams. Children may be taught by the same teachers for two or three years.

2. *Integrated day.* The classroom is organized into various centers, for math, science, and the arts. The teacher moves from one child or center to another as needed. Play is often the central activity, with an emphasis on follow-through with children's ideas and interests as they arise.

3. *Underlying concept.* There is a fundamental belief that the process of thinking takes precedence over the accumulation of facts. Learning how to think rather than stockpiling data is encouraged. How to identify and solve problems is valued more than having a finished product. Teachers focus on the child's current learning rather than on the future.

Psychology

The roots of early childhood education are wonderfully diverse, but one tap root is especially deep: the connection with the field of psychology. In this century particularly, the study of people and their behavior is linked with the study of children and their growth. Initially, child development was mostly confined to the study of trends and descriptions of changes.

Since World War II, the scope and definition of child development have changed radically. Developmental psychologists now study the process associated with those changes. Specifically, child development focuses on language acquisition, the effect of early experiences on intellectual development, and the process of attachment to others. Such is the world of early childhood—it is no wonder that we are so closely tied to the world of psychology.

There is no one theory or name that encompasses all of developmental psychology. Indeed, there are many. The major theories, their creators, and their influence on early education will be discussed in depth in Chapter 4.

THEMES IN EARLY CHILDHOOD EDUCATION

When reviewing the colorful and rich history of early childhood education, three major themes emerge. These same themes reappear and are reflected in the ensuing thought and theory of each age.

1592–1670	Johann Amos Comenius (E) (*Orbis Pictus*, 1657)
1712–1788	Jean Jacques Rousseau (E)
1746–1826	Johann Heinrich Pestalozzi (E) (*How Gertrude Teaches Her Children*, 1801)
1782–1852	Friedrich Wilhelm Froebel (E)
1804–1894	Elizabeth Peabody (E)
1843–1916	Susan Blow (E)
1856–1939	Sigmund Freud (P)
1858–1952	John Dewey (E) (*My Pedagogic Creed*, 1897)
1860–1931	Margaret Macmillan (E)
1868–1946	Patty Smith Hill (E)
1870–1952	Maria Montessori (M)
1874–1949	Edward L. Thorndike (P)
1878–1958	John B. Watson (P)
1880–1961	Arnold Gesell (M) (*The Preschool Child*, 1923)
1896–1980	Jean Jacques Piaget (P) (*The Language and Thought of the Child*, 1926)
1902–	Erik H. Erikson (P) (*Childhood and Society*, 1950)
1903–	Benjamin Spock (M) (*Baby and Child Care*, 1946)
1904–	B.F. Skinner (P) (*The Behavior of Organisms*, 1938)
1913–	Abagail Eliot (E)
1915–	Jerome Bruner (P)
1918–	T. Berry Brazelton (M) (*Infants and Mothers*, 1969)
1925–	Albert Bandura (P)
1929–	Jerome Kagan (P)
1929–	Burton White (M)

(E): Educator
(P): Psychologist
(M): Medical person

FIGURE 1.7 The timeline of influential people in early childhood education stretches across the centuries and includes the works and ideas of the influential educators throughout history.

Ethic of Social Reform

The first theme is that of the ethic of social reform. Early childhood education programs often have had the expectation that schooling for the young will lead to social change and improvement. Montessori, the Macmillans, and Head Start all tried to improve children's health and physical well-being by attending first to the physical and social welfare aspects of children's lives. Educators today still assert that tired, undernourished children are not ready to learn or to be educated. Social reform can go a step further, such as with Head Start, improving the whole family situation and involving the community in its efforts.

Importance of Childhood

The second theme is the importance and uniqueness of childhood. Before 1700 or so, Western society showed little concern for children. Infanticide was persistent, if not actually accepted. Once families and society began to value children, life changed dramatically for the young. As people accepted the importance of childhood, they began

Year	School and Founder	Location
1837	First kindergarten, Froebel	Germany
1856	First American kindergarten, Schurz	Wisconsin
1873	First American public school kindergarten, Blow	Missouri
1907	Casa di Bambini, Montessori	Italy
1911	Deptford School, Macmillan Sisters	England
1919	Bank Street School, Johnson	New York
1921	Columbia Teacher's College Laboratory School, Hill	New York
1921	Iowa Research Station	Iowa
1921	Summerhill, Neill	England
1922	Merrill-Palmer Institute, White	Michigan
	Ruggles Street Nursey School, Eliot	Massachusetts
1926	Smith College Nursery School	Massachusetts
	Vassar College Nursery School	New York
	Yale Guidance Nursery, Gesell	Connecticut
1927	Mills College Nursery School	California
1943	Kaiser Child Care Centers, Stolz	Oregon
1946	Bing Nursery School, Stanford, Dowley	California
1965	Head Start	United States
1967	British Infant Schools	England

FIGURE 1.8 Since the early 1900s, early childhood education has provided children with excellent schools both here and abroad.

to take on the responsibility for a quality life for children. Society began to provide for the health and physical welfare of children and came to understand the necessity to care for their minds.

Modern early childhood teachers believe the early years form the foundation for later development, physically, intellectually, socially, and emotionally. Children need special attention during these years. Childhood is fundamentally different from adulthood; it needs to be understood and respected as such. Public recognition of that need has created a wealth of programs for the young not dreamed of at any other time in history.

Transmitting Values

The third recurrent theme in our educational heritage is that of transmitting values. What children should ultimately *do* and *be* is at the core of all child-rearing practices, whether in the home or the school. Values—be they social, cultural, moral, or religious—have been the essence of education for centuries. For example, the Puritan fathers valued hard work and Biblical theology. Therefore, schools of their time taught children to read in order to learn the Bible. Rousseau, Froebel, Montessori, and Dewey valued the child. Their work reflected a belief in the worth and dignity of childhood. They transmitted these values into the educational thought and practices we have inherited. Finally, the initiators of Head Start realized the child's self-worth would be enhanced by valuing cultural heritage. Therefore, an awareness and appreciation of ethnic heritage became an integral part of the Head Start curriculum.

Teaching children to live in a democratic society has always been valued in the United States. In the curriculum from kindergarten through college, this belief is reflected as we educate our children for citizenship. It is how we define these values and how we teach them that are the critical issues in education.

FIGURE 1.9 Childhood is a special time of life.

These three themes have been at the center of early education for centuries. Occasionally, one theme dominates, as it did in the 1960s when the desire for social reform led to the creation of Head Start. At other times they seem indistinguishable from one another. Together, they have shaped the direction of early childhood education as we know it today. As we learn more about children, society, and ourselves, the 1980s will be a time to reconsider and redefine our aims and directions. It is a formidable challenge—and a worthy one.

SUMMARY

This chapter traces the roots of early childhood education from ancient times. Knowing this history gives teachers a sense of support and inspiration. An historical overview offers insights that illuminate present program and societal needs and prevent future mistakes. It helps us appreciate the legacy left by others.

Early childhood education involves children from infancy through the primary years. The term itself offers its own professional challenges:

EARLY: How do YOUNG children grow and learn best?

CHILDHOOD: How do CHILDREN think, feel, learn?

EDUCATION: How can children LEARN and be TAUGHT?

These questions have been addressed by educators in Europe and America throughout history. Their answers have influenced educational philosophy and practice and, in turn, have been affected by the social and political forces of the day. The most notable modern developments in this country have been the advent of nursery schools and kindergartens, the Kaiser Child Care Center in World War II as a day care model, and Head Start.

Early childhood education itself is an interdisciplinary field. Important contributions have come from medicine, education, and psychology.

Certain themes emerge in early childhood education with a study of its history. The ethic of social reform, the importance of childhood, and the transmission of values have been at the core of this field throughout history.

The contributions of many pioneers leave us dreams for the young children of our society. This can give meaning to our lives as teachers as we continue to create a climate for the child who will make history tomorrow.

Review Questions

1. Identify and describe five key people who influenced the field of early childhood education.

2. Match the name with the appropriate phrase:

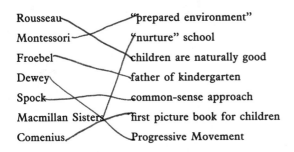

Rousseau — "prepared environment"
Montessori — "nurture" school
Froebel — children are naturally good
Dewey — father of kindergarten
Spock — common-sense approach
Macmillan Sisters — first picture book for children
Comenius — Progressive Movement

3. Define early childhood education in your own words. Include age ranges and what you believe to be its purpose.

4. Name three institutions or living persons who are influencing the history of early childhood today.

5. Maria Montessori made several contributions to education. What are some of her theories and how did she adapt them for classroom use?

Learning Activities

1. Find out when and by whom the school or center in which you are student teaching was started. What were some of the social, economic, and political issues of those times? How might they have affected the philosophy of the school?

2. Write your own pedagogic creed. List five of what you consider to be the most important beliefs you hold about educating young children. How do you see those beliefs expressed in school today?

3. Make a list of the values you think are important to teach children. In an adjoining column, add the ways in which you would help children learn those values. In other words, list the materials and curriculum you would use.

Bibliography

Braun, S.J., and Edwards, E.P. *History and Theory of Early Childhood Education.* Belmont, Calif.: Wadsworth Publishing Co., 1972.

Brazelton, T. Berry, M.D. *Toddlers and Parents.* Delacorte Press, 1974.

Broman, Betty L. *The Early Years in Childhood Education.* Chicago: Rand McNally College Publishing Co., 1978.

Cohen, Dorothy H., and Randolph, Marguerita. *Kindergarten and Early Schooling.* Englewood Cliffs, N.J.: Prentice-Hall, 1977.

Deasey, D. *Education Under Six.* New York: St. Martin's Press, 1978.

Dewey, John. *Democracy and Education: An Introduction to the Philosophy of Education.* New York: Macmillan, 1916.

Evans, Ellis D. *Contemporary Influences in Early Childhood Education.* New York: Holt, Rinehart and Winston, 1975.

Froebel, F.W. *The Songs and Music of Frederich Froebel's Mother Play.* Arranged and prepared by Susan Blow. New York: Appleton & Co., 1895.

Gesell, A.L.; Ames, L.A.; and Ilg, F.L. *The Child From Five to Ten.* New York: Harper and Row, 1977.

Hymes, James L., Jr. *Early Childhood Education: Living History Interviews.* Carmel, Calif.: Hacienda Press, 1978.

Katz, Lilian. "Early Childhood Education as a Discipline." *Young Children,* December 1970, pp. 82–90.

Lazerson, M. "The Historical Antecedents of Early Childhood Education." In Gordon, I.J. (ed.), *Early Childhood Education (Part II).* National Society for the Study of Education, University of Chicago, 1972.

Macmillan, M. *The Nursery School.* New York: E.P. Dutton and Co., 1919.

National Association for the Education of Young Children. *Montessori in Perspective.* Washington, D.C.: 1966.

Read, Katherine, and Patterson, June. *The Nursery School and Kindergarten.* New York: Holt, Rinehart and Winston, 1980.

Robison, Helen. *Exploring Teaching in Early Childhood Education.* Boston: Allyn and Bacon, 1983.

Spock, Benjamin. "Taking Care of a Chid and a Home: An Honorable Profession for Men and Women." *Redbook Magazine,* April 1976, pp. 22, 25, 115.

Spodek, Bernard. *Teaching in the Early Years.* Englewood Cliffs, N.J.: Prentice-Hall, 1972.

2

Types of Programs

Questions for Thought

- What are some of the different types of early childhood programs?
- What basic principles are common to most programs for young children?
- What is the range of early childhood education, and which programs correspond to the various age levels?
- Why is there an increase in the number of infant/toddler programs?
- Around which programs are there controversies—and why?
- How does the role of the teacher differ in each of the early childhood settings?
- What criteria affect programs in early childhood?
- How do Head Start and Follow-Through differ from other early childhood programs?

Outline

I. Diversity of Programs
  A. Some Common Factors

II. The Core of Early Childhood Education
  A. The Traditional Nursery School
  B. Day Care Centers
    1. Day Care Controversy
    2. Family Day Care
    3. Employer-Sponsored Child Care
  C. Laboratory Schools
  D. Parent Cooperatives
  E. Church-Related Schools
    1. Role in Day Care
    2. Academic Church Schools
  F. Other Schools

III. Schools with a Message
  A. Head Start
    1. Beginnings
    2. Guiding Objectives and Principles
    3. Evaluating Head Start's Effectiveness

  B. Follow-Through
  C. Open Schools
  D. Montessori
    1. The Program
    2. The Controversy

IV. Extending the Age Range
  A. Infant/Toddler Programs
    1. Philosophy of Infant/Toddler Care
    2. What Is Good Infant/Toddler Care?
    3. Issues
  B. Kindergarten
  C. After-School Programs

V. Criteria Affecting Programs

VI. Summary

VII. Review Questions

VIII. Learning Activities

IX. Bibliography

DIVERSITY OF PROGRAMS

From the types available to the numbers of children who attend these schools, the name of the game in early childhood programs is diversity. Early childhood programs abound; every community has some type of schooling for the young child. The range can encompass a morning nursery school for toddlers, an infant–parent stimulation program, or a full day care service for three-to-six-year-olds. Some programs run for only a half-day; others are open from 6:00 A.M. until 7:00 P.M. Still other centers accept children on a drop-in basis. Churches, school districts, community-action groups, parents, governments, private social agencies, and businesses may run schools.

Schools exist to serve a number of needs:

1. caring for children while parents work

2. enrichment programs for children

3. educational programs for parent and child

4. an activity arena for children

5. academic instruction

Programs generally reflect the needs of society as a whole. Millions of mothers of children under six are in the labor force as never before. Early childhood schools provide a wide range of services for children from infancy through eight years of age to meet some of that need.

In the human life cycle, early childhood is a period of maximum dependency. The various programs available reflect this in a number of ways. The teacher–child ratio varies in relation to the child's age; infants, at the higher end of the dependency scale, require more teachers per child in a classroom than do five-year-olds. The program itself reflects the age group it serves. The size of the group, the length of the program, and the equipment used relate to the enrolled children's capabilities and needs. Even the daily schedule mirrors the dependent relationship between the child and the teacher. Bathrooming, snack and meal routines, as well as clothing needs, call for longer periods of time in a toddler group than in a class of four-year-olds.

Diversity is apparent, too, in the philosophy expressed by the specific program. Some schools, such as Montessori programs, follow a very clear, precise outline based on a philosophical approach developed by Maria Montessori at the turn of the century. Other schools are more eclectic; they draw from a number of theories, choosing those methods and ideas that best suit their needs.

Some Common Factors

Preschools vary greatly in their educational goals and practices, their methods of instruction, and even in the kind of social "mood" or atmosphere they create. Yet, varied as they are, most early childhood programs share some common principles. In their research on Follow-Through programs, Maccoby and Zellner (1970) found that most programs agree on six major points, fundamental tenets to any preschool desiring to teach and nurture young children:

1. Children's education must start where the child is—on the child's level of learning at the outset of the program.

2. Teaching should be individualized as much as possible.

3. The right conditions must exist in order for the children to learn; a child's failure to learn stems from the methods and procedures of the programs, not from the child.

4. Any program for young children must be specific and detailed in its goals.

5. Children ought to enjoy the learning process and feel successful in school.

6. Children should learn specific school-appropriate behaviors like attending to tasks, motivation, and how to behave.

Other additions include the importance of helping children learn to have successful social relationships with adults and children; the necessity of helping children develop a strong sense of self-worth; giving children an opportunity to develop strong physical skills; and helping children live and learn and work in groups.

THE CORE OF EARLY CHILDHOOD EDUCATION

What do programs for the young child look like? How are the similarities and differences expressed in school settings? What marks a program as unique? The answers to these questions can be found by looking at some of the most common programs in early childhood education.

The Traditional Nursery School

At the core of early education is what is labeled *traditional nursery school:* a place for 2½-to-five-year-olds designed for educational experiences. This includes nursery schools, the variations of day care centers and their sister programs, laboratory schools, and parent cooperatives.

The philosophy of these schools is best described by Katherine Read in her now classic book, *The Nursery School: A Human Relationships Laboratory.* First published over 35 years ago, this book serves as an encyclopedia of the traditional nursery school, its methods, and its philosophy.

The idea of a school as a place of human activity mirrors the thoughts of Dewey, Piaget, Erikson, and others. Read develops this philosophy fully, with an educational model that emphasizes the human needs, growth patterns, and relationships in a young child's life. Developmentally, a traditional nursery school focuses on social competence and emotional well-being. The curriculum encourages self-expression through language, creativity, intellectual skill, and physical activity. The basic underlying belief is the importance of interpersonal con-

nections children make with themselves, each other, and adults.

In theory, the objectives of traditional nursery schools are prescribed. The schools have some general characteristics in common, like the daily schedule (see Figure 2.1). The schedule reflects the values for the school. For example, large blocks of time are devoted to free play, emphasizing the importance of play. In this way, children learn to make their own choices, select their own playmates, and work on their interests and issues at their own rate. A dominant belief is that children learn best in an atmosphere free from excessive restraint and direction.

A typical daily schedule also indicates an awareness of the developing child's characteristics and needs. Programs attend to the physical and health needs, (toileting, snacks, fresh air). There is a balance of activities (indoors and out, free choice, and teacher-directed times). Closer inspection of the environment reveals a wide variety of activities (large- and small-muscle games, intellectual choices, creative arts, social play opportunities).

Then, too, there is the clear acknowledgment of change and the time it takes children to make and adjust to changes. Children must have plenty of time for arrival and departure from school, greetings, cleanup, and transition times between activities. The amount of time given to any one part of the day's activities directly reflects the values the school endorses.

9:00	Children arrive at school
9:15–9:45	Free play (indoors)
9:45	Cleanup
10:00	Singing time (large group)
10:15–10:30	Toileting/snack time (small groups)
10:30–11:30	Free play (outdoors)
11:30	Cleanup
11:45	Story time
12:00	Children leave for home

FIGURE 2.1 A sample schedule for traditional half-day nursery schools

There are also aspects of the traditional model that are not immediately evident by looking at a daily schedule. The role of the teacher and methods of teaching are important. Nursery schools assume that young children need individual attention and should have personal, warm relationships with important adults. Therefore, the groups of children are generally small, often fewer than 20 in a class. The teacher–child ratio is low, as few as six to ten children for each teacher. Teachers learn about children's development and needs by observation and direct interaction, rather than from formalized testing. They work with children individually and in small groups (perhaps three or four) and often teach through conversation and materials. Always, the teacher encourages the children to express themselves, their feelings, and their thinking. And, as Read puts it:

> . . . A large part of the teacher's role is helping children learn to learn. Some teaching may be done through games that encourage the use of the senses, the imagination, and problem-solving capacities. Throughout her teaching, the teacher respects the individual interests, styles, and rates of learning of the children.
> (Read and Patterson, 1980)

FIGURE 2.2 Interactions aid children's social, emotional, even physical development. (Courtesy of Family Service Agency of San Mateo County, Calif.)

Such rapport between teacher and pupil fosters self-confidence, security, and belonging. Proponents of the traditional nursery school believe that these feelings promote positive self-image, healthy relationships, and an encouraging learning environment.

There are several programs within the traditional preschool framework. Three important variations on the theme are: day care centers, laboratory schools, and parent cooperative nursery schools.

Day Care Centers

Some of the first nursery schools in England operated from 8:00 A.M. until 4:00 or 5:00 P.M. It was only later in America that the nursery school evolved into a part- or half-day program. Day care, then, is not a modern phenomenon. Day care center patterns differ from those of half-day nursery schools. By definition, a *day care center* is a place for children who need care for a greater portion of the day. The school schedule is extended to fit the hours of working parents. The program roughly models what ordinarily happens in the routines of a child's day at home. Therefore the adults who work in a day care center have somewhat different responsibilities and training. Day care centers are for infants and toddlers, as well as for the 2½-to-five-year-old range. In this section, the focus is on those centers for the nursery school age range.

Day care has a number of unique qualities.

Scheduling. Compare the nursery school schedule to the day care schedule (see Figure 2.3). The morning starts slowly. Children arrive early since their parent(s) must go to work. The center will usually supply breakfast; midmorning and midafternoon snacks supplement a noon lunch. A nap period for one to two hours for all the children gives a needed rest and balances their active, social day with quiet, solitary time. The program also includes extended experiences outside the school—field trips, library story hour, or swimming lessons—since children spend the major portion of their waking hours onsite. As the day draws to a close, children gather together quietly, with less energy and activity.

Licensing. There are no national standards or policies regarding licensing of child care facilities. Many local and state governments, however, do require licensing of child care centers and family day care homes. Nor is there one central licensing agency. Depending upon the state, a license may be issued by the Department of Health, Department of Education, or Department of Social Welfare. Certification of child care workers is again left to local options. Early childhood education professional groups are calling for increased standardization of licensing procedures to ensure that children are being given the best possible care in safe and healthy environments.

While professionalization of centers is worthwhile, implementation is controversial and costly. The question arises as to which agency should rightfully evaluate licensing and enforce the policies and procedures established by law. Many see it as a natural extension of the state Department of Education. Others argue equally for the Department of Social Welfare or Board of Health.

7:00–8:30	Arrival/breakfast; limited indoor play
8:30	Large group meeting
8:45–9:45	Free play (inside)
9:45	Cleanup/toileting
10:00	Snack time (small groups)
10:15–11:30	Free play (outside)
11:30	Cleanup/handwashing
12:00	Lunch
12:30	Toothbrushing/toileting
1:00–2:00	Nap time
2:00–3:00	Free play (outside)
3:00	Group time
3:15	Snack time (small groups)
3:30–5:00	Inside and outside free play/library hour
5:00	Cleanup
5:15–5:30	Departure

FIGURE 2.3 A typical day care schedule. Day care programs combine education and caring for basic needs.

Until government and professionals can agree on implementation, enforcement, and funding, licensing of day care facilities and personnel will remain an unsolved issue.

Staffing. What does day care mean for teachers? First, they must be aware of and trained to deal with the parenting side of teaching. The children may need more nurturing, clearer consistency in limits, and established routines. At the same time, they need individual flexibility and understanding and regular private time with caring adults.

Parents' needs also may be greater and require more of the teachers' time. Teachers should communicate with and support parents effectively. Parents want to trust their children's teachers and be relaxed with them. Teachers in a day care center find it valuable to take the time to be good listeners and clear communicators to parents about their child; this builds the trust and support that is so vital when working with young children. Day care parents may require extra effort; they have full-time jobs as well as child-rearing responsibilities draining their energies. It takes a strong team effort on the part of the teacher and the parent to make sure the lines of communication stay open.

The teaching staff undoubtedly has staggered schedules, perhaps a morning and an afternoon shift. Administration of this type of program is therefore more complex. An effort must be made to ensure that all teachers get together on a regular basis to share the mutual information and details about the children in their care. Both shifts must be aware of what happens when they are not on-site in order to run the program consistently.

Day care in the United States used to be primarily *custodial,* providing basic health and physical care. But times have changed. Full day care is an American way of life, providing enriched programs for total development. Thousands of families rely on day care centers. By 1980, 58 percent of mothers were in the work force compared with only 19 percent in 1947 (Collins, 1983). The rising divorce rate, single-parent families, the women's movement, and the economy have all contributed to a greater need than ever for child care.

Good day care provides educational experiences and guidance, health services and makes available social services as needed by the child and his family. It safeguards children and helps parents to maintain the values of enriched family life.

(National Committee for Day Care of Children, 1965)

Day Care Controversy

Day care issues are continually debated. Some see child care outside the traditional home setting as undermining the role of mother, family, and therefore society. Many question the effects on children who spend so much of their early years in group care.

The issue is complex and related to economic trends as well as social forces. Families need and want child care. Day care exists as a response to the trend toward working mothers. It is a solution to economic and social pressures, not a cause.

The impact of day care on children, families, and the community is not yet fully understood. Some experts continue to urge mothers to stay at home with their young children (White, 1981). Yet over a dozen studies investigating day care found "no consistent adverse effect of out-of-home child day care" (O'Connell, 1983). Ongoing research can help answer the critical questions regarding the effect of day care on a child's development, on parent–child relationships, and on the quality of child care.

Work in day care is long and intense coupled with undesirable wages. This creates high staff turnover and low morale. Full-time day care is expensive. Sometimes it is too costly for poorly paid or underemployed parents to pay for quality child care. Occasionally, a center will cut corners to keep tuition reasonable, but the results of these shortcuts are usually detrimental to children.

Regardless of disagreements about the effects, child care outside the home is a fact of life for millions of children. It is the only choice for many parents, and the most sensible one for others. Therefore, the issue is not whether there should be day care, but how to provide the highest quality care. Two variations in day care may provide some of the solutions.

Family Day Care

This type of service cares for children in ways reminiscent of an extended family grouping. The day care provider takes in small numbers of children in the family residence. The group size can range from two to twelve, but recent research shows that most homes keep a low adult–child ratio, enrolling fewer than six children (Stevens, 1982).

The home setting, sometimes right within the child's own neighborhood, offers a more intimate, convenient, and possibly less expensive service for working parents. The children in a *family day care* home can range from infants to school-age children who are cared for after regular school hours.

Advantages. Family day care has many advantages. It is especially good for children who do well in small groups or whose parents prefer them in a family-style setting. Women who want to remain at home with one or more children of their own have found family day care meets this need while giving them a chance to increase the family's income. And those who have begun careers in this area feel a sense of budding professionalism.

Disadvantages. Family day care has its disadvantages, too. Many homes are unregulated; that is, they are not under any sponsorship or agency that enforces quality care. Many offer little more than baby-sitting or custodial care. In a review of recent research about family day care, agency- or group-regulated homes had the best care (Stevens, 1982). In such homes, the day care providers interacted more frequently with the children than did those in unregulated homes. The quality of these interactions and the types of activities offered were more stimulating and beneficial to the children's growth and development. The environment as a whole, in the regulated day care homes, was more satisfactory: the food was more nutritious and the providers taught and helped the children more. Significantly,

FIGURE 2.4 Day care must involve more than basic health and physical care.

the day care providers in these regulated homes also had more training in early childhood education.

The overwhelming majority of family day care is provided by women in unregulated homes, according to Stevens' review. Blacks, Hispanics, and Caucasions share equally as day care providers. Sponsorship of a regulating agency, be it by government or a family service association, proved to be positive in terms of both quality of child care and training of providers.

This type of care could be a star in the galaxy of child care options. Small and personalized, it offers parents an appealing choice of home-based care. It is obvious, though, that further regulation of standards, availability of training for providers, and an awareness of the advantages of family day care need to be addressed. For those who need child care, this should be a viable alternative; for those who want to work at home, this type of career should be given serious consideration.

Employer-Sponsored Child Care

Employer-sponsored child care refers to child care facilities on or near the job site and supported by the business or industry. Hospitals, factories, colleges, and military bases often provide this service.

The role of industry and business in group day care has an outstanding, if brief, history. The most notable example in this country is the Kaiser Shipyard Centers during World War II. When child care was equated with a national cause—winning the war—government and industry joined forces to provide quality child care in industrial settings. Recently this model has been examined as one way businesses can support working parents' efforts to find quality child care.

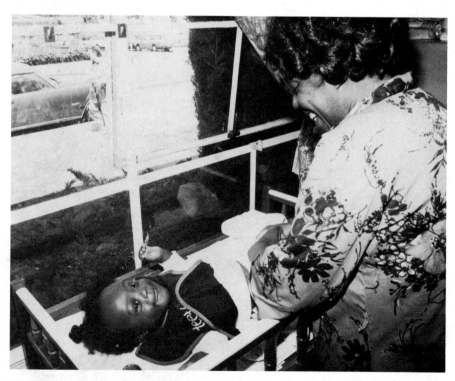

FIGURE 2.5 Family day care can be within the child's own neighborhood. (Courtesy of Family Service Agency of San Mateo County, Calif.)

FIGURE 2.6 Some corporations help parents by offering on-the-job child care. (Courtesy of Stride Rite Children's Centers, Cambridge, Mass.)

The number of women working outside the home and the increase in single-parent families encourage us to look at the workplace as a logical solution for child care needs. Advocates claim many benefits for both industry and people. They suggest that:

- Absenteeism drops when stable and convenient child care is available on or near the parent's work site.

- Employees are likely to stay on the job longer and employers will need to do less recruiting by offering child care services at reasonable cost and close to work.

- There can be tax advantages to businesses that provide child care services.

- There is a greater sense of loyalty because employees feel more positive about working for companies that provide this benefit.

- There is a greater opportunity for parents to spend more time with their children, going to and from work, during breaks, and at lunch time.

- Children understand their parents' role outside the home when these two worlds are brought into relationship with one another.

The most common disadvantage cited is that of cost; child care is not profitable nor cost-effective in business terms. There is also some concern that the location of the center, in highly commercialized areas, could expose children to industrial pollution (Verzaro-Lawrence et al., 1982).

The critical issue is not concerned so much with on-site facilities for care of employees' children. (For instance, employers who do not have their own programs could provide vouchers for child care in other settings. They could also offer, as a benefit to attract working parents, reimbursement for some portion of their employees' child care.) Helping parents with placement in other centers or offering flexible time schedules is as much a part of the issue as child care itself.

However, an even larger issue addresses women in the work force and parents' relationships to their families. A small but growing number of businesses deal with this issue of balancing work and parenthood in a unique way: around the country in corporate boardrooms, parenting seminars are available to employees during business hours. Led by qualified child development specialists, parents discuss some of the difficulties they face as working people who are also mothers and fathers (Collins, 1983). Early childhood professionals must explore new avenues with business and industry to assist the working parent, especially the working mother, that will be of mutual benefit.

Laboratory Schools

The college and university laboratory schools were among the first preschools established in the United States. They usually focus on teacher training, research, and innovative education. These schools serve as standards for model programs in early childhood education. They add to our knowledge of children, child development, and teaching methods. An important part of education in the United States, they are often supported or subsidized by the college.

As part of the child study movement, laboratory schools gathered information previously unknown about children and child development. Early ones include Bank Street School in 1919, begun by Harriet Johnson, and the laboratory nursery school at Columbia Teacher's College, also started in 1921 by Patty Smith Hill. In the late 1920s, Vassar, Smith, and Mills colleges all opened laboratory schools. Shortly after World War II, Edith Dowley started the Bing Nursery School at Stanford University. Much more recently, community-college campuses have followed the lead of these pioneers. Campus child care centers have begun to combine child care services with the laboratory function of teacher training in one setting. The types and roles of the schools vary, depending on the educational philosophy and needs of the college and its students.

Regardless of their specific purposes, laboratory schools enlarge our understanding of children. They are often excellent places for beginning teachers to learn ways of teaching children. They encourage the joining of psychology, medicine, and other related fields to early education, and they serve as professional models for the public at large for what is good in child care and education.

The isolation of college campuses sometimes restricts the number and type of children who enroll. The program itself is tailored to meet the needs of student teachers who, under the guidance of skilled people, do much of the teaching. College calendars may be unable to accommodate the needs of children for full-time and year-round care. In addition, teachers trained in a laboratory school atmosphere will have to adjust to the realities of subsequent school settings.

Parent Cooperatives

Parent cooperatives are those schools organized and run by parents. This type of early childhood setting offers a unique opportunity for parents to be involved in the education of their child. The very first parent cooperative, the Chicago Cooperative Nursery School, was started in 1915 by faculty wives at the University of Chicago.

Parent cooperative schools generally hold half-day sessions and are usually nonprofit organizations.

FIGURE 2.7 Lab schools are good vehicles for student teachers.

They are similar to other nursery schools, with two notable exceptions. First, parents organize and maintain the school: they hire the teachers, buy supplies and equipment, recruit members, raise funds, influence school philosophy, and manage the budget. Second, and more important, each parent must participate in the classroom on a regular basis.

Cooperative schools work well for many reasons. Popular with young families, they have low operating costs, the appeal of being with parents in similar circumstances, and the mutual support that is generated among members of a co-op. Friendships grow among parents who share child rearing as participants in their own and in their child's education. But what a co-op does not cost in dollars, it may cost in time. By their very nature, cooperatives can exclude working parents unless another adult is able to substitute for them in classroom participation. Maintenance is very much the parents' responsibility; they must regularly schedule work parties to refurbish the facility.

Depending upon the size of the school, parents hire one or more professional teachers. These teachers must be able to work well with adults, have curriculum-building skills, and model good guidance and discipline techniques. Since many parent cooperatives require a weekly or monthly parent meeting, the teaching staff must also be competent in parent education. Child development and child-rearing topics are part of almost any cooperative nursery school discussion and require a practiced teacher to lead. The role of the teacher in this setting, then, is two-fold: to provide for a sound educational experience for young children and to guide and direct parents in their own learning.

Church-Related Schools

Church-related schools are those owned or operated by an individual congregation or other recognized church organization. Many different denomi-

FIGURE 2.8 Parent co-ops actively involve parents.

nations sponsor a variety of educational and child care programs.

Throughout this nation's history, churches have demonstrated their concern for the welfare of children and their families. It was the churches that established many of the early schools, advocating the education of children. At the turn of the century, church day nurseries and settlement houses cared for children of immigrants and poor working mothers. Later, hospitals and orphanages were founded, and churches spoke out for children's rights and the creation of child labor laws. In each era, depending on social and economic conditions, the churches have responded to the needs of children.

Role in Day Care

It is no surprise, then, to find that churches are deeply involved in child care today: they are probably the single largest group of day care providers in the country. They also play an indirect part as landlords to programs not under church sponsorship (Lindner et al., 1983).

Church-housed programs are broad-based. Toddler groups, full- and part-time nursery classes, day care, and after-school care are typical. Some churches sponsor programs for children with special needs and children of migrant farm workers. They serve the community-at-large and rarely restrict participation to their own congregations or denominations.

Religious or spiritual development is not the explicit aim of the majority of programs for preschoolers. Churches are committed to caring for children of working parents, providing a warm and loving environment to help children develop positive self-esteem (Lindner et al., 1983). The teaching of religious values to children in this age group is not common practice in most day care settings. The policy will vary, however, with each individual setting.

Academic Church Schools

For those parents who seek alternative education in a religious context, church schools fill the need. Many denominations serve children from early childhood through senior high. The relationship with the individual church organizations and the academic philosophy will vary from setting to setting.

Other Schools

To serve the scope of human needs today, some early childhood programs focus on caring for children in a very specific context. Many high schools now have on-campus child care programs. Some serve as laboratory facilities to introduce adolescents to child care principles and practices before they become parents.

Others are part of a growing trend to provide support services to teenage parents. Young mothers are encouraged to complete their high school education by returning to campus with their young children. Parents are required to participate in parent education classes along with regular academic subjects where they discuss child-rearing policies and parent concerns. They also spend time in the children's classroom, applying their skills under the supervision of professional child care workers.

The aim of this program is to help meet the long-term needs of adolescent parents by providing educational skills necessary to secure a job. At the same time, valuable support and training for parenthood helps teenagers deal with the reality of the young children in their lives.

Hospitals also provide group settings for children who are confined for a period of time. Schools for the handicapped address the needs of specific disabilities, offering a combination of educational, medical, and therapeutic services. Children who attend these schools may or may not be mainstreamed part-time into other school settings.

SCHOOLS WITH A MESSAGE

Head Start

Beginnings

Head Start began as part of this country's social action against poverty in the mid-1960s (see Chapter 1). The implication of this program was clear: if underprivileged, disadvantaged, poverty-stricken children could be exposed to a program that enhanced their schooling, their intellectual functions might increase, and these gains would help break the poverty cycle. To that end, the Office of Economic Opportunity created Head Start, a federally funded school program for low-income children and their families. Head Start served youngsters from ages two to five in both half-day and full-day classes. The schools were administered by any one of several agencies: the local government, school districts, or Model Cities projects.

One of Head Start's most valuable contributions was its *comprehensive* program. Beyond intellectual development was a concern for health, nutrition, and physical growth. The child was seen as a whole, requiring medical, dental, and nutritional assessment as well as intellectual growth.

Head Start was for children *and* their families. Parents were required to be involved at all levels: in the classroom as teacher aids and on governing boards. Parents helped to define and direct each Head Start center; parent involvement was a major underlying philosophy.

Community interest and support is an ongoing Head Start objective. Head Start attempts to involve neighborhood resources and functions under local rule. Programs reflect not only the child but the culture as well. The curriculum encourages activities that enhance self-esteem, especially as it relates to the child's ethnic heritage and cultural background.

Guiding Objectives and Principles

- Improve the child's physical health and physical abilities.

- Help the emotional and social development of the child by encouraging self-confidence, spontaneity, curiosity, and self-discipline.

- Improve the child's mental processes and skills with particular attention to conceptual and verbal skills.

- Establish patterns and expectations of success for the child that will create a climate of confidence for his future learning efforts.

- Increase the child's capacity to relate positively to family members and others, while at the same time strengthening the family's ability to relate positively to the child and his problems.

- Develop in the child and his family a responsible attitude toward society and foster constructive opportunities for society to work together with the poor in solving their problems.

- Increase the sense of dignity and self-worth within the child and his family.

(Evans, 1975)

These objectives could apply to any good nursery or kindergarten class. They take on an added dimension, though, when viewed as part of the total effort of Project Head Start. Administration, education, social services, health services, parent involvement, and career development were the six major components of Head Start (Evans, 1975).

Evaluating Head Start's Effectiveness

Has Head Start fulfilled its promise? As soon as the program began, so did the research to evaluate its effectiveness. Evaluating any program is complicated, and Head Start is no exception. Research findings take on great importance when large numbers of children and governmental dollars are at stake. Three research studies demonstrate the types of controversies and the variety of findings.

The first major evaluation is known as the Westinghouse study, which looked at the intellectual and personal/social development of primary grade children who had attended Head Start programs. This group was compared to other groups of children who had not attended Head Start, but who were the same age, grade, and from the same socioeconomic backgrounds. Four tentative conclusions were drawn:

1. No persistent gains were found in either the intellectual or personal/social development in summer session groups.

2. Full-year programs gave more improvement in reading readiness; no significant changes in the personal/social area.

3. Children from both summer and full-year programs remained below average in language and scholastic achievement tests.

4. Parents of Head Start children strongly approved of the program and participated in it regularly.

(Evans, 1975)

On the surface, these results seem discouraging. Head Start was no miracle cure for the poor child, the underachiever, or the failure in school. The Westinghouse study has been criticized; there was not an assessment of skills taken before the children entered Head Start programs, so that a clear picture of gains children made was not possible. Nonetheless, its results were sobering.

Evans (1975) summarized the research that took place between 1970 and 1975. His conclusions are:

1. For most children, especially males, any type of Head Start program is better than none.

2. Positive gains in academic/intellectual areas, when achieved within Head Start, usually dissipate when special services are terminated and children move on to "regular" classrooms.

3. Upon formal school entry, Head Start children generally manifest a slight advantage over their non–Head Start peers on "school socialization," which includes adjusting to classroom routines, self-care skills, sharing behavior, and following teacher directives.

4. Only in unusually well-designed and executed programs for basic skill learning is the overall rate of disadvantaged children's educational development much accelerated.

5. Disadvantaged children who achieve and maintain cognitive advantages more generally attend schools that have a low proportion of low-income children in the overall student body.

These findings suggest that early intervention seems to help some children, but not radically.

In another study, 2,400 former Head Start families were contacted to discover what happened to the children, who by now were in their twenties. Over 87 percent responded with the following information about their lives after Head Start:

- *School achievement.* At no time through twelfth grade did the Head Start children fall below the control group (children similar in age, socioeconomic status, and background, who did not attend Head Start classes) in intellectual achievement. Furthermore, significantly fewer Head Start graduates were put in special classes or held back.

- *Teenage years.* Although the same proportion of Head Start girls got pregnant as of the control girls, almost all of the Head Start girls went back to school. The others did not. For boys, the Head Start group was far less likely to get involved with the law than the control group.

- *College.* Less than three percent of the control group has gone beyond high school. Twenty-five percent of the Head Start group are in college or some post–high school education.

(Lazar et al., 1978)

It would appear that Head Start was both cost-effective and worthwhile. The studies point out some of the positive long-term effects of this national program. It will surely be written in history books as one of the most ambitious efforts ever on behalf of young children in America.

Follow-Through

Once Head Start got underway, its children began to graduate and continue on into elementary school. Project Follow-Through is a set of federally funded programs for children from kindergarten through third grade. Many of the gains children made in intellectual achievement during their Head Start years were lost a year or two later. People asked: What is happening to the "head start" these children had in school? Can the whole idea of compensatory education work at all? Or is there something about elementary school that fails to build upon the gains made in preschool?

Project Follow-Through attempts to answer the last question by providing some model programs for impoverished grade-school children. Follow-Through, started in 1968, is a smaller project than Head Start—and more experimental. The programs operate across the country, in both urban and rural settings. The children in any one group come from a variety of ethnic backgrounds, or from a single population. Sponsors include universities, research centers, and communities.

Educational models of Follow-Through differ widely in philosophy and teaching techniques. The Bank Street Model uses a classic child development approach, while the Direct Instruction Model is academically oriented. The Tuscon Early Education Model emphasizes language development, the Florida Project concentrates on parents and infants in the home, and the Behavior Analysis Model uses behavior-modification principles. Each separate model is striking in its diversity, yet contributes to an interesting experiment in planned variations.

How have these programs helped children? Attempts to evaluate Follow-Through are as complicated as those for Head Start. Generally, it seems that programs tend to be successful in meeting their particular goals. For example, the Cognitively Oriented Curriculum Model (based on Piaget's theory) has been successful in meeting its stated goal of increasing children's use of verbal language. The

Florida Project demonstrates how early education begins in the home. It appears that the more specific the program format, the greater the chance for success.

A nationwide study (Stanford Research Institute, 1971) analyzed the project by looking at two questions: First, which program was the most efficient and what did it do? Second, can education help change the effects of poverty on children?

The results showed that the effects of Follow-Through varied from program to program and that more time is needed to answer the first question. As for the social issue, a fairly definitive set of data emerged. Children at all grade levels showed greater gains in school achievement, greater changes in attitudes toward school and toward their teachers and children. Parents had a higher awareness of their children's program, and teachers and staff were positive about the programs.

A more recent study of the original Follow-Through program in Philadelphia (Goodwin, 1981) had similar results. In this study, the children in Follow-Through outperformed non-Follow-Through children significantly in both reading and math at every grade level. The need for social services was high and the rate of referral equally as great. The compensatory nature of the program was as effective as in the SRI study.

Regardless of any one survey outcome, however, compensatory education is a difficult process. There are no easy solutions to the problems of poverty, the realities of ghetto life. Continued support of experimental research and educational programs is one way to try to find ways to help our children—all our children—succeed.

Open Schools

Open education—sometimes called open schools or informal education—is a term used to describe child-centered learning environments often associated with the British infant schools. It is based on the belief that children learn and grow at different rates, that they are eager and curious about learning, and that they learn best when they are able to pursue their own interests. Open school philosophy uses play as the principal means for learning. Not only do children learn from each other as they play in a mixed-age group, they grow through a rich and varied learning environment.

The emphasis in an open classroom is on the integration of the total curriculum, rather than on the separate subject matter. Academic skills—reading, writing, number concepts—comprise a natural part of all learning. Music can include math and counting; science discussions develop language arts; and dramatic play can spur writing. The stress is on the learning process—what happens when child and materials meet. Their play encourages children to explore, manipulate, and construct; classroom space encourages this. Activity areas, or centers of interest, are set up throughout the room. Children self-select where and with whom they want to spend their time, be it with clay, at woodworking, or at one of the table games.

Teachers facilitate, or guide, setting up the environment to promote independence and self-sufficiency so that they are free to interact with children. Team teaching is ideal for the open classroom; several teachers can provide the amount of supervision, organization, and planning necessary for success. "Good informal instruction is hard work." (Elkind, 1982)

If this description sounds vaguely familiar, it should since it applies to many typical nursery schools and kindergartens. The philosophy has a familiar ring to it. Didn't John Dewey speak of self-initiated learning, social cooperation, active education, and respect for the individual? And before him, Comenius, Rousseau, Pestalozzi, and Froebel all promoted similar concepts. In some ways, open education is the Progressive Movement revisited.

The British aided the revival of open education in the United States today since many schools pattern themselves after the British infant school model. American educators, excited by the British response to open learning, helped to revive local commitment to those principles. Numerous American educators trekked to England to see how open schools worked there, and so they reappeared in the United States education scene in the 1970s. Several Follow-Through models—the Bank Street Model and the EDC Open Education Model—use the open school approach to learning. The open school has come to mean an approach, a philosophy, that is practiced in many types of early childhood settings—nursery schools, day care centers, and elementary schools.

The open school is not without criticism, much of which centers around the lack of formal instruction. The deemphasis in direct instruction of reading and writing is questioned. Supporters of open schools counter that the child-centered approach in fact leads to a high motivation to read and write.

While loosely structured classrooms may prove challenging and stimulating to some children, others may find the lack of structure difficult. More traditional programs offer clear goals that are measured by evaluation and testing. The open school's approach includes the children in the planning and evaluation of some of the learning that takes place. If the experiences in an open classroom are not integrated into the total curriculum and the learnings not related in some meaningful way, they remain merely good—but isolated—experiences for the child. "Done well," says Elkind, "open education can be a model of truly humanistic education; done poorly, it can be a disaster." (Elkind, 1982)

Open education allows for a child to respond individually and personally to the experience. The freedom of choice, the development of problem-solving skills, the respect for initiative, are based on the strong belief that allowing children this kind of involvement reflects back to them their worth and dignity. For that reason alone, open classrooms continue to exemplify the best in humanistic education.

FIGURE 2.9 Open education provides freedom and room for individuality.

Montessori

Maria Montessori began working with slum children in the early 1900s in Rome, Italy. Her school, the Casa di Bambini, was open to children from the ages of 2½ to seven years. Montessori's approach to learning has had a continuing influence in education since those early years. Of her work, three features stand out: (1) adapting school work to the individual rather than molding the child to fit the curriculum; (2) insisting on freedom for children in selection of materials and choice of activities; and (3) training of the senses and practical life issues.

The Program

The most striking feature of the Montessori classroom is its materials. Many are made of wood and designed to stress the philosophy of learning through the senses. Color, texture, and quality of craftsmanship of the materials appeal to the hand as well as the eye; they demand to be touched. "Smooth" and "oval" take on new meaning as a child runs a finger around Montessori-designed puzzle shapes.

Montessori materials have other unique characteristics besides their tactile appeal. They are self-correcting—that is, they fit together or work in only one way so that children will know immediately whether or not they are successful. Montessori curriculum presents the materials in a sequence, from simplest to most difficult. Many of the learning tasks have a series of steps and must be learned in a prescribed order. Whether sponging a table clean or using the number rods, the child is taught the precise order in which to use the materials. Montessori developed curriculum materials and tasks that related to real life. "Practical life" activities range from cleaning tasks (hands, tables) to clothing tasks (lacing, buttoning, or tying garment closures).

In a Montessori classroom, children work by themselves at their own pace. They are free to choose the materials with which they want to "work"—the word used to describe their activity. Children must accomplish one task before starting another, one including the replacing of the materials on the shelf for someone else to use.

The prepared environment in a Montessori program has child-sized furniture and equipment—one of Froebel's ideas that Montessori used. Materials are set out on low shelves, in an orderly fashion, to encourage children's independent use. Only one set of any materials—their shape, form, and the way they are presented for children to use—are the vehicles for learning.

The teacher in the Montessori setting has a prescribed role, one of observing the children. Teachers become familiar with skills and developmental levels, then match the child to the appropriate material or task. There is little teacher intervention beyond giving clear directions for how to use the materials. Group instruction is not common; learning is an individual experience.

The Controversy

Much controversy surrounds the Montessori method, its schools, its training. Limitations of the Montessori philosophy most frequently cited follow. They highlight the difference between the Montessori system and the mainstream of American education.

- *Lack of social interaction among children and between teachers and children.* Notably, the absence of dramatic play equipment that would foster peer interchange.

- *Lack of self-expression.* Children are discouraged from exploring and experimenting with materials in their own way. Creative arts are not part of the pure Montessori method. No vehicle is provided for self-expression through fantasy, imagination, or creative play.

• *Lack of stimulation for language development.* Since children are encouraged to work alone and teachers interact with them in fairly structured ways, many opportunities for verbal exchange are lost. Again, creative arts and dramatic play provide options, if they are available.

• *Lack of large-motor equipment or emphasis.* Only fine-motor skills are emphasized in most of the Montessori materials. Outdoor play is not an integrated part of the Montessori curriculum.

In a review of the research (Chattin-McNichols, 1981), it was found that the Montessori programs have positive results in divergent thinking and school readiness. Montessori was regarded as inferior to other programs in the areas of vocabulary recognition, verbal-social participation, and Piagetian conceptual development. Montessori performs as well as any other program in general intelligence achievement in academic areas, attention, concentration, and distractability strategies. Both sides of the issue call for continued research concerning the effects of a Montessori school experience.

Today, this country is interpreting Montessori education differently. Many Montessori schools are adding curriculum areas of art, dramatic play, and large-motor development. There is also greater teacher flexibility to promote social interaction.

Maria Montessori has found her way into nearly every early education program in existence today. Many schools regularly use materials she designed: the alphabet sandpaper letters, the graduated cylinders, and the number rods are common in preschools and elementary math labs. Whether labeled so or not, much of the material and equipment as well as many of the teaching techniques in use today originated with this dynamic woman nearly one hundred years ago.

She is firmly established in early childhood history of the past and of the future. The Montessori method should be weighed in light of contemporary knowledge and be tailored to meet the needs of vigorous, eager, often needy children of the 1980s and 1990s.

EXTENDING THE AGE RANGE

Infant/Toddler Programs

There has been a dramatic rise in recent years in the demand for and availability of group care for infants and toddlers. The early 1970s produced a great deal of research concerning the infant/toddler, enhancing public awareness of the potential of children this age. Greater resources and information became available, creating an awareness of the implications for programs that focus specifically on the infant or toddler. Research by Brazelton, White, Honig, Caldwell, Keister, and others has informed us where and how and why we can offer enrichment and learning opportunities to the youngest of children. And we know that this can take place in group care settings under professional guidance.

The trend toward group care for infants and toddlers is affected by the rising number of women in the work force who combine child rearing and careers and by the increasing single-parent families where the parent must work.

Gonzales-Mena and Eyer (1980) define the infant/toddler age group: Infancy is from babyhood until the child learns to walk. Then he or she is called a toddler until almost three years old.

Infant/toddler centers fall into several categories. They may be full day care centers or they may be part-time. They may be more educational, with parent involvement programs, than centers for group care. Most are a combination of physical care coupled with intellectual stimulation and parent development.

Parent relationships are an important part of any program for young children, but especially so when babies and toddlers are involved. The general intention of these centers is to provide care that is supplemental to family life and that supports the child's family structure. In order to do that, the caregiver at an infant/toddler center involves the parents in the everyday decisions about the care of their child, provides them with information about the child's day, and strengthens the child's sense of belonging to that particular family.

Philosophy of Infant/Toddler Care

Current research has enlarged the understanding of the growth process of babies. Piaget defined this time as the sensorimotor stage, and Erikson states that trust and autonomy are the critical lessons to be learned at this age (see Chapter 4). Through these insights, we have come to view the infant more and more as an involved person, one who experiences a wide range of intellectual and emotional abilities. The prevalent philosophy of quality infant/toddler programs recognizes the "personhood" of the baby (Honig, 1981). This means that the infant/toddler is treated with the same consideration as any child. Although they may appear to be helpless beings, babies are in fact persons with feelings, rights, and an individual nature. Gonzales-Mena and Eyer (1980) hold that the infant/toddler deserves "respect as a full human being regardless of age of helplessness."

This philosophy implies that taking care of infants or toddlers is not just a case of thrusting bottles in their mouths when they are hungry or putting them in a playpen to amuse themselves. The caregiver in a quality infant/toddler center understands that feeding, diapering, and playing are, in fact, the curriculum of this age group. The challenge for the caregiver is to find ways to use these daily routines to interact, develop trust and security, and provide educational opportunities. The term "educaring," coined by Magda Gerber, describes the combination of factors that "stress the importance of respectful, responsive, and reciprocal adult–infant interaction" (Gonzales-Mena and Eyer, 1980).

FIGURE 2.10 Toddlers struggle to achieve autonomy.

In many cases, the caregiver's (or educarer's) role extends to helping parents use these same common occurrences to promote the optimum development of their child.

What Is Good Infant/Toddler Care?

Just what is meant by "quality" infant/toddler care? What are the factors that combine to provide the best environments for these youngsters? The following are some of the most important elements found in good infant/toddler centers:

- A low ratio of caregiver to child, the optimum being one to three (Willis and Ricciuti, 1975). The National Day Care Study suggests a ratio of one to four for children under three (Slaughter, 1981).

- The total group size should be between eight and 10 infants/toddlers with the appropriate number of caregivers (Willis and Ricciuti, 1975).

- Programs should be designed to allow for caregivers to spend between 10 and 15 percent of their time on a one-to-one basis with each of the children in their care (Slaughter, 1981).

- The stability and continuity of the staff is important. There should be a minimum amount of staff turnover, with plenty of time allotted for introduction of new personnel to the children.

- The quality and training of caregivers is a key factor. They should be responsive adults who are sensitive to the awakening social, emotional, and intellectual needs of the infant/toddler.

Issues

There are many important issues surrounding quality infant/toddler care. First, good care costs money. The factors that combine to make a quality program—low teacher/child ratio, small groups, individual attention—raise the costs to make infant/toddler care one of the most expensive child care programs. Second, critics of day care—any day care—raise even greater fears about the negative effects on family life and the harmful aspects of group care for the very young. Ignoring the statis-

tics, they do not seem to realize that the question is hardly one of whether or not day care should exist. The need for day care for young children is well documented. According to the Children's Defense Fund (1983), the availability of child care lags behind the need: by 1990 at least one half of all preschool children will have mothers who work outside the home. That means 11.5 million preschoolers will need some kind of child care service (Children's Defense Fund, 1983).

So the question of infant day care is actually several questions: How do we provide quality child care? What aspects of infant/toddler care foster positive growth and development in children? What are the effects of day care on the infant/toddler? On the parents? On the family? On society? How are the disadvantages of day care minimized?

Research can offer some answers to these questions. However, where infants/toddlers are concerned, the conclusions are mixed and still tentative. The long-term effects of group care on babies are not yet available.

Ramey (1981) concluded from his own research in an infant/toddler center that children from low-income families can be cared for in group settings without adverse affects on the child's health, the mother's attitude toward the child, or the child's attachment to the mother, and that high-quality day care influences substantially a broad range of cognitive abilities.

Slaughter's review (1981) of recent research on infant/toddler group care concluded that the bond between parent and child is not unfavorably affected and that intellectual development can benefit. In a statement reflecting the criteria for infant/toddler care, Slaughter acknowledges that the child's social, emotional, and cognitive development will be normal in group care if the care is stable and of high quality. She cites the need for further research regarding the effect of mother's employment on the infant/toddler.

Federal regulations, standards, and funding for infant/toddler programs lead us into the political arena. The issues are again cloaked in controversy. According to Slaughter (1981), the government seems indifferent to the needs of children: "Even after 10 years of concentrated public effort, more than 3 million children . . . under 14 . . . are in programs which have no national standard of child care that even minimally reflects the child development research."

The task for the early childhood professional seems clear. Learn what the issues are, defend policies that reflect high standards, and be prepared to further influence group care for infants and toddlers that is of the highest quality.

Kindergarten

Today's kindergartens reflect a broad picture. Kindergartens are found in elementary schools, churches, private schools, and as part of preschool day care centers. The school day may be 2½ hours long, a half-day, or (of increasing frequency) a full-day session. Age of enrollment varies from 4½ to six years old. Children may be required to attend school every day or just part of the week. Teachers may be trained in elementary school methods, in nursery school, or in a specialty, such as Montessori methods. There may be supportive services, such as library visits, art, and music lessons, or none at all. Classes range in size from a very small group of less than six, to an average of 20 to 25 children and even up to 45 (Ramsey and Bayless, 1980).

Kindergartens at the present time vary from relatively permissive, socializing classes to highly structured, academically oriented programs. The more permissive approach tends to focus on social adjustment to school as a whole and focuses on developmental patterns. Creativity is valued, large blocks of free-play time are provided, and process is emphasized over content.

The second approach is one that has emerged strongly in the last two decades. Usually called an instructional or cognitive model, development in mathmatics, language, and reading is stressed. Direct teacher instruction is common. Behavioral objectives may be established and behavior modification used. Product is emphasized over process.

Most kindergartens are probably a blend of these two models. With the pressure of developing children's intellectual powers, it is common for kindergartens nowadays to offer direct instruction of some academic content. The curriculum of the kindergarten is becoming more comprehensive with commercially packaged kits, instructional aides such as computers, and workbooks. At the same time, giving children free-play time, opportunities to use concrete objects, and attention to social and emotional adjustment, still concerns most kindergarten teachers.

So the issues and controversies are set. Today's child faces a world of unbelievable complexity. All kinds of values are changing, from the roles of men and women, to the growing scarcity of resources, to the real threat of extinction. No one innovation, either in materials or approaches, has shown itself to be the answer to society's—or kindergarten's—problems. Recent research and evaluation have begun to pose questions that need answers. As those answers emerge, keep in mind that

> . . . kindergarten is a beginning, a beginning of school experience. It must be just that—a beginning. Kindergarten is not first grade; it is not supposed to 'hurry up' the maturation process so that children will be able to perform at a superior level when they reach first grade. Kindergarten should be a place where each child is recognized as an individual and where individual needs are met.
>
> (Ramsey and Bayless, 1980)

After-School Programs

After-school programs are designed for children after they finish their regular academic day. This type of care is usually available for children in kindergarten through third grade. Some family day care homes provide this service, as do individual programs designed specifically for the five-through-eight-year-old.

Generally, by the time children reach the age of eight or nine, they stay at home or engage in extracurricular activities at school or in the community. Younger children need adult supervision and access to appropriate materials and activities when they finish their school day. There is a critical need for safe, recreational programs for children of this age. It is estimated that there are over three million five-year-olds in the nation, most of whom have only half-day kindergarten (Carlson et al., 1980). The number of six-to-eight-year-olds is even higher, and more and more these children have parents who both work or have only one parent who *must* work.

What happens to these children after school? For the kindergartener, school may be over at noon. From 1:30 to 3:00 P.M., first-, second- and third-graders are released from their school day. Too often these children are sent home with a house key around their necks or in their pockets. They are instructed to look after themselves and possibly a younger sibling until the parent (or parents) comes home from work. These *"latch key" children,* as they are known, are a young and vulnerable population. The early childhood community has embraced their obvious need for good after-school programs.

The essentials of after-school care reflect the needs of the parents, teachers, and children involved. Flexible hours, reasonable tuition rates, and clear lines of communication are of primary importance to parents. To ensure continual care, scheduling must take into consideration the elementary school calendar. Holidays, conference times, and minimum-day schedules of public schools must be considered. Opportunities to extend the after-school program can originate from the use of community resources such as library story hours, swimming facilities, and parks.

In planning, the teaching staff must be aware of how their program differs from the rest of the child's normal school day. Knowing that this is probably the third environment, set of rules, and adult supervision that the child has faced that day is uppermost in the minds of the teachers. Carlson et al. (1980) identify four components necessary for success. Children need:

- *A time for sharing.* Small conversational groups where children can relate the day's happenings

with an interested adult and their after-school friends.

- *To control the experience.* Children actively participate in group planning of short- and long-term projects and activities. Children move freely, choosing between indoor and outdoor activities, with many choices in a supervised, guided, free-play environment.

- *Vigorous activity.* Outdoor play, indoor climbers, slides, and other large-motor equipment are popular. Self-directed chasing games are important.

- *Challenging curriculum.* Craft materials requiring increasingly complex fine motor and planning skills are successful with this age group. Table activities, such as origami, checkers, Chinese checkers, marbles, card games, charades, and puppetry add to the necessary stimulation.

Children need the safety, the creative opportunity, and the emotionally supportive relationships that after-school care can provide. As the trend of working mothers continues, more of these programs will appear as a natural extension of responsible child care.

CRITERIA AFFECTING PROGRAMS

There are many factors that determine exactly what type of program will best serve the young child. Some of these variables emerged through the descriptions of the many kinds of settings available for children today. Programs in early childhood are defined by the elements listed in Figure 2.12. Any one program is a combination of these factors. At one time or another, each factor was given specific and serious consideration regarding its impact on the program desired.

SUMMARY

Educational facilities for young children reach a broad population. They serve children from in-

FIGURE 2.11 After-school programs must provide interests and challenges beyond the child's regular school day.

fancy through elementary-school age. There is an array of programs available, which varies for philosophical reasons as well as because of ages of children enrolled. Early childhood teachers have a wide range of programs from which to choose—as do parents.

The traditional nursery school and its sister programs of day care, laboratory schools, and parent cooperatives form the core of early childhood programs. The intervention models of the 1960s and 1970s—Head Start and Follow-Through—are vari-

ations on the theme. They are specific attempts to provide early education and intervention to children caught in poverty's cycle. Other schools, such as Montessori or behavior analysis programs, are based on clearly stated principles with outlined procedures for teachers and children.

In reflecting the needs of society, it is no wonder that extended day programs have been created. Not only are children being cared for in group situations before and after school hours, they are being placed in the group settings at an earlier age. The

Criteria Affecting Programs	For Example
1. The age of the children served	Is it a toddler group? Infant care? A specific age group? A multiage group?
2. The philosophy expressed	Is there one overriding philosophy, such as Montessori or behavior analysis? Is it an eclectic school, combining several approaches?
3. The goals of the program	Are the objectives academic preparation? Custodial care? Enrichment for preschoolers? Socialization? Parent education?
4. The purpose for which it was established	For profit? As a laboratory for research? As a place for parents to meet? As a social service vehicle?
5. The sponsoring agency and its requirements	To whom is the program responsible? The federal government? A family service agency? School district? Church board? Employer? Private individual? How does that agency influence and affect the program?
6. The quality and training of the teaching staff	Do all teachers have degrees or credentials in early childhood? What kind of experience is required? Is there an opportunity for in-service training and continuing education?
7. The physical environment	What is the amount and shape of space available indoors and out?
8. The general population served	What is the ethnic makeup of the surrounding community? What languages are spoken? What are the economic status and family patterns in the neighborhood? Will it serve the handicapped and disabled?
9. The financial stability	Is money available for equipment and supplies? Is the budget sufficient to pay child care workers reasonable salaries? Is the financial base sound? Will funding end?

FIGURE 2.12 Chart of criteria affecting programs.

1970s gave rise to numerous infant/toddler programs. After-school care is becoming common in many communities.

As varied as they are, there is also a certain similarity among all programs for young children. Consideration must be given to a number of factors when reviewing the needs of young children and their families. Some of these elements are the ages of the children the program will serve, the qualifications and experience of the teaching staff, the funding base and financial support available, and the goals of the program to meet the needs of all children and their families. With so many choices, those who desire child care will find options that suit their specific needs.

Review Questions

1. Match the program with the appropriate description:

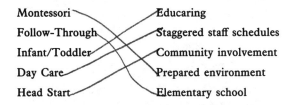

Montessori — Educaring
Follow-Through — Staggered staff schedules
Infant/Toddler — Community involvement
Day Care — Prepared environment
Head Start — Elementary school

2. Name and describe the three sister programs within traditional preschool boundaries.

3. Why are some early childhood programs called "intervention" schools?

4. Are there differences among preschool and kindergarten programs? What are they?

5. What are some of the criteria that affect all children's programs?

Learning Activities

1. Choose one program and describe how you would operate that type of class. Include the daily schedule, number and skill level of teachers, types of parent contacts, and the activities for children.

2. Consider how each of these problems might be handled in each of these different programs:

   Problems: One child hits another
   Parent doesn't pay tuition on time
   A child who withdraws from social contact
   A child who wanders

   Programs: Montessori
   Day care
   Parent cooperative

3. What role would children's social skills play in these settings:
   Traditional nursery school
   Montessori
   Kindergarten
   Infant/Toddler

4. What are the licensing regulations for child care in your area? Describe the steps necessary in your town to open a
   • nursery school.
   • day care center.
   • family day care home.

5. Which government agencies are involved in the licensing procedure?

Bibliography

Banta, Thomas J. "Montessori: Myth or Reality?" In Parker, Ronald (ed.), *The Preschool in Action*. Boston: Allyn & Bacon, 1972.

Carlson, Nancy A., et al. "After-Kindergarten Day Care: A Challenge to the Community." *Young Children,* November 1980, pp. 13–20.

Chattin-McNichols, John P. "The Effects of Montessori School Experience." *Young Children,* July 1981, pp. 49–66.

Children's Defense Fund. *A Children's Defense Budget.* Washington, D.C.: Children's Defense Fund, 1983.

Cole, Luella. "Basic Ideas of the Montessori Method." In Coopersmith and Feldman (eds.), *The Formative Years.* San Fransisco: Albion Publishing Co., 1974.

Collins, Glenn. "Employers Offering Seminars to Help the Working Parent." *New York Times,* June 23, 1983.

Elkind, David. "Humanizing the Curriculum." In *Early Childhood Education,* Annual Edition. Guilford, Conn.: The Dushkin Publishing Group, 1982.

Elkind, David. "Montessori Education: Abiding Contributions and Contemporary Challenge." *Young Children,* January 1983, pp. 3–10.

Evans, Ellis. *Contemporary Influences in Early Childhood Education.* New York: Holt, Rinehart and Winston, 1975.

Gonzales-Mena, Janet, and Eyer, Dianne W. *Infancy and Caregiving.* Palo Alto, Calif.: Mayfield Publishing Co., 1980.

Goodwin, Judy. "Evaluation of the Original Follow-Through Program." In ERIC Document #ED 202 607. Philadelphia: Office of Research and Evaluation of the School District of Philadelphia, March 1981.

Honig, Alice. "What Are the Needs of Infants?" *Young Children,* November 1981, pp. 3–10.

Hymes, James L., Jr. *Early Childhood Education—The Year in Review.* Carmel, Calif.: Hacienda Press, 1982.

Lazar, Irving, et al. *Summary: The Persistence of Preschool Effects.* Washington, D.C.: U.S. Department of Health, Education, and Welfare, 1977.

Lindner, Eileen; Mattis, Mary C.; and Rogers, June. *When Churches Mind the Children.* Ypsilanti, Mich.: High/Scope Press, 1983.

Maccoby, Eleanor E., and Zellner, Miriam. *Experiments in Primary Education: Aspects of Project Follow-Through.* New York: Harcourt Brace Jovanovich, 1970.

Moore, Shirley G., and Kilmer, Sally. *Contemporary Preschool Education.* New York: John Wiley and Sons, 1973.

National Committee for Day Care of Children. *Newsletter,* Spring 1965.

O'Connell, Joanne Curry. "Research in Review: Children of Working Mothers: What the Research Tells Us." *Young Children,* January 1983, pp. 62–70.

Ramey, Craig T. "Consequences of Infant Day Care." In Weissbourd and Musick (eds.), *Infants: Their Social Environment.* Washington, D.C.: National Association for the Education of Young Children, 1981.

Ramsey, Marjorie, and Bayless, Kathleen. *Kindergarten: Programs and Practices.* St. Louis: C.V. Mosby Co., 1980.

Read, Katherine, and Patterson, June. *The Nursery School and Kindergarten.* New York: Holt, Rinehart and Winston, 1980.

Slaughter, Diana T. "Social Policy Issues Affecting Infants." In Weissbourd and Musick (eds.), *Infants: Their Social Environment.* Washington, D.C.: National Association for the Education of Young Children, 1981.

Soar, Robert S., and Soar, Ruth M. "Am Empirical Analysis of Selected Follow-Through Programs." In Gordon (ed.), *Early Childhood Education,* Seventy-First Yearbook of the National Society for the Study of Education, Part II. Chicago: University of Chicago Press, 1972.

Stanford Research Institute. "Longitudinal Evaluation of Selected Features of the National Follow-Through Program." ERIC Document # 067 266 and 057 267, 1971.

Stevens, Joseph H., Jr. "The National Day Care Home Study: Family Day Care in the United States." *Young Children,* May 1982, pp. 59–66.

Verzaro-Lawrence, Marce, et al. "Industry-Related Day Care: Trends and Options." *Young Children,* January 1982, pp. 4–10.

White, Burton L. "Viewpoint: Should You Stay Home with Your Baby?" *Young Children,* November 1981, pp. 11–17.

Willis, Anne, and Ricciuti, Henry. *A Good Beginning for Babies.* Washington, D.C.: National Association for the Education of Young Children, 1975.

SECTION II

WHO IS THE CHILD?

K. Eileen Allen

WHO IS THE CHILD? In attempting to respond to that question, it might be wise to first ask a counterquestion—Who are we? The answers to both questions will be quite different today than in the 1960s, and different again from the answers given in the 1940s. In the course of these years, our perspective as practitioners in the field of early childhood education has changed appreciably, and so have our attempts to answer "Who is the child?"

In the 1940s, we were entering into an age of smugness, even conceit, about our knowledge of the young child. The genetic-maturationist theory of development governed most of our thinking. The evidence of the times was so convincing that few of us questioned the prevailing thesis—that the underpinnings of all development lay in sequential, biological changes based upon specific hereditary information mapped out at the moment of conception. And so, when asked "Who is the child?" we glibly answered that the child was the product of its genes, and everything that the child could ever be was determined at the moment of conception.

Such a deterministic philosophy was a forerunner of the normative movement. Researchers, led by Gesell, assessed groups of infants and children during the first months and years of life and charted the rate and sequence of their development at each age level. Armed with these data, we began a process that, in retrospect, can only be called naive. We gave ourselves over to "ages and stages" stereotyping. Catch phrases, such as the Terrible Twos, the Trusting Threes, and the Fearless Fours, became the banners of our trade. We never questioned the elitist quality, the homogeneity, the relatively small numbers of children on whom the normative data were based. Nor did we examine the often unwarranted conclusions derived from those data.

In spite of oversubscribing to an "ages and stages" theory of development, we did learn a great deal about developmental sequences, and especially about the acquisition of motor skills. And even though the importance of the maturationist theory faded into relative obscurity, the whole issue of heredity and its possible impact on a wide range of behaviors is reemerging today as an important area of study.

In the early 1960s, an about-face occurred in answer to the question, "Who is the child?" With almost one voice came the answer that the child was a product of

Who Is the Young Child?

the environment. Everything a child could ever be was dependent upon the kind of environment in which he or she spent the first year of life. Where did such a notion come from?

Learning theorists (starting way back with John Locke's *tabula rasa,* or "blank slate," concept of development) had been slowly but surely building a case for the role of the environment in determining a child's developmental outcome. Research began to demonstrate conclusively that the *result* of a child's behavior was the crucial factor in determining what a child learned. Study after study showed that children tended to acquire behaviors that produced success or positive results, and that they avoided experiences that ended in failure or negative results.

Again, another period of naivete and oversubscribing—this time to the theoretically baseless assumption that the child was little more than a puppet, a passive recipient of whatever the environment provided, or failed to provide. To the credit of all, this fallacy was short-lived. Learning theory subsequently broadened its theoretical base to focus on social learning and observational learning. Research that analyzed social interactions, like the mother–infant studies, yielded evidence that the human infant was far from being a passive creature. From the earliest hours of life, the infant learned from observation and was a remarkably good imitator of the mother's facial expressions. The neonate was shown to be an active observer, imitator, and responder who evoked additional respones from significant persons in the environment, thereby prompting further responding from the infant. Of course, the interaction may or may not be benign. A placid, cuddly baby who expresses needs clearly and at regular times is likely to have quite a different experience from a colicky infant who is tense, fussy, and unpredictable in crying, eating, and sleeping patterns.

Almost concurrent with these analyses of development came a changing view of intelligence. No longer was intelligence viewed as fixed and innate, unfolding in ways comparable to a child's developing physical capacities. Instead, the theory, as put forth by Piaget, was that the development of intelligence—or cognition—was analagous to a layering or building block process. In this process, interaction with the environment provided critical nourishment for the child's intellectual development. J. Mc V. Hunt, theorizing further from Piaget's writings, described cognitive development as the direct result of the child's exploration of the environment. By actively playing with or manipulating a variety of objects and events that were familiar in many respects, but which also contained elements just a bit beyond the child's immediate knowledge base, cognitive development thrived. And so an interactionist theory of development, a melding of maturational and environmental forces, began to take form.

Other forces, both social and political, were at work, too. The Civil Rights Movement and its exposure of the inequities in our educational system, together with the repudiation of a wholly deterministic viewpoint of development, led to compensatory early education programs for minority and poverty children. Not long after, we came to recognize that the needs and rights of handicapped children must also be respected. These children, and those in our poverty sector, were as much a part of the answer to "Who is the child?" as were the vast majority of children who were fortunate enough to be spared physical or environmental trauma and deprivation.

The inclusion of poor children, minority children, and handicapped children in our response to "Who is the child?" expanded our understanding of developmental processes. True, even at the height of our "ages and stages" period, we touted the need to recognize individual differences among children, and to value each child's uniqueness. But did we really believe it, especially if the child was unkempt or poor, slow or from a different culture? I think not. Today, having broadened our developmental perspective, there is wide recognition that every child is a special child with a unique personality, learning style, and interest. Every child is deserving of genuine respect for the uniqueness of his or her family history and cultural background.

With this growing esteem for the differences among children, families, and cultures, we also began to develop a different attitude toward parents. Instead of viewing ourselves as the experts—and parents as humble targets or objects of our expertise— we came to see parents as partners, *senior partners,* in promoting a child's development. We faced up to the reality that it is they, not us, who will continue to provide support and carry the primary responsibility for the child's socialization and developmental progress. We came to recognize, too, that the more delayed or the more impaired the child, the greater the need for us to listen to parents, seek their help, and work in close partnership with them.

What else have we learned from broadening our definition of the child to include *all* children, regardless of physical, cognitive, or social-economic differences? Most notable is a reaffirmation that the child is, indeed, more than a sum of its parts. True, we have always espoused the "whole child" or holistic approach to development, but the concept tended to be didactic rather than applied. Only through the combination of service, research, and clinical training activities in interdisciplinary settings devoted to retarded, handicapped, and high-risk infants and children did rigorous evidence of the essential interrelatedness of all areas of development come to light. In such settings, we came to see how futile it was to view any problem from a single perspective. We learned that more often than not, a language delay, for example, stemmed from physical, neurological, nutritional, psychological, and social factors interacting in complex combinations with other events in the child's environment.

Where does all of this leave us in formulating an answer to "Who is the child?" The here and now of child development in the 1980s most assuredly boasts a broad knowledge base. But history has taught us to be cautious. It seems that the more we know about the developing child, the more we have to learn. Perhaps the best answer to the question is that we are still searching for the answer.

K. EILEEN ALLEN has been involved in the field of early childhood at many levels—as a lay teacher in a parent cooperative, as the head teacher in the Developmental Psychology Laboratory Preschool at the University of Washington, and as Coordinator of Early Childhood Education, Research, and Teacher Training in the Child Development and Mental Retardation Center, also at the University of Washington. Currently, she is Professor of Human Development at the University of Kansas, Lawrence, Kansas.

During the more than three decades that Mrs. Allen has been in the field, she has been deeply involved in many "firsts" in child development and early childhood education. Among other projects, she helped design and implement one of the earliest training programs for Head Start teachers, and she conducted some of the first service, training, and research programs related to an interdisciplinary approach with young handicapped children. She also directed one of the first First Chance Network Model preschools, which demonstrated the value of mainstreaming handicapped children.

More recently, she was selected as a Congressional Science Fellow by the Society for Research in Child Development and the American Association for the Advancement of Science. Much of Mrs. Allen's university teaching and public lecturing now focuses on social policy, while she continues hands-on activities with children.

3

Defining the Young Child

Questions for Thought

- What is the age range for early childhood?
- What are some of the basic characteristics of each age?
- How does the development of one area of growth affect other areas?
- What are the implications for teaching children of varying levels of development?
- What are some cautions to take when interpreting age-level characteristic charts? How are they useful?
- Who is the whole child?
- Who are special-needs children?
- What are some of the common types of handicaps found in preschoolers?
- What is mainstreaming?

Outline

DEFINING THE CHILD

Children Can

Who can crawl under a table
Who can sit under a chair?
Who can fit their feet in little shoes
And sleep most anywhere?

Who can play very much longer,
Play very much harder than grown-ups ever
    dare?
You're a child so you can do it.
You can do it anywhere.

Who can wake up every morning
And be ready right away?
Who can notice all the tiny things
That other people say?

Who can make the things they play with
Something different for every single day?
You're a child and you can do it.
Children do it any way.
    © 1969 by Fred M. Rogers;
    used by permission.

Children—who are they? When entering a classroom, questions arise in teachers' minds about the youngsters they see:

- What do children say?
- What can children do?
- What do children think?
- How do children feel?

Glancing around the room brings an awareness of the group as a whole. Individuals blur among a number of children, all the same size and same age. At this point, they are hardly more than a list of names with ages attached. Quickly, however, a teacher becomes conscious of a single child here and there. In this assortment of small people, different sizes, shapes, and colors emerge.

Through the Teacher's Eyes

Physical Impressions

Teachers usually begin to define children by their physical characteristics. Initially, their differences are most obvious by the way they look.

Eric is a tall blonde. He is much larger than his just-three age would indicate. He has long slender fingers and arms to match. His movements are fluid; he lopes across the room toward the easel.

Lamar's short stocky build and constant swagger lend the impression that he is a pretty tough

FIGURE 3.1 Children: anywhere, any way.

character. His coffee-and-cream complexion, soft, curly hair, and smile offset that image.

Natalie at four is a study in perpetual motion. Green eyes flashing, arms and legs waving, she ignores the bulk of her diaper as she propels herself down the slide. There is little indication that the mild case of spina bifida she has inhibits her motor activities. It certainly hasn't affected her daring.

Nothing will heighten an awareness of the individuality of each child more than working in the classroom. Teachers quickly learn what makes each child special. By watching and observing children, teachers accumulate a great deal of detailed information. Adults learn what children really look like as children move their bodies, change expressions and assume a posture. A teacher can sense whether Sonja is happy, hurt, or hurried by the way she moves and how she looks. Rodrigo's face mirrors his distress or his delight. The observant teacher learns to read children for evidence of their social, emotional, physical, and intellectual growth. Children quite naturally express these characteristics with their whole body; each child's response is unique.

Children's Behaviors

Children's behaviors are so individual; they show their own personal responses to life. They relate to people in ways that express their original nature. Dina has an ability to get her peers to wait on her; Sean trails the teachers for constant companionship. Their responses to the classroom environment are also singular. Ginny becomes overstimulated and loses control; Clark stands and watches other children for long periods of time before he joins in. Teachers become aware of individual differences in the skill level of children. They notice that of the five children at the art table, for instance, only one of them is holding scissors correctly and cutting paper.

How Children Are Alike

The similarities of the many children in a class are striking. The more they are different, the more

they are the same. There seems to be a natural discrepancy here. Teachers can see the differences—wide differences—yet there are common characteristics within the age group itself. Six toddlers working on an art project exhibit six different personal styles, yet typically, they all become distracted and leave their projects half finished. Observation of children—how they look and how they act—helps the teacher see each child as an individual. When many children in a classroom are observed, behaviors common to that age become clear. There is enough standard behavior appropriate to certain age levels that allows for some generalizations about children's behavior.

Descriptions of these common characteristics date back to a classic collection of research by Gesell and Ilg. Beginning on page 68 are a series of "word pictures" depicting these *age level characteristics* from infancy through age five. In looking at individual children or a group, these descriptions are helpful in understanding the nature of the child and normal growth.

How Children Differ

Watching and working with children exposes how very different each child is. What makes children differ so, especially when they have so many features in common? Megan gives the tire swing a big push. Ariel shrieks with delight, but Hans bursts into tears and screams to get off. What accounts for the wide range of behaviors evident when you observe any group of children?

Genetic Makeup. This certainly accounts for some of the differences. Each child is a unique combination of *genes* that "contributes to the emergence and nature of every human trait from the color of the eyes . . . to the individual's ultimate intelligence and creativity" (Gardner, 1982).

Environment. The effects of the world on inherited genes also play a role. The number and kinds of experiences children have affect how they develop. The attitudes with which children are raised, their culture, socioeconomic status, and their com-

FIGURE 3.2 Even within one classroom, children have many different sizes and shapes.

munity combine in countless ways to affect growth. Good, nutritious food, adequate play space, interested and stimulating adults, the quality of life in the neighborhood, and family stability and relationships affect individual development. Whether a child lives in the South Bronx or Beverly Hills, environmental factors interact with genes to create a single, individual person.

The small child who stands at the classroom door is the sum total of the physical, intellectual, social, and emotional factors of home and heredity. What nature provides, the world shapes and bends. Using intelligence as an example, Gardner (1982) states the interdependency of environment and genetics this way: "The limit of intelligence is fixed by genetics, but the actual intelligence achieved reflects the diverse environments."

There are three other factors concerning the developmental scheme of things that account for individual differences.

Children Grow and Develop at Different Rates. Each child has an inner mechanism for monitoring growth. It is a timetable that varies from child to child. It means that each child is ready to learn at a given time, which may or may not coincide with the rest of the group. This readiness factor must be respected.

Development Is Predictable and Follows a Sequence. Periods of rapid growth and activity are followed by periods of calmness and consolidation. *Behavioral swings* at the half-year mark are common in many children. The pleasant, well-balanced three-year-old may become shy and begin to stutter at three-and-one-half. The age at which this occurs is not as important as the sequence in which it happens. The important thing to remember is that children will exhibit markedly different behaviors in the period of one short year. Teachers prepare for these times and appreciate them as a normal course of events for the growing child.

There Is a Set of Developmental Tasks. These challenge children at every stage in their growth. Teachers will recognize where children are in the mastery of these tasks, knowing that normal development will account for the inherent differences in children.

Implications for Teaching

The differences in children's development must be accounted for when planning a program for a group. How do teachers take all these factors into consideration? How do they meet the needs of the individual child while addressing the concerns and interests of the total group?

Program Planning. Teachers generally begin by planning individual and group activities according to the age level of the class they teach, knowing that certain behavior patterns exist. Planning begins around the known similarities, the developmental tasks and age-appropriate behavior common to that group of children. Goals are set for the children based on these general characteristics. As the school year progresses, teachers observe individuals and the group and change the developmental goals as needed. Individual differences in children are incorporated into the planning; activities selected allow for a variety of responses from children at different stages of development. A pasting activity encourages creativity in the most adept three-year-old and still allows the less-skilled two-year-old to explore the feel of the paste on fingers and hands. Programs are planned to meet the needs and challenges of the whole group.

Grouping of children by rigid age levels seems contrary to our understanding of individual rates of growth, readiness factors, and wide ranges of abilities. It is a convenient, though arbitrary, system of teaching children. The implication for teachers is clear: plan for the age level with the understanding and appreciation of the variations in development even within a one-year span. Know the child; know

what to expect and what development has taken place. Look at the stages of growth for the age level just below and just above the one in which you teach.

Teachers' Response. The key word for teachers is *acceptance*. Teachers must not only accept the differences in children, they must plan for them. In doing so, they show respect for the individuality of each child in the class. Accepting the way children reveal themselves fosters the uniqueness that makes each one a special person.

Through Children's Eyes

Another way to define children is to look at them from their own point of view. What does it mean to look at the world through children's eyes? What is a child's perspective on the world?

Adults carry into the classroom a great many perceptions about children. Having the advantage of many more years of experience, they tend to forget how much they know! The child they see is sometimes blurred through a great many filters. These filters are attitudes, concepts, experiences, and prejudices. What looks mundane to an adult, such as a trip on the subway, fills children with the joy and wonder of discovery.

To view a classroom through the eyes of a child, one must set aside the filtered lenses of the grown-up world. The young child in the classroom is of the here and now and likes what is familiar and known. The preschooler takes pleasure in common, everyday experiences, learns by doing, and uses all five senses. Though aware of a great many things, the young child is a "superficial learner" (Moore and Kilmer, 1973) who is not interested in depth of learning. This may be due to a short attention span or because there is just so *much* to learn about.

The teacher learns to look through children's eyes—what interests them, what they avoid, who their friends are, how they respond in a variety of situations, and how they learn. When Kitty must play it safe with a friend who is less timid than

FIGURE 3.3 Teachers capitalize on each child's uniqueness.

she or Jacques puts together facts in ways that make sense to him, the teacher recognizes these as expressions of individuality.

Adults find that by looking at the world through the eyes of a child, they gain a different and valuable perspective as teacher.

AGES AND STAGES

Each developmental phase has characteristic traits. In the following pages some of the classic normative data collected by Gesell is combined with theories of Piaget, Elkind, and Erikson to demonstrate what children have in common at various ages. Despite the wide range of individual differences at all ages, there are some characteristics children share that are worth keeping in mind. These common behaviors help teachers prescribe programs and plan activities and curricula. They lend perspective. Word pictures of a child, taken from age-

level charts, help teachers know what to expect and when to expect it. By using the charts as a reference, teachers lessen the risk of expecting too much or too little of children at any given age. If, for instance, four-year-olds typically "tell tall tales," teachers' responses to their stories reflect that awareness. The fun of making up a story and the use of imagination is acknowledged, but there is not a concern that the child is lying. Age-level characteristics give a frame of reference with which to handle daily situations and a basis for planning appropriate guidance measures.

Most classes are labeled "the two's," "the three's," and so on. Schools enroll children according to a chronological order based on whether a birthday falls before or after an *arbitrary* deadline. Yet most child development texts no longer use the narrow one-year age span when setting out behavior characteristics. Larger, more inclusive groupings of Infant, Toddler, Preschooler, and so on are common. The reason for this change is "that

FIGURE 3.4 Understanding children requires a youthful perspective.

individual differences are so great and growth patterns so diverse that any delineation of common characteristics for a particular age level is bound to be deceptive and misleading" (Elkind, 1978). That point of view has merit; age-level charts can be misunderstood unless used with discretion.

One consideration is what use teachers will make of the charts. It is important to know what range of behaviors occur and to be able to recognize them as normal patterns of growth. That helps to define and interpret the child's action in light of what is considered typical. Guidance and discipline are based on an awareness of the expected behaviors common to a given age range. Many so called "problem behaviors" are normal behaviors of the age in which they occur. This does not imply a passive approach; teachers and parents do not ignore undesirable behavior because the child is "going through a stage." Instead adults seek to guide and direct children in ways that enhance their overall growth. Four-year-olds test limits and are resistant to con-

trols. The wise teacher accepts the testing of power and individuality, yet still maintains necessary limits to behavior.

Use the charts with care. A profile of the whole child is helpful, but avoid the tendency to overclassify. Look and listen to the children in the classroom in order to interpret theory. Balance your impressions with classroom experience of real children.

The Value of Word Pictures

There are several things to keep in mind for the age-level charts to be a valuable teaching tool. It is very important to realize that these norms of development refer to average or typical behavior. They cannot be applied to an individual child too literally. If you were to look at a class of six-year-olds using the profiles, for instance, you would find that probably half of the children would fit the majority of the description. Some of them would not yet have reached this level of development and some would have already gone through this stage. Shawna might well fit the general description of the six-year-old at a physical level. Her language and intellectual levels may be closer to a seven-year-old, while her social skills may be typical of many four-year-olds. There may very well be characteristics that Shawna will *never* exhibit. It won't work to use the chart as a measuring stick, comparing one child to another, since children develop at their own rates and in their own ways.

Remember that children probably go through most of the stages described, and in the same sequence. But they will do so in ways that reflect their own rate of growth and their own background. Use these characteristics not to pit children against each other to see who is developing faster, but to compare the child to himself. Looking at Dwayne, it helps to know where he is in relation to most two-year-olds, but more important, where he is now, six months from now, a year from now, and what he was like a year ago. A clear picture of his rate of growth emerges. His recent change of behavior, for instance, might be attributed to the 2½-year-old stage of *disequilibrium,* even though Dwayne is chronologically two years, nine months.

The following word pictures are designed to help classroom teachers. Characteristics listed are:

- behaviors most common to the age group
- those that have implications for children in group settings
- those that suggest guidance and disciplinary measures

Word Pictures

Four basic developmental areas are included in the word pictures:

- *Physical/Motor Development.* Includes gross motor, fine motor and perceptual motor.
- *Language Development.* Includes children's utterances, pronunciation, vocabulary, sentence length, and the ability to express ideas, needs, and feelings. It includes receptive language (do they understand what they hear?) and verbal levels (what do they say?)
- *Intellectual Development.* This generally means the ability to perceive and think. Includes curiosity, memory, attention span, general knowledge, problem solving, analytical thinking, beginning reading, computing skills, and other cognitive processes.
- *Social-Emotional Development.* Includes a child's relationship with himself and others, self-concept, self-esteem, and the ability to express feelings.

=== **NOTE** ===

The word picture charts on pp. 68–74 are adapted from the following texts: Ames and Ilg, *Your One-Year-Old, Your Two-Year-Old, Your Three-Year-Old, Your Four-Year-Old, Your Five-Year-Old;* Gesell and Ilg, *Infant and Child in the Culture of Today;* Hurlock, *Child Development;* and Stone and Church, *Childhood and Adolescence.* See Appendix A for word pictures of the six-, seven-, and eight-year-old.

SOCIAL-EMOTIONAL

6–8 weeks: social smiles
2 months: begins social games
3 months: distinguishes familiar faces;
turns head toward human voice;
smiles in response to a smile;
kicks, smiles, waves in response;
cries when left alone;
recognizes parent
4 months: genuine laugh;
smiles when spoken to;
loves attention
5 months to 1 year: stranger anxiety
6 months: distinguishes between voices;
smiles, babbles at strangers;
develops attachment;
begins to play imitation games;
plays peek-a-boo;
sensitive to parental moods
9 months: screams to get own way
10 months: recognizes self in mirror

Play is activity only for present moment.
Fears unfamiliar: people, places, things.
Beginning sense of separate self.

PHYSICAL/MOTOR

By 1 year: grows 8 inches, gains 15 lbs., lengthens
by 40%, doubles brain size, grows full
head of hair
Bounces in crib
Uses whole-body motions
4 months: sees, grasps objects
5 months: examines fingers;
sits when propped
6 months: rolls over;
discovers feet;
teething begins
7 months: crawls
8 months: sits up unaided;
pulls to standing position;
pincer grasp established
9 months: creeps
10 months: feeds self with spoon
11 months: stands alone; cruises
12 months: first steps
Late infancy: can move hands in rotation to
turn knobs

LANGUAGE

At birth: cries
6–8 weeks: coos
Gestures to communicate:
pushes objects away, squirms,
reaches out to people, pouts,
smacks lips, shrieks, points
2 months: voluntary vocal sounds
3 months: babbles
6–12 months: imitation sound games

Responds to variety of sounds.
Makes vowel sounds.
Acquires receptive language.

INTELLECTUAL-COGNITIVE

At birth: senses function, especially pain, touch
10 weeks: memory is evident
4 months: smiles of recognition
7–10 months: solves simple problems (knocks over
box to get toy)
8 months: begins to believe in permanence of
objects
8–12 months: intentionality in acts
11 months: begins trial-error experimentation
12 months: plays drop/retrieve games

Explores with hands and fingers
Smiles, vocalizes at image in mirror

FIGURE 3.5

FIGURE 3.5 Within the first year, the infant learns to recognize himself.

SOCIAL-EMOTIONAL

Almost totally egocentric
Likes to be noticed; loves an audience
Lacks inhibitions
Insists on own way
Insists on doing things by self
Becomes demanding, assertive
Adapts easily
Plays by self in playpen
Refers to self by name
Grabby about possessions
Laughs loudly at peek-a-boo
Cries when left alone
Somewhat asocial
Relates to adults better than children
Not interested in other children
Talks mostly to self

LANGUAGE

Enjoys vocalizing to self
Says first meaningful word
Babbles in own jargon
Uses "eh-eh" or "uh-uh" with gestures
Names closest relatives
Repeats adults' words
Points to communicate needs, wants
Shakes head "no" to respond
Responds to directions to fetch, point
Obeys verbal requests
Answers "What's that?"
Understands simple phrases

PHYSICAL/MOTOR

Awkward coordination; chubby body
Tottering stance
Creeps when in a hurry
Walks with increasing confidence
Walks with feet wide apart, arms out, head forward
Finds it difficult to turn corners
Goes up and down stairs on hands and knees
Backs into chair to sit down
Can squat for long periods of time
Motor-minded: constant motion
Loves to pull objects

Runs with stiff, flat gait
Uses whole-arm movements
Fumbles, drops objects
Scribbles
Turns pages two or three at a time
Zips/unzips large zipper
Likes holding objects in both hands

INTELLECTUAL-COGNITIVE

Points to objects in a book
Matches similar objects
Fits round block in round hole
Loves opposites: up/down, yes/no
Imitates simple tasks
Interest shifts quickly
Short attention span
Follows one direction
Gives up easily
Conclusions are important: close doors, shut books
Thinks with feet; action-oriented
Builds tower of three to four small blocks

FIGURE 3.6 The 18-month-old child shifts interests quickly.

SOCIAL-EMOTIONAL

Self-centered
Unable to share
Clings to familiar; resistant to change
Ritualistic; insists on routines
Dependent
Likes one adult at a time
Quits readily; easily frustrated
Goes to extremes
Impulsive; shifts activities suddenly
Easily distracted
Pushes, shoves
Finicky, fussy eater
Refers to self by given name
Treats people as inanimate objects
Dawdles; slow-geared
Plays parallel
Watches others
Likes people
Excited about own capabilities

LANGUAGE

Uses two- or three-word sentences
Telegraphic sentences: "Throw ball"
Has difficulty in pronunciation
"Mine" most prominent pronoun
Spontaneous language; rhythmic, repetitive
Constant talking; interested in sound
Sings phrases of songs, not on pitch
Can't articulate feelings
Frustrated when not understood
May stutter
Asks "Whassat?" about pictures
Can match words with objects
Repeats words and phrases

PHYSICAL/MOTOR

Uses whole-body action
Pushes, pulls, pokes
Climbs into things
Leans forward while running
Climbs stairs one by one
Dependent on adults for dressing
Can help undress

Grasps cup with two hands
Awkward with small objects
Lugs, tumbles, topples; unsteady
Alternates hands; preference developing
Can rotate to fit objects
Expresses emotions bodily
Sensory-oriented
Cuts last teeth
Has difficulty relaxing

INTELLECTUAL-COGNITIVE

Investigates with touch and taste
Intrigued by water, washing
Likes to fill, empty things
Has limited attention span
Lives in present
Only understands familiar concepts
Colors and numbers are meaningless
Needs own name used
Doesn't recognize problems
Does one thing at a time
Remembers orders of routines
Recalls where toys are left
Knows, points to: arms, nose, mouth, feet, eyes

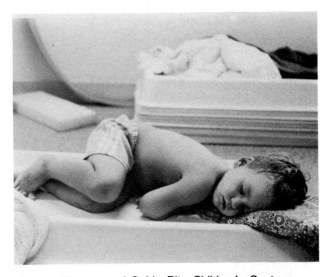

FIGURE 3.7 Sometimes the two-year-old has trouble relaxing. (Courtesy of Stride Rite Children's Centers, Cambridge, Mass.)

SOCIAL-EMOTIONAL

Highly imitative of adults
Wants to please adults; conforms
Responds to verbal suggestions
Easily prompted, redirected
Can be bargained with, reasoned with
Begins to share, take turns, wait
Avid "me-too"er
Exuberant, talkative, humorous
Has imaginary companions
Has nightmares, animal phobias
Plays consciously, cooperatively with others
Plays spontaneously in groups
Dramatizes play
Goes after desires; fights for them
Asserts independence often
Often stymied, frustrated, jealous
Sympathizes

LANGUAGE

Talkative with or without a listener
Can listen in order to learn
Likes new words
Increases use of pronouns, prepositions
Uses "s" to indicate plural nouns
Uses "ed" to indicate past tense
Uses sentences of three or more words
Says "Is that all right?" a lot
Talks about nonpresent situations
Puts words into action
Moves and talks at the same time
Substitutes letters in speech: "w" for "r"
Intrigued by whispering

PHYSICAL/MOTOR

Well-balanced body lines
Walks erect; nimble on feet
Gallops in wide, high steps
Alternates feet in stair climbing
Suddenly starts, stops
Turns corners rapidly
Swings arms when walking
Jumps up and down with ease
Uses toilet alone

Rides a tricycle
Puts on, takes off wraps with help
Unbuttons buttons
Has some finger control with small objects
Grasps with thumb and index finger
Holds cup in one hand
Pours easily from small pitcher
Washes hands unassisted
Can carry liquids
Has activity with drive and purpose

INTELLECTUAL-COGNITIVE

Enjoys making simple choices
Alert, excited, curious
Asks "why?" constantly
Understands "It's time to . . ."
Understands "Let's pretend . . ."
Enjoys guessing games, riddles
Has lively imagination
Often names block buildings
Has short attention span
Carries out two to four directions in sequence
Often colors pages one color
Can't combine two activities
Names and matches simple colors
Has number concepts of one and two
Sees vague cause/effect relationships
Can recognize simple melodies
Distinguishes between night and day

FIGURE 3.8 The three-year-old is alert, excited, and curious.

SOCIAL-EMOTIONAL

Tries out feelings of power
Dominates; is bossy, boastful
Assertive, argumentative
Shows off; is cocky, noisy
Can fight own battles
Hits, grabs, insists on desires
Explosive, destructive
Easily over-stimulated; excitable
Impatient, intolerant in large groups
Cooperates in groups of two or three
Develops "special" friends
In-group develops; excludes others
Shifts loyalties frequently
Resistant; tests limits
Exaggerates, tells tall tales
Alibis frequently
Teases, outwits; has terrific humor
May have scary dreams
Tattles frequently
Has food jags, food strikes

LANGUAGE

Has more words than knowledge
A great talker
Likes words, plays with them
Has high interest in poetry
Able to talk to solve conflicts
Responds to verbal directions
Enjoys taking turns to sing along
Interested in dramatizing songs, stories
Exaggerates, practices words
Uses voice control, pitch, rhythm
Asks "when?" "why?" "how?"
Joins sentences together

PHYSICAL/MOTOR

Longer, leaner body build
Vigorous, dynamic, acrobatic
Active until exhausted
"Works," builds, drives, pilots
Can jump own height and land upright
Hops, skips
Throws large ball, kicks accurately
Can't throw overhand
Stands on one foot

Races up and down stairs
Turns somersaults
Walks backward toe–heel
Accurate, rash body movements
Copies a cross, square
Can draw a stick figure
Holds paint brush in adult manner
Can lace shoes
Dresses self except back buttons, ties
Has sureness and control in finger activities

INTELLECTUAL-COGNITIVE

Does some naming and representation in art
Gives art products personal value
Can work for a goal
Questions constantly
Interested in how things work
Interested in life–death concepts
Has an extended attention span
Can do two things at once
Dramatic play is closer to reality
Judges which of two objects is larger
Has concept of three; can name more
Has accurate sense of time
Full of ideas
Begins to generalize; often faulty
Likes a variety of materials
Calls people names
Has dynamic intellectual drive

FIGURE 3.9 Dramatic play is a way of life when you are four.

SOCIAL-EMOTIONAL

Poised, self-confident, self-contained
Sensitive to ridicule
Has to be right; persistent
Has sense of self-identity
May get silly, high, wild
Enjoys pointless riddles, jokes
Enjoys group play, competitive games
Aware of rules, defines them for others
Chooses own friends; is sociable
Gets involved with group decisions
Insists on fair play
Likes adult companionship
Accepts, respects authority
Asks permission
Remains calm in emergencies

LANGUAGE

Uses big words
Uses complete sentences regularly
Can define some words
Spells out simple words
Takes turn in conversation
Has clear ideas and articulates them
Uses words to give, receive information
Insists "I already know that"
Asks questions to learn answers
Makes up songs
Enjoys dictating stories

PHYSICAL/MOTOR

Completely coordinated
Has adultlike posture
Has tremendous physical drive
Likes to use fine-motor skills
Learns how to tie bow knot
Has accuracy, skill with simple tools
Draws a recognizable person
Dresses self completely

Enjoys jumping, running, doing stunts
Rides a two-wheeler
Balances on a balance beam
Jumps rope
Runs lightly on toes
Likes to dance; is graceful, rhythmic
Sometimes roughhouses, fights

INTELLECTUAL-COGNITIVE

Curious about everything
Wants to know "how?" "why?"
Likes to display new knowledge, skills
Somewhat conscious of ignorance
Attention span increases noticeably
Knows tomorrow, yesterday
Can count 10 objects
Sorts objects by single characteristic
Knows name, address, town
Makes a plan, follows it

FIGURE 3.10 At five, it is fun to show off new skills.

The Whole Child

The concept of the "whole child" . . . is based upon an understanding that all aspects of human development are inter-related, and that considering single areas in isolation would be absurd, except for its convenience for purposes of study.

(Lancaster and Gaunt, 1976)

Each Child Is Unique

There are several reasons to consolidate different developmental areas into one person. The first is the uniqueness of children. Each one is a sum total of all those parts and, as such, is different from anyone else. Individual natures and learning styles affect the way teachers will teach two children of the same age in the same class.

Growth Is Interrelated

The second reason is that one area of development affects the other. "Behavioral development, like physical growth, demands emotional and cognitive support and stimulation" and ". . . motor development overlaps and intermingles with cognitive and perceptual development." (Stone and Church, 1979) A child with a hearing loss is likely to have language delay as well; thus, the physical development affects the language part of growth. The child who has trouble making friends (social) is likely to exhibit his unhappiness (emotional) in the school yard (physical) and in the math period (intellectual). The interdependence of the areas of development have some positive aspects as well. The child who has a good breakfast and starts the school day with parent interest is ready to tackle new puzzles and new relationships. The kindergartener who masters using scissors is ready to try printing: the fine-motor skills enhance the cognitive task of learning the alphabet.

One way for new teachers to look at this concept of development is to plot the relationships visually. Think of each area of development as a circle. There are four of them: physical-motor, language, intellectual, and social-emotional. Try to connect them so that they intersect one another, as shown in Figure 3.11.

Think how each area might affect or interact with the others. Can physical development affect how children feel about themselves? Of course; children who appreciate their body and its power feel confident in what they can do. How do intellectual skills interact with language development? When children have mastered their primary language, they can then clarify some of their thought processes. Stone and Church emphasize the "inescapable circularity" of the child's development (1979).

"Normal physical development," for instance, "can take place only when the child's physical and psychological needs are adequately met." (Stone and Church, 1979) Social development is aided by the ability to communicate verbally; a well-developed attention span helps the child develop fine motor skills; relating to others is more successful

if intellectual problem-solving skills are already mature.

Three-year-olds frequently pose the question, "Why?" as part of their intellectual curiosity. A teacher matches that understanding with the age-level characteristic of "listening in order to learn" and knows that the child understands some explanations. Thus, intellectual and language development areas influence one another.

Two-year-old Gabe, who has difficulty relaxing, responds better at naptime if allowed to cling to a familiar object or toy. Motor and emotional growth interact with each other in this case.

Valuing Wholeness

The whole-child approach is seen from a medical point of view as well. *Holistic* medicine is basically an attempt to view health care from a "wellness" rather than illness perspective. From this comes the idea of preventive medicine, which attempts to maintain the body in a healthy state, rather than wait for treatment until infection or disease has invaded.

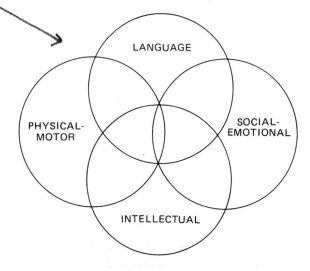

FIGURE 3.11 How areas of growth are interrelated: Each area of growth is affected by and influences every other area of development.

What does this have to do with educating children? It is an attitude that begins with a belief in the "wellness" of children, their innate goodness and trustworthiness. A two-year-old who says, "No!" exhibits signs of "wellness" and is to be accepted as behaving normally. Young children wiggle and squirm during naptime. The deadly quiet of 25 kindergarteners in a room may indicate anxiety and concern rather than accomplishment. In other words, rather than viewing behavior as "wrong," it is important to notice and value whether what a child is doing is a sign of "wellness."

The concept of the whole child strongly suggests the uniqueness of the person. Although they are often discussed separately, the areas of development (social, emotional, physical, and intellectual) cannot be isolated from one another. They each make a valuable contribution to the total child.

CHILDREN WITH SPECIAL NEEDS

Two types of children come under the category of children with special needs. The handicapped child and the gifted child extend the definition of "Who is the child?". They are discussed separately in this section.

The Handicapped Child

More and more of the children in early childhood classrooms have a handicap or disabling condition. Five-year-old Pete, blind from birth, has been in nursery school for three years. Chrissy, a multi-handicapped four-year-old, has her daily program in a special school supplemented by attending the day care center three afternoons each week. Travis is a child with *Down's syndrome,* and this is his first experience in a school not restricted to *atypical* children.

These children have some obvious characteristics that qualify them for special-needs status. Other children with less apparent handicaps also fall into this category. The term *special needs* includes a great many handicapping conditions that may or may not be noticeable.

Allen (1980) suggests three conditions under which a child is considered handicapped. To be so designated, a child's normal growth and development is (1) delayed; (2) distorted, atypical, or abnormal; or (3) severely or negatively affected. This definition includes the physical, mental, emotional, and social areas of development.

Attention to the problems of the handicapped in our society has reached national proportion only recently. Since the mid-1960s there has been significant public recognition of and the advent of public funding for the educational programs for the handicapped. Prior to that, public—and private—attitudes seemed to be ones of shame and segregation. Past generations hid the handicapped in their homes or secluded them in institutions. Slowly, reform took place. Keeping the handicapped out of sight gave way to providing separate opportunities for them. Schools, classes, and recreational programs were started exclusively for handicapped persons. Public consciousness is now sufficient to understand that many disabled people can lead useful and productive lives, and that all people with handicaps are not retarded. The current practice of integrating the handicapped into ongoing programs in schools —the mainstream of American life—is not only more humane, but practical as well.

Over the years a small number of schools had routinely accepted children with special needs. The idea gained national attention in 1972 when Head Start required that a minimum of 10 percent of its enrollment be reserved for handicapped children. Head Start led the way toward large-scale mainstreaming. In 1975, Public Law 94–142, the Education for All Handicapped Children Act, passed. This so-called "Bill of Rights for the Handicapped" guarantees free public education to those from three to 21 years of age who are handicapped. An individualized program for each person is mandatory, to be worked out in concert with the child's parents. Early childhood educators are fulfilling the requirements of that legislation. Public school systems faced with providing preschool programs for handi-

FIGURE 3.12 Handicapped child in classroom setting with other children. (From Machado and Meyer, *Early Childhood Practicum Guide,* Delmar Publishers, 1984, p. 150. Used with permission.)

capped and disabled children are turning to private preschools to fill the need when their own services are unavailable or inadequate.

In the course of normal development, any one area of a child's growth is affected by the development of the whole child. This is true for the handicapped child also; the disability may have resulted in problems in other areas of growth. A child with a profound hearing loss is often delayed in speech production or language abilities and suffers social isolation due to the inability to hear and speak with peers. A Down's syndrome child may have the intellectual capacity to put simple puzzles together but not yet have the language to engage verbally in songs and fingerplays.

Some disabilities are in and of themselves multihandicapping, affecting several growth areas. A typical Down's syndrome child, for instance, may have congenital heart defects, mental retardation, eye abnormalities, poor physical coordination, and speech disorders (Robinson and Robinson, 1965). Children who have *cerebral palsy,* a central nervous system disorder, often have other disabling conditions, such as mental retardation, epilepsy, and hearing, visual, and speech problems (Kiernan et al., n.d.).

Figure 3.13 lists some typical handicaps found in early childhood classes. For further information concerning a specific handicap or disability, the student will want to consult a special education text book.

Mainstreaming

The term *mainstreaming* refers to the process of integrating handicapped children into classrooms with the nonhandicapped. Children disabled by physical, intellectual, or emotional problems enroll in classes with other youngsters their age who are not handicapped.

Placement in the classroom is not all there is to mainstreaming. Planning and care must be given to ensure that

- Teachers foster interactions between handicapped and nonhandicapped children that promote healthy social relationships.
- Teachers recognize that every handicapped child has strengths as well as deficits and build upon those strengths.
- Teachers receive training and guidance in the critical task of working with handicapped and *developmentally disabled* children in their classes.
- Teachers work with parents to plan and implement the child's program.
- Handicapped children are actively involved and accepted in the total program.
- Handicapped children are helped to take advantage of, to the fullest extent of their capabilities, all the activities the school has to offer.
- Children's individual handicaps are addressed and taken into consideration in program planning and that procedures and curriculum are adapted to fit the children with special needs.

Mainstreaming is an important concept for all children. For the nonhandicapped it is an opportunity to learn to accept differences in people. In the early education center much of the curriculum is

Social-Emotional
Self-destructive behavior
Severe withdrawal
Dangerously aggressive to
    self and others
Noncommunicative
Moodiness
Tantrums
Hyperactive
Severely anxious
Depressed
Phobic
Psychotic
Autistic

Physical/Motor
Visual impairment
Blindness
Perceptual motor
Orthopedic handicaps:
    Cerebral palsy
    Spina bifida
    Loss of limbs
    Muscular dystrophy
Hearing impairments
Deafness

Speech and Language
Hard of hearing
Deafness
Stuttering
Articulation problems
Cleft palate
Chronic voice disorders
Learning disabilities

Intellectual
Mental retardation
Brain injury
Brain dysfunction
Dyslexia
Learning disabilities

Health Impairments (of a chronic nature or requiring prolonged
                        convalescence)
Severe asthma
Epilepsy
Hemophilia
Congenital heart defects
Severe anemia
Malnutrition
Diabetes
Tuberculosis
Cystic fibrosis
Down's syndrome
Sickle-cell anemia
Tay Sachs

FIGURE 3.13 A variety of handicapping conditions. (Adapted from Kiernan et al., n.d.)

directed toward fostering the child's self-esteem and self-worth. Teaching is dedicated to helping youngsters see themselves and others as important and valuable. Mainstreaming the handicapped presents an opportunity to extend that principle to the full range of human characteristics.

For the handicapped child in a mainstreamed classroom, the large numbers of children who serve as age-appropriate behavior models is important. Many handicapped children have not had an opportunity to hear the language of their normal peer group. They may not know how to play with another child or how to communicate in socially acceptable ways. In the mainstreamed classroom, with sensitive and knowledgeable teachers, handicapped children are helped to realize their potential as growing and learning children.

Teachers are a key factor in the successful integration of the handicapped. Their attitude is critical; they must be committed to teaching all children, regardless of their intelligence or skill levels, with equal caring and concern.

Handicap legislation makes strong demands on parents to be intimately involved with their child's program. Parent involvement greatly improves the child's chances for success (Allen, 1980). Teachers and parents work together on a planned, consistent set of expectations. The childs confidence is reinforced at home and at school for the same achievements. Parents of handicapped children find support from other parents since they share common child-rearing concerns. Teachers learn a great deal about handicaps from the parents of the children who are mainstreamed. This helps them become more effective teachers and aware of the special needs of the handicapped child.

Fortunately, the classroom teacher rarely needs to face the task of mainstreaming alone. Almost every early childhood center has access to a team of professionals who can provide the child, the family, and the teaching staff with effective therapeutic activities. Their combined knowledge helps teachers understand the specific handicap and plan an appropriate curriculum for each child. Together, teachers, clinicians, and parents work out a well-rounded program. This is called an *interdisciplinary approach* to teaching.

Early childhood educators of the 1980s would be wise to avail themselves of special education courses in order to meet the challenges of mainstreaming. Many states now require such course work before awarding early childhood certification. This training enhances job opportunities as well as

teaching abilities when the teacher is faced with issues related to mainstreaming children in the classroom.

The Gifted Child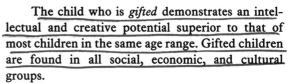

The child who is *gifted* demonstrates an intellectual and creative potential superior to that of most children in the same age range. Gifted children are found in all social, economic, and cultural groups.

At the preschool level, formal testing procedures to identify gifted and talented children are not common. Therefore, early childhood educators should be aware of some traits gifted children display so they can recognize potentially gifted children in their care.

In intellectual and academic areas, gifted children have long attention spans, learn rapidly, have good memories and advanced vocabularies. They ask a lot of questions and are able to express their ideas easily. Independent and imaginative, gifted children may be bored by normal activities.

Socially, the gifted child is sought after by peers yet may be uneasy about relationships with other children. Planning and organizing skills are evident in their artwork and other creative endeavors. The gifted child is content to be alone, spending time in purposeful activity. Their use of humor is more advanced than children the same age; originality is typically characteristic of the gifted.

Gifted children, once identified, need to be challenged. In some cases the children may be advanced to an older group, moving on to kindergarten or first grade. A more common approach in early childhood has been in the area of curriculum enrichment. In this way the child remains with age-level peers in order to develop social skills. Some schools segregate gifted children by placing them in special classes exclusively for those identified as being gifted.

The teacher's role with the gifted preschool child is that of providing challenge and stimulation. Curriculum areas are developed in more complex ways. The gifted child is ready to learn in greater depth; the teachers provide added materials and activities that will help the child probe the extent of their interests. The nongifted children in the same classroom benefit from this enrichment; each responds according to his or her abilities. Teachers of children who have special gifts and talents can meet their unique needs in a regular school setting at the same time they provide a rich curriculum for the nongifted student.

SUMMARY

The child in early childhood programs ranges from the dependent infant to the outgoing eight-year-old. In those few short years teachers witness tremendous physical, intellectual, social, and emotional gains.

The child learns to crawl, walk, run, climb, throw a ball, write with a pencil, use scissors, hold a spoon, and manipulate toys. Both large and small muscles are called into play throughout each stage of development.

Language development is equally impressive. The nonverbal infant becomes fluent, sometimes in more than one language. Intellectual gains coincide as children become able to express thoughts, solve problems, and exhibit growth in their reasoning powers.

Socially, the child learns to relate to family members, schoolmates, teachers, and other adults. Every range of human emotion is developed during these early years as children learn appropriate ways to express and release their feelings.

Teachers notice that children share many common characteristics at the same time they display wide individual differences. Profile charts—word pictures—describing normal development help teachers understand when a particular behavior is likely to occur. With advance notice, then, teachers can plan activities and curricula that appeal to children at every age level; disciplinary and guidance measures can match the child's specific level of development.

Yet it is obvious that growth and development do not proceed normally for all children. Two groups of children have special needs within the early childhood classroom. The handicapped who are mainstreamed require particular attention to their individual disabilities, and teachers need special skills to help them integrate handicapped and nonhandicapped children. Gifted children also require attention; their exceptional abilities must be challenged and stimulated within the regular early childhood program.

Review Questions

1. Match the word picture to the age group in which it belongs:

Plays peek-a-boo	fours
"Me" is prominent pronoun	fives
Draws recognizable man	threes
Avid "me-too"er	threes
Grasps cup with two hands	twos
Beginning to share	infants
Silly, loves nonsense	twos
Time concept is now	fours
A great talker	twos
Smiles at self in mirror	infants

2. Name one way children are alike and one way they differ from each other.

3. One area of development affects another. List two ways that social or emotional problems can affect other areas of growth.

4. What are some of the reasons for using the concept of the whole child in early education?

5. What are some of the advantages of mainstreaming children with special needs?

Learning Activities

1. Select two children who are approximately the same age. Compare their physical and social development. How are they alike? How are they different? What do you think accounts for these differences?

2. Observe a handicapped child who has been mainstreamed. How does the teacher promote social interaction? Define the type of handicap.

3. Look at the word picture for a three-year-old. Compare it with a three-year-old you know. What behavior do you see that falls within the range of the chart? What is different?

Bibliography

Allen, K. Eileen. *Mainstreaming in Early Childhood Education.* Albany, N.Y.: Delmar Publishers, 1980.

Allen, K. Eileen; Holm, V.A.; and Schiefelbusch, R.L. *Early Intervention—A Team Approach.* Baltimore: University Park Press, 1978.

Ames, Louise B., and Ilg, Frances L. *Your One-Year-Old.* New York: Dell, 1983.

———. *Your Two-Year-Old.* New York: Dell, 1976.

———. *Your Three-Year-Old.* New York: Dell, 1976.

———. *Your Four-Year-Old.* New York: Dell, 1976.

———. *Your Five-Year-Old.* New York: Dell, 1979.

———. *Your Six-Year-Old.* New York: Dell, 1979.

CRC Education and Human Development, Inc. *Mainstreaming Preschoolers.* Belmont, Mass.: U.S. Government Printing Office, series.

Elkind, David. *A Sympathetic Understanding of the Child.* Boston: Allyn and Bacon, 1978.

Elkind, David. "Humanizing the Curriculum." In *Early Childhood Education,* Annual Edition. Guilford, Conn.: The Dushkin Publishing Group, 1982.

Gardner, Howard. *Developmental Psychology.* Boston: Little, Brown and Co., 1982.

Gesell, Arnold, and Ilg, Frances L. *Infant and Child in the Culture of Today.* New York: Harper Brothers, 1943.

Hurlock, Elizabeth. *Child Development.* New York: McGraw-Hill, 1972.

Kiernan, Shari, et al. *Mainstreaming Preschoolers: Children with Orthopedic Handicaps.* Washington, D.C.: U.S. Department of Health, Education, and Welfare, n.d.

Kitano, Margie. "Young Gifted Children: Strategies for Preschool Teachers." *Young Children,* May 1982, pp. 14–24.

Lancaster, Janet, and Gaunt, Joan. *Developments in Early Childhood Education.* London: Open Books, 1976.

Moore, Shirley G., and Kilmer, Sally. *Contemporary Preschool Education.* New York: John Wiley and Sons, 1973.

Robinson, H.B., and Robinson, N.M. *The Mentally Retarded Child.* New York: McGraw-Hill, 1965.

Rogers, Fred, and Head, Barry. *Mister Rogers Talks with Parents.* New York: Berkley Books, 1983.

Stone, Joseph L., and Church, Joseph. *Childhood and Adolescence.* New York: Random House, 1979.

4

Developmental and Learning Theories

Questions for Thought

- What psychological theories are basic to early childhood education today?
- Who are the main speakers for each school of thought?
- What are the psychosocial stages of early childhood?
- What are the tenets of behaviorist theory?
- How does a cognitive theory explain children's thinking processes?
- What is the hierarchy of human needs?

Outline

INTRODUCTION

Early childhood education draws from several fields of study. The connection with the field of psychology is particularly strong. Much of what we know about children today comes from child development and child psychology research. As educators, we apply those findings in the classroom. Our knowledge base comes directly from psychological studies.

- How do children develop?
- What do they learn, and in what order?
- What do people need in order to be ready to learn?
- What affects learning?
- Do all people develop in the same ways?
- What are the similarities and differences in growth and development?

Psychologists and educators have been asking themselves these questions for years. In the twentieth century a great deal has been discovered about these issues. The basic quest for knowledge about learning and development has given early educators much to consider in developing their own ideas about children.

Initially, the study of child development was mostly confined to the study of trends and descriptions of age changes. As this century has progressed, the scope and definition of child development have changed radically. Developmental psychologists now study how psychological processes begin, change, and develop. Specifically, child development focuses on language acquisition, various early effects on later intellectual development, and the process of attachment to others. Early childhood teachers should know how children develop and how they learn. Therefore, it is important to have a background in both developmental psychology and learning theories.

There is no one set of principles that encompasses all developmental and learning theories. We have chosen three theories that are commonly ac-

cepted as major components of the child development field. A fourth, though it does not always appear in child psychology texts, highlights some of the processes of working with children. The four theories we will outline are commonly known as (1) psychodynamic theory; (2) behavior theory; (3) cognitive theory; and (4) humanistic theory.

Imp.

Since the field of child development is broad, encompassing a wide variety of opinion and fact, not all the experts agree, or even think alike. Indeed, there are differences among them about how children grow, think, and learn, and what motivates them. Each theory describes children and their processes in a different way. The teacher thus has a diversity of thought on which to establish a professional philosophy.

PSYCHODYNAMIC THEORY

Psychodynamic theory is about personality development and emotional problems. Dr. Sigmund Freud first put forth this theory, and his ideas were expanded upon by Anna Freud (his daughter), Carl Jung, Karen Horney, and others. The psychoanalyst whose ideas have most affected early childhood education is Erik Erikson.

Erik Erikson

Erik Homberg Erikson is perhaps the most influential psychoanalyst alive today, certainly a key figure in the study of children and development. His interest in children and education has been a lifelong one, including a teaching background in progressive and Montessori schools in Europe. After clinical training in psychoanalysis, he remained interested in the connections between psychotherapy and education. Erikson became the first child analyst in the Boston area. He continues to work in various universities in this country, without any formal degree of his own.

Erikson's Theory of Human Development

Erikson's theory of human development, like those of Freud and Piaget, states that life is a series of stages through which each person passes, with each stage growing from the previous ones. He proposes eight stages of psychosocial development, each representing a critical period for the development of an important quality or virtue. Positive growth allows the individual to integrate his or her physical and biological development with the challenges that the social institutions and culture present. Each stage is characterized by a pair of basic emotional states; the formation of a balance between these is the basis for personality strength.

In other words, every growing organism passes through certain developmental stages. A stage is a period during which certain changes take place. What one achieves in each stage is based on the developments of the previous stages, and each stage presents the organisms with certain kinds of problems to be solved. When children succeed, they go on to attack new problems and grow through solving them.

Everyone has certain biological, social, and psychological needs that must be satisfied in order to grow in a healthy manner. Medicine has learned much about physical needs—diet, rest, exercise. There are also basic intellectual, social, and emotional needs that must be met for an organism to be healthy. Psychology, such as Eriksonian theory, can speak to these needs. Whether these needs are met or unfulfilled will affect development.

Stage 1: Trust vs. Mistrust (Birth to One Year)

Erikson's first stage is roughly the first year of life and parallels Freud's oral-sensory stage. Attitudes important to development are the capacity to trust—or mistrust—inner and outer experiences. By providing consistent care, parents help an infant develop a basic sense of trust in self and an ability to trust other people. They give affection and emotional security as well as provide for physical needs. Inconsistent or inadequate care prevents the infant from trusting the world. In extreme cases, as shown by Spitz's classic studies on infant deprivation

Stage	Description	Challenge
Stage One	The newborn	Trust vs. mistrust
Stage Two	Toddlers	Autonomy vs. shame and doubt
Stage Three	Childhood	Initiative vs. guilt
Stage Four	School	Competence (or Industry) vs. inferiority
Stage Five	Adolescence	Search for identity vs. role confusion
Stage Six	Young adulthood	Intimacy (love and friendship) vs. isolation (loneliness)
Stage Seven	Grown-ups	Caring for the next generation (generativity) vs. stagnation
Stage Eight	Old age	Integrity vs. despair

FIGURE 4.1 Erikson's theory of psychosocial development centers on basic crises that people face from birth to old age. This stage theory of development proposes that these conflicts are part of the life process, and that successful handling of these issues can give a person the "ego strength" to face life positively. (Adapted from Hubley and Hubley, 1976)

(Spitz, 1946), lack of care can actually lead to infant death. A less extreme case might form isolation or distrust of others, such as in schizophrenia. Given a solid base in early trust, though, the infant develops the virtue, or strength, of hope.

Stage 2: Autonomy vs. Doubt (Two to Three Years)

The second stage, corresponding to the second and third years of life, parallels the muscular-anal period in Freudian theory. The child learns to manage and control impulses, and to use both motor and mental skills. To help a child develop a healthy balance between autonomy and shame, parents should consider how to handle their toddlers' toilet training and growing curiosity to explore. Restrictive or compulsive parents may give the child a feeling of shame and doubt, causing a sense of inse-

curity. Successful growth in this stage gives a child the strength of will.

Stage 3: Initiative vs. Guilt (Three to Five or Six Years)

The third stage of Eriksonian theory corresponds to the preschool and kindergarten years and parallels Freud's genital stage of development. Out of a sense of autonomy grows a sense of initiative. The child is ready to plan and carry out thoughts and ideas. The parent can encourage the child's natural curiosity to plan and execute activities that are constructive and cooperative. An overly restrictive parent may raise a child with an excessive sense of guilt and inhibition. On the other hand, parents or teachers giving no restraints signal to the child no clear idea of what is socially acceptable and what is not. The key strength that grows out of this stage is purpose.

FIGURE 4.2 An Eriksonian crisis in a young child's life. The child who has successfully mastered the first of Erikson's psychosocial conflicts will then be able to cope with future challenges. In this instance, the child who takes initiative (grabbing a toy) also can feel guilt (returning it).

Applying Theory to Work with Children

How can teachers apply Erikson's theory of psychosocial development to young children? First, Erikson has a clear message about the importance of play. Second, the theory helps shape guidelines for the role of adults in children's lives.

Nursery school teachers have long held that play is a critical part of children's total development. Most schools for children under six have periods of time allotted for play called "choice time" or "free play." Erikson supports these ideas explicitly by stating that the sense of autonomy and of initiative are developed mainly through social and fantasy play. He suggests that child's play is "the infantile form of the human ability to deal with experiences by creating model situations and to master reality by experiment and planning. . . . To 'play it out' in play is the most natural self-healing measure childhood affords" (Erikson, 1964).

The adult, from a psychoanalytic point of view, is primarily an emotional base and a social mediator for the child. That is, the adult is "an interpreter of feelings, motives, actions; and assists the child in solving his social problems. The adult assesses the emotional make-up of the child and his progress through each developmental crisis." (Charlesworth, 1983) Since the infant must learn to trust the world, the parent needs to be responsive and satisfy the basic needs of food, warmth, and love. In a toddler's world, the teacher and parent must allow the child, in Erikson's words:

. . . to experience over and over again that he is a person who is permitted to make choices. He has to have the right to choose, for example, whether to sit or whether to stand, whether to approach a visitor or to lean against his mother's knee . . . whether to use the toilet or to wet his pants. At the same time he must learn some of the boundaries of self-determination. He inevitably finds that there are some walls he cannot climb, that there are objects out of reach, that, above all, there are innumerable commands enforced by powerful adults.

(Erikson, 1969)

In preschool and kindergarten, a teacher allows children to take initiative and does not interfere with the results of those actions. At the same time, teachers and parents provide clear limits so that the children can learn what behaviors are unacceptable to society.

The issues of early childhood, from Erikson's theory, are really our own issues. Since the remnant of these crises stay with us all our lives, teachers must be aware of their own processes to fully appreciate the struggles of children.

BEHAVIORIST THEORY

Behaviorism is the most pragmatic and functional of the modern psychological ideologies. Developed during the 1920s and continually modified today, behaviorism is "the most distinctively American contribution to psychology" (Suransky, 1982). There are countless developmental psychologists and researchers who have defined and expanded upon this idea, several of whom are mentioned later in this chapter. To summarize the behaviorist theory, we have chosen four theorists: John Watson, Edward Thorndike, B.F. Skinner, and Albert Bandura.

The Behaviorists

What is known today as "behaviorism" begins with the notion that a child is born with a "clean slate," a *tabula rasa* in John Locke's words, on which events are written throughout life. The conditions of those events cause all important human behavior.

John B. Watson was an American theorist who studied the experiments of Russian scientist Ivan Pavlov. He then translated those ideas of conditioning into human terms. In the first quarter of this century, Watson made sweeping claims about the powers of this classical conditioning. He declared that he could shape a person's entire life by controlling exactly the events of an infant's first year. One of his ideas was to strictly discourage emotional ties between parents and children, though he later modified this. Nonetheless, he gave scientific validity to the idea that teachers should set conditions for learning and reward proper responses.

Edward L. Thorndike also studied the conditions of learning. After working with animals and their problem-solving abilities, he decided that people took an active part in their learning. He set forth the famous "stimulus-response" technique. A stimulus will recall a response in a person; this forms learned habits. Therefore, it is wise to pay close attention to the consequences of behavior and to the various kinds of reinforcement.

B.F. Skinner took the idea of "tabula rasa" one step further. He created the doctrine of the "empty organism." That is, a person is like a vessel to be filled by carefully designed experiences. All behavior is under the control of one or more aspects of the environment. Furthermore, Skinner maintains that there is no behavior that cannot be modified.

Behaviorists often insist that only what can actually be observed will be accepted as fact. Only behavior can be treated, they say, not feelings or internal states. This contrasts to the psychodynamic approach, which insists that behavior is just an indirect clue to the "real" self, that of inner feelings and thoughts.

Skinner's ideas have probably stirred up more controversy, and caused more emotional response, than those of any other psychologist of our time. Some people might argue that Skinnerian concepts tend to depersonalize the learning process and treat people as puppets. Others say that behaviorist psychology has made us develop new ways to help people learn and cope effectively with the world.

Albert Bandura has developed another type of learning theory, called social learning. As behaviorists began to accept that what peope said about their feelings and internal state was valid data, they looked at how children became socialized. Socialization is the process of learning to conform to social rules. Social-learning theorists watch how children learn these rules and use them in groups. They study the patterns of reinforcement and reward in socially appropriate and unacceptable behavior.

From this arose a new concept known as modeling. This is what used to be known as learning and teaching by example. For instance, children who see their parents smoking will likely smoke themselves. Any behavior can be learned by watching it, from language (listening to others talk) to fighting (watching violence on television).

Theory of Behaviorism and Learning

What is behavior, or learning, theory all about? Many texts have been written on this set of principles; every child development text of the day cites behavior and social-learning concepts. Most early education texts will make mention of the system of positive reinforcement; that is, how to praise children so that they are likely to repeat the desired behavior.

Learning takes place when an organism interacts with the environment. Through experience, behavior is modified, or changed. In the behaviorist's eyes, three types of learning occur: (1) classical conditioning; (2) operant conditioning; and (3) observational learning or modeling. The first two are based on the idea that learning is mostly the development of habit. What people learn is a series of associations, forming a connection between a stimulus and response that did not exist before. The third is based on a social approach.

Classical Conditioning

Classical conditioning can be explained by reviewing Pavlov's original experiments. A dog normally salivates at the sight of food, but not when he hears a bell. By pairing the sound of a bell with the sight of food, the dog "learns" to salivate when he hears the bell, whether or not food is nearby. Thus, the dog has been conditioned to salivate (give the response) for both the food (unconditioned stimulus) and the bell (conditioned stimulus).

Operant Conditioning

Operant conditioning is slightly different from classical conditioning in that it focuses on the response rather than the stimulus. It also involves reinforcers, or those things that are likely to increase behaviors that produce pleasant results. Most people are likely to increase what gives them pleasure (be it food or attention), and decrease what gives them displeasure (such as punishment, pain, or the withdrawal of food or attention). The behaviorist tries to influence the organism by controlling these kinds of reinforcement.

For example, you would like Claire to begin to use a spoon instead of her hands to eat. Before conditioning, you talk to her whenever she eats. During the conditioning period, you can give attention, (a positive reinforcer) each time she picks up a spoon during feeding times, and ignore her when she uses her hands. Afterward, she is more likely to use a spoon, and less often her hands. This is an example of a positive reinforcer, something that increases the likelihood of the desired response.

The reinforcers can be both positive and nega-

tive. Circle time is Jimmy's favorite activity at school. Yet he has difficulty controlling his behavior and consistently disrupts the group. Before conditioning, he is told that if he talks to his neighbors and shouts responses at the teacher, he will be asked to leave the circle. During the conditioning period, Jimmy is praised whenever he pays attention, sings songs, and does not bother those around him (positive reinforcement). When he begins to shout, he is told to leave and return when he can sing without shouting (negative reinforcement). A negative reinforcer is used to "stop a child from acting in a particular way . . . by arranging for him to terminate a mildly adversive situation immediately [his having to leave the group] by improving his behavior" (Krumboltz and Krumboltz, 1972). Jimmy, by controlling his own behavior, could end his isolation from the group.

Reinforcement, both positive and negative, is a powerful tool. It is important for adults to realize

FIGURE 4.3 A shared smile is a simple and powerful social reinforcement.

that it can be misused. It is wise to be careful, particularly in the case of negative reinforcement. An adult may not be gentle with a negative reinforcer when angry with a child's inappropriate behavior. Educators and parents should be aware of the possibilities and check their own responses.

Modeling

The third kind of conditioning is called "observational learning" or "modeling." Social behavior is particularly noteworthy to early childhood professionals, as most work with children in groups and thus witness social behavior constantly. Any behavior that involves more than one person can be considered social. One of the most negative social behaviors is aggression. It is this type that Albert Bandura researched, finding that much of it is learned by watching others.

Aggression is a complex issue, involving various definitions and behaviors. To illustrate social-learning theory, Bandura and others interpret aggression to mean behavior intended to inflict harm of discomfort to another person or object. Bandura showed a short film of aggressive behavior to young children. The original mid-1960s studies are summarized below:

Each child in Bandura's experiment viewed one of three films. In all three films, a man hit, kicked, and verbally abused an inflated Bobo doll in ways that young children are unlikely to do spontaneously. The films differed in what happened to the model after the aggressive sequence. In one film the model was lavishly rewarded with praise and foods that appealed to preschoolers, such as candy and caramel popcorn. In another film the model was punished in a dramatic way, including severe scolding and a spanking. The third film simply ended after the model's aggressive behavior, with no consequences following the aggression. After viewing one film, each child in the experiment was allowed to play in a room with a Bobo doll, all the toys used in the aggressive film, and a variety of other toys.

(McClinton and Meier, 1978)

The results are most impressive, especially to those working with young children. The level of aggression was directly related to what the children saw as the consequences in the film. When offered prizes, they imitated almost exactly what their model had done. Also, children appeared more likely to attack another child after viewing the attacks on the Bobo doll in film. Further studies have shown that children's level of aggression is higher right after viewing the film, but less so when shown it again six months later (McClinton and Meier, 1978). Regardless of the controversy that may surround any study of children's aggression, or the effects of watching filmed violence on youngsters, the social-learning theory deserves serious consideration.

	Classical Conditioning	Operant Conditioning	Social Learning
Kind of behavior	Reflexive	Voluntary	Voluntary
Type of learning	Learning through association	Learning through reinforcement	Learning through observation and imitation
Role of learner	Passive	Active or passive	Active

FIGURE 4.4 Behaviorist learning processes. Classical conditioning, operant conditioning, and social learning are three ways to develop learned behavior. Each describes how certain kinds of behavior will be learned and what role the learner will take in the process.

Applying Theory to Work with Children

Behaviorist theories make a strong case for how the environment influences our behavior. A teacher, a parent, any adult who works closely with children, can use this knowledge to arrange the environment in such a way that positive learning is enhanced. Thus, early childhood educators pay close attention to how to arrange furniture, materials, the daily schedule. The way teachers interact with children is critical to changing their behavior.

Adults are powerful reinforcers and models for children. A learning situation is comprised of many cues; it is up to adults to know what those cues are and how to control them. Teachers who use behavior modification techniques know both what children are to do and how they will be reinforced for their behavior. The issues of using this kind of control, and the ethics involved, are of deep concern to everyone. The extremes of behaviorist theory suggest programmed instruction and interaction that many early educators reject. Each teacher and program must consider the impact of this theory and how to apply it to classroom and client.

COGNITIVE THEORY

Adult: What does it mean to be alive?
Child: It means you can move about, play—
      that you can do all kinds of things.
Adult: Is a mountain alive?
Child: Yes, because it has grown by itself.
Adult: Is a cloud alive?
Child: Yes, because it sends water.
Adult: Is wind alive?
Child: Yes, because it pushes things.
           (Peters and Willis, 1978)

How can we tell what children are thinking? How do children learn to think, and what do they think about? Once we begin to ask these questions, we enter the realm of knowledge about how people "know" and "think," and how they learn to do it.

Jean Piaget

Jean Jacques Piaget (1896–1980) was one of the most exciting research theorists in child development. A major force in child psychology, he studied both thought processes and how they change with age. Jean Piaget's ideas serve as our guide to the cognitive theory because of the thoroughness of his work. He had great influence on child psychology, theories of learning, intellectual development, even philosophy. He became the foremost expert on the development of knowledge from birth to adulthood.

How did Piaget find out about such matters? A short review of his life and ideas reveals a staggering volume of work and a wide scope of interests. Born at the turn of the century, Piaget built on his childhood curiosity in science and philosophy by working with Dr. Simon at the Binet Laboratory (Simon and Binet devised the first intelligence test). While recording children's abilities to answer questions correctly, he became fascinated with children's incorrect responses. He noticed that children tended to give similar kinds of wrong answers, and that they made different kinds of mistakes at different ages.

Thus, Jean Piaget launched into a lifelong study of intelligence. He believed that children think in fundamentally different ways from adults. He also developed a new method for studying thought processes. Rather than using a standardized test, he adapted the psychiatric method of question and response. Called the "methode clinique," it lets people's answers guide the questions. Therefore, it focuses on the child's own natural ways of thinking.

Piaget then began studying children's thought processes. With his wife, one of his former students, he observed his children. He also began to look closely at how actively children engage in their own development. He studied the development of logic and looked at children's understanding of scientific and mathematical principles. In his final works, he returned to his original interest, that of the study of knowledge itself. Prolific his entire life, Jean Piaget has given us a complex theory of intelligence and child development that will influence us for some time. He has recorded, in a systematic way, how children learn, when they learn, and what they learn.

Theory of Cognitive Development

What are the concepts of cognitive theory? Detailing all Piaget's ideas is impossible. What follows are several tenets that explain the nature of intelligence and its functions.

Piaget's theory relies on both maturational and environmental factors. It is called maturational because it sets out a sequence of cognitive (thinking) stages that are governed by heredity. For example, heredity affects our learning by (1) how the body is structured biologically, and (2) automatic, or instinctive, behavior, such as an infant's sucking at birth. It is an environmental theory because what experiences children have will directly influence how they develop.

Thinking and learning is a process of interaction between a person and the environment. Piaget also sets out that all species inherit a basic tendency to organize their lives and adapt to the world around them. In doing so, an organism "figures out" what the world is all about, and then works toward surviving in that world. Regardless of their age, all people use two basic processes of adaptation, accommodation, and assimilation. Figure 4.5 demonstrates how these processes work.

Piaget theorizes that thinking develops along certain lines. This coincides with his idea that people tend to organize themselves, and the stages of thinking are the psychological structures that go along with trying to adapt to the environment. Such a series of stages goes beyond individual differences in thinking styles. It focuses on internal structures rather than on external conditions as behavioral theory does. Piaget identifies four major stages of cognitive development:

Sensorimotor stage	zero to two years
Preoperational stage	1½ to six or seven years
Concrete operational	six to 12 years
Formal operational stage	12 years to adulthood

Each person of normal intelligence will go through these stages in this order, although the rate will change depending on the individual and his or her experiences. Figure 4.6 details the stages of early childhood.

Children progress from one stage to the next, changing their thinking depending on their level of maturation and experience with the environment. Certain physical skills, such as fine-motor coordination, will determine how much a child is capable of doing. Environmental factors, such as the kinds

Assimilation: Taking new information and organizing it in such a way that it fits with what the person already knows.

Example: Annie sees an airplane while walking outdoors with her father. She knows that birds fly. So, never having seen this flying thing before, she calls it a "bird." This is what we call *assimilation.* That is, she is taking in this new information and making it fit into what she already knows.

Accommodation: Taking new information and changing what is already thought to fit the new information.

Example: Aaron is at the grocery store with his mother and newborn baby. He calls the lady in line "pregnant" although she is simply overweight. After being corrected, he asks the next person he sees, "Are you pregnant or just fat?" This is what we call *accommodation.* That is, having learned that all large people with large bellies aren't pregnant, he changes his knowledge base to include this new information.

FIGURE 4.5 In Piagetian theory, the processes of assimilation and accommodation are basic to how all people organize their thoughts and therefore to all cognitive development.

Stage	Age	What Happens
Sensorimotor	Birth to 1½ to 2	Initial use of inherent reflexes (sucking, crying)—at birth.
		Out of sight, out of mind, at the beginning; object permanence is learned by experience by around one year.
		Movements from accidental and random to more deliberate and intentional—throughout stage.
		Learns to coordinate perceptual and motor functions (such as seeing object and then grabbing it).
		Learns relationship between means and ends (pushes aside barrier to get a toy).
		Beginning forms of symbolic behavior (opens and closes mouth when doing same to a jar).
Preoperational	2 to 6–7	Gradual acquisition of language (new words, like "yummed it up," or "my ponytail was keeping me in bothers").
		Symbolic (play doll as baby, stick as sword).
		Egocentric (not aware of another point of view, only one's own).
		Physical characteristics, such as size, judged by appearance only (a ball of playdough *looks* bigger when made into a long roll, so therefore it *is* bigger).
		"Conservation" develops slowly; ability to reverse operations is not understood (the milk cannot be visualized as being poured back into the first glass).
		Inability to think of the whole and its parts at the same time (given a set of blue and red wooden beads, the child will say that the blue beads will make a longer necklace than the red beads).
Concrete operational	6 to 12	Begins to "conserve" (can see that quantity, size, length, volume, remain the same no matter how they are arranged).
		Can handle several ideas at the same time (given an array of objects of various colors and shapes, can find all the "red, square, small ones").
		Starts to remove contradictions (can understand and follow rules, and make up own).
		Can understand other points of view, although needs to be in real situations, rather than abstract ones.

FIGURE 4.6 In their early childhood, children will pass through the sensorimotor and preoperational stages and enter the stage of concrete operations.

of experiences adults and the world provide, influence the rate of growth. Throughout the process, both accommodation and assimilation are at work in a child's mind. Children take in new knowledge and decide how it fits with what they already know.

Applying Theory to Work with Children

What can teachers learn from this complicated theory? Piaget's writings do not apply directly to classroom methods or subject matter per se. In fact, he never claimed to be an educator. However, Piaget's theories provide a framework, or philosophy, about children's thinking. Piagetian theory has some implications for both environment and interactions.

Materials

Children need many objects to explore, so that they can later incorporate these into their symbolic thinking. Such materials need to be balanced among open-ended ones (such as sand and water activities, basic art and construction materials), guided ones (cooking with recipes, conducting experiments, classification and seriate materials), and self-correcting

ones (puzzles, matching games, such as some of the Montessori materials). It is important to remember that young children need to be involved with concrete objects and to explore and use them in their own ways, which include both sensorimotor and beginning symbolic play.

Scheduling

Children need lots of time to explore their own reality, especially through the use of play. A Piagetian classroom would have large periods of time for children to "act out" their own ideas. Also, there should be time scheduled for imitation of adult-given ideas (songs, fingerplays, and stories).

FIGURE 4.7 Young children need materials and time to explore the world on their own.

Teachers

Children need teachers who understand and agree with a developmental point of view. The teacher who knows the stages and levels of thinking of the children will be one who can guide that class into new and challenging opportunities to learn and grow.

Awareness

Perhaps more important is the awareness on the part of all adults that all children have the capability to reason and be thinkers if they are given appropriate materials for their stage of development. Teachers must remember that young children

1. Do not think like adults.

2. Need many materials to explore and describe.

3. Think in a concrete manner and often cannot think out things in their heads.

4. Come to conclusions and decisions based on what they see, not necessarily on what is sensible and logical.

5. Need challenging questions, and the time to make their own decisions and find their own answers.

The thoughts and ideas of Jean Piaget are impressive, both in quantity and quality. The collective works of this man are extremely complex, often difficult to understand. Yet they have given us a valuable blueprint. Clearly, Jean Piaget has provided unique and important insights into the development of intelligence and children.

It is Piaget's genius for empathy with children, together with true intellectual genius, that has made him the outstanding child psychologist in the world today and one destined to stand beside Freud with respect to his contributions to psychology, education, and related disciplines. Just as Freud's discoveries of unconscious motivation, infantile sexuality, and the stages of psychosexual growth changed our ways of thinking about human personality, so Piaget's discoveries of children's implicit philosophies, the construction of reality by the infant, and the stages of mental development have altered our ways of thinking about human intelligence.

(Elkind, 1977)

HUMANISTIC THEORY

The Humanists

As the field of psychology began to develop, various schools of thought arose. By the middle of this century, two "camps" dominated the American psychological circles. The first, known as psychodynamic, included the Freudians and is best known to us through the works of Erik Erikson. The second, called behaviorism, began with Watson and Thorndike, and was later expanded by Skinner and Bandura.

In 1954, Abraham Maslow published a book that articulated another set of ideas. He called it

. . . the Third Force (or Humanistic Psychology), which is developing a new image of man, . . . the work of *many* men. Not only this, but it is also paralleled by independent advances and discoveries in other fields as well. Thus, there is rapidly developing a new image of society and all of its institutions. So, also, there is a new philosophy of science, of education, of religion, of psychotherapy, of politics, of economics, etc, etc, etc. Taken together these developments can be called single aspects of a comprehensive philosophy of *everything*.

(Goble, 1970)

This theory has a place in early childhood education because it attempts to explain how people are motivated. Specifically, humanistic theory is centered on people's needs, goals, and successes. This was a change from the study of mental illness, as in psychotherapy, or the study of animal behavior, in the case of much behaviorist research. Instead, Dr. Maslow studied exceptionally mature and successful people. Others, such as Carl Rogers, Fritz Perls, Alan Watts, and Erich Fromm added to what was known about healthy personalities. The humanists developed a comprehensive theory of human behavior based on mental health.

Maslow's Theory of Human Needs

Maslow's theory of self-actualization is a set of ideas about what people need in order to become and stay healthy. He asserts that every human being is motivated by a number of basic needs, regardless of age, sex, race, culture, or geographic location. According to Maslow (1962), a basic need is something:

- Whose absence breeds illness.
- Whose presence prevents illness.

- Whose restoration cures illness.
- Preferred by the deprived person over other satisfactions, under certain conditions (such as very complex, free-choice instances).
- Found to be inactive, at a low ebb, or functionally absent in the healthy person.

These needs, not to be denied, form a theory of human motivation. It is a hierarchy, or pyramid, because there is a certain way these needs are interrelated, and because the most critical needs form the foundation from which the other needs can be met.

Applying Theory to Work with Children

The basic needs are sometimes called "deficiency needs" because they are critical for a person's

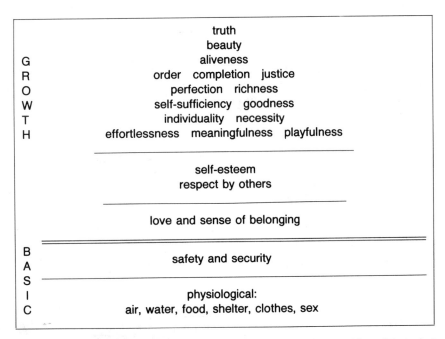

```
                        truth
                        beauty
G                       aliveness
R          order    completion    justice
O              perfection   richness
W            self-sufficiency   goodness
T              individuality   necessity
H     effortlessness  meaningfulness  playfulness
      _____

                    self-esteem
                  respect by others
      _____

               love and sense of belonging
      ========================================
B
A                  safety and security
S      _____
I
C                    physiological:
          air, water, food, shelter, clothes, sex
```

FIGURE 4.8 Abraham Maslow studied healthy personalities and found that what people need for growth is universal. One tenet of humanistic psychology is the hierarchy of basic and growth needs. (Adapted from Maslow, 1954)

survival, and a deficiency can cause a person to die. Until those are met, no other significant growth can take place. How well a teacher knows that a hungry child will ignore a lesson, or simply be unable to concentrate. A tired child often pushes aside other learning materials and experiences until rested. The child who is deprived of basic physiological needs may be able to think of those needs only; in Maslow's words, "such a man can fairly be said to live by bread alone" (Maslow, 1954). The humanists would strongly advocate a school breakfast or lunch program, and support regular rest and naptimes in programs with long hours.

Once the physiological needs are satisfied, the need for safety and security will emerge. Maslow points at insecure and neurotic people as examples of what happens when these needs are left unfulfilled. These people act as if a disaster is about to occur, as if a spanking is on the way. Given an unpredictable home or school, a child cannot find any sense of consistency, and so is preoccupied with worrying and anxiety. Maslow would advise teachers to give freedom within limits, rather than either total neglect or permissiveness.

The growth needs begin to emerge when the basic needs have been met. Higher needs are dependent on those primary ones. They are what we strive for in order to become more satisfied and healthy people.

Love and Belonging

The need for love and belonging is often expressed directly and clearly by the young children in our care. A lack of love and sense of belonging stifles growth. In order to learn to give love later in life, one has to learn about love by receiving it as a child. This means learning early about the responsibilities of giving as well as receiving love.

The Esteem Needs

The need for esteem can be divided into two categories: self-respect and esteem from others. "Self-esteem includes such needs as a desire for confidence, competence, mastery, adequacy, achievement, independence, and freedom. Respect for others includes such concepts as prestige, recognition, acceptance, attention, status, reputation, and appreciation." (Goble, 1970)

Self-Actualization

Self-actualization is what gives a person satisfaction in life. From the desire to know and understand the world and people around us comes a renewal of self-knowledge. For the early childhood educator, these needs are expressed in the enthusiasm, curiosity, and natural "drive" to learn and try. In meeting these needs, a person finds meaning for life, an eagerness to live, and a willingness to do so.

Children must have their physical and basic emotional needs met before these requirements of higher cognitive learning can be fulfilled. Moreover, the child who seems stuck in a particular "needs area" will likely stay there until that basic need is satisfied. A hungry, insecure, or hurt child is a poor learner. Teachers must continually advocate better physical and social conditions for all children.

OTHER PSYCHOLOGISTS

We complete our discussion of psychology and early education by mentioning the contributions of several others. All have added to our knowledge of children and learning.

Jerome Bruner

Jerome Bruner is another rich resource of knowledge about learning and thinking. What makes him special is his interest in education. A professor at Harvard, in 1959 he directed a group of intellectual scholars that produced a book on the study of the process of education. It is this involvement in the educational field and the practical issues that provide a critical and all-too-rare link between psychology and education.

Jerome Kagan

Jerome Kagan has researched a variety of issues related to child development for more than 20 years. He has written works on children's play, achievement, and readiness, and coauthored one of the most widely used child development texts.

Eleanor Maccoby

Eleanor Maccoby is a developmental psychologist whose work has revealed the realities—and myths—surrounding sex differences and their effect on behavior from infants to adults. Her work has provided a forum for open-minded discussion of how people grow and the complex interaction between heredity and environment that makes child development so fascinating.

David Weikart

David Weikart has directed research and development in cognitive theory and its application to education since the late 1960s. He initiated the Ypsilanti Perry Preschool Project, a longitudinal study of how preschool affects disadvantaged children. He has been instrumental in developing a cognitively oriented approach to teaching and curriculum, using Piagetian theory.

Burton White

Burton White is best known for his work with infants. His research has helped establish descriptive data about children from newborns to three years of age—and how to work with them.

CONCLUSION

As a beginning teacher, it is important for you to think about what *you* believe about children, development, and learning. When you do, try to avoid the pitfall of taking sides. Your job is to integrate theory into your daily work with children. To do so, a comparison of the major developmental and learning theories is helpful.

Similarities Among the Theories

All four theories we have discussed attempt to explain how children grow, more in the socioemotional and cognitive areas than in the physical and motor areas. In other words, these theories do not try to explain the workings of the body as much as the mind and heart. In general, the theories do not dictate curriculum for the classroom, though behaviorism does recommend teaching/learning techniques. Each theory posits that learning follows an orderly, if not always smooth, path from birth to adulthood. They all see later learning as growing from previous experiences. They all agree that learning must be real, rewarding and, except in extreme cases, connected to an important person or people in early life.

Differences Among the Theories

More obvious are the differences among the four sets of ideas. All four have a particular focus, but not the same one. In developmental terms, Erikson covers the psychosocial area. The behaviorists and Piagetians tend to concentrate on cognitive growth. Maslow builds a framework including physiological, affective, and intellectual needs. Three of the four are developmental theories; that is, they describe changes in children as the result of combination of growth (controlled mostly by maturation and heredity) and interaction with the environment. Maslow's theory of self-actualization is less developmental than descriptive of overall human needs, though it is clear that in early childhood the basic needs predominate over higher ones that occur later in life.

Behaviorist theory emphasizes changes that occur in the environment. Cognitive and psychosocial ideas are stage theories, explaining growth as a series of steps through which all children pass, regardless of environment. Behaviorists spell out how the child learns no matter what age or stage they may have achieved, while the two stage theorists claim that what and how a child learns is tied to his stage of development. Humanists tend to look at learning as paralleling the child's internal affective state, rather than a stage of growth or external environmental conditions.

Most early childhood educators are eclectic in their theoretical biases. That is, they have developed their own philosophies of education based on a little of each theory, as summarized in Figure 4.9. Each teacher has an obligation to develop a clear set of ideas of how children grow and learn. We are fortunate to have choices. Most educators agree on some basic tenets based, in part, on theories of development and learning.

1. The child's basic physiological needs and needs for physical and psychological safety must be met satisfactorily before he can experience and respond to "growth motives." [Maslow]

2. Children develop unevenly and not in a linear fashion as they grow toward psychosocial maturity and psychological well-being. A wide variety of factors in children's lives, as well as the manner in which they interpret their own experiences, will have a bearing on the pattern and

Theory	Major Theorists	Important Facts
Psychosocial	Erik Erikson	Maturational emphasis Stage theory of social and emotional development Crises at each level Teacher: Emotional base, social mediator
Behaviorist	John Watson Edward Thorndike B. F. Skinner Albert Bandura	Environmental emphasis Stimulus-response Conditioning (classical and operant) Reinforcement (positive and negative) Modeling Teacher: Arranger of environment and reinforcer of behavior
Cognitive	Jean Piaget	Maturational and environmental emphasis Assimilation and accommodation Stage theory of cognitive development Teacher: Provider of materials and time and supporter of children's unique ways of thinking
Humanist	Abraham Maslow Erich Fromm Fritz Perls Carl Rogers	Environmental emphasis Mental health model Hierarchy of human needs Teacher: Provider of basic and growth needs
Others	Jerome Bruner Jerome Kagan Eleanor Maccoby David Weikart Burton White	Learning and thinking Child development research/text Sex differences research Cognitive-oriented curriculum Infant research

FIGURE 4.9 Each of the major theories of development or learning describes children and their growth in a different way.

rate of progress toward greater social and emotional maturity. [Erikson, the behaviorists]

3. Developmental crises that occur in the normal process of growing up may offer maximum opportunities for psychological growth, but these crises are also full of possibilities for regression or even negative adaptation. [Erikson]

4. Children strive for mastery over their own private inner worlds as well as for mastery of the world outside of them. [Erikson, Piaget]

5. The child's interactions with significant persons in his life play a major part in his development. [Erikson, the behaviorists, Piaget, and Maslow]

Developmental Research Results

To keep in mind the real child underneath all these theories, teachers apply developmental research to their own classroom settings. Figure 4.10 consolidates what developmental research has found and how it can be put into practical use with young children.

Conditions for Learning

Teachers also look for the best conditions for learning. Caring for children means providing for total growth, in the best possible environment. Developmental theory helps define conditions which enhance learning and from which positive learning environments are created. Research on all theories extends the knowledge of children and learning.

Coupled with practical application, both theory and research have helped all to recognize that:

1. *Learning must be real.* We teach about the children's bodies, their families, their neighborhoods, and their school. We start with who children are and expand this to include the world, in their terms. We give them the words, the ideas, the ways to question and figure things out for themselves.

2. *Learning must be rewarding.* Practice makes better, but only if it is all right to practice, to stumble and try again. We include the time to do all this, by providing an atmosphere of acceptance and of immediate feedback as to what was accomplished (even what boundary was just overstepped). Also, practice can make a good experience even better, as it reminds children in their terms of what they can do.

3. *Learning must build on children's lives.* We help connect the family to the child and the teacher. We know important family events and help the family support happenings at school. For children learning goes on wherever they may be, awake and asleep. Parents can learn to value learning and help it happen for their child.

4. *Learning needs a good stage.* Healthy bodies make for alert minds, so good education means caring for children's health. This includes physical health, and emotional and mental health, too. Psychological safety and well-being are theoretical terms for the insight, availability, and awareness teachers bring to their classrooms. On the lookout for each child's successes, we prevent distractions in the way furniture is arranged, how noisy it is, how many strangers are around. Mental health is both emotional and intellectual. We try to have a variety of materials and experiences, and a flexible schedule, when someone is pursuing an idea, building a project, finishing a disagreement. As long as we care for children, we will have our hands full. With the theoretical underpinnings presented here, we have the tools with which to make our own way into the world of children and of early childhood education.

SUMMARY

The twentieth century has been called "the century of the child." Developmental and learning theories of this century form the cornerstone of our knowledge about children. What we know about how children grow, learn, and adapt to the world

Developmental Research Tells Us:	Teachers Can:
1. Growth occurs in a sequence.	Think about the steps children will take when planning projects. Know the sequence of growth in their children's age group.
2. Children in any age group will behave similarly in certain ways.	Plan for activities in relation to age range of children. Know the characteristics of their children's age group.
3. Children grow through certain stages.	Know the stages of growth in their class. Identify to family any behavior inconsistent with general stages of development.
4. Growth occurs in four interrelated areas.	Understand that a person's work in one area can help in another. Plan for language growth, while children use their bodies.
5. Intellectual growth: Children learn through their senses. Children learn by doing; adults learn in abstract ways, while children need concrete learning. Cognitive growth occurs in four areas: perception (visual, auditory, etc.)	Have activities in looking, smelling, tasting, hearing, and touching. Realize that talking is abstract; have children touch, manipulate, act out what they are to do. Provide materials and activities in matching, finding same/different, putting a picture with a sound, taste, or with a symbol.
language	Provide opportunities to find and label things, talk with grown-ups, friends, tell what it "looks like," "smells like," etc.
memory	Know that by three, a child can often remember 2–3 directions. Know that memory is helped by seeing, holding objects and people.
reasoning	Recognize that it is just beginning, so children judge on what they *see,* rather than what they reason they should see. Be sure adult explanations aid in understanding reasons. Practice finding "answers" to open-ended questions such as "How can you tell when you are tired?"
6. Social growth: The world *is* only from the child's viewpoint. Seeing is believing.	Expect that children will know their ideas only. Be aware that the rights of others are minimal to them. Remember that if they cannot see the situation, they may not be able to talk about it.
Group play is developing.	Provide free-play sessions, with places to play socially. Understand that group play in structured situations is hard, because of "self" orientation.

FIGURE 4.10 Developmental research tests theories of growth and learning to find out about children and childhood.

Developmental Research Tells Us:	Teachers Can:
Independence increases as competence grows.	Know that children test to see how far they can go. Realize that children will vary from independent to dependent (both among the group, and within one child).
People are born not knowing when it is safe to go on.	Understand that children will need to learn by trial and error.
Adult attention is very important.	Know the children individually. Be with the child, not just with the group.
Young children are not born with internal mechanism that says "slow down."	Move into a situation before children lose control.
7. Emotional growth: Self-image is developing.	Watch for what each person's self-image is becoming. Give praise to enhance good feelings about oneself. Know that giving children responsibilities helps self-image. Talk to children at eye level. Children learn by example. Model appropriate behavior by doing yourself what you want the children to do.
8. Physical growth: Muscle development is not complete. Muscles cannot stay still for long. Large muscles are better developed than small ones.	Not expect perfection, in either small- or large-muscle activity. Plan short times for children to sit. Give lots of chances to move about, be gentle with expectations for hand work.
Hand preference is being established.	Watch to see how children decide their handedness. Let children trade hands in their play.
A skill must be done several times before it is internalized.	Have available materials to be used often. Plan projects to use the same skill over and over.
Bowel and bladder control is not completely internalized.	Be understanding of "accidents." If possible, have toilet facilities available always, and keep them attractive.

FIGURE 4.10   Cont.

around them is critical in our quest for greater understanding of the people we serve. Our field is greater for the contributions of several schools of study. Psychoanalyst Erik Erikson's theory of psychosocial development gives us insight into children's feelings and how their emotional and social lives affect their learning. The behaviorists, a distinctively American group of psychologists, demonstrate how much we can learn of human affairs by applying the methods of science. Jean Piaget, a "giant in the nursery school" (Elkind, 1977), opens our eyes to a stage theory of growth and shows us how active children are in their own learning. Abraham Maslow, a humanistic psychologist, establishes a hierarchy of needs, reminding us that the basic physical and psychological needs must be met before higher learning can take place.

In learning about these theories, we are more able to formulate our own philosophy of education. By tracing our roots to these learning theories, we show our willingness to make a commitment to children. What we know about growth and development helps us fight for our most important resource—our children.

FIGURE 4.11 Research to examine theory and psychological processes will further our knowledge of child development.

Review Questions

1. Match the theorist with the appropriate description:

B.F. Skinner   Sex differences *maccoby*

Abraham Maslow   Social learning *Bandura*

Jean Piaget   Psychosocial development *erikson*

Albert Bandura   Behaviorism *skinner*

Eleanor Maccoby   Cognitive theory *Piaget*

Erik Erikson   Self-actualization *maslow*

2. Describe Piaget's four stages of cognitive development.

3. Name at least three psychologists who have contributed to the knowledge of development.

4. Given four theories of learning and development, which one would most likely advocate large blocks of free play? An early academic program? Open-ended questioning by teachers? Regular early mealtime?

Learning Activities

1. You are a teacher in a large urban day care center. Your children arrive by 7:00, and usually stay until after 5:00 each day. What would you do first thing in the morning? Use Maslow's hierarchy of needs to justify your answer.

2. What do you think of cartoons? From a social learning perspective, what kind of television would you have your daughter watch?

Bibliography

Charlesworth, Rosalind. *Understanding Child Development.* New York: Delmar Publishers, 1983.

Elkind, David. "Giant in the Nursery School—Jean Piaget." In Hetherington, E.M., and Parke, R.D. (eds.), *Contemporary Readings in Psychology.* New York: McGraw-Hill, 1977.

Erikson, E.H. "A Healthy Personality for Every Child." In Mussen, Paul H.; Conger, John J.; and Kagan, Jerome (eds.), *Child Development and Personality,* 3rd ed. New York: Harper and Row, 1969.

Erikson, E.H. *Childhood and Society,* 2nd ed. New York: W.W. Norton and Co., 1963.

Erikson, E.H. "Toys and Reasons." In Haworth, M.R. (ed.), *Child Psychotherapy: Practice and Theory.* New York: Basic Books, 1964.

Ginsberg, Herbert, and Opper, Sylvia. *Piaget's Theory of Intellectual Development.* Englewood Cliffs, N.J.: Prentice-Hall, 1969.

Goble, Frank G. *The Third Force: The Psychology of Abraham Maslow.* New York: Grossman Publishers, 1970.

Hubley, John, and Hubley, Faith. *Everyone Rides the Carousel.* Santa Monica, Calif.: Pyramid Films, 1976.

Krumboltz, John, and Krumboltz, Helen. *Changing Children's Behavior.* Englewood Cliffs, N.J.: Prentice-Hall, 1972.

McClinton, Barbara S., and Meier, Blanche G. *Beginnings: Psychology of Early Childhood.* St. Louis: C.V. Mosby Co., 1978.

Maslow, Abraham H. *Motivation and Personality.* New York: Harper and Row, 1954.

Maslow, Abraham H. *Toward a Psychology of Being.* New York: D. Van Nostrand, 1962.

Murphy, Lois B., and Leeper, Ethel M. "Conditions for Learning." Washington, D.C.: U.S. Department of Health, Education, and Welfare, 1973.

Peters, Donald L., and Willis, Sherry L. *Early Childhood,* Life-Span Human Development Series. Monterey, Calif.: Brooks/Cole Publishing Co., 1978.

Spitz, R.A., and Wolf, K.M. "Anaclitic Depression: An Inquiry into the Genesis of Psychiatric Conditions in Early Childhood, II." In Freud, A., et al. (eds.), *The Psychoanalytic Study of the Child,* Vol. II. New York: International Universities Press, 1946.

Suransky, Valerie Polakow. "A Tyranny of Experts." *Wilson Quarterly,* Autumn 1982, pp. 53–60.

SECTION III

EFFECTIVE TEACHING: A COMMITMENT TO OPTIMAL CHILD DEVELOPMENT

Joseph H. Stevens, Jr.

Effective teaching with young children requires commitment, knowledge, and skill: commitment to assisting children's optimal development; knowledge of the factors which promote that development; and skill in behaving and arranging the environment in ways consistent with that knowledge. To do this well requires some self-awareness: insight about one's own competencies, as well as an ability and willingness to formulate a professional point of view–an open, working philosophy. Construct that point of view. Inform it through study of research and theory. Hone it by reflecting on your experiences with children and your teaching practices. Have coworkers scrutinize it. Work to enlarge it. Expect it to change.

Consider the following incident and what you would do were you the teacher in this classroom.

Timmy and Kwansa, two black five-year-old boys, have been building with Lego blocks for about ten minutes. Jeff, one of two white children in the class, walks over, points to Kwansa's building, and says, "That's my house!" Kwansa looks up, stares dead at Jeff, and shouts, "No, it's not!" He pauses, then, "You're not building with me!" Timmy and Kwansa turn back to their work. Jeff continues to look as they work; he sits down about two feet away, looks over at the box of Legos, then glances back at Kwansa, and says, "I hate you!" No reply from Timmy or Kwansa as they talk, smile at each other, and add more buildings. Five minutes later they have three blocks of houses, stores, and garages. Jeff has moved off to the side with some Rig-A-Jigs and has started building an airplane.

Not so cute, but certainly revealing. If you had overheard this incident, what would you have done? Why? What hypotheses about the social development and

Who Are the Teachers of the Young Child?

G U E S T E D I T O R I A L

social skills of Timmy, Kwansa, and Jeff does this incident generate? If this behavior is typical of Jeff, what might be appropriate learning objectives for him? How would you arrange the materials, equipment, daily schedule, learning activities, and grouping of the children to achieve these? How would you intervene—directly or indirectly? What social behaviors would you model, suggest, or praise? With which ones do you begin? How do you assist parents in working toward similar objectives at home? Are there alternative strategies? What do research and theory say about the relative effectiveness of the alternatives? What do you do tomorrow with Timmy, Kwansa, and Jeff? How will you know if it works? This is the business of teaching.

Many competencies are required of the effective early childhood teacher. Some are: keen observational skills; knowledge of child development; adherence to a strong ethical code; commitment to educational experiences that support cultural diversity and literacy; deftness in constructing, implementing, and evaluating activities targeted to foster specific developmental growth; participation in activities to foster one's own professional development; and skill in integrating the classroom program with the child's life at home.

Skill in assessing children's behavior and their perspective of the world, as well as those environmental factors that influence their behavior, is a cornerstone of good teaching. Children teach adults about child development and about education when those adults are sensitive and systematic observers. I like to remember Maria Montessori's description of how she developed the Method—through watching how children played with materials.

The burgeoning knowledge base in child development continually challenges us to judiciously apply what we learn. For example, consider what we know now about the effects of divorce, how children learn to read, how nutrition affects learning and development, and the teacher's role in promoting oral language. Extensive research on the development of infant attachment has provided guidance about key caregiving behaviors infant workers need to manifest. This research has also convinced us that infant day care need not be detrimental to a child's emotional development. Research on the long-term consequences of high-quality preschool education for low-income children has affirmed for state and national legislators the importance of early education. Effective application requires regular reading of professional journals like *Young Children, Child Care Quarterly, Journal of Applied Developmental Psychology,* and *Topics in Special Education,* among others.

Increasingly, children in early childhood programs represent a variety of ethnic and cultural backgrounds. A major task for teachers is to increase children's literacy about their and others' cultures without promoting stereotypes. A starting point is attitudinal—recognition that each ethnic group has a distinct culture (customs, language, dress, values, often a world view) and sense of peoplehood that distinguish it from its cultural counterparts. Promoting cultural literacy among children means helping them gain first-hand knowledge about these cultural aspects of various groups. We can help expose children to these broad cultural themes, and at the same time, we can help children see the diversity *within* cultures and the diffusion of cultural practices.

A central task of the teacher is curriculum development. All teachers must assess children's development, plan instruction, implement those plans, and evaluate whether the objectives were achieved; this process is curriculum development. It is through this systematic process that we are most likely to provide programs that promote children's development—programs that are effective. It is on this process that teachers must focus that commitment, that knowledge, and that skill. This is clearly no mean endeavor, one that anyone can do. It *is* one in which skilled professionals can make a difference.

PROFESSOR STEVENS was a teacher in a research and demonstration program for preschool children and was administrator of a prekindergarten program. For the past several years, he has been actively involved in early childhood teacher education. His research has examined the effectiveness of home-based early childhood programs, the influence of teenage and adult parents' social support systems on their childrearing skill, and factors related to the socialization of parenting from early adolescence through adulthood. He is currently Professor of Education and (by courtesy) Professor of Psychology and Human Development, George Peabody College for Teachers, Vanderbilt University.

5

The Teacher's Role

Questions for Thought

- What makes the teacher's role complex?
- What qualifications does a good teacher possess?
- What is team teaching in early childhood?
- What are the essentials for successful team relationships?
- How does my own personal development relate to my growth as a teacher?
- How do I make the most of my student teaching experience?
- What are some of the common problems associated with student teaching, and how can I avoid them?
- What does it mean to be a member of the teaching profession?

Outline

I. Who Are the Teachers of the Young Child?
  A. Comparison to Teaching in Other Educational Settings
    1. Differences
    2. Similarities

II. The Teacher's Role
  A. Definitions
  B. In the Classroom
    1. Interacting with Children
    2. Managing the Classroom
    3. Setting the Tone
  C. Outside the Classroom
    1. Paperwork
    2. Meetings
    3. Other Responsibilities

III. The Teacher as a Person
  A. Personal Qualities
  B. Self-Awareness
  C. Attitudes and Biases

IV. The Teacher as a Team Member
  A. Team Teaching
    1. Team Functions
    2. Rationale for Team Teaching
    3. Types of Teaching Teams
    4. Ten Essentials for Successful Team Teaching

V. The Teacher as a Professional
  A. Attitudes and Background
  B. Professional Development
    1. Developing a Professional Code of Ethics
    2. Continuing Education
    3. Setting Professional Goals
    4. Professional Affiliations

VI. The Student Teacher
  A. Orientation to the Role of Student Teacher
    1. Before School Starts
  B. Guidelines for Beginning
    1. Student Behavior
    2. Interacting with Children
    3. Relating to Other Adults

VII. The Whole Teacher

VIII. Summary

IX. Review Questions

X. Learning Activities

XI. Bibliography

WHO ARE THE TEACHERS OF THE YOUNG CHILD?

Group time for the 3½-year-olds is about to begin. The teacher, Paul, is well prepared and ready. He has chosen dinosaurs as his topic after hearing two children arguing about how to pronounce tyrannosaurus the day before. That morning, Paul gathered pictures of dinosaurs, small plastic models of prehistoric animals, a record with songs and stories about dinosaurs and several picture books. He put pictures of dinosaurs on the wall, borrowed a copy of "Danny and the Dinosaur" from another classroom, and learned a fingerplay about dinosaurs from his coteacher Margarita.

But where are the children? Group time was scheduled to begin five minutes ago. Two or three at a time, children begin to join Paul on the rug. They are coming in from outdoors; some are going to the bathroom before they sit down. Kendra, another teacher, is with them. "Has anyone here ever seen a dinosaur?", Paul asks. Before the words are out, Phillip wanders in from outside, his face covered with sand, and crying softly. Margarita takes him to the bathroom where Kendra will help him clean up.

Paul begins again but the children are restless. Angelo puts his arm around Fatima and she pushes him away. Erika and Andrew, sitting close by, are watching them with avid interest. No one responds to Paul's question. Some of the children are looking at him, some seem lost in their own thoughts, and others are still pulling at the velcro of their shoes. Several are making faces and noises at their neighbors. For Max, the lull is too tempting, and he launches into a monologue about his sister's new toy. Paul simultaneously nods encouragement to the children who are watching him, frowns at Angelo, tells Max to listen, and brings out a picture of a dinosaur. Margarita has rejoined the group in time to hear them shout, "I saw one of those!", "I have one at home like that!", "They scare me—", "I don't like them."

Capitalizing on the children's interest, Paul and Margarita pass around the small plastic

dinosaurs. Willie refuses to share them with anyone, Marcus growls and shoves one near Jennifer's face. She screams; Kendra, who has brought the last child from the bathroom, moves near to comfort Jennifer and control Marcus. All 25 children are now in place and Paul continues leading a discussion about dinosaurs. The book sits unused, the fingerplay forgotten, as the teachers invite the children to join them in a dinosaur dance. Thus, five to eight minutes have passed in the lives of three early childhood teachers.

Teachers of young children come into early childhood for many reasons. Paul spent several years with emotionally disturbed children and wants to gain some experience with normal youngsters. Margarita began as a Head Start teacher, and Kendra was active in a parent cooperative school. The teachers in the next classroom have different stories. Elva, mother of two elementary-school children, wanted part-time work to earn extra income. During high school, Karen worked part time at a day care center and thought she might like to make a full-time career of child care. Roger helped raise his younger brothers and sisters, while Ann and Al always wanted to be teachers.

All of these people had different motivations, but all were drawn into the early childhood classroom. What prompted that decision may have had something to do with the nature of teaching at this early age.

Comparison to Teaching in Other Educational Settings

Differences

The nature of teaching in the early years is unlike that of other age groups. Early childhood teachers are more involved in small-group activity than many elementary- and secondary-school teachers. The bulk of teaching and learning in the preschool takes place through teacher–child interactions rather than through lectures and demonstrations. Play is the learning medium in a classroom for preschoolers, but reserved for recess time in other grades. Children in early childhood settings generally have a choice of activities, while schools for older children are structured so that all the students do the same thing at once. Outdoor play periods in the preschool actively involve the teachers since young children require more supervision than older ones. Even the classrooms are set up differently. There is an abundance of materials and child-sized equipment to invite children's interest and interaction; no rows of desks line up neatly in the early childhood room.

Working closely with other adults is an unusual aspect to teaching in the early years. A staff, a team of teachers, is common to many preschools, whereas a fourth- or fifth-grade teacher generally teaches alone most of the day. Being sensitive to the role of the secretary, bus driver, cook, and janitor is important in an early childhood setting where everyone on the staff works together to create the best possible program for children.

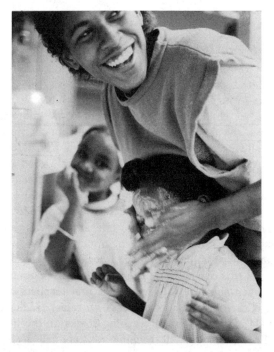

FIGURE 5.1 Early childhood teachers simply enjoy being with young children. (Courtesy of Stride Rite Children's Centers, Cambridge, Mass.)

Teachers in early childhood education have close and frequent contact with parents of the children they teach. Regularly scheduled parent conferences, parent assistants/volunteers in the classes, and daily contact with parents when they deliver and pick up their children combine to give the early childhood teacher an opportunity to develop closer home–school relations. (Parent–teacher relations will be discussed more fully in Chapter 8.)

Similarities

At first glance, the differences in teaching preschool and older children outweigh any similarities. There is one common element, however, that links the two. Early childhood teachers teach what other teachers teach. The curriculum in the early years is as rich in math, science, social studies, history, language, art, and geography as it is in any other grade. Academic content is presented in the preschool in ways appropriate to the age and developmental level of the students.

THE TEACHER'S ROLE

Definitions

Over the years the teacher's role in the early childhood classroom has been defined in many ways. The number and variety of tasks teachers perform are innumerable and hard to label. Hilliard says:

> . . . Teaching is many things . . . learning all that is possible to be learned about each child . . . modeling learning, modeling curiosity, modeling excitement, and modeling care . . . managing one's self as a tool, the primary tool . . . being aware of one's changing self and its changing impact on children.
>
> (Spodek, 1974)

Beyer (1968) calls the teacher a "viewer of children, a catcher of their signals, and a perceptive responder." Spodek (1972) lists teacher tasks:

> . . . (the teacher) functions as lecturer, story teller, group discussion leader, traffic director,

mediator of conflicts, psychological diagnostician, custodian, assigner of academic work, and file clerk.

An early pioneer in the field, Jessie Stanton, takes a more humorous view:

> . . . She should have a fair education. By this I mean she should have a doctor's degree in psychology and medicine. Sociology as a background is advisable. She should be an experienced carpenter, mason, mechanic, plumber, and a thoroughly trained musician and poet. At least five years practical experience in each of these branches is essential . . . Now at 83, she's ready!
>
> (Beyer, 1968)

It would be difficult to improve on any and all of these job descriptions. They are accurate and awesome, yet this diversity is exactly what makes

teaching in the early years so appealing. The multiple roles a teacher plays add challenge to the job. Nor are these descriptions exhaustive; the list could include adult educator, parent resource, faculty member, chief purchasing agent, nurse, program planner, staff supervisor, business manager, treasurer, personnel director, employee, and employer. (The role of the teacher in relationship to parents and programs as a whole will be further discussed in Chapters 8 and 10, respectively.)

Perhaps the job would seem more manageable and less overwhelming to the new teacher if some of the responsibilities were categorized. What teachers do with children is not all there is to teaching. Much of the work takes place outside the classroom. It is helpful to look at the teacher's role in another way. What are the things a teacher does with children? What are the things a teacher does after the children go home? How does the teacher interact with other adults in the early childhood setting?

In the Classroom

Interacting with Children

It is no secret that most teachers find their greatest satisfaction and challenges in the first role—who and what they are with children. The teacher–child interactions, the spur-of-the-moment crisis, the intense activity, the on-the-spot decisions, the loving and nurturing, go far in making one "feel" like a real teacher. Helping Rhonda get a good grip on the hammer, soothing Josh and Benno after they bump heads, and talking with Alexa about her drawing are at the heart of teaching young children. These encounters are enjoyable and provide moments for interactive teaching opportunities. These times help establish good relationships with the children. It is during these spontaneous, anything-can-happen-and-probably-will times that teachers display their "mastery of professional tools" (Hilliard, 1974). The real art of teaching comes on the floor of the classroom. All teaching skills are called upon in short order. Responses are automatic and sometimes unplanned. Teachers intuitively call upon their knowledge base, their experience, and their

FIGURE 5.2 Teachers model learning, listening, and loving.

proven techniques. Almost unconsciously, they reach back in their minds for all those things they know about children. Throughout the school day they apply that combination of knowledge and know-how.

Managing the Classroom

A teacher spends a lot of time being a classroom manager. Being a successful manager is a little like being a successful juggler. Both require the ability to think about and react to more than three things at once. With a simple gesture, a significant look, or merely moving nearby, the teacher maintains the ongoing activity.

Anticipating a clash between Nathan and Julie, the teacher Miriam intervenes, redirects them, and moves away. At the same time she has kept a watchful eye on Bobby at the bathroom sink. Passing close to Francie, she touches the child's shoulder in brief acknowledgment, smiling down as Francie struggles with the doll's dress. Miguel and Lea run up to her, grab her by the skirt and hand, and pull her toward the science display. They need to ask her something about the snake . . . NOW! Jake, the handyman, has come into the classroom wanting to know exactly which of the climbers needs repair. Sarah, the parent volunteer, waves to her; it's time to check on the corn bread baking in the kitchen. Quickly, the teacher files a mental note of the names of the children who accompany Sarah to the kitchen. As she reaches for a copy of *Ranger Rick* (the one with the great snake pictures in it), she observes Angie and her father entering the room. They both look upset. Telling Miguel and Lea she will return, the teacher walks over to greet the latecomers. As she moves past Doug, the student teacher, she comments on how well his language game is going and suggests he continue for another five minutes. Glancing at the clock, she realizes it is almost cleanup time. Her assistant, Chuck, watches her. She looks his way, and a nonverbal signal passes between them. Without a word, they both understand that snacks will be a little late today. Angie's

father begins to explain their delay as the teacher bends down to invite the child to come and look at the new snake cage with her.

In this setting, the teacher has a major role in supervising a number of people. Aides and volunteers, student teachers, and visitors add to the richness of a program. But it is the teacher who coordinates and supervises their various functions. From the description, it is clear that the teacher's role as a supervisor and manager includes being:

- a liaison and communicator with parents
- on-site supervisor for student teachers
- on-the-spot teacher trainer for students, aides, and volunteers
- observer of and listener to children
- caretaker for a safe environment

Setting the Tone

Teachers, obviously, are at the center of activity. Directly or indirectly they control much of the action. Since teachers are responsible for what occurs in the classroom, they must have a finger on its pulse at all times. As part of the juggling act, the teacher takes that pulse while moving around the class or yard. But something else happens. Throughout the day, from the moment of arrival, the teacher puts into effect another vital element. The teacher *sets the tone,* creating an atmosphere in which teachers and children will work and play. The skill with which it is done can make the critical difference between a classroom that is alive and supportive and one that is chaotic or apathetic. Because personality has such impact in the early childhood setting, the teacher creates more than an environmental mood, does more than provide the setting and the learning activities.

The teacher establishes what will be the *emotional framework.* This is done with body movements, by the tone of voice, facial expressions or lack of them, and nonverbal as well as verbal gestures. The way the children respond reflects this tone.

This interaction between the atmosphere the teacher creates and the child's behavior sets the tone. Young children are very sensitive to adult moods and attitudes. The teacher who is upset or angry invites the children to react with their own tense brand of activity. A teacher who exudes calm and confidence, strength and support, will inspire a more relaxed, comfortable atmosphere in which children can learn and grow. If the teacher is punitive and harsh, the tone of the classroom will reflect that. On the other hand, if teachers act on their beliefs that children deserve respect and are intelligent, capable human beings, they will create an entirely different climate. And the children will respond in kind.

Normal behavior for the young child includes tantrums, crying, resistance, curiosity, impatience, emotional swings, noise, and self-centeredness. This is the time to achieve a sense of their own separate self. They need a place to work through the developmental stages that their needs and nature indicate. The atmosphere that a teacher creates is a key element in that process.

The way teachers handle fights, react to tears, the words they use, and the voices raised communicate a direct message to the child. The understanding, the soothing, the warmth, the acceptance, create a climate where children feel safe, secure, and guided. This requires teachers who respect childhood, the individuality of children, their growing patterns, their emerging feelings, and their special capacity to learn. The end result is that preschoolers will thrive in an atmosphere influenced by teachers who understand this time of tension and growth in their lives.

Outside the Classroom

But what of those after-hours tasks that are a part of any total teaching effort? There are quite a few of these responsibilities that may be taken for granted. This part of the job may not be as gratifying as working directly with children, yet teachers must understand why it is important.

A good classroom is often dependent on how teachers spend their time away from the children.

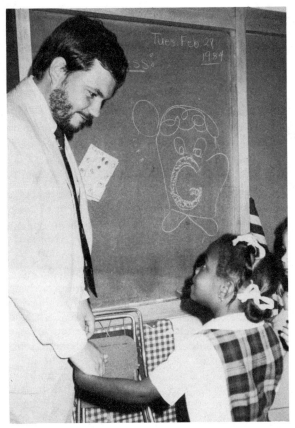

FIGURE 5.3 Teachers create a supportive atmosphere. (Courtesy of St. Mark's Episcopal School, Ft. Lauderdale, Fla.)

Many of the tasks that give added strength and depth to a teacher's curriculum are those which, out of necessity, must be accomplished after hours. The two most obvious jobs that fall into this category are paperwork and meetings.

Paperwork

Preschool teachers keep records on a variety of subjects; the type and kind will vary from school to school. The philosophy of the school, the number of children, the background of the teaching staff, and the purpose for the records will determine the amount the teachers will write. In schools that rely on government funding, record keeping is not optional. The children's progress, the teacher's performance, the program itself, must be evaluated on a regular basis. The data collected will be used to justify the continuation of the program; thus, the paperwork becomes critical to survival. Laboratory schools, teacher training centers, and other programs consider developmental reports as a natural part of teaching; they guide the teacher in more objective ways than casual observations.

While report writing and record keeping may be considered time-consuming, they are essential to any good early childhood program. The ultimate reason for collecting data is to give a more complete and up-to-date picture of each child. Once teachers understand the importance and value of ongoing records, they set about the task readily.

Children's progress reports demonstrate a school's commitment to good child development practices. Teachers see them as a means for parent education and information. Curriculum plans and learning activities sprout from such reports and records. It wasn't until such data was collected for entry into first grade that the kindergarten teachers realized most of the children were not sufficiently skilled with the scissors. They were able to plan curriculum experiences around this need and provide an opportunity for the classes to learn a necessary task.

Teachers also find that the social-emotional growth recorded periodically provides information from which insight and interpretation can develop. It may be just a brief note taken on the run, a thoughtful anecdote written at length after class, or a checklist of the child's favorite activities. All of these serve to give teachers a greater understanding of the role they play. If maintaining reports after school hours supports that role, they accept the job willingly.

FIGURE 5.4 Teachers' responsibilities extend beyond the classroom.

Staff Meetings

Held usually once a week for individual teaching teams. Purpose is to plan curriculum, set goals, and discuss children's progress. Faculty meetings for all school personnel may be held less frequently.

Professional Meetings

Attendance at workshops, seminars, in-service training. Local, state, and national conferences are sponsored by the National Association for the Education of Young Children, Association for Childhood Education International, and Child Care Coordinating Council.

Parent–Teacher Conferences

May be offered on a scheduled basis or they may be called by either parents or teachers as needed. Each school defines its own policy as to the number and frequency of parent contacts.

Student–Teacher Conferences

In schools used as training sites, teachers arrange time with individual students assigned to their class.

Parent Education Meetings

Many schools offer evening programs for parents. Teacher attendance may or may not be required.

Home Visits

May or may not be optional. Some schools schedule them before opening day. Otherwise teachers must arrange them on their own time.

FIGURE 5.5 Teachers attend many different types of meetings.

Meetings

Meetings are probably the most time-consuming of all out-of-class jobs. The teacher may need to communicate with the other people who are involved in the lives of the children, directly or indirectly. Parents, other teachers, baby-sitters, doctors, and social workers are some of the people with whom a teacher may want to confer. Teachers attend many different kinds of meetings. Figure 5.5 lists the most common.

Other Responsibilities

Some of a teacher's after-hours activities are intended to fortify and vitalize the classroom. Therefore, teachers:

- Organize and collect materials for use in class. They might collect space shuttle books from the library, find out if the bagel factory will allow field trips, or cut 18 pumpkin shapes while watching television. Teachers are also responsible for maintaining an orderly classroom. They might add pictures to the bulletin board, obtain new books and records, or replenish curriculum materials.

- Purchase materials and equipment that cannot be ordered. They know that the kitchen needs new mixing bowls, the supply room is low on red construction paper, and someone has to pick up fabric for pillow covers.

- Make phone calls. This is a quick and efficient way of keeping in touch. Teachers may call parents to check on children who are sick or absent. For children with special needs, teachers may need to contact doctors, therapists, and other specialists.

These duties are a part of the job of teaching young children but many will be shared with other teachers on the team or at the school. Though time-consuming, these responsibilities add to the creativity and care that teachers express for their classes.

THE TEACHER AS A PERSON

Personal Qualities

A teacher's personality has influence and impact. When a teacher exhibits a sense of trust, security, and support, the children echo those feelings and behaviors. Children learn to trust by being trusted; they learn respect by being respected. Children learn to understand others by being understood themselves. They learn responsibility by being treated as responsible human beings. The personal qualities of their teachers should include traits that foster those learnings.

Good teachers should have dedication, compassion, insight, flexibility, patience, energy, and self-confidence. Teachers should also be happy people who can laugh and use their sense of humor wisely. Liking children is part of wanting to work with them; teachers then feel that the job they are doing is important. Teachers need to be fair-minded, showing concern for all, regardless of color or creed. Physical and mental well-being are important, as is a demonstrated sense of responsibility and reliability. Teachers who can be both warm and loving, yet firm when expressing disapproval, have good teaching qualities.

Today, the well-rounded teacher, while maintaining a professional commitment, has other interests as well. Good teachers have an involvement with the world outside the walls of the child care center. They want to help children understand some of the real-life issues and concerns. They know that their interest in the world at large transmits itself to children.

Quality teachers personalize teaching, integrating their individuality into their work in appropriate ways. By exposing the human qualities they possess, teachers strengthen the bond between themselves and the children.

This basic description is a framework, a checklist of personal attributes, a place to begin to look at the human side of teaching. Men and women who are able to nurture and comfort children treat them as real persons and value them as children.

Expressing this takes practice so that teachers do not intrude on children's well-being. Teachers do not have to sentimentalize childhood or tolerate misbehavior because it is "cute." Children deserve teachers who understand their nature and respect the limits of behavior.

Self-Awareness

To be the best teacher possible, understanding and accepting oneself is vital. *Self-awareness* will make a difference in the way teachers relate to children. Each teacher must ask, "Who and what and why am I? And how does knowing this bring some meaning into my life? How does it affect my life as a teacher?"

FIGURE 5.6 Teachers may recognize themselves within the children.

Teachers may also begin to realize something about themselves. They know how and why children learn as they do, but what do they know about themselves as learners? How do teachers communicate an authentic appreciation of learning unless they have a sense of it in their own lives? Teachers might well ask themselves: "Do I see myself as a learner? Where does my learning take place? How? What happens to me when something is hard or when I make a mistake? Do I learn from other teachers? Do I learn from children?" Teachers' recognition of themselves as learning, growing persons gives an added degree of sincerity to teaching.

Self-knowledge—examining values and personal qualities—takes courage and a willingness to risk oneself. Children, other teachers, and parents will respond. Accepting oneself is where to begin in accepting children.

Attitudes and Biases

Facing *prejudices* about children may be one of the most difficult things for a beginning teacher. Personal histories are filled with biases. Most people are not familiar with ethnic cultures other than their own and therefore may be uncomfortable with persons who are different. They have been raised to know what is "good" behavior (at least what their family thinks is such) and what is "naughty." Teachers have strong opinions, born of their own experiences, as to how parents should treat their children. Children who are messy, who have odors, whose clothes are too big or too small, bother some teachers. Some of these biases can be resolved. Home visits and parent demonstrations of ethnic, religious, and cultural observances, can awaken an appreciation for the diversity of humankind. Sometimes teachers may be forced into further soul searching and reflection before they can untangle their anxiety and attitudes. Our feelings show in our contacts with children, and we do not want those feelings to damage their self-acceptance or self-appreciation. The question is not one of liking or disliking any child, it is one of teacher understanding and acceptance. By achieving that sense of acceptance, teachers are better able to accept all the children with whom they work, regardless of their "likeability."

THE TEACHER AS A TEAM MEMBER

The teaching role is not restricted to working with children. Numerous adults must be met, tolerated, dealt with, and included in the total teaching picture. A teacher may work with any or all of the following:

- other professional teachers
- teacher's aides
- student teachers
- program directors and administrators
- clerical and secretarial staff
- food service personnel
- maintenance staff
- bus drivers
- volunteers
- parents
- consultants and specialists
- research sponsors and assistants
- community representatives

These diverse people are connected through *children.* This network is made of people with different skills, styles, and backgrounds. Everyone has something to contribute, though each will have a different reason for and level of involvement with children and the educational process. The relationships that beginning teachers form with the other members of this team are crucial to the optimal development of the children for whom they care. One of the most important relationships is with the other teachers working in the early childhood setting.

Team Teaching

The beginning teacher will likely be joining a team of teachers, who together will shape, direct, and participate in the early childhood program. Regardless of the background of those who form the team, there are certain characteristics that are common to most teaching teams.

Team Functions

Teaching teams are formed with specific purposes in mind:

Sharing Information. In a teaching situation, important information centers around activities in the classroom and the children themselves. Information about children and their families is also shared by team members, as are child development strategies to foster continuity in the teaching approach.

Example: "Sheila's grandmother died yesterday, so she may need some extra attention and support for a while."

Contributing New Ideas. A vital team is one that offers new ideas for curriculum, behavior management, parent–school relationships, professional growth, and the like. New ideas keep the team and the teaching alive and fresh.

Example: "A friend of mine is a marine biologist. I'm sure she would be glad to come and talk with the children about the different kinds of fish, and it would be a nice extension to the unit we did on water creatures."

Solving Problems and Resolving Conflicts. Every team, every organization, every classroom will encounter problems at some time. Differences in opinion, approach, personality, and style among adults or children are inevitable whenever two or more people work together. Effective teams recognize and accept such problems and conflicts as part of their challenge, and work together to solve them.

Example: Meg, the teacher's aide who has been with the preschool for a year, constantly belittles the new student teacher's efforts to conduct group time and refuses to do her share when they are assigned to the same activity center. The head teacher confronts Meg privately about her attitudes and performance.

Making Decisions. In team teaching, many decisions are made by the members together. An issue is raised, discussion follows, and a decision is reached by mutual agreement or consensus. Decisions on class policy or behavior management are often made this way. Other decisions may be deferred to the team leader or director, and many decisions will be made by individual team members. The successful team recognizes these different levels of decision making. By being clear on who makes the decisions, the team members learn to trust themselves and each other to handle each situation appropriately.

Example: At a recent staff meeting, Jackie, the head teacher, decided to consult with the director about recommending a psychologist to Tammy's family. At the same time she left it to the rest of the team to decide where to go on the spring field trip.

Supporting Other Team Members. Team members share both the workload and the satisfactions of a job well done. Teaching is a demanding, intense profession; it can be a draining experience. Teaching on a team can bring support in time of need and inspiration to those working with young children every day. Supportive interactions are a part of the joy of team teaching.

Example: "Here, why don't I change Darian? You've been at the diapering table all morning."

Rationale for Team Teaching

There are many reasons why team teaching is such an integral part of so many early childhood programs.

State Law. First, many state regulations mandate a minimum number of adults in the classroom. This number varies with the ages of the children. The prescribed ratio of adults to children changes as children mature and become more independent of

FIGURE 5.7 Everyone on a team has something to contribute.

adults. For example, California state law dictates that publically subsidized programs for three- to six-year-olds maintain a ratio of one adult for every eight children (California State Education Code, Section 8288, 1984). Since the adult–child ratio is mandated by law, larger groups of children will be taught and supervised by more than one adult.

Adult Role Models. A team of teachers provides a wide range of adult models for children. Teachers who are male, female, young, middle-aged, older, or of varying ethnic backgrounds bring to the teaching experience equally diverse attitudes, approaches to children, interests, skills, and knowledge to share. In the team-teaching setting, teachers have an opportunity to model good social relationships for children in the way they treat each other. Children learn how to accept differences in people as they watch adults interact with others on the team.

Support for Children. Team teaching is supportive for children. The absence of one teacher is not as disruptive when the children can count on other familiar faces. Children learn to trust the teaching environment, since someone they know is always there. In this way, they are introduced to change in a less abrupt manner.

Support for Teachers. Team members can share problems with each other and be understood. Learning to work together on a team promotes admiration and respect for one another. This can be a great teaching tool: adults working cohesively, communicating with one another, and being friends.

Workload Reduction. Teams lighten the workload. There are more people available to do the paperwork and record keeping, to maintain the room and yard, and to help clean up and set up. There is a sharing of the teaching tasks, whether it is curriculum planning, parent conferencing, or teaching and caring for the children.

Program Enrichment. Team teaching adds richness to the program. A team of teachers can share talents and resources. All team members can teach to their strengths, and can work on weaknesses with the support of the team. Clara may be superb with small groups of children but ineffective at music. Jon loves music, plays a guitar, and dances with the children. These two teachers can learn from each other.

Types of Teaching Teams

Teaching teams may differ in their makeup. They may include two or more teachers who share teaching responsibilities for one class, or they may be made up of two or more teachers in the same school who teach the same grade level, but in different classrooms. Despite their physical separation in two classrooms, these teachers may plan activities together, consult one another, or sometimes combine their classes. Another form of team teaching involves a *resource teacher*—someone who has a special knowledge to share (for example, in music, gymnastics, or computers). Such a teacher might travel from classroom to classroom and from group to group, coordinating activities with many individual teachers.

Some of the usual teacher combinations in the early childhood setting are:

- teacher–teacher (professional equals)
- teacher–aide (less experience and training)
- teacher–parent (volunteer or hired aide; less experience)
- teacher–volunteer (wide range of qualifications; generally not trained)
- teacher–student (entry level skills; needs support and guidance)

Most teams have a leader and an established course to follow. The leadership styles of teams may differ, however, and a team's course or purpose may change over time. In the early childhood setting, a head or supervising teacher often is responsible for directing and planning the types of activities and for implementing the program's goals within a particular classroom. Sometimes this leadership responsibility is rotated among team members; other

teaching teams may have coleaders. Most often there is one designated leader for each team. The way a team learns to work together is, in large measure, determined by the leader's style. As direction from the leader decreases, team members assume increasing responsibility and initiative. As a team member, it is important for the beginning teacher to be aware of the possible leadership styles and their effect on his or her teaching role. See Appendix B for a table of leadership styles and their effect on other members of the teaching team.

On a teaching team, the one-to-one relationships between individual team members is important. The effectiveness of the team and its leadership is dependent on several key factors that are essential to any working relationship.

Ten Essentials for Successful Team Teaching

Team teaching clearly has its advantages and its place in early childhood education. Working with other teachers is not without its difficulties, however. Communication problems and conflicts beset most teams, affecting the members as well as their leaders. To avoid such stumbling blocks, there are ten essential steps for effective team teaching.

1. Open Communication. The ability and opportunity to communicate thoughts, concerns, and feelings to other team members are perhaps the most important factors in promoting effective teamwork. Communication can take several forms; it may be verbal (either written or spoken), or it may be nonverbal, using *body language* instead of words. Whatever form it takes, all communication involves the sharing of information and requires both a sender and a receiver. The message sent must be clear, and the person to whom it is sent must be ready to receive it.

Knowing the various means of communication is not sufficient, in itself, for effective team communication, however. Rather, team members must seek out *opportunities* to communicate with their coworkers, either formally or informally. For many teachers, this means making the most of the set-up and clean-up times when children and families are not at school. Maintaining ongoing, if brief, verbal contact with one's coworkers during the class session keeps communication flowing. To be effective, teams must have the opportunity to plan curriculum, discuss issues, resolve conflicts, and plan strategies for handling particular behaviors or family situations.

Beginning teachers would do well to ask themselves: What methods of communication do I use? Do I communicate what I am truly thinking and feeling? Am I a good listener? What can I do to foster dialogue with my fellow team members?

2. Self-Awareness. Beginning teachers may feel inadequate at first in their relationships with the other members of their teaching team. How well they perform as members of a team will depend, to some extent, on their self-perceptions. When teachers gain insight into and accept themselves, they can then apply this insight and acceptance to their relationships with their coworkers.

To promote teamwork in teaching through self-knowledge, teachers might ask themselves: What are my strengths and weaknesses, and how do they complement or conflict with those of my fellow team members? Do I prefer to follow or lead, to plan programs or carry out plans developed by a coworker? In what teaching situations do I feel uncomfortable, and why? What have I done lately to learn more about myself?

3. A Satisfying Role. Each team member must have a satisfying role to play on the team. That means each person must be appreciated for the "special something" he or she brings to the group. Beginning teachers must consider: Is there a place on my team that is uniquely mine? In what way can my special talents and experiences contribute to the success of my team's efforts?

4. Mutual Respect and Acceptance. All members of a teaching team have an obligation to learn about the people with whom they work. Knowledge of team members' diverse personalities, experiences, strengths and weaknesses, teacher developmental stages, educational philosophies, and social and cultural values—and acceptance of their individuality—is as important to team functioning as it is in working with children. This knowledge is also the basis for resolving differences to promote smooth functioning of the teaching team. The climate of trust and the nonthreatening atmosphere gained through mutual respect allow each team member to contribute openly and innovatively to the team.

In the interest of developing a respect for, and acceptance of, the "uniqueness" of team members, teachers should ask themselves: What do I have in common with my coworkers, and what unique qualities do they bring to the team? What do I expect from my fellow team members: Emotional support? Intellectual stimulation? Candid feedback?

5. Team Spirit and Empathy. A sense of "teamness" happens not by accident, but by conscious

FIGURE 5.8 How do my special talents contribute to the teaching team?

effort. Each member of the teaching team must be committed not only to the day-to-day working of the team, but also to the long-term goals of the early childhood program. This commitment means being *empathetic* to the moods, feelings, and needs of coworkers. This may mean sharing the workload, being tactful in disagreements, and positive in suggesting change.

To develop empathetic and supportive relationships with fellow team members, teachers should ask themselves the following questions: How can I relate to and be supportive of my coworkers? Have I ever been in their shoes? What did I feel like when I lost control of the children in my activity center? What strategy worked for me when I had to deal with Kim's destructive behavior? What can I do to promote and sustain high morale among my coworkers?

6. Flexibility. Just as it is important to change with and adapt to the varying needs of children, so too it is crucial to respond to the needs of team members with a give-and-take approach. Flexibility involves a willingness to offer and accept negotiation and compromise in order to preserve the effectiveness of the team effort.

Beginning teachers should ask themselves: Do I demonstrate a willingness to change with the changing needs of my team members, or do I adhere rigidly to preset plans or attitudes? Am I open to new ideas proposed by my coworkers? Am I sufficiently prepared to handle changes within the classroom setting?

7. A Willingness to Share the Spotlight. Unless held in check, tension among staff members can arise from a sense of competition, which may appear in subtle ways. We must be willing to admit that other teachers are just as dedicated to children and deserving of their affections as we are. As a member of a team, we must be willing not only to share the credit for progress, but also to share the responsibility for resolving problems when they arise. We should ask ourselves: How do I feel when another teacher is praised by a parent, or preferred by a

child? Am I quick to acknowledge my coworkers' achievements?

8. Clearly Defined Roles. An understanding of the roles of each member on a teaching team is essential for the smooth functioning of that teaching unit. A checklist or job description may be helpful in reinforcing the appropriateness of the actions taken or the responsibilities assumed by team members. Besides understanding one's own role, a knowledge of what others' jobs entail is also helpful in fostering team efficiency and in avoiding duplication of effort. Clearly defined teacher roles also serve as a guard against legal and ethical problems. Teachers should ask themselves: Do I know my role assignment and my appropriate place on the teaching team? Do I often overstep the bounds of my teaching knowledge or skills? Do I fulfill my responsibilities as a team member, or do I allow others to take over some of my least-liked responsibilities?

9. Professionalism. Professional attitudes and behavior are a critical part of team teaching. Personal grievances must be kept out of the classroom. Teachers should be encouraged to relate to one another as peers, colleagues, and professionals, whatever the level of their development. There is no place in the early childhood setting for petty gossip, ill will, or exclusive cliques. Most schools have established appropriate channels through which individual problems can be resolved. Taking personal differences to someone who can help solve them usually means going directly to the person in question, not complaining about that individual in the teachers' lounge. Everyone on the team can model ways of professional behavior for other team members. Teachers should ask themselves: Do I behave in a professional manner? Can I keep confidences? Do I confront those with whom I have differences in an attempt to work them out?

10. Evaluation. No team can declare itself an effective teaching unit unless provisions are made for ongoing evaluation. Judging other members of the team, and being judged, is part of the privilege of being a member of the teaching profession. Evaluations should provide a teacher with a clear picture that confirms strengths and pinpoints potential areas for growth. Assessment of a team member's performance should be communicated in an affirming, rather than in a criticizing, manner. (Evaluation of programs and people is discussed more thoroughly in Chapter 10.) Teachers should ask themselves: Do I evaluate my team members fairly and share my assessment with them in a supportive way? Do I accept evaluation as an essential part of teaching? Am I responsive to the thoughts and opinions of others?

THE TEACHER AS A PROFESSIONAL

Attitudes and Background

There is a body of knowledge, an educational foundation, that is assumed of anyone entering the early childhood profession. There are also some basic teaching skills that are necessary. These include methods and techniques appropriate for teaching the very young child. Yet there is more if one is to be called a true *professional*.

Being a member of the teaching profession goes beyond an accumulation of methods, coursework, and teaching experiences. Being a professional teacher suggests an attitude about teaching. It is not simply an eight-hour-a-day job, or an occupation chosen lightly. Teachers are called to the profession when they believe they can indeed make a difference in the lives of the children. While that may at first sound *altruistic,* it reflects a dedication to teaching that exceeds the desire for a job or a steady paycheck.

There are professional expectations, starting with having a common background with others in the field. This includes studying child development and human behavior, family relations, parent education and development, and curriculum planning. Some practical teaching experience under the guid-

ance of a master teacher is assumed, as is a familiarity with observation and recording techniques. This foundation of knowledge and experience provides the framework for professional development. Teachers gradually acquire further skills on the job. They learn to juggle three or four interactions with children at once and develop the skill of stopping an argument by a mere look or a quick gesture. Thus, the process of becoming a professional teacher is an orderly progression along a continuum of development.

This progression of teaching skills has been described by Lilian Katz (1977) as consisting of four distinct stages of teacher development. See Appendix C for a description and definition of each stage.

FIGURE 5.9 Teaching's benefits are intrinsic and individual. (Courtesy of Stride Rite Children's Centers, Cambridge, Mass.)

Professional Development

Developing a Professional Code of Ethics

As teachers mature, they turn their attention to issues and concerns outside themselves. Many of these issues, whether they are called so or not, are related to ethical conflicts and moral principles. Teachers are, after all, human beings, and that entails genuine conflict about behavior. Doing what is right becomes difficult at times; knowing what is right may be elusive. Even identifying what is right—an ethical conflict—may not be obvious. Some everyday examples that fall into this category follow:

A teacher takes a disruptive child out of the classroom. Two witnesses tell you later they saw the teacher shake the child severely. *What do you do?*

A teacher tells you she is pregnant and plans to stay for only a few months into the school year for which she has just been hired. Fearing the loss of her job, she asks you to keep her secret and not tell the director. *What do you do?*

A child comes to school with marks across her forehead. The child states that her father hit her with a belt. *What do you do?*

A teacher who has not been rehired for the following year begins to pull parents aside and share his grievances with them. *What do you do?*

These are problems that occur daily in any teacher's life. They are not problems of an abstract or impersonal nature. They are concerns teachers face at work every day. J.D. Andrews defines *ethics* this way:

. . . Ethics are the genuine smile on your face . . . treating the custodian like a human being . . . cooperating with the teacher with whom you have a personality conflict. It is showing . . . that other people are . . . worthy of respect and consideration.

. . . Children learn ethics by our behavior and our attitudes toward other people. There-fore we need to exercise care about the behavioral model we present. Young children will see it like it is, and they will set their standards accordingly.

(Katz and Ward, 1978)

Teachers may find it helpful to discuss their ethical concerns with colleagues. Some schools provide in-service programs for the staff where these issues are raised. Other schools have a code of ethics for their employees to follow. In Appendix D there is an Initial Code of Ethics for early childhood educators.

Continuing Education

Creative and stimulating classes are the product of teachers who continue to learn more about how to teach. After the initial stage of teaching, many teachers begin to seek new challenges and new ways to improve the quality of their teaching. Usually, this leads to some form of *continuing education,* such as participation in workshops, courses, or seminars. If time to pursue continuing education is not built into a teacher's schedule, there may be other options:

- In-service training programs may be brought into the school setting. Resource people can be invited to lead the staff in discussions about children's behavior, parent relationships, assessment charts, or science curriculum.

- Various members of the teaching staff can develop a program of their own, offering their expertise to fellow faculty at an in-service meeting.

- A computer specialist, art resource teacher, or movement expert can be invited to visit the classrooms, instructing children and providing staff with some useful ideas and plans.

- A family therapist can be invited to speak at a staff meeting about strategies for supporting families in crisis.

- A library for teachers, stocked with professional books, journals (such as *Young Children*), and newspapers (such as *Education Week*) can provide a teacher with the means to keep up with current trends and practices and to improve teaching skills in the classroom.

- Parents who are professionals in a variety of fields can be utilized whenever possible to enrich the knowledge and skills of the staff.

Setting Professional Goals

As teachers raise their sights beyond "How will I survive?" to "Where am I going?", they begin to set goals for themselves and their teaching career. They develop both long- and short-term objectives for themselves, establishing a framework for professional growth.

The goals that are set will vary with individual teachers. For Jim, this could mean developing a brand new curriculum for his class of two-year-olds. Susan might choose to work toward having greater parent support in her classroom. Thea and Frank might decide to develop a workshop on sensorimotor skills. Stephanie wonders about using her skills with children and computers to go into business for herself. Cassie would like to create a calendar of parent meetings and events for the school year. Whether in the area of children's programs, administration, staff relations, or their own professional development, teachers can learn, grow, and change. (See Chapter 10 for evaluation and goal-setting techniques.)

Professional Affiliations

Teachers who are beginning to perceive themselves as professionals may choose to join one of the professional organizations related to the early childhood field. One of the largest, the National Association for the Education of Young Children (NAEYC), has local and state affiliate groups through which one can become a member. NAEYC offers a range of services to its members, including conferences and publications such as the journal, *Young Children*. The Association for Childhood Education International (ACEI) has a similar function, whereas the Society for Research in Child Development (SRCD) focuses on child psychology, research, and development.

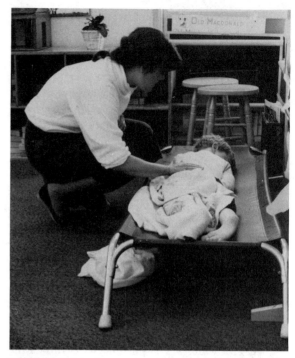

FIGURE 5.10 The student teacher has many responsibilities.

THE STUDENT TEACHER

Beginning teachers of young children cannot expect to successfully blend all of the many facets of a teacher—personal, team, and professional identity—at once. Certainly, teaching young children carries with it the obligation to understand and accept the many roles and responsibilities associated with the title of "teacher." However, beginning teachers must also be committed to the time and energy needed to *become* that total teacher.

Student teaching can be a great deal of fun as well as a unique learning experience. Textbook theories come alive as children naturally demonstrate child development concepts. Student teachers expect to learn about individual child growth and development; many are surprised to discover that they also learn how children function in groups and with adults. For students in a teacher training program, *practice teaching* may be the first hands-on opportunity to work directly with children.

Planning and executing activities that fit the needs and abilities of the child are another part of the student teacher's role. They provide an opportunity to test curriculum ideas, to see what happens when child meets materials. Working with an experienced teacher who models highly polished skills is an important part of the experience. The student becomes part of a faculty for a short period of time. Identification with a number of professionals can help the student find a teaching identity, and working as part of a team is supportive to the beginning teacher.

Yet we know that student teaching is not always fun. It is a time for intensive self-searching and self-revelations. Many students' own school experiences loom before them and intimidate their confidence. Planning lessons takes long hours. Students may still have doubts about being a teacher at all. It is uncomfortable to feel judged and criticized by others. This is a time of anxiety for most beginning teachers. But remember, even the poised, confident, and always-does-the-right-thing master teacher was once a beginning teacher.

Orientation to the Role of Student Teacher

Beginnings for student teachers are just as important as they are for young children. A child's first days of school are planned very carefully: Attempts are made to ease the separation process for parents and child, new children are shown where to put their belongings, daily schedules are explained, the locations of the bathroom and drinking fountain are pointed out, and the basic rules of the child care center are outlined.

Likewise, there are some strategies for easing the transition from student to student teacher. The key to making the most of an initial teaching experience is to anticipate some of the common pitfalls and develop a plan for dealing with them if they arise.

Before School Starts

The following guidelines will help to make the first days of your student teaching assignment a satisfying and positive experience:

- Contact the teacher before the first day of school. Try to meet together before school begins. Find out where the class meets and at what time. Be sure to ask at what time to arrive and when to leave. Are there any meetings to attend? If so, when and where are they held? What is the age group, the size, and the makeup of the children in the class? Are there special children and what are their needs? Get a copy of the daily schedule.

FIGURE 5.11 Student teaching combines learning with teaching.

- Find out what is expected during the first few days. Will you observe or actively participate? Will you be assigned to follow another teacher for a day or so? Ask these questions to learn the general format of the school day and to get a feeling for the student participant's role. Then relax and concentrate on the children.

- Visit the room to which you will be assigned to become acquainted with its layout. Tour the yard as well. Continue to look around the rest of the school if there is time. The janitor's room, the kitchen, nurse's office, and storeroom are all important places to identify.

- Share with the teacher any special skills or talents you may have, such as playing the harp or knowing how to use sign language. The teacher can help utilize these skills in new ways with young children. Sharing something of importance with young children is one way to establish closer relationships and adds confidence that will carry over into other areas of teaching. Let the teacher know about any other experiences with children: babysitting, camp counseling, or eight younger brothers and sisters.

- At some point in this initial meeting, the teacher will probably ask about goals for the student teaching experience. What would you like to get out of the time you spend in this classroom? It may be just a desire to work with children or a more definite goal to work with children for a specific reason. There may be short-term goals: to be at ease in a classroom setting. Some may be long term and specific: do a cooking activity in three weeks or lead a group time by the end of the semester. By establishing some common goals, the teacher will be able to guide a course so that those goals will be realized.

- Evaluation is an important part of the goal-setting process. Suggestions, constructive criticism, and feedback can be looked at more objectively when goals are clear. Students need to know how their work is affecting the classroom, the children, and the other teachers. Set a time together for receiving feedback; this may be each day after class or only every few weeks.

Guidelines for Beginning

After the first few sessions, things will begin to go more smoothly. The routine will become second nature. Most of the children's names will be familiar, and the student teacher will assume a place in this group of children and adults. Background information from the teacher and class participation help ease the adjustment. Once this level of comfort is reached, some of the more challenging aspects of working with young children can be addressed. The following suggestions will help ease the first week's anxieties.

Student Behavior

Dress Appropriately. Be sure to dress for the job and the season. A teacher who is worried about getting paint or clay on clothes will not be relaxed with the children. Dress warmly for the outdoors in cold weather. Wear sturdy, waterproof shoes when it is wet. Summer clothing should be equally practical. Smocks or aprons are quite common when supervising some of the messier activities.

Be Prompt. Arrive at school on schedule. Five or ten minutes late can make the difference between a well-organized day and one that never quite makes it. Don't spend the day trying to catch up. It is the student's responsibility to inform the teacher if he or she will be absent. As a member of a teaching team, a student's presence is very important. The team needs to know in advance if the student will be absent in order to make adjustments. Get the master teacher's home phone number as well as the school office number.

Know Where Things Are. Find out where equipment and materials are stored—the glue, construction paper, art supplies. Look at what scrounge materials are available, where the key to the rabbit cage is kept, and where the laundry room is located.

Use Professional Ethics. Children and parents are not to be discussed outside of the school setting. Their privacy is to be protected at all times. The way Carlos described the guinea pig or Andrea's original songs make amusing stories, but be sure to change the children's names to protect their privacy.

Interacting with Children

Move in Slowly. When interacting with children, move in slowly. Make a practice of sitting back and watching to see what children are doing before getting involved.

Maintain Your Role as Teacher. Do not play games with the children or entertain them. When that happens, it becomes an adult-centered activity instead of a child-centered one. Help the children keep their attention focused on the game they are playing, the other children, or on the materials they are using. It is easy to fall into the trap of becoming the center of their interest. One of the lessons student teachers learn is how to be with children in interesting and meaningful ways, yet not be the focus of their attention.

Give Children Time. Allow plenty of time for children to do for themselves. Let them help as much as possible, whether it is putting away the music instruments or pulling on their snow pants. Give them time to do as much as they can possibly do without help. Children will vary; some will need five minutes to struggle into their boots, and others will have coats on and zippered in less than one.

Help Children Wait. It is almost impossible for children to wait, but there are some ways to help them when it becomes necessary. Make sure that the next activity is ready to go. Have some fingerplays or songs ready if children get restless while waiting. If possible, have an area of the schoolroom available for quiet reading for those who finish first.

FIGURE 5.12 The teacher's primary role is with the children.

Be Alert to the Whole Group. Know where the children and other teachers are and what they are doing, even when they are not in the immediate area. Develop this skill by consciously thinking about where all the children are and what is happening in the rest of the room or yard. This takes practice but it is never too soon to start.

Never Leave Children Unsupervised. Notify the teacher in charge if you must leave the area, and work out an arrangement that will provide full coverage of all the activities.

Maintain the Environment. Keep the room and yard in order as the day moves along. Involve children in the clean-up process. Model a sense of social concern with a few simple acts. Wipe finger paint off the front of the sink before another child comes along. Pick up the sand toys, and put them on the shelf in an attractive arrangement for the next class. These thoughtful deeds show children another aspect of living in a group and caring about one another. Remember, however, the first priority is to be with children.

Use Your Voice and Tone Effectively. Go over to a child, bend down, and speak quietly, but distinctly. Children are more likely to listen to an adult who is close and low than to one that shouts from across a room. Learn to use verbalizations to get children to cooperate. Listen to other teachers in the room. See what works for them.

Never Shove or Use Force. Avoid picking up children to get them where they are supposed to go. Such acts show great disrespect for children and their sense of growing up in a world populated by people so much larger. Do not undermine their budding feelings of strength and competency.

Relating to Other Adults

Never Interfere When Another Teacher Is Solving a Problem. Unless specifically invited to join in, allow other teachers the courtesy of dealing with the situation alone. It can be confusing to children to have too many adults involved and runs the risk of giving the children mixed messages.

Ask Questions. It is not always possible for others to know of difficulties; be sure to ask for help when needed. It may not be clear how a teacher handled an argument between Chloe and her mother or why the room was rearranged. Be sure to ask since the school staff is there to help the student learn. In most teacher training centers, the staff is used to being challenged. Many teachers enjoy a chance to respond to, "Tell me why you did it that way."

Maintain Communication. Keep other team members informed of significant events or problems that occur. The teacher in charge will want to know the details of Aaron's fall from the climber or Sarita's sand-throwing episode. Some problems will require the assistance of another teacher. Parent questions and concerns should be redirected to the staff.

Consult Your Master Teacher. In planning a lesson or activity, consult the teacher so plans can be integrated into the established curriculum. Work together on selecting age-appropriate activities and the best time and place for them. Ask for help to evaluate the lesson; get some feedback from a staff member who saw the activity. Many times students are overcritical of their initial efforts. An experienced teacher can help draw out the positive aspects as well as look at what didn't work so well.

Keep these guidelines in mind to avoid some of the common pitfalls of student teaching. But remember, they are only guidelines. Students must add their own experiences, insights, and interpretations. With the support of the teaching staff, confidence will grow, together with an understanding of what it means to be a total teacher.

THE WHOLE TEACHER

"Teachers deliberately build their programs on their best knowledge of why they are teaching, whom they are teaching, what they are teaching

FIGURE 5.13 Through the teaching experience, the whole teacher emerges.

and how they are teaching." (Hymes, 1974) This integration of knowledge and training, experience and life, is referred to by several names. Some say "real" teachers. Others refer to the "total" teacher. A common phrase is the "whole" teacher. Any one of these terms is an apt reflection of the relationship between how teachers view children and how they see themselves. There is a meshing of the emotional, physical, intellectual, and social aspects of each human being, adult or child.

What happens when this blending occurs? During the first few years in the classroom, teachers consolidate their various official functions—merging their teacher training and experience with their personal style and nature. To discover and define the role of a teacher means to develop a personal teaching style. This is the sum of one's response to teaching, and it is unique to each teacher. When it happens, a beginning teacher becomes aware of "feeling" like a teacher. The strengths and convictions one has as a person blend with those one has as a teacher; they become inseparable. What teachers do and what teachers are become woven to-

gether. And in adding the personal teacher to the professional teacher, the sum becomes greater than two, allowing the whole teacher the freedom to grow in insight and understanding.

SUMMARY

Teachers of young children share with other teachers a variety of subject matter. The curriculum in the early childhood school is rich in math, science, language, social studies, geography, and the like. The format for these learning experiences is a "hands-on" approach. Teachers set out materials, equipment, and activities that invite children's interest and interaction.

In some areas the early childhood teacher differs from others in the field of education. Team teaching, teacher–child interactions, small-group emphasis, and adult relationships are more common in the early years than in other types of schools.

Team teaching is common in most early childhood programs. A group of teachers guide the program by sharing information, contributing ideas, solving problems, and making decisions. They share the responsibilities as well as the workload. In many states, team teaching is mandated by law to ensure the proper teacher–child ratio in a program. By keeping in mind ten essentials for successful team teaching, early childhood educators assure themselves of optimal working conditions on a staff.

Early childhood teachers have multiple roles. They supervise and manage the classroom, interact with children and a number of adults, and they set the emotional tone. Much of what they do occurs away from children. There are meetings to attend, reports to write, parent conferences to hold, and materials to purchase. These after-hours duties add to the depth of classroom experiences the teacher provides for the children.

The student teacher gains valuable experience working directly with children under the supervision of a mature teacher. Some of the initial anxieties are overcome by following general guidelines for student teaching. Further help comes from looking at some common problems and ways to avoid them.

As they grow and gain confidence, teachers pass through several stages of professional development and search for ways to be more effectively challenged. As they integrate teaching style and personality, they become whole teachers.

Review Questions

1. What do you think are the five most important qualifications a teacher of young children should have?

2. Make a line down the center of a paper. On one side write a list of what you like about teaching. On the other side, list those aspects of teaching that you don't like. How can you address those that you don't like and make them more positive?

3. Give several reasons why team teaching is important in the early years.

4. List some of the common problems associated with student teaching. How can you avoid them?

5. Describe a teacher you would want to teach your own child.

6. Finish the following statement: "Teaching is _____."

Learning Activities

1. Draw a picture of the first classroom you remember. Place furniture in it and note where your friends sat, where you sat, where the teacher sat. Down one side of the paper write one-word descriptions of what you felt when you were in that classroom.

2. Write an advertisement for yourself as a teacher.

3. Have you ever had a teacher who was "different"? Describe the person. What did you like most about that teacher? What did you like least? Would you hire that teacher? Why?

4. Write your own code of ethics.

5. Read the ethical situations posed on page 123. Think about how you would solve them. Discuss your answers with a member of your class, a teacher, and a parent.

6. Define team teaching. How does this relate to the teaching situation in which you are working? What are the differences? Similarities?

Bibliography

Beyer, Evelyn. *Teaching Young Children.* New York: Western Publishing, 1968.

Gordon-Nourok, Esther. *You're a Student Teacher!* Sierra Madre, Calif.: Southern California Association for the Education of Young Children, 1979.

Hilliard, Asa G., III. "Moving from Abstract to Functional Teacher Education: Pruning and Planting." In Spodek, Bernard (ed.), *Teacher Education—Of the Teacher, by the Teacher, for the Child.* Washington, D.C.: National Association for the Education of Young Children, 1974.

Hymes, James L., Jr. *Teaching the Child Under Six.* Columbus, Oh.: Charles E. Merrill, 1974.

Katz, Lilian G. *Talks With Teachers.* Washington, D.C.: National Association for the Education of Young Children, 1977.

Katz, Lilian G., and Ward, Evangeline H. *Ethical Behavior in Early Childhood Education.* Washington, D.C.: National Association for the Education of Young Children, 1978.

Lasher, Miriam G. *Preschool Organization: Key to Better Teaching.* Medford, Mass., n.d.

Spodek, Bernard. *Teaching in the Early Years.* Englewood Cliffs, N.J.: Prentice-Hall, 1972.

Spodek, Bernard, ed. *Teacher Education—Of the Teacher, by the Teacher, for the Child.* Washington, D.C.: National Association for the Education of Young Children, 1974.

Spodek, Bernard, ed. *Teaching Practices/Reexamining Assumptions.* Washington, D.C.: National Association for the Education of Young Children, 1977.

6

Observation: Learning to Read the Child

Questions for Thought

- Why is observing children an important teaching tool?
- How do observations help us understand people and their behavior?
- What is the difference between fact and inference?
- How can observations be used to compare individual behavior and general developmental growth?
- What are some of the ways to record observations?
- What are the guidelines to following when observing and recording behavior?

Outline

131

INTRODUCTION

Children are fascinating. They are charming, needful, busy, creative, unpredictable, and emotional. At school, at home, in the grocery store, and in the park, children demonstrate a variety of behaviors. There is the happy child pumping hard on the swing. The angry, defiant child grabs a book or toy and runs away. The studious child works seriously on a puzzle.

These pictures of children flash through the mind, caught for an instant as if by a camera. These minipictures of children working, playing, and living together can be very useful to teachers. Good observing skills can help teachers capture those moments in a child's life. Memory leaves just the impression. The written word is an opportunity to check impressions and opinions against the facts.

What Is Observation?

Teachers learn to make mental notes of the important details in each interaction:

That's the first time I've seen Karen playing with Bryce. They are laughing together as they build with clocks.

FIGURE 6.1 Observing children is the first step in getting to know them.

Teddy has been standing on the fringes of that group for five minutes now. He has refused all invitations to join in the play.

Antonio stops climbing each time he reaches the top of the climbing frame. He looks quickly around and if he catches a teacher's eye, he scrambles down and runs away.

Through their behavior, these three children reveal much about their personalities. The teacher's responsibility is to notice all the clues and put them together in meaningful ways. The teacher sees the obvious clues as well as the more subtle ones. The way observations are put together with other pertinent information becomes critical. The first child, Karen, has been looking for a special friend. Now that she has learned some ways to approach other children that don't frighten and overwhelm them, children want to play with her. Teddy's parents divorced two weeks ago. It appears he is just beginning to feel some of that pain and has become withdrawn at school. At home, Antonio is expected to do things right the first time. At school, he generally attempts only what he knows he can do without making a mistake.

These simple observations, made in the midst of a busy morning at school, give vital information about each child's abilities, needs, and concerns. It is a more developed picture. Children are complex human beings who respond in many ways. Teachers can observe these responses and use their skills to help each child grow and learn.

Seeing Children Through Observation

Play is the work of childhood. It is the way children express themselves and how they show what they are really like. By observing play, teachers can see children as they are and as they see themselves. Much of what children do gives clues to their inner beings.

The stage is set; the action begins as soon as the first child enters the room. Here, teachers can see children in action and watch for important behavior. All that is needed is to be alert to the clues and make note of them:

Allison, normally a cocky, competent three-year-old wavers in her confidence as she enters school. She knows her best friend, Andy, will be absent today.

Charlie, full of bravado in the play yard, refuses to perform a simple coloring task. He tells the teacher, "I can't do it. I don't know how."

Developing sound observational skills enables teachers to better meet the social, emotional, and intellectual needs of each child.

What are children telling us about themselves? Which actions are most important to note? The teacher makes a point to observe children at critical moments. An alert teacher will notice the way a child enters school each morning. Tina always clings to her blanket after her Dad leaves her at school. Lasauna bounces in each day ready to play the moment she walks in the door. David says good-bye to his grandmother, then circles the room, hugging each adult before settling into an activity. These children show the observant teacher something about their needs. A good observer will continue to watch, taking note of these early morning scenes. One can interpret these behaviors later, seeing how they apply to each child and how behavior changes over time.

Another important behavior to watch is how children use their bodies. The basic routines of eating, napping, toileting, and dressing show how they take care of themselves. Whether Chris learns how to put his jacket on by himself indicates his skills in other areas requiring initiative and self-sufficiency. It also shows whether or not children are developing an awareness of themselves as separate, independent beings.

Seeing children in relation to other people is a third area to notice. Teachers see whom children choose as playmates and whom they avoid. They can tell what children will look for in friends. The observant teacher will also make note of the adults in each child's life. Who does the child seek for comfort? For questions? Who takes care of the child outside of school? Who picks the child up from school each day?

FIGURE 6.2 Observing children closely reveals their feelings and needs.

Finally, in selecting play materials and equipment, children show what they like to do, how well they use the environment, and what they avoid. Teachers observe whether or not a child picks materials that are challenging. Bethany starts each morning in the art area, then plays with puzzles before taking care of the animals. Conor prefers the blocks and dramatic play areas and lately has been spending more time in the cooking corner. Observing children at play and at work can tell us how they learn and what methods they use to gain information.

Why Observe?

To Become More Objective

Observing children helps teachers become more objective about the children in their care. When making observation notes, teachers look first at what the child is doing. This is different from looking at how a child ought to be doing something. The teacher becomes like a camera, recording what is seen without immediately judging it. This *objectivity* can balance the intense, personal side of teaching.

Teachers are influenced in their work by their own early childhood experiences. They have notions about how children learn, play, grow, or behave because of the way they were raised and trained. Moreover, when teachers are in the thick of activity, they see only a narrow picture. To pull back, take some notes, and make an observation gives the teacher a chance to see the larger scene.

Teams of teachers help each other gain perspective on the class, an individual, a time of the day. Observations can be a means of validating one teacher's point of view. By checking out an opinion or idea through systematic observation, teachers get a sense of direction in their planning.

Additionally, all teachers develop ideas and impressions about children when they spend time with them. Some children seem shy, some helpful, some affectionate, aggressive, cooperative, stubborn, and so on. These opinions influence the way teachers behave and interact with children. The child thought to be aggressive, for instance, is more likely to be blamed for starting the quarrel when one occurs nearby. It is no accident that the children teachers consider more polite are the ones who are often given special considerations. The problem stems from teacher biases, and these can be misleading. Assumptions made about a child often stereotype the child (or the group) rather than illuminate it. This gives both teachers and children a narrow view of themselves and others.

Suggesting that teachers become careful observers is to be part scientist (Cohen and Stern, 1978). A good observation makes a clear distinction between fact and *inference*, between real behavior and an impression. That does not mean teachers have to become aloof; their eyes can reflect both warmth and a measure of objectivity at the same time. The picture of the child from a teacher's view is often based on one or two events, not necessarily repeated or typical of the child. Thus, it is not a true picture of the child at all.

No one can be free from bias, nor is that the point. The impressions and influences made can provide valuable insights into children. The important first step in observation, though, is to separate what children *do* from what teachers think or feel about it. This can only be done with an awareness of one's own biases. Knowing personal influences and prejudices, coupled with observation and recording skills, prepares teachers to focus on actual behaviors.

To Link Theory with Practice

Observations are a link between theory and practice. All teachers gain from making this connection. New teachers can see the pages of a textbook come alive as they watch a group of children. They can match what they see with what they read. By putting together psychology and medical research with in-class experiences, teachers gain a deeper understanding of the nature of children.

FIGURE 6.3 Observations bring words to life.

To Help Parents

Parents benefit from observations. A collection of notes about an individual child can be used in parent conferences. The teacher shares fresh, meaningful examples that demonstrate the child's growth and abilities. The child's teachers also gain a perspective when the notes are accumulated and discussed with the parents. Problems become more clear and plans can be made to work together. Results can be further tested through continuing observation.

To Use as an Assessment Tool

Notes, time samplings, and running records serve as an informal way to assess children's skills and capabilities. The results lead directly into curriculum planning for the class. Teachers observe the room arrangement and use of space. Does the traffic flow easily or are children stuck in play areas and can't get out? Many classroom problems can be solved if teachers will take time to make observations. They can observe what happens in the block corner at cleanup time. Who always cleans up? Who avoids it? Or they look at play patterns and find out who children play with or who plays alone. Observations can clarify which children are having problems and give teachers a sense of when and where the trouble starts.

More frequently teachers are called upon to set specific goals for the children in their classes and for the overall class performance. They justify what they do and why and document children's progress. In this way teachers are accountable to their clients: the children, the parents, and the public. Learning to assess children's skills and behavior and to document it is becoming increasingly important to the early childhood educator.

UNDERSTANDING WHAT WE OBSERVE

The goal of observing children is to understand them better. Teachers, students, and parents collect a great deal of information by watching children. Observational data helps adults know children in several significant ways.

Children as Individuals

How do children spend their time at school? What activities are difficult? Who is the child's best friend? By watching individual children, teachers help them learn at their own pace, at their own rate of development, in their own time. By watching carefully, they find out each child's learning style. When teachers know how each child functions, they can choose activities and materials to match interests and skills. This is called *individualized curriculum:* tailoring what is taught to what a child is ready and willing to learn.

Observing helps a teacher spot a child's strengths and areas of difficulty. Once these are known, teachers plan intervention measures, helping to make the school experience successful for the child. The following example shows how individualizing the curriculum can bring about changes in behavior that help children succeed.

The teachers were concerned about Jody, age 4½, who had minimal small-motor skills. She used scissors in a "hedge-clippers" fashion and had an awkward grip when using a pencil. Jody also found it difficult to fit puzzle pieces together. She avoided all areas that required the use of those skills: art, table toys, woodworking, and cooking. A check with her parents revealed two important facts: Jody had trouble handling table utensils and couldn't button her sweater. They said there was no provision at home for her to pursue any fine motor activities. Knowing of Jody's interest in airplanes, the teachers used that to draw Jody into areas of the curriculum she didn't ordinarily pursue. Small airplanes were added to the block corner and airplane stencils were placed near the art table. A large mural of an airport was hung on the fence and children were invited to paint on it. One day children cut airplane pictures out of magazines and used them on a collage. Simple airplane puzzles were placed on the puzzle table. Felt shapes and small plastic airplanes in the water table helped draw Jody toward activities requiring fine motor skills. Jody's parents supplied her with a special art box at home, full of crayons, scissors, pens, water colors and stencils. As her small-motor skills increased and refined, Jody became a more confident and happier child. By the end of three months she was a regular participant in all areas of the school and seemed to be enjoying her new-found interest in art materials.

Children in General

When recording behavior, teachers see growth patterns emerge. These trends reflect the nature of human development. Both Jean Piaget and Erik Erikson used this technique to learn how children think and develop socially and emotionally. Gesell studied large numbers of children to get developmental *norms* of physical growth. Parten and Dawes watched hundreds of preschoolers and arrived at the definitive description of children's play patterns and quarreling behavior. For today's early childhood educator, observing children can provide the answer to these questions:

- What might you expect when a two-year-old pours juice?

- How will the class respond to a change in the daily routine?

- What will children do when their parents leave them at school the first day?

- What is the difference between the attention span at storytime of a two-year-old and a five-year-old?

- What kind of social play is typical for the four-year-old?

Observation gives a feeling for group behavior as well as a developmental yardstick to compare individuals within the group. Teachers determine age-appropriate expectations from this. It is important, for example, to know that most children cannot tie their own shoes at four, but can be expected to pull them on by themselves. A general understanding aids in planning thoughtful and challenging

curriculum. Teachers in a class of three-year-olds, for instance, know that many children are ready for eight- to 10-piece puzzles, but that the 20-piece jigsaw will most likely be dumped on the table and quickly abandoned.

Finally, knowledge of children in general gives teachers a solid foundation upon which to base decisions about individuals. From observing many children comes an awareness of each child's progression along the developmental scale. Teachers learn that it is typical of four- and five-year-olds to exclude others from their play because they will have seen it happen countless times. The 3½-year-old who is sure she is "too little" to use the toilet won't convince the knowledgeable teacher that this is developmentally appropriate behavior! Decisions about single children come from watching and knowing many children. This understanding is a valuable asset when talking to parents.

Developmental Relationships

Observing brings about an understanding of the various developmental areas and how they are related. Development is at once *specific* and *integrated*. Children's behavior is a mix of several distinct developmental areas and, at the same time, an integrated whole whose parts influence each other. Reference to the *whole child* implies a consideration of how development works in unison.

When observing children, one must focus on these different developmental areas. What are the language abilities of three-year-olds? What social skills do preschool children acquire? Which self-help skills can children learn before six? How does fine-motor development interact with intellectual growth? Does large-motor skill effect successful cognitive learning? How does self-concept relate to all of the other areas?

Observing these separately brings a specific definition to the term "growth." Teachers see how the pieces fit together. When teachers have an understanding of children's thought processes, they can see why children have difficulty with the concept of dual-identity, for instance. When given a

FIGURE 6.4 Understanding the child is the goal of observation.

set of blocks in various sizes, colors, and shapes, a four-year-old will have no difficulty finding the red ones or square ones, but may be puzzled when asked to find those that are both red and square. No wonder that same child has difficulty understanding that someone can be their best friend and like someone else at the same time.

Practiced observation will show that a child's skills are multiple and varied and have only limited connection to age. Derek has the physical coordination of a 4½-year-old, language skills of a six-year-old, and the social skills of a two-year-old—all bound up in a body that just turned three. A brief picture such as this "whole child" can be helpful to both parents and teachers.

Influences on Behavior

Careful observation in the classroom and on the playground benefits an understanding of child growth and behavior. This includes an understanding of the influences and dynamics of that behavior.

Danny has a hard time when he enters school each morning, yet he is competent and says he likes school. Close observation reveals that his favorite areas are climbing and outdoor games. Danny feels least successful in the construction and creative arts areas, the primary choices indoors, where Danny's school day begins.

Mari, on the other hand, starts the day happily but cries frequently throughout the day. Is there a pattern to her outbursts? Watch what happens to Mari during the transition from free play to group time. She falls apart readily when it is time to move outdoors to play, time to have snacks, time to nap, and so on. Transitions seem difficult for her and she resists changes in any activity.

Environmental influences impact on the behavior of both of these children. Mari's and Danny's behaviors are directly affected by the restraints imposed by the daily schedule.

Adult behavior affects and influences children. Annika has days of intense activity and involvement with materials; on other days she appears sluggish and disinterested. After a week of observation, teachers find a direct correlation with the presence of a student teacher. On the days the student is in the classroom, Annika calls out to him to see her artwork and watch her various accomplishments. It is on the days that the student is absent that Annika's activity level falls. A pattern emerges when adults as well as children are observed.

Understanding of Self

Observing children can be a key to understanding ourselves. People who develop observational skills notice human behavior more accurately. They become skilled at seeing small but important facets of human personality. They learn to differentiate between what is fact and what is *inference*. This increases an awareness of self as teacher and how one's biases affect the perceptions of children.

The values and benefits of observation are long-lasting. Only by practicing observations—what it takes to look, to see, to become more sensitive—will teachers be able to record children's behavior fully and vividly, capturing the unique qualities and personality of each child. According to Dr. Edith Dowley, observation of children can be made at three levels. First, report exactly what the child *does*. Second, express how the child seems to feel about what happened. Last, include your own impressions and interpretations. Each level describes a separate level of child development and builds on successful mastery of the previous level to insure accurate reporting. The challenge of observation is high, but the benefits are well worth the effort.

RECORDING OBSERVATIONS

Once teachers and students understand why observing is important, they must then learn how to record what they see. While children are constantly under the teacher's eyes, so much happens so fast that critical events are lost in the daily routine of classrooms. Systematic observations aid in recording events and help teachers make sense of them.

Common Elements of Observations

All observational systems have certain elements in common:

Focus

1. What do you want to know?

2. Whom/what do you want to observe?
   Child? Teacher? Environment? Group?

3. What aspects of behavior do you want to know about?
   Motor skills? Social development? Problem-solving?

4. What is your purpose?
   Study the environment?
   Observe the daily schedule?
   Evaluate a child's skills?
   Deal with negative behavior?
   Analyze transitions?
   Do research?
   Conference with parents?
   Train teachers?

System

1. What will you do?

2. How will you define the terms?

3. How will you record the information you need?

4. How detailed will your record be?

5. Will you need units of measure? What kind?

6. For how long will you record?

Tools

1. What will you need for your observations?

2. How will you record what you want to know?
   Video or tape recorder? Camera? Pencil? Chart?

Environment

1. Where will you watch?
   Classroom? Yard? Home?

2. What restraints are inherent in the setting?

Using these building blocks of observational systems, four major methods of observing will be discussed:

• Narratives (diary descriptions, running records, specimen descriptions, anecdotal notes)

- Time sampling
- Event sampling
- Modified child study techniques (Checklists, rating scales, shadow study)

Types of Observations

Narratives

At once the most valuable and most difficult of records, narratives are attempts to record nearly everything that happens. In the case of a young child, this means all that the child does, says, gestures, seems to feel, and appears to think about. Narratives are an attempt to actually recreate the scene by recording it in thorough and vivid language. Observers put into words what they see, hear, and know about an event or a person. The result is a full and dynamic report.

Narratives are the oldest and often most informative kind of report. Historically, they were used to set basic developmental norms (Arnold Gesell). They are a standard technique in anthropology and the biological sciences. Irwin and Bushnell (1980) provide a detailed historical background that traces the narrative back to Pestalozzi (1700s) and Darwin (1800s). Jean Piaget watched and recorded in minute detail his own children's growth. His observations resulted in a full report on children's thought processes and development of intelligence. *"Baby biographies,"* narratives written by parents, were some of the first methods used in child study and reached their peak of popularity in the early 1900s.

Diary descriptions are one form of narrative. Just as the term implies, they are, in diary form, consecutive records of everything children do and say and how they do it. The process is a natural one. In the classroom this means describing every action observed within a given time period. It might be a five-minute period during free play to watch and record what one child does. The child who is a loner, the child who wanders, and the child who is aggressive are prime candidates for a diary description. Another way to use this type of *running record* is to watch an area of the yard or room, then record who is there and how they are using the materials.

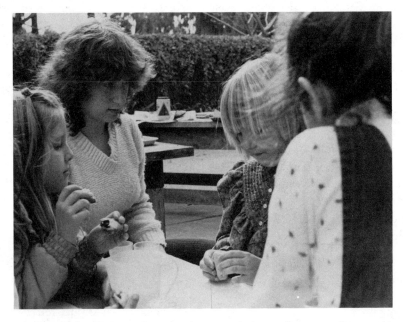

FIGURE 6.5 Narratives can be recorded anywhere, any time.

A more common form of the narrative is a modified version of a running record, or a *specimen description* as it is often called in research terms. The procedure is to take-on-the-spot notes of a specific child each day. This task lends itself easily to most early childhood settings. The teachers carry with them a small notebook and pencil, tucked in a pocket. They jot down whatever seems important or noteworthy during the day. They may focus on one specimen at a time:

- A part of the environment—how is the science area being used?

- A particular time of day—what happens right after naps?

- A specific child—how often is Lucy hitting out at other children?

This system may be even less structured with all the teachers taking "on-the-hoof" notes as daily incidents occur. These notes then become a rich source of information for report writing and parent conferences.

Another form of narrative is a *log* or *journal*. A page is set aside for each child in the class. At some point, teachers write in details about each child. Since this is time-consuming and needs to be done without interruption, it helps to write immediately after school is over. Sometimes teaching teams organize themselves to enable one member of the staff to observe and record in the journal during class time. The important point is that each child's general behavior is recorded either while it is happening or soon afterward.

The challenging part of this recording technique, the narrative, is to have enough detail so the reader will be able to picture whole situations later. Using language as a descriptive tool requires a large vocabulary and skillful recorder. Whatever notes the teachers use, however brief, need to be both clear and accurate. At the same time teachers are recording in a graphic way, they need to be aware of the personal biases that can influence one's recording. Figure 6.6 shows two observations that illustrate this point.

In summary, narratives are an observational technique with roots in psychology, anthropology, and biology. They can follow several formats and are an attempt to record all that happens as it happens. There are many advantages to this type of observation. Narratives are rich in information, provide detailed behavioral accounts, and are relatively easy to record. With a minimum of equipment and training, teachers can learn to take notes on what children do and say. The main disadvantages are the time they can take, the language and the vocabulary that must be used, and the biases the recorder may have. Still, the narrative remains one of the most widely used and effective methods of observing young children today.

Time Sampling

This method collects information other than that which a narrative provides. It is less descriptive, more specific, and requires different observational skills. A time sample is an observation of what happens within a given period of time. Developed as an observational strategy in laboratory schools in the 1920s, time sampling was used to collect data on large numbers of children and to get a sense of normative behaviors for particular age groups or sexes.

Time sampling "appears to be indigenous to research in child development" (Wright, 1967). It has been used to record autonomy, dependency, task persistence, aggression, and social involvement. Time sampling has also been used to study dependent, independent, and solitary play patterns and to record nervous habits of school children, such as nail biting and hair twisting (Prescott, 1973, and Irwin and Bushnell, 1980). The definitive study using time sampling is Mildred Parten's observation in the 1930s of children's play. (The codes developed in this study have become classic play patterns: parallel, associative, and cooperative play.)

In a time sample, behavior is recorded at regular time intervals. To use this method, one needs to sample what occurs fairly frequently. It makes

Poor Observation	Analysis and Comments
A. Julio walked over to the coat rack and dropped his sweater on the floor. He is shy (1) of teachers, so he didn't ask anyone to help him pick it up. He walked over to Cynthia because she's his best friend (2). He wasn't nice (3) to the other children when he started being pushy and bossy (4). He wanted their attention (5), so he nagged (6) them into leaving the table and going to the blocks like four-year-old boys do (7).	(1) Inference of a general characteristic. (2) Inference of child's emotion. (3) Observer's opinion. (4) Inference with no physical evidence stated. (5) Opinion of child's motivation. (6) Observer's inference. (7) Overgeneralization; stereotyping.

Good Observation	Analysis and Comments
B. Emilio pulled out a puzzle from the rack with his right hand, then carried it with both hands to the table nearby. Using both hands, he methodically took each piece out of the frame and set it to his left. Sara, who had been seated across from Emilio with some table toys in front of her, reached out and pushed all the puzzle pieces onto the floor. Emilio's face reddened as his eyes stared directly at Sara with his mouth in a taut line. His hands turned to fists, his brow furrowed, and he yelled at Sara in a forced tone, "Stop it! I hate you!"	Emilio was clearly *angry* as demonstrated in his facial expressions, hand gestures, and body movements. What is more, the way a child speaks is as revealing as what a child says when one wants to determine what a child is feeling. Muscular tension is another clue to the child's emotions. But the physical attitude of the child is not enough; one must also consider the context. Just seeing a child sitting in a chair with a red face, one doesn't know if he is embarrassed, angry, feverish, or overstimulated. We need to know the events that led to this conclusion. Then we can correctly assess the entire situation. By attempting to rid ourselves of some of these biases, we begin to see the child more clearly.

FIGURE 6.6 Two observations. Example A contains numerous biases; these are underlined in the left column and numbered with explanations in the right column. Example B has good descriptions and is relatively bias free.

sense to choose those behaviors that might occur, say, at least once every 10 minutes. Figure 6.7 demonstrates a time-sampling procedure.

Time sampling has its own advantages and disadvantages. The process itself helps teachers define exactly what it is they want to observe. Certainly it helps focus on specific behaviors and how often they occur. Time sampling is ideal for collecting information about the group as a whole. Finally, by defining behaviors clearly and developing a category and coding system, the problem of observer bias is reduced.

Yet by diminishing this bias one also eliminates some of the richness and quality of information.

It is difficult to get the whole picture when one divides it into artificial time units and with only a few categories. The key is to decide what it is teachers want to know, then choose the observational method that best suits those needs. When narratives or time samplings won't suffice, perhaps an event sampling will.

Event Sampling

This is one of the most fascinating and intriguing techniques. With this method, the observer defines an event, devises a system for describing and coding it, then waits for it to happen. As soon as

	Time Unit																	
Child	**9:00**			**9:05**			**9:10**			**9:20**			**9:25**			**9:30**			**Total**
	P	A	C	P	A	C	P	A	C	P	A	C	P	A	C	P	A	C	

PLAY WITH OTHERS
P = Parallel
A = Associative
C = Cooperative

FIGURE 6.7 Time sampling of play with others involves defining the behavior and making a coding sheet to tally observations.

it does, the recorder moves into action. Thus, the behavior is recorded as it occurs naturally.

The events that are chosen can be quite interesting and diverse. Consider Helen C. Dawes' classic analysis of preschool children's quarrels. Whenever a quarrel began, the observer recorded how long the quarrel lasted and what took place (Irwin and Bushnell, 1980).

Other researchers have studied dominance and emotions. Teachers can use event sampling to look at these and other behaviors such as bossiness, avoidance of teacher requests, or withdrawal.

Like time sampling, event sampling looks at a particular behavior or occurrence. But the unit is the event rather than a prescribed time interval. Here again the behavior must be clearly defined and the recording sheet easy to use. Unlike with time sampling, the event to be recorded may occur a number of times during the observation.

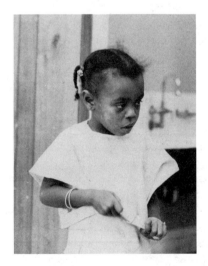

FIGURE 6.8 Teachers develop systems for recording significant events. (Courtesy of Stride Rite Children's Centers, Cambridge, Mass.)

For these reasons, event sampling is a favorite of classroom teachers. They can go about the business of teaching children until the event occurs. Then they can record the event quickly and efficiently. By prescribing the context within which the event occurs, some of the quality often lost in time sampling is regained. The only disadvantage is that the richness of detail of the narrative descriptions is missing.

Modified Child Study Techniques

Since observation is the key method of studying young children in their natural settings, it makes good sense to develop many kinds of observational skills. Each can be tailored to fit the individual child, the particular group, the kind of staff, and the specific problem. Teachers who live in complex, creative classrooms have questions arise that need fast answers. Modified child study techniques can define the scope of the problem fairly quickly. Some of the techniques are: checklist systems, rating scales, shadow studies, and modified processes that reach both the group and the individuals in it.

Checklists contain a great deal of information that can be recorded rapidly. A carefully planned checklist can tell a lot about one child or the entire class. The data is collected in a short space of time, usually about a week. Figure 6.9 is an example of

Observer _____ Date _____ Time _____

Learning Center	Anna	Charlie	Leticia	Neroko	Mat	Josie	Totals
Indoors							
Science Area					|		1
Dramatic Play	|	|	|			|	4
Art	|		|	|			3
Blocks		|					1
Manipulatives			|	|	|		3
Easels				|			1
Music			|		|		2
Outdoors							
Water/Sand/Mud		|	|			|	3
Blocks				|	|		2
Wheel Toys		|				|	2
Climbers	|		|			|	3
Woodworking				|			1
Ball Games	|						1
Animal Care	|	|				|	3
Totals	5	5	6	5	5	4	

FIGURE 6.9 An activity checklist. With data collected for a week, teachers have a broad picture of how children spend their time at school and what activities interest them.

an activity checklist. With data collected for a week, teachers have a broad picture of how these children spend their time and what activities interest them.

If, however, teachers want to assess children's motor skills, a yes/no list is preferable. Figure 6.10 illustrates the use of such a chart.

Checklists can vary in length and complexity depending on their functions. To develop one, teachers first determine the purpose of the observation. Next they define what the children will do to demonstrate the behavior being observed. Finally comes designing the actual checklist, one that is easy to use and simple to set aside when other duties must take precedence.

Rating scales are like checklists, planned in advance to record something specific. They extend checklists by adding some quality to what is observed. The advantage is that more information is gathered. A potential problem is added, since the observers' opinions are now required and could hamper objectivity.

Rating scales differ from checklists in several ways. Instead of simply recording where children are playing, the rating scales require the teacher

---

Motor Skills Observation (ages 2–4)   Child _____
        Date _____   Observer _____ Age _____

Eating: Yes   No
1. Holds glass with one hand
2. Pours from pitcher
3. Spills little from spoon
4. Selects food with pincer grasp

Dressing:
1. Unbuttons
2. Puts shoes on
3. Uses both hands together (such as holding jacket
   with one hand while zipping with the other)

Fine Motor:
1. Uses pincer grasp with pencil, brushes
2. Draws straight line
3. Copies circles
4. Cuts at least 2″ in line
5. Makes designs and crude letters
6. Builds tower of 6–9 blocks
7. Turns pages singly

Gross Motor:
1. Descends/ascends steps with alternate feet
2. Stands on one foot, unsupported
3. Hops on two feet
4. Catches ball, arms straight, elbows in
   front of body
5. Operates tricycle

FIGURE 6.10 A yes/no checklist gives specific information about an individual child's skills.

to decide how they are playing. What is the extent of their involvement and the frequency or degree of their play? A rating scale may use word phrases ("always," "sometimes," "never") or a numerical key (1 through 5).

Developing a rating scale is simple. After deciding what to observe, teachers then determine what the children will do to demonstrate the action. To measure attention at group times, a scale might include the categories in Figure 6.11. Each teacher's rating scale could include a series of checkmarks that record each group time for a period of two weeks. The staff pools information by comparing notes. The result is a detailed description of (1) each child's behavior as each teacher sees it; (2) the group's overall attention level; and (3) an interesting cross-teacher comparison.

The *shadow study* is a third type of modified technique. It is similar to the diary description and focuses on one child at a time. An in-depth approach, the shadow study gives a detailed picture.

Each teacher attempts to observe and record regularly the behavior of one particular child. Then after a week or so the notes are compared. Although the notes may be random, it is preferable to give them some form and organization. Divide a sheet of paper in half lengthwise, with one column for the environment and the other column for details about the child's behavior or response. This will make it easy to glance at 15-minute intervals to collect the data. Figure 6.12 illustrates this process.

The data in a shadow study is descriptive. One interesting side effect often noted is how the behavior of the child being studied improves while being observed. The disruptive behavior seems to diminish or appear less intense. It would appear that in the act of focusing on the child, teacher attention has somehow helped to alter the behavior. Somehow the child feels the impact of all this positive, caring attention and responds to it.

Modified child study techniques are particularly useful because they are tailored to fit the specific needs and interests of the teachers. Teachers know what it is they want to observe and can develop a method of recording that matches their needs and the time available during school. Devising

---

NEVER ATTENDS (wiggles, distracts others, wanders away).

SELDOM ATTENDS (eyes wander, never follows fingerplays or songs, occasionally watches leader).

SOMETIMES ATTENDS (can be seen imitating hand gestures, appears to be watching leader about half the time, watches others imitating leader).

USUALLY ATTENDS (often follows leader, rarely leaves group, rarely needs redirection, occasionally volunteers, usually follows leader's gestures and imitations).

ALWAYS ATTENDS (regularly volunteers, enthusiastically enters into each activity, eagerly imitates leader, almost always tries new songs).

FIGURE 6.11 A rating scale measuring attention at group times requires data in terms of frequency, adding depth to the observation.

Child's Name *Jonah*

Time	Setting (where)	Behavior/Response (what and how)
9:00	Arrives—cubby, removes wraps, etc.	"I can put on my own nametag" (enthusiastically). Uses thumb to push sharp end of pin; very proud of himself. Goes to teacher, "Did you see what I did?"
9:15	Blocks	Precise, beautiful work with small cubes on top of block structure which he built with James. "Those are the dead ones," pointing to the purple cubes outside the structure. Cries and hits Kate when her elbow accidentally knocks tower off.
9:30	Wandering around room	Semidistant, slow pace. Stops at table where children are preparing snack. Does not make eye contact with teacher when invited to sit; Ali grabs J.'s shirt and tugs at it. "The teacher is talking to you!" J. blinks, then sits and asks to help make snack. Stays 10 minutes.

FIGURE 6.12 A shadow study will profile an individual child in the class. This method is especially useful for studying children who seem to be having trouble in school.

a new technique is neither easy nor quick. It takes hard work and dedicated teachers committed to improving their observational skills to record accurately what they see.

Summary

The key ingredients to all types of observations used in recording children's behavior are: (1) defining and describing the behaviors; and (2) repeating that technique over several criteria, be it time, number of children, or activities. The end result is a collection of observational data, an opportunity for teachers to see more clearly what is happening, and the knowledge that what they do with what they record can make a significant difference to children.

HOW TO OBSERVE AND RECORD

Learning how to observe is a serious activity and requires a great deal of concentration. Some preparations can be made beforehand so that full attention is focused on the observation. Thinking through some of the possible problems helps the teacher get the most out of the experience.

Observing While Teaching

To make observing workable at school, it is important to keep in mind that there is no one right way to observe and record. Some teachers find certain times of the day easier than others. Many prefer

Method	Observational Interval	Recording Techniques	Advantages	Disadvantages
1. Narratives Diary description	Day to day	Using notebook and pencil; can itemize activity or other ongoing behavior; can see growth patterns	Rich in detail; maintains sequence of events; describes behavior as it occurs	Open to observer bias; time-consuming.
Specimen descriptions/ running record	Continuous sequences	Same	Less structured	Sometimes need follow-up
Journal	Regular, preferred daily/weekly	Log, usually with space for each child; often a summary of child's behavior		
"On-the-Hoof" Anecdotes	Sporadic	Ongoing during class time; using notepad and paper in hand	Quick and easy to take; short-capture pertinent events/details	Lack detail; need to be filled in at later time; can detract from teaching responsibilities
2. Time Sampling	Short and uniform time intervals	On-the-spot as time passes; prearranged recording sheets	Easy to record; easy to analyze; relatively bias free	Limited behaviors; loss of detail; loss of sequence and ecology of event
3. Event Sampling	For the duration of the event	Same as for time sampling	Easy to record; easy to analyze; can maintain flow of class activity easily	Limited behaviors; loss of detail; must wait for behavior to occur
4. Modifications Checklists	Regular or intermittent	Using prepared recording sheets; can be both during or after class	Easy to develop and use	Lack of detail; tells little of the cause of behaviors
Rating scales	Continuous behavior	Same as for checklists	Easy to develop and use; can use for wide range of behaviors	Ambiguity of terms; high observer bias
Shadow study	Continuous behavior	Narrative-type recording; uses prepared recording sheets	Rich in detail; focuses in-depth on individual	Bias problem; can take away too much of a teacher's time and attention

FIGURE 6.13 A summary chart of the major observational techniques that the early childhood professional can use to record children's behavior. (Adapted from Irwin and Bushnell, 1980)

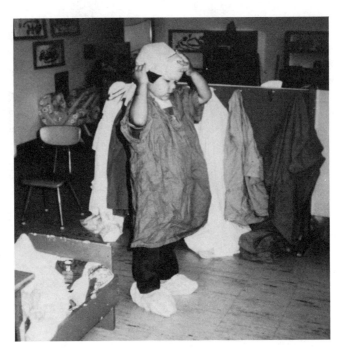

FIGURE 6.14 Various observational methods translate the child's play behavior to the child's personality.

to watch during free play, while others find it easier to watch individual children during directed teaching times. While some teachers keep a pencil and paper handy to write their observations throughout the day, others choose to record what they see after school is over for the day. The professional team that is committed to observation will find ways to support its implementation.

Finding an opportunity for regular observations is difficult. Centers are rarely staffed so well that one teacher can be free from classroom responsibilities for long periods of time. Some schools ask for parent volunteers to take over an activity while a teacher observes. In one center the snack was set up ahead of time to free up one teacher to observe during group time. The environment can be arranged with activities that require little supervision when a teacher is interested in making some observations.

Teachers practice observations and recording techniques outside the classroom. Staff meetings take on an added dimension when teachers role play, devise word games, and draw up observation forms together. At home, observation strategies are used to compare notes on a segment of a television program.

The teacher who makes notes during class time has other considerations. The need to be inconspicuous while note taking is important when trying to teach and record simultaneously. Wear clothing with at least one good pocket. This insures the paper and pencil is available when needed and the children's privacy is protected. Take care not to leave notes out on tables, shelves, or in cupboards for others to see. They should be kept confidential until added to the children's records.

Respect the privacy of the children and their families at all times. Any information gathered as part of an observation is treated with strict confidentiality. Teachers and students are careful not to use children's names in casual conversation. They do not talk about children in front of other children or themselves. It is the role of the adults to see that children's privacy is maintained. Carrying tales out of school is tempting, but unprofessional.

The Beginning Student Observes

In some schools, observers are a normal part of the school routine. In colleges where there are laboratory facilities on campus, student observers are familiar figures. They have only to follow established guidelines for making an observation.

Many times students are responsible for finding their own places to observe children. If so, the student calls ahead and schedules a time to observe that is convenient. Be specific about observation needs, the assignment, the ages of children desired, the amount of time needed, and the purpose of the observation.

Whenever an observation is planned, it is wise to look at some practical matters before settling into the classroom. When arriving at the school, students should:

- Make themselves known to the principal, director, or teacher.
- Find out where to store personal belongings and wraps.
- Take into class only what is necessary.

The success of the observation depends on how inconspicuous the observer can be. Children are more natural if the observer blends into the scenery. By sitting back, one can observe the whole scene and record what is seen and heard, undisturbed and uninfluenced. This distancing sets up a climate for recording that aids the student in concentrating on the children.

How to Observe Effectively

There are two main reasons for an observer to be *unobtrusive*. First, it allows for a more accurate recording of the children's activities. Second, it does not interfere with the smooth functioning of the classroom, the children, or the teachers. The following suggestions help effective observing:

- Enter and leave the area quietly. Ask the teacher where to sit. Keep in the background as much as possible. The good observer is so skilled at this that both children and teachers forget the presence of a stranger.

- Sit down in a low chair in an out-of-the-way place. Sit where the activity of the children is unobstructed. By keeping low, observers call less attention to themselves. Take care to sit outside traffic patterns so children will be able to carry on with play without interference or interruption.

- Sit at the edge of an activity rather than right in the middle of it. Against a wall or around the perimeter of the room are good vantage points for sitting. Outside, if no chair is available, blend against a wall, a fence, or a tree.

- Sometimes it may be necessary to follow children as they move from place to place. When that happens, be as inconspicuous as possible and be prepared for times when, for good reasons, the teacher might object.

- Children may occasionally ask, "What is your name? What are you doing? Why did you come here?" If asked a direct question, answer in a truthful, friendly manner, but be as brief as possible. A good response is, "I'm working." Avoid initiating conversations with children. Be as natural as possible if a child talks to you but appear to be busy writing and observing.

- It is difficult to be in a busy classroom with children without being amused by them. Avoid a degree of response that will attract the children's attention. Laughing at them, smiling, talking, meeting their eyes, distracts them from play. It also makes the observer the center of their attention rather than their work or playmates.

- Avoid talking to other adults while observing. Sitting apart from others draws less attention to the tasks and lessens the temptation to chat. Request a brief conference before leaving to check accuracy.

FIGURE 6.15 Students learn subtle ways of recording behavior.

- There is one time when it might be necessary to get involved with the children. If a child is in obvious danger and no one else is around, the observer should step in. Call for a teacher only if there is time. A child running out the gate toward the street or in the way of a swing needs immediate help. Two children fighting over a truck might need a teacher but are not in immediate danger.

SUMMARY

Systematic observation and recording of children's behavior is a fundamental tool in understanding children. What children do and say and how they think and feel are revealed as they play and work. By learning to observe children's behavior, teachers become more aware of the children's skills, needs, and concerns.

The ability to observe is a skill in itself; teachers examine their own lives and attitudes in order to achieve a measure of objectivity. Recording the observations is another skill, one that requires facility with the written word and an understanding of the purpose for observing. For an observation to be successful, teachers first decide what it is they want to find out about the child(ren).

Key ingredients to successful observations include clear definitions of the behaviors to be observed and techniques for observing and recording them. These provide the tools for gaining a deeper understanding of individual children and the group. They also enhance knowledge about the interrelationships of developmental areas. Too, one gains insight into the dynamics of child behavior and what influences are brought to bear on it. Finally, observing children can give insight and greater understanding of self.

The general types of observational techniques explored in this chapter include narratives, time sampling, event sampling, and modified child study techniques, such as checklists, rating scales, and shadow studies.

As teachers observe and record the behavior of young children, they are aware of professional guidelines that protect children. The guidelines help insure accurate observation and help the observer respect the privacy of the individual or group.

Review Questions

1. List four observational methods. Describe the advantages and disadvantages of each. Which would you prefer? Why? Which one(s) might best suit a beginning teacher? A parent? An experienced teacher? The director of the school?

2. Observe a child for 10 minutes. Using language as your paintbrush, make a written picture of that child's physical appearance and movements. Include a comparison of the child's size, body build, facial features, and energy level to those of other children in the class. Record as many of the body movements as you can, noting seemingly useless movements, failures, partial successes, as well as final achievements.

3. Perceptions of a person's character are in the eyes of the beholder. These perceptions affect how teachers behave with children. What color are your glasses tinted? Divide a piece of paper in half, lengthwise. On one side, list some words to describe your feelings about childhood, school, teachers, children, authority, making friends, losing friends, hitting, playing. On the other side, describe how these feelings may have influenced your teaching and helped create your own biases.

4. Teachers have noticed that several children consistently interrupt at storytime with seemingly irrelevant questions and constantly grab onto children seated nearby. What's happening—and why? What observational tools would you use to find out? What clues from individual behavior would you look for? How would you look at the group as a whole? What other information would you need?

5. What do you consider to be the three most important guidelines to follow when observing young children? Why?

Learning Activities

1. Try a time sample of children's play in your classroom. Observe 10 children for one minute each during free-play times, and record the type(s) of social behavior they show. Using Parten's categories, your chart would look like the one on p. 152. Compare your results with the impressions of the other teachers with whom you work. Did you come to any conclusions on how children develop socially?

2. If you can, try a shadow study on a child in your class. Choose a child you don't know much about, you have trouble working with, or who is exhibiting inappropriate behaviors. How did this study help you to see the class and school from that child's point of view?

3. Observe one child in your class and jot down a brief description of her language skills. Are they typical of her age level? How could you tell? Compare your notes with the perceptions of your supervising teacher.

4. Choose two children, one you think is doing well and one who is having trouble. Observe the adult–child interactions of each. What are the differences from the *children's* point of view in the quantity and quality of those relationships? What generalizations about the importance of such relationships in the early years can you make?

Child/Age	Unoccupied	Solitary	Onlooker	Parallel	Associative	Cooperative
1.						
2.						
3.						
4.						
5.						
6.						
7.						
8.						
9.						
10.						

Totals

5. Observe a children's quarrel. What was happening for *you* when you watched? What does this tell you about your own influences in childhood? How did the teaching staff intervene? How would you? Why?

Bibliography

Boehm, A. *The Classroom Observer.* New York: Teachers College Press, 1977.

Cohen, D.H., and Stern, V. *Observing and Recording the Behavior of Young Children.* New York: Teachers College Press, 1978.

Dowley, Edith M. *Cues for Observing Children's Behavior.* Unpublished paper.

Irwin, D.M., and Bushnell, M.M. *Observational Strategies for Child Study.* New York: Holt, Rinehart and Winston, 1980.

Mattick, I., and Perkins, F.J. *Guidelines for Observation and Assessment.* Washington, D.C.: Day Care and Child Development Council of America, 1972.

Phinney, Jean. *The Observational Study of Children.* Unpublished paper.

Prescott, Elizabeth. *Who Thrives in Group Day Care? Assessment of Child-Rearing Environments: An Ecological Approach.* ERIC Accession No. ED 076 229. Pasadena: Pacific Oaks College, 1973.

Stallings, J. *Learning to Look.* Belmont, Calif.: Wadsworth, 1977.

Wright, H.F. *Recording and Analyzing Child Behavior.* New York: Harper and Row, 1967.

7

Understanding and Guiding Behavior

Questions for Thought

- Why do children misbehave?
- What are some ways in which the classroom environment affects children's behavior?
- What do teachers need to know about themselves so they can guide children with control and concern?
- What is the difference between discipline and punishment?
- Are behavior goals the same for all children? Why?
- What are some common problem behaviors found in young children?
- What are some effective ways to deal with behavior problems?

Outline

UNDERSTANDING BEHAVIOR

Allie leans across the table and scribbles on Beth's paper.

Nicole dashes from the block area after knocking over Joey's building.

Joel bursts into tears when the teacher stops him as he strikes out at Pablo.

These are typical scenes in any early childhood center. No matter how plentiful the materials, how many or well-trained the adults, or how preplanned the program, conflicts are sure to occur. In this chapter, students will look at ways to recognize and handle such problems; how to understand and guide children's behavior in ways that will help them deal more effectively with their feelings. Helping children learn how to cope with their anger, their fears, their frustrations, and their desires is one of the most challenging jobs for a teacher.

To teach children to respect themselves and each other is a complex and difficult task. It takes experience, skill, and love and is a critical part of caring for children. Look at the examples again. What do they say about children in general? What do they say about Allie, Nicole, and Joel? How should teachers respond to these children, and how does that response influence future behavior?

Theories

To guide children's behavior, a teacher must first understand it. This requires a solid background in child development, skills in observing, and understanding about *why* children behave and misbehave.

There are several ways of explaining what people do and why. One idea is that people's behavior is mainly a result of heredity (nature). Another is that experience and environment shape behavior (nurture). A third theory suggests that children go through "stages" at certain times of their lives regardless of their genes or home background.

Both sides have valid arguments in the nature/nurture debate. It is useful to remember that both heredity and experience affect behavior. Age and stage theory is also familiar. People speak of the "terrible two's" or say that all four-year-old girls are silly. There may be some truth to those generalities, but that does not excuse the inappropriate behavior of the various developmental stages. Teachers and parents cannot ignore misbehavior just because children are the "right" age or because of their home situations. That attitude implies adults are powerless to help children form new behavior patterns. Not true!

Adults can do something about children's behavior if they understand what is happening to the child. Where does inappropriate behavior come from? Why do children misbehave?

Understanding Misbehavior

Dreikurs' Goals of Misbehavior

Psychiatrist Rudolf Dreikurs has classified children's *misbehavior* into four categories. Since the child has something to gain from each type of misbehavior, Dreikurs labels them "goals"—the goals of misbehavior. Read through the four goals and reflect again on the incidents cited at the beginning of the chapter. Try to pinpoint the purpose and the results of the misbehavior rather than focus only on what the child did.

Attention. Nearly all children want attention. They prefer to get it in positive ways, but if that doesn't work, they will try to gain attention, any attention, even if it is negative. There are several appropriate responses possible. First, try to pay attention to children when they are not actively seeking attention, that is, when it is not being demanded. This will emphasize the giving nature of attention rather than the getting. Next, attend to the child's positive behavior. This shows children that their useful acts get them attention, not their negative ones. Finally, ignore their bids for attention when they misbehave or try to respond in ways children do not expect. An example of the latter would be to keep the dawdling Cleo inside until she puts on her coat, even though the rest of the class is already outside.

Power. Everyone likes to feel important and powerful. Power-seeking children, though, seem to think that they are important only if they are "the boss." Adults must avoid a power struggle; getting angry or using power tactics only defeats the child and shows that power over others is, in fact, valuable. Rather, choose carefully what to say and do, following through with limits or decisions calmly and deliberately. Enlist children's help; give them some valid power. By empowering these children with chances for positive leadership, their behavior can turn into something productive.

Revenge. Usually children who seek revenge feel unlovable and unimportant. Often they think others are treating them unfairly or have decided that this treatment is what they deserve. They are hurt and they try to hurt back; only by hurting others can they be important. Adults must try not to retaliate; this will only reinforce the children's belief that they are, indeed, being hurt and are unlovable.

A Display of Inadequacy. All children who misbehave are discouraged. The children who display *inadequacy* probably feel the most helpless. They have given up any idea of succeeding, rarely try anything new, and will not persist in any activity for long. They may also say, "I don't know" in order to keep people from expecting anything of them. Adults may get impatient or easily discouraged, or give up hope. Instead, teachers and parents should try to eliminate any criticism and praise any attempt the child makes. Do not wait for the child to succeed; praise the effort of trying.

Figure 7.1 outlines Dreikurs' four goals of misbehavior. These goals can apply to adult–child relationships as well as child–child interactions.

Factors That Affect Behavior

Knowing what affects children's behavior and feelings helps adults understand and manage the misbehaving child. Teachers can anticipate problems instead of waiting for them to occur; preventive guidance measures are part of guiding children's behavior.

There are three factors that affect behavior: developmental factors, environmental influences, and individual or personal styles. They are a combination of the nature/nurture and ages/stages theories.

Developmental Factors

Children's growth is constant if not always smooth. Adults who work with children should be aware of developmental theory in order to know what type of behavior to expect of children at various ages.

Case Study #1
All the children are outdoors playing, just before lunch. Chris, who turned three years old last week, is at the sand table, when 5½-year-old Benjamin arrives. "Stop! We're the bosses here!" Benjie states with a frown. Chris returns the angry glare, hunches his shoulders, and sits down. "You can't have any sand. Get out of here. And you just messed up our road, you dummy!" shouts Benjie. Chris stands up quickly and throws sand at Benjie. They start hitting each other. (See Figure 7.2.)

The facts are that these children have been in a group setting for more than three hours and it is nearly lunch time. One child is over five years of age; the other barely three. The teacher knows that preschoolers cannot be expected to be in control of themselves over extended periods of time. Conflicts and disagreements are to be expected in any group of children. Hungry children are often ineffective problem solvers; the same situation might not be as *volatile* after lunch. It is also clear to the teacher that three-year-olds do not have the language or social development skills to talk problems out with other children. Five-year-olds tend to dominate a younger peer to exercise their well-developed cognitive, social, and language skills.

Taking all of these developmental factors into consideration, the teacher *intervenes* to stop the fighting and takes both boys over to the hose to clean the sand out of their faces. In the process, the teacher encourages the children to help each other by holding the hose when the other one

Child's Goals	Child's Faulty Belief	Child's Action	Adult Responses
Attention	I belong only when I am being noticed or served.	Nags, demands, interrupts.	Pay attention when child doesn't seek it; praise child when possible; ignore inappropriate behavior; do not wait on child.
	Example: "Thanks for waiting while I talked to Cindy's mother. Now let's go find a place where the two of us can talk."		
Power	I belong only when I am in control or am boss, or when I am proving no one can boss me.	Argues, disagrees, talks back.	Do not argue back or give in; remain calm and in control when setting limits; enlist child's help toward solution.
	Example: "Paul, I said you would have to leave the table if you threw food again. Go to your room until you are ready to come back and eat your dinner."		
Revenge	I belong only by hurting others like I feel hurt; I cannot be loved.	Hurts others, destroys their property or creations.	Avoid punishment and retaliation; protect others from being hurt; find something lovable about child and show/say it.
	Example: "Lamar, the other children don't like to play with you when you tear up their paintings. Gloria and Esther's paintings were special. Put the paper and paint back on the table so they can make a new one. You can make a special one, too. Would you like me to watch while you paint?"		
Display of inadequacy	I belong only by convincing others not to expect anything from me; I am unlovable; I am helpless.	Says, "I can't," gives up easily, withdraws, cannot consider alternatives.	Do not criticize, help child focus on trying; find one thing child does well and praise it.
	Example: "I'm glad to see you trying to pull those pants up. I know it's hard to do, but you are really trying."		

FIGURE 7.1 Four goals of misbehavior. Understanding why children misbehave is the first step in guiding them. (Adapted from Dinkmeyer and McKay, 1976)

washes. The conversation at this time revolves around how hungry everyone must be as lunch time approaches. Benjie is encouraged to find a place for Chris; Chris is given words to use to tell Benjie where he wants to play in the sand. Benjie is asked to assume a role in helping Chris find a place; his leadership skills are put to positive use.

Developmental theory helps teachers anticipate what children will do and how they will behave. To see behavior as predictable is to understand it more completely. This guides teachers in solving behavioral problems.

FIGURE 7.2 "We're the bosses here!"

Environmental Factors

Environment for the young child is primarily home, school, or day care settings. The term environment has three distinct parts: the physical, the *temporal* (timing and scheduling), and the interpersonal. Each has an impact on children's behavior.

Materials. In addition to arrangement of room or yard, materials affect how children behave, whether in a family day care home or an after-school sports program. The materials provided can challenge children, overwhelm them, or bore them. If materials and equipment are suitable, children will feel more at ease with themselves and be more willing to accept adults' limits and controls. The materials and equipment allow appropriate outlets for children's natural tendencies; they capture interest and atten-tion, and this helps prevent many opportunities for misbehavior. When children are occupied with stimulating, age-appropriate materials, the amount of conflict and disruption lessens.

Time. The temporal structure (Mattick and Perkins, 1974) describes the sequence of a program. When there are blocks of time to choose activities, children can proceed at their own pace without feeling pushed or hurried. They feel free to work, move, and play and are able to accept the teacher's control when it is necessary. The physical needs of eating, sleeping, and toileting are met by careful scheduling so that children are able to play without concern for the necessities of life.

A consistent daily plan helps promote a feeling that the world is predictable and understandable.

Children need time to work out their own problems. Hurrying and wondering what happens next create tension that results in behavior problems.

Relationships. These need special consideration because they determine how learning takes place. The interpersonal environment refers to all the "people" factors. An atmosphere of trust and support helps to create a sound learning environment. In early childhood centers the significant relationships are those between teacher and child, children and other children, teacher and parents, and teacher and other teachers. Each type of relationship affects and influences children's behavior. When children sense a feeling of mutual support and acceptance, their play reflects that tone. Tension among adults is quickly transmitted to children, and their behavior patterns adjust to the negative influence.

Other influences affect behavior. Weather seems to affect children. Wild, windy, gray, rainy days seem to stimulate children into high and excitable behavior. Bright, sunny days also seem to influence a child's mood and temperament. Problems that upset adults can make an impression on a child. A family crisis, a new baby, or a recent divorce have impact. Sharing a room, visits from relatives, illness, television and movie shows, brothers and sisters, nutrition and health, cause children to behave in many different ways. The longer teachers work with children, the more adept they become at seeing how these various factors shape the behavior of the individual children in their class.

Case Study #2
It is late in the afternoon at the day care center, and it has been raining all week. Several children are playing with hollow blocks on the covered patio. Shouts and screams fill the air. Three-year-old Jonathan holds firmly to a steering wheel mounted on a large block. "It's mine! It's mine!" he yells. Sam, a four-year-old and Justo, who is 2½, pull the block toward their building. Scowling, Justo reaches toward Jonathan, grabs his arm, and raises it to his face. The teacher arrives just in time to prevent Justo from biting Jonathan.

FIGURE 7.3 "It's mine! It's mine! I got it first!"

The facts are that children find waiting and sharing difficult. When they are able to play with attractive equipment for only short periods of time, they become frustrated, resulting in more arguments over play materials. Two- and three-year-olds are just developing social skills and learning to share; they do not have the abilities of a four-year-old to negotiate for equipment. Two steering wheel blocks may not be enough for the number of children in this particular group; perhaps more should be added so that children do not have to wait as long for a turn. The rain has kept the children confined to small spaces indoors and on the patio; that adds to the tension everyone feels. Jonathan has been at school only a week, and Justo helped to celebrate his sister's first birthday yesterday. Both of these children carry with them remnants of emotional adjustments they are making.

The teacher grabs Justo's arm to prevent him from biting Jonathan. "I will not let you bite children, Justo. Biting hurts. I won't let you hurt children, and I won't let you be hurt," says the teacher. Jonathan is invited to tell his side of the story and the teacher helps the children negotiate a time limit for using the steering wheels and for playing on the patio.

Environmental factors can add to the stress of behavior expectations. In this example, the amount of time, the weather, and levels of social development combined to create a situation that frustrated the children and resulted in their inappropriate behavior.

Individual Styles

People seem to come equipped with a style all their own. Pregnant women can describe a child's personality while the baby is still in the womb. Mothers know of the special way infants behave that sets them apart. Parents often comment on the differences among their own children. Raised by the same parents in the same house and neighborhood, each child is a singular and original being.

Each child in a classroom is also unique, an individual like no other. All have a personal style that needs to be acknowledged and valued. Children who are not accepted for themselves may learn to hate themselves or not to trust their own instincts. A broken or timid spirit creates a timid or rebellious person.

Case Study #3
It is midmorning at the preschool, nearing the end of free-play time indoors. Zachary has been cruising the room for 10 or 15 minutes. He has stepped on Sergio's hand as he shuffled past and he "accident'ly" knocked over Megan's five-story garage in the block corner. Now he comes to the art table where children are using water colors. To Steven and Lydia he says, "Those are ugly pictures." The teacher reminds him that hurtful words bother other people. He shouts back, "I don't care. You can't make the words go back in my mouth. And I'm not helping at cleanup time either."

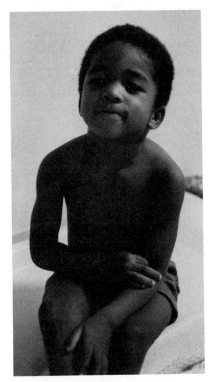

FIGURE 7.4 "You can't make the words go back in my mouth." (Courtesy of Stride Rite Children's Centers, Cambridge, Mass.)

The facts are that Zachary's personal style is that of a five-year-old full of himself and his power as one of the leaders in the class. He is a verbal and strong child who likes to have the last word. He is also enthusiastic and plunges into activities spontaneously, sometimes without looking ahead or surveying the wreckage he leaves behind. Zachary's teacher is aware that he can be personable and cooperative if he is given options and a chance to make decisions. As they talk together about this incident, the teacher offers Zachary a valid choice: leading the bucket brigade to empty the water table or moving chairs to clear space for a movie (one of Zachary's favorite group activities). Both find satisfaction in working together in ways that acknowledge and respect Zachary's personal style.

Common Behavioral Problems

Guidance, *discipline*, and behavior management refer to the adult's role in working with children and their behavioral problems. A teacher observes what the child says and does and identifies how that needs to change.

Behavior is the acting-out, unspoken language of the young child. Until children learn to express themselves vocally, they will employ a variety of behaviors to communicate distress, anger, anxiety, fear, hurt, jealousy, and so on. Figure 7.5 lists some of the most common ways children indicate they are troubled.

The inappropriate ways children use to express themselves are the hardest for teachers to handle. These are the behaviors that cannot be ignored and that demand a response. How a teacher reacts will depend on the particular child and the situation.

GUIDING BEHAVIOR

Discipline

Discipline is one of the most common and persistent concerns of teachers and parents. Listen in the teacher's lounge or at the park and sooner or later the discussion turns to children's behavior.

Why won't Emily make her bed?

What should I do when Carl refuses to take the garbage out?

Crispin is such a whiner!

I wonder why Dominic never comes to school on time.

I wish Peggy wouldn't disrupt group time with her silliness.

How can teachers be more effective in helping children change the way they behave? "How can I get better results? What should I do now? I've tried everything," is the lament. When the subject is discipline, feelings and frustrations run high.

What Is Discipline?

Some of those strong feelings stem from the association of *discipline* with the word *punishment*. Discipline is generally thought of in negative terms. To many people, the words *discipline* and *punishment* are synonymous.

What does discipline mean and why does it cause uncertainty in teachers and parents? Why is there so much confusion about it?

The word discipline stems from disciple: a pupil, a follower, a learner. This suggests an important concept, that of following an example versus following rules. Children try to be like the adults they see; adults serve as models for children. How children see adults behave tends to become part of their own behavior. Adults help children learn appropriate behavior by setting good examples.

Discipline and guidance are used interchangeably. Discipline is guiding and directing children toward acceptable behavior. This includes everything parents and teachers do, everything they say, in an attempt to influence the child. Discipline is something you do with children; it is an interaction, not something adults do *to* children. In caring and understanding ways, the effective teacher helps children gain control over their own behavior. To accomplish this, teachers maintain that delicate bal-

1. Immature Behavior:	Hyperactive, impulsive, silly, messy, pouty, overdependent and self-centered behavior. May also include clowning and daydreaming. Child has short attention span, seeks attention, and uses time poorly.
2. Insecure Behavior:	Child is hypersensitive to criticism, worries, tells tall tales, and may be domineering, jealous, shy, compulsive, fearful, a perfectionist. Has low self-esteem; may resort to baby talk, bribery.
3. Peer Problems:	Child may be aggressive, cruel, and a social isolate. Resorts to name calling. Feels sibling rivalry.
4. Habit Disorders:	May experience thumb-sucking, nail biting, bed wetting, stuttering, and tics. Child may have sleep disturbances and eating problems.
5. Antisocial Behavior:	Child disobeys, throws temper tantrums, uses bad language, runs away, bites others, and is destructive. May exhibit prejudices.

FIGURE 7.5 Common behavioral problems. The five groups cover a wide variety of behaviors that are typical in young children. (Adapted from Schaefer and Millman, 1981)

Discipline	Punishment
Emphasizes what the child should *do*	Emphasizes what the child should *not* do
Is an ongoing process	Is a one-time occurrence
Sets an example to follow	Insists on obedience
Leads to self-control	Undermines independence
Helps children change	Is an adult release
Is positive	Is negative
Accepts child's need to assert self	*Makes* children behave
Fosters child's ability to think	Thinks *for* the child

FIGURE 7.6 Discipline vs. punishment. A disciplinary approach encourages children's interaction; punishment is something done *to* a child.

ance between children's attempts to be independent and their need for outer controls.

It is not so much the word discipline that is significant as it is the form it takes. Children are robbed of their self-respect when they are treated harshly and made to feel they have no ability to control themselves. Shame, disgrace, and embarrassment have no part in good disciplinary procedures.

One of the goals of discipline is to help children achieve self-discipline. This happens only if adults lead in ways that support children's developing ability to control themselves. Teachers who are sensitive to this will decrease the amount of control they exercise. By gradually handing over to children the opportunity to govern their own actions, adults communicate trust. For young children, with their urge to prove themselves, their drive toward initiative, this is an important step to take. With added responsibility and trust comes an added dimension of self-respect and self-confidence. Such children feel capable and worthwhile.

Along with self-respect, the child must taste the freedom that comes with a lessening of adult controls. Children do not learn to handle freedom by being told what to do all the time. Only when they have an opportunity to test themselves, make some decisions on their own, will they know their capabilities. Young children must learn this in safe places, with adults who allow them as much freedom as they can responsibly handle.

The essence of good discipline is summed up by Jenkins (1971) in the following way:

> . . . Good discipline is not an end in itself but a means toward providing a healthy atmosphere in which children may grow and learn. Good discipline is neither too much freedom nor too little freedom, neither complete lack of control nor authoritarianism.

The Language of Discipline

Discipline has a language all its own. As beginning teachers gain experience in handling problem behaviors, they learn to use that language. The result, in most cases, is a startling *interdependence:* the more practiced teachers become in the language of discipline, the more comfortable they become in developing their own approach to disciplinary problems. And the more comfortable they are in that approach, the more effectively they use language to solve behavior problems.

The language and communication techniques in discipline are both spoken and unspoken. Teachers discover how potent the voice can be; what words will work best and when. They become aware of facial expressions and what a touch or a look will convey to children. How they use their body reflects a distinct attitude and approach to discipline. New teachers should know how to use these tools in ways that will work best for them and the children.

Voice. Some adults feel that when they are speaking to children they must assume a different voice from the one they normally use. This "teacher voice" often occurs when disciplinary issues are at stake. The teacher's voice becomes tight, high-pitched, the tone increasingly strained. Teaching requires no more than a normal speaking voice. Talk to children in the same way you talk to other people. Learn to control the volume and use good speech patterns for children to imitate. In order to be heard, get close enough to speak in a normal tone; get down to the child's level.

Words. Children have torrents of words rained upon them in the course of a school day. Teachers fall into the trap of overusing words. Where behavior is concerned and anger or frustration aroused, some adults seem to gain release from a string of verbage. This works against good disciplinary practices. Children tend to turn off people who are excessively verbal with them. Their eyes glaze over, they become fidgety or even frightened, and the incident looses significance.

The fewer the words, the better. Simple, clear statements, spoken once, will have more impact. The child will be able to focus on the real issues involved. A brief description of what happened, a word or two about what behavior is acceptable and what isn't, and a suggestion for possible solutions are all that is necessary.

Choose words carefully. They should convey to the child exactly what is expected. "Richy, move the block closer to the truck. Then Sarah won't bump into it again," tells Richy in a positive, concrete way what he can do to protect his block building. If he had been told, "Richy, watch where you are building," he would not know what action to take to solve the problem.

Body Expressions. When working with small children, it is important to be aware of body height and position. Show children that respect for their size by speaking with them face to face. Sit, squat, or kneel—but get down to their level. It is difficult to communicate warmth, caring, and concern from two or three feet above a child's head.

Good discipline is founded on a loving, caring relationship between child and adult. In order to help children gain control over their impulses and monitor their own behavior, teachers must establish a sense of trust and well-being with children. The way teachers use their bodies invites or rejects close relationship and familiarity. A child will find teachers more approachable if they are seated low, with arms available, rather than standing, with arms folded.

By making full use of the senses, the impact of words can be softened. A firm grip on the hand of a child who is hitting out, a gentle touch on the shoulder, tells children the adult is there to protect them from themselves and others. Eye contact is essential. Teachers learn to communicate the seriousness of a situation through eye and facial expressions. They also show reassurance, concern, sadness, and affection this way.

Physical presence should convey to the child a message that the teacher is there, available, and interested.

Attitude. This is part of the unspoken language of discipline. Attitudes are derived from experience. Most adults who take care of children reflect how their own parents treated them and how they were disciplined. Some people react against the way they

FIGURE 7.7 Trust and caring: foundations for discipline.

were raised; others tend to follow the model their parents established. Teachers find it useful to look at the way they were disciplined as youngsters and acknowledge their feelings about it. As they begin to inhibit the behavior of the children in their classes, teachers should be aware of their own attitudes. The following questions may help that process:

- Do you accept the fact that all children will have problems, misbehave, and will make mistakes?

- Do you believe children are capable of solving their own problems, and do you involve them in the process?

- Do you accept the child's right to independence and actively encourage self-reliance?

TIME

_____ Does the daily schedule provide enough time for unhurried play?

_____ Are those periods that create tension—transitions from one activity to another—given enough time?

_____ Is cleanup a leisurely process built in at the end of each activity, with children participating?

PROGRAM PLANNING AND CURRICULUM

_____ Is there enough to do so that children have choices and alternatives for play?

_____ Is the curriculum challenging enough to avoid boredom and restlessness?

_____ Is the curriculum age appropriate for the children in the class?

_____ Are there activities to help children release tension? Do the activities allow for body movement, exploration, and manipulation of materials?

ORGANIZATION AND ORDER

_____ If children are expected to put things away after use, are the cabinets low, open, and marked in some way?

_____ Are the materials within easy reach of the children, promoting self-selection and independence?

_____ Are there enough materials so that sharing does not become a problem?

_____ Are the areas in which activities take place clearly defined so that children know what happens there?

_____ Does the room arrangement avoid runways and areas with no exits?

_____ Do children have their own private space?

PERSONNEL

_____ Are there enough teachers to give adequate attention to the number of children in the class?

_____ Is the group size and makeup balanced so that children have a variety of playmates?

_____ Are the teachers experienced, and do they seem comfortable in setting limits and guiding children's behavior?

_____ Do teachers use their attention to encourage behavior they want, and do they ignore what they want to discourage?

_____ Do all adults enforce the same rules?

FIGURE 7.8 Classroom checklist. By anticipating children's needs and growth patterns, teachers set up classrooms that foster constructive and purposeful behavior.

- Do you help children accept the responsibility for their own actions without blaming them?
- Are you optimistic that problems can be solved and that you and the child can work it out together?

Good Disciplinary Practices

Children's behavior is influenced by more than just their own impulses, needs, or reactions. The three case studies show that factors beyond the scope of childhood can cause misbehavior. There are several areas over which adults have control that may cause problems for children. Three of the most common are the classroom environment, setting limits on children's behavior, and the teacher's role in guidance.

Consider the Classroom

Since it promotes or detracts from positive interactions and appropriate behavior, the classroom is the first place to look for ways to improve guidance and disciplinary techniques. The goals for behavior management should be reflected in the classroom setting. Too many times good intentions are defeated by the physical environment. Use the checklist (Figure 7.8) to see how environment relates to disciplinary values. Children should be told clearly and directly by the physical environment how to act in that setting. That makes it easier for them to know what is expected and how they should behave.

Consider the Limits

When teachers discipline children for unacceptable behavior, they are setting the *limits* on that behavior. Limits are the absolute control the adult puts on the child's behavior. They are the constraints set up to help children know what will or will not be tolerated. Teachers generally have two reasons for setting limits: (1) to prevent children from injuring themselves or others; and (2) to prevent the destruction of property, materials, or equipment.

Limits are a necessary part of any group or society. Every group has its bottom-line rules—rules that must be kept to ensure order and living in accord. The early childhood classroom is no exception; teachers make it clear to children what rules determine the conduct within that group. Teachers plan curriculum, arrange rooms, and follow good disciplinary practices so that a great number of rules are not necessary. Frequent exclamations of "Don't do this . . ." or "Don't do that . . ." need not be a part of the early childhood classroom when one understands the nature of setting limits.

Limits are like fences; they are protective structures that help children feel secure. Limits define the boundaries of behavior just like fences outline property lines. Fences and limits are erected and maintained to help people know how far they can go.

Fences—or limits—set up a framework in which everyone knows the rules. There is no guess work, no vague or hidden boundaries, no invisible lines to cross over. When children know where fences are, what limits, what rules apply, they do not have to continually try to find out *if* fences are there and *where* they are. "Inside those fences . . . children . . . have the complete freedom to move, to experience, to shift and change, to grow and shrink, to rest and have fun; to live, if you will." (Long, 1977)

A natural part of growing up is to stretch those limits and push those fences aside. This happens as children grow and mature; fences move in an ever-widening pattern. The womb first holds and protects the growing fetus; the infant is protected in the confines of the crib. The toddler has safe space defined in a playpen. The preschool child plays first in small, protected yards before moving on to the large, open playground in elementary school. Physical limits expand as the child is able to handle more freedom, more space, more responsibility. It is the same with behavioral limits.

When Setting Limits	For Example
1. Make sure that the limit is appropriate to the situation.	"Yes, that's a beautiful truck, Andrew, but it has to stay in your cubby until it's time to go home. When other children see it, they want to play with it too. Why don't you show Eddie and Heather how it works? Then I'll help you find a special place in your cubby where it will be safe."
2. Fit the limits to the individual child's age, history, and emotional framework.	"Sheila, you've interrupted the story too many times today. Please find a place at the puzzle table until we are finished. Remember, I told you earlier that you wouldn't be able to hear the end of the story if you yelled again." "Jamal, I know it's your first day back since you broke your arm, but it is time to listen to the story now. You and Sascha can talk together in a few minutes."
3. See that the limits are consistently applied by all adults.	"I know you want to ride the red bike now but both teachers have said you already had a long turn today."
4. Reinforce the same rules consistently.	"Judy, remember everyone *walks* inside. You can run outside."
5. Follow through; support your words with actions.	"I can't let you tear the books. Since this is the second page this morning, you'll need to make another choice instead of the book corner." If child does not leave, begin to pick up books. Lead child firmly to another activity.
6. Use simple statements; be clear and state limits positively.	"You need to use a gentle voice indoors so that people can be together and think. We call this an inside voice."
7. Respect the child's feelings and acknowledge them when you can.	"I know you want your mom to stay. She has to go to her job now. I'll stay with you while you feel sad and I'll take care of you until she comes back."
8. Act with authority; be sure of your purpose and be confident.	"I can't let you hurt other people. Put the block down," instead of "I wish you wouldn't do that."
9. Be ready to accept the consequences; have a plan for the next step, if needed. Maintain the limit. Don't avoid the situation or give in if the child threatens to fall apart or create a scene.	"I'm sorry, Sarah, but you missed your ride to school. When you play with your food it keeps you from getting dressed on time. Remember, Mrs. Allen said she wouldn't wait one more time. Screaming and kicking won't get her to turn the car around. Let's go feed the cat and think about what you might do at home today."

FIGURE 7.9 Guidelines for setting limits. Children feel safe when appropriate limits are set on their behavior.

Children may not like fences; they may resist attempts to limit their behavior. The beginning teacher must learn to set and maintain limits with confidence and authority. Children respond to how limits are set as much as to the limits themselves. Figure 7.9 illustrates positive ways to set limits when working with young children.

For the child, limits are self-protective. Young children have not yet learned the skills to control themselves in all situations. Their behavior easily goes out-of-bounds. Children are just beginning to exert that inner pressure (self-control) that will help them monitor their own actions. Until then, they need adults to help them learn when and how to

FIGURE 7.10 Limits are like fences: they help children feel secure.

apply self-restraint. Limits keep them from going too far. Children can frighten themselves and others with anger, frustration, fear. They need adults who care to stop them from doing physical or emotional harm to themselves. Well-considered limits give the child freedom to try out, test, and explore avenues of self-expression in ways that will promote growth and protect budding autonomy. Children feel more secure with adults who will stop them from going too far and who help them learn to gain control.

Consider the Teacher's Role

A teacher has direct and indirect influence on children's behavior. Some of the ways teachers deal directly with discipline is by what they say and what they do. Indirectly, a teacher's influence is felt just as strongly. Room arrangements and time schedules, attitudes and behavior can work for or against good disciplinary practices.

Teachers who are well grounded in the developmental process know that problem behaviors are normal and occur in every early childhood setting. They realize that growing children must have a safe, secure place in which to test themselves against the world.

Wise teachers do not attempt to prevent children from stretching limits and controls. Instead, they help children understand and accept their feelings and learn that they can live within limits. Acting with confidence, the teacher involves children in the disciplinary process, discussing with them alternatives and options for how they act. Children learn they are held accountable for their actions and can help determine how they want to handle themselves and change their own behavior.

The teacher as a behavior model is an important element in discipline. Children pattern their responses after adult behaviors. They are aware of how teachers respond to anger, frustration, and aggression; how they solve problems and conflicts. Adults must be sure to model the desired behavior around the children they teach. To be successful models, teachers should be aware of their emotions and feelings; they do not want to compound a problem by their own reaction.

Being consistent is one of the key elements in good disciplinary practices. If adults want to develop mutual trust, the rules must be clear, fair, and enforced consistently and regularly. At the same time, children need to know what will happen if rules are not followed. This, too, should be consistent.

Children have a right to express negative feelings and air their grievances, but what about teachers? Is it ever appropriate for a teacher to show anger? If so, what are the considerations? Children are very sensitive to adult emotions. It is better to acknowledge the feeling, label it, and then discuss it together. Once it is identified, it becomes more manageable for both. Adults who express negative feelings to children must proceed carefully, stating their position clearly, honestly, and objectively:

It bothers me when you call Roberto a dummy.

You don't need to yell at me. I can hear you from right here. Tell me again in a quieter voice.

I'm serious about this . . . no biting.

Sometimes I get mad when children try to hurt each other.

It makes me sad to see all that food going to waste. Please put just enough on your plate so that you will eat it all.

Remember that children are frightened by strong feelings; do not overwhelm them.

Sometimes teachers have unrealistic expectations for children, either too high or too low. They presume children have abilities and skills they do not yet possess. This may cause children to respond in inappropriate ways. It can be helpful to rehearse with children how they are expected to act. Practice sessions are especially useful when introducing a new topic or plan. One teacher rehearsed the children for their first bus ride. They practiced singing, looking out the windows, having snacks, talking with friends. A large outline of a bus was drawn with chalk on the patio floor. The children pretended to board the bus, walk down the narrow aisle, find a seat, and remember to take big steps getting up and down the steps. When the field trip day arrived, children knew several appropriate ways of behaving while on the long bus trip.

Many times children are asked to do jobs that are too complicated for them. The young child who is just learning to put on jackets and pants or to make a bed is a good example. Children may not be able to accomplish the entire job at first; it is helpful to them if the task is broken down into smaller steps. Straighten the sheet and blanket for Gordon, then let him pull the spread up over the pillow. Little by little have Gordon assume more of the bed-making job as he becomes capable.

Teachers can learn a great deal about the cause and effect of their discipline and guidance techniques if they are active observers in their own classrooms. When teachers observe, they can time intervention; they do not want to interfere too soon. Observations can be used to show children their actions and the consequences they have for others.

There are many varieties of guidance techniques and ways to deal with disciplinary problems. Figures 7.11 and 7.12 illustrate some of them.

Three Guidance Approaches

The following approaches, while not specifically outlined, are woven throughout the discussion of discipline and behavior management. They have many similar components. Each requires some advance thought on the part of the adult, and allows for consequences that are predictable and immediate. These methods follow good disciplinary practices by encouraging less talk and more action. Adults and children will not need to spend time arguing the situation when the outline of response is so clear.

Parent Effectiveness Training (P.E.T.)

This outlines two techniques that have proved most helpful in child guidance. These are (1) active listening, and (2) the use of "I" messages (Gordon, 1970).

Parents and teachers can learn the art of *active listening* in order to respond to a child's feelings as well as words. The technique encourages sensitive, atuned hearing—checking on the accuracy of what is being said. To do this, teachers or parents listen carefully, trying to understand what the child is saying beyond the words being used. Then they reflect back in their own words what it is they think the child has said. The child has an opportunity to correct any misinterpretations. Further dialogue helps to clarify what it was the child meant. An example is:

Rita: I hate school!
Teacher: Sounds like you are really disappointed you didn't get a turn cooking today.
Rita: I *really* wanted to help make pancakes.

If This Is The Behavior	Try This
Whining	Ignoring
Playing cooperatively	Positive reinforcement
Refusing to cooperate	Provide a choice
Restlessness, inattentiveness	Change the activity
Daydreaming	Indirect suggestion
Arguing over the ownership of a toy	Active listening
Dawdling, late for snacks	Natural consequences
Pushing, crowding, running inside	Change room arrangement
Unable to take turns, to wait	Review daily schedule, equipment
Boisterous play	Positive redirection

FIGURE 7.11 Varieties of disciplinary responses. The astute teacher selects from the options available and individualizes disciplinary methods.

ABOUT CHOICES

–Give children choices whenever possible. This allows some control over themselves so they do not feel continually dominated by adults and helps them practice self-reliance, self-direction, and self-discipline. "Looks like there is plenty of room at the easels or at the lotto games, Seth. Where would you like to play?"

–Only give choices when you mean for the children to have a choice. Be prepared to accept their answer when a choice is offered. Make sure you present choices to children only when they really have one. "Some of the children are going inside for music now. Would you like to join them?" Do not ask, "Would you like to go home now? Clean up?" when it is not an option.

–Suggest two choices when there is the possibility of resistance. Let children know you expect them to comply with your request, but allow some decision on their part. Do not box them into a corner. "It's time to go home now. Would you like to get your artwork before or after you put on your jacket?"

–Make the choice real and valid. Acknowledge children's growing ability to deal with responsibility and help them practice making reasonable choices. "There are several kinds of nails, Stacey. Try them out to see which ones work best for you."

BEING POSITIVE

–Tell children what it is you want them to do. Make directions and suggestions in positive statements, not in negative forms. "Walk around the edge of the grass, Hilla, so you won't get hit by the swing," instead of, "Don't get hit!"

–Reinforce what children do right, what you like, and what you want to see repeated. This helps build the relationship on positive grounds. "Good job, Sammy. You worked hard on that puzzle."

–Give indirect suggestions or reminders, emphasizing what you want children to do. Help them refocus on the task without nagging or confrontation. "I know you are excited about the field trip, Mickey. Looks like you are almost finished putting on your jacket so we can go," instead of "Hurry and button that jacket so we can go."

–Use positive redirection whenever possible. Suggest another acceptable way for the child to do the same thing or achieve the same results. This shows children how to meet their needs by addressing the problem in direct ways. Redirection differs from diverting the child's attention to something else. It does not avoid the issue, but confronts it with an alternative

FIGURE 7.12 Effective techniques for guiding children. Good disciplinary methods are rational, consistent, and fair.

method. "You two really seem to want to wrestle. Let's get the mats out so you can wrestle with each other and not interfere with music," instead of "Stop that wrestling and find something else to do."

–Give reasons for your request. Let children know in simple, straightforward statements the reasons behind your request. Children are more likely to cooperate when they can understand the reason why. "Tom, if you move those chairs, then you and Dee will have more room to dance," instead of "Move the chairs, Tom."

PLAN AHEAD

–Allow plenty of time for children to respond. Give them an opportunity to decide their course of action.

–Review limits and rules periodically. Modify them as children's growth and maturation indicate. Change them as circumstances change; be flexible.

–Encourage children to talk things over. Be open to their point of view even if you cannot accept it. Let them know you are willing to listen to all sides of the conflict.

–Become aware of the climate in the room or yard. Anticipate the need for a change of pace or a different activity BEFORE children become bored or troublesome.

–Remember, it takes time and numerous opportunities for changes in behavior to occur. By using consistent guidance techniques, you will help children practice new behavior repeatedly.

ALWAYS AVOID

–Methods that will shame, frighten, or humiliate children.

–Physical abuse.

–Comparisons among the children. This fosters competitiveness and affects self-esteem.

–Carry-overs from the incident. Once it is over, leave it behind; do not keep reminding children about it.

–Consequences that are too long, too punitive, or postponed. Children benefit most from immediate, short consequences.

–Lots of rules. Set only enough to ensure a safe environment for all children.

–Making promises you cannot keep.

–Being overly helpful. Let children do as much as they can by themselves, including solving their own conflicts.

–Threatening children with the loss of your affection.

FIGURE 7.12 Cont.

"I" messages are an adult's way of reflecting back to children how their actions have affected others. According to Gordon, a "parent simply tells a child how some unacceptable behavior is making the parent feel" (1970).

> Parent: When you scream indoors, it really hurts my ears.
>
> Parent: I feel sad when you tell me you don't like me.

"I" messages are honest, nonjudgmental statements that place no blame on the child, but which state an observation of the behavior and its results. They avoid accusing statements, such as "You made me . . ." and call for a framework that allows adults to state their feelings to the child.

Natural and Logical Consequences

These enhance children's ability to take responsibility for themselves. As implied, this approach lets children experience the natural consequences of their actions. This approach, designed by Rudolf Dreikurs, emphasizes the opportunity children have to learn from the way their environment functions:

> If Libby does not eat her dinner, she can expect to be hungry later.
>
> If Kara puts her hand on a hot stove, she is likely to get burned.
>
> If Tony grabs the book away from Ben, Ben may hit him.

This method allows adults to define the situation for children without making judgments, and lets children know what to expect. The consequences are a natural result of the child's own actions. *Logical* consequences, on the other hand, are a function of what adults impose. A logical consequence of disrupting group time is removal from the group. For the adult, this means a commitment to follow through; consequences, once stated, must be enforced. It is important to give children an opportunity to choose a course of action for themselves

once they have some understanding of what is likely to happen.

Behavior Modification

This is an organized approach based on the premise that behavior is learned through *positive and negative reinforcement* or rewards. The belief is that children will tend to repeat behavior for which they get the desired results (positive reinforcement) and are likely to avoid doing things which have undesirable consequences (negative reinforcement). Positive reinforcement is used to teach new and different behaviors to a child, and

FIGURE 7.13 Children can choose their own course of action.

help the child maintain the change. Negative reinforcement may simply involve ignoring or withdrawing attention when the child acts inappropriately. Initially, the reinforcement (or reward) must be swift and consistently applied, as often as the behavior occurs. If the desired behavior, for instance, is for Janie to always hang her coat on the hook, praise and appreciate the effort each time Janie hangs up her wraps. Once this is a well-established routine, the reinforcement (praise) becomes less intense.

Reinforcers, or rewards, must be individualized to meet the needs of the child and the situation. Social reinforcers, such as smiling, interest and attention, hugging, touching, and talking, are powerful tools with young children. Food, tokens, and money are also used as reinforcers in home and school settings. The goal is that inner satisfaction will become its own reward, no matter the type of reinforcer one might use initially.

To succeed, the adult will focus on only one behavior change at a time. If parents want to use behavior modification methods to help their children arrive at the dinner table on time, then Dad does not nag about homework or Mom about a messy room. The behavior that is targeted for change becomes the primary concern until it is successfully altered.

Parents and teachers often take for granted the positive, desirable behavior in children and may forget to acknowledge these behaviors frequently. Behavior modification helps to correct that oversight. Whenever adults focus on a negative aspect of a child's behavior and make an attempt to change it, they also look at the positive qualities the child possesses and reinforces them. This keeps a balanced perspective while working on a problem.

Behavior modification enables adults to invite children to be part of the process, giving them an active part in monitoring their own behavior. Children are capable of keeping a chart of how many times they finished their plate, made the bed, or fed the dog. This chart serves as a natural reinforcer.

Each of these methods is a valuable tool for teachers. These approaches influence children to modify their behavior because they place the responsibility where it belongs: with the child. The adult informs children of the results of their actions and trusts their willingness and abilities to cooperate in a solution. The child's self-respect is left intact because no one has placed blame. By integrating these methods into a disciplinary approach, teachers enlarge the child's capacity to become increasingly self-directed and self-reliant.

SUMMARY

The early childhood educator provides opportunities for children to express their feelings in appropriate ways and to solve their social problems constructively. Children are incapable of controlling their own impulses all the time, so caring adults are needed to guide them toward self-control. Teachers base their methods and disciplinary principles on an understanding of why children misbehave and what factors influence behavior.

Most guidance techniques begin by accepting the feelings the child expresses and verbalizing them. Then the adult sets limits on what form the behavior may take, guiding the action as needed and following through to conclusion.

The most effective methods of discipline are clear, consistent, and fair rules that are enforced in consistent, humane ways. Children should be aware of the consequences if the rules are broken.

Good disciplinary practices emphasize the positive aspects of a child's behavior, not just the problem behaviors. Guidance measures have greater meaning to children if they are encouraged to take responsibility for their own actions and are part of the problem-solving process.

Review Questions

1. What are some of the goals of children's misbehavior? What techniques can adults use to deal with children who exhibit these goals?

2. What developmental factors affect children's behavior? What environmental factors? How does a child's individual style affect behavior?

3. How would you solve Case Study #3 if Zachary refused to make a choice between emptying the water table and moving chairs?

4. What is your own definition of discipline?

5. Why do teachers have to set limits on children's behavior? How does it help the child?

Learning Activities

1. Your three-year-old daughter always interrupts when you talk on the telephone. She cries for you to play with her, hits her brothers, and crawls into cupboards. What is she doing and why? What is your reaction? How will you solve the problem?

2. List activities that channel aggressive feelings into acceptable ways to play. After each, note the emotion or feeling the specific activity might release. *Example:* Clay—anger, frustration

3. Finish this sentence: "When I was four-years-old, the *worst* thing I ever did was . . ." How did the adults around you react? What would you do if you were the adult in charge? Discuss and compare responses with a classmate.

4. Children's literature helps us focus on disciplinary and behavior problems. Select a book from the following list. Define the problem behavior and the person creating the problem. Do you agree with the author's way of handling the situation? Suggest alternatives. When and with whom might you use this story?

Suggested books: *Noisy Nora*/Rosemary Wells
The Man Who Wouldn't Wash His Dishes/Phyllis Krasilovsky
Pierre/Maurice Sendak
Nobody Asked Me If I Wanted A Baby Sister/Martha Alexander
Benjamin and Tulip/Rosemary Wells
Bread and Jam for Frances/Russel and Lillian Hoban
Ira Sleeps Over/Bernard Waber
Where the Wild Things Are/Maurice Sendak
The Bundle Book/Ruth Krauss
And to Think That I Saw It on Mulberry Street/Dr. Seuss
Alexander and the Terrible, Horrible, No Good, Very Bad Day/Judith Viorst

Bibliography

Dinkmeyer, Dona, and McKay, Gary. *Systematic Training for Effective Parenting.* Circles Pines, Minn.: American Guidance Service, 1976.

Dreikurs and Grey. *A New Approach to Discipline: Logical Consequences.* New York: Hawthorne Books, Inc., 1968.

Gordon, Dr. Thomas. *Parent Effectiveness Training.* New York: Peter H. Wyden, 1970.

Jenkins, Gail Gardner. *Helping Children Reach Their Potential.* Glenview, Ill.: Scott, Foresman and Co., 1971.

Long, Dr. Barbara Ellis. *Freedom Versus Limits.* Unpublished paper. 1977.

Mattick, Ilse, and Perkins, Frances J. *Guidelines for Observation and Assessment: An Approach to Evaluating the Learning Environment of a Day Care Center.* Washington, D.C.: Day Care and Child Development Council, 1974.

Schaefer, Charles, and Millman, Howard. *How to Help Children with Common Problems.* New York: Van Nostrand Reinhold, 1981.

8

Parents and Teachers: Partners in Education

Questions for Thought

- Why is it important to have good working relationships with parents?
- What are teachers expected to share with parents?
- What will parents share with teachers?
- How do parents get interested and involved in the classroom?
- What are the ingredients for a good parent program?
- What are the ingredients for a successful parent–teacher conference?
- What is the teacher's role in providing a supportive atmosphere for parents?

Outline

HISTORICAL PERSPECTIVE

Working with parents can be one of the teacher's most satisfying responsibilities, or it can be one of the most frustrating. It is usually both. The potential is clearly present for a dynamic partnership between the most important adults in a child's life. The common goal is obvious: the welfare of the child. Each has knowledge, skills, and a sense of caring to bring to that relationship. Each has a need for the other. Partnerships usually begin with such a need. So, parents and teachers become coworkers, colleagues in a joint effort to help the child develop fully.

There is a historical *precedent* for the partnership between parents and teachers. Pestalozzi and Froebel, early eighteenth-century educators, detailed many of their procedures for home use. The involvement of the mother in the education of the child was considered important even then. When kindergartens were organized in this country, classes for parents and mothers' clubs were also started. The National Congress of Mothers evolved from that movement. Today it is the National Congress of Parents and Teachers (Spodek, 1972). This well-known organization is an integral part of most school systems and continues to promote a union between home and school, teachers and parents.

There was a period of time during the 1930s when parental involvement in education was actively discouraged. Teachers were seen as experts who wanted to be left alone to do their job. In many cases, teachers felt they did little but remedy parental mistakes. Parents in or near the classroom were barely tolerated. That trend ended in the 1940s when the need for parent support and encouragement was recognized. Closer relationships between teachers and parents were established. This view of a need for closer ties between teacher and parents, although nearly 50 years old, stands today as a commonly accepted principle.

Teacher training curricula began to reflect the change. Teachers were exposed to courses that would help them appreciate and utilize parents as coworkers in the child's development. By the 1960s,

Head Start programs required parental involvement and set about developing parent education and parent training programs. Their commitment to children included a commitment to the parents of those children.

The most recent influences are still felt today. Early childhood teachers all over the country, regardless of the setting, believe in the necessity of the parent–teacher relationship. There is general agreement that at no other age is such a relationship more important than in the years before school. Teachers have come to appreciate the role parents can play and no longer fear their interference. Parents have accepted the responsibility, too. The way, then, is paved for this partnership to be successful. By changing some of their assumptions about one another, parents and teachers now stand together to support and promote children's development.

PARTNERSHIP IN EDUCATION

Parents have a unique contribution to make in the child's schooling. They have different knowledge about the child from what the teacher has. They know the child's history: physical, medical, social, and intellectual. They know the child as a member of a family, and the role that child plays in the total family group. Through parents, teachers learn about the home life of the children in their classes: who they live with, in what kind of family situation, and what their life style is like. Parents bring with them a sense of continuity about the child: they provide the context with which the teacher can view the whole child. As the teacher will soon learn, the parents already know what makes their child happy or sad, or how they react to changes in routines. Thus, parents have a wealth of intimate knowledge about their child that the teacher is only just beginning to discover.

Teachers bring to the partnership another perspective. As child development professionals, they see the child in relation to what they know are normal milestones and appropriate behaviors. They no-

FIGURE 8.1 Parents and teachers share knowledge and insights.

tice how each child plays with other children in the group, what seems to challenge Elizabeth and when Patrick is likely to fall apart. Unlike parents, teachers see individual children from a perspective that is balanced by the numerous other children they have taught. They observe how the child behaves with a variety of adults, sensing children's ability to trust other adults through interactions with them at school. When parents need help for themselves or for their child, teachers become resources. They may work with the parents to find psychologists, hearing and speech specialists, or other educational programs, if warranted.

By pooling their knowledge of a child, both parents and teachers gain a more complete picture of the whole child. By becoming aware of the role each plays in the life of the child, teachers and parents grow in their understanding of one another. They can respect each other's unique contribution. As they recognize their need to share valuable information, they can support one another.

The Value of Working Together

The very first contact between parents and teachers is likely to take place within the early childhood education setting. If parents feel welcome and important, the stage is set for ongoing involvement in their child's education. By working closely with parents, teachers establish a pattern that can be re-

What Parents Share	What Teachers Share
Intimate knowledge of their child	Knowledge of child development; milestones, normal behavior
Information about home life	
Family background	Knowledge of the child's strengths and weaknesses
Child's health history and growth record	
Changes in the family routine: job loss, death, divorce, illness, trips, moves	Discipline and guidance techniques
	School and community resources
Specific skills and talent	Observational skills
A unique viewpoint: subjective	Language as a tool and a method
	A unique viewpoint: objective

FIGURE 8.2 Parents and teachers share valuable information and, in doing so, form a partnership that benefits the child.

peated as the child grows. Parents should be involved in the school life of their child at all grade levels. Their introduction to this world of schools and teachers, then, is important.

For the Parents

Parents are the child's teachers too. They teach by word, by example, and by all they say and do. Some parents are better teachers than others. Through close home–school relationships, parents can find ways to become more effective. They can observe teacher's modeling techniques that are successful. Teachers can support parents' efforts in many ways:

- By praising parents when they teach their children to dress themselves.
- By posting notices about special events the whole family can enjoy.
- By sponsoring a "games night" when parents get together to make inexpensive educational games for home use.
- By providing book lists for bedtime reading.
- By making sure parents have copies of the children's favorite songs.
- By supplying parents with some easy-to-do cooking recipes to try at home with children.
- By providing lists of snacks to serve as alternates to sweets.

- By involving parents in teaching their children safety habits for fire drills at home.

One of the greatest values of a strong parent program is the opportunity for parents to meet each other. They find that they share similar problems and frustrations, and that they can support one another in finding solutions. Friendships blossom based on mutual interests and concerns about their children.

For the Teachers and School

Active parent involvement benefits the teacher and school, too. Parents are an untapped resource in most schools. The skills and talents in a group of parents multiply the people resources available to children. Some parents will want to work directly in the classroom with children; others may volunteer to help in the office, the schoolyard, or the kitchen. Parents who have jobs can sometimes arrange to take some time off to accompany a class on a field trip. There are parents who are willing to work at home, either sewing, typing, mending, building, or painting. Parents will vary in their willingness to become involved. Some may be unable to participate because of work schedules, small children to care for at home, or lack of transportation.

For the Children

The children whose parents choose to take an active part in the school reap the rewards of such

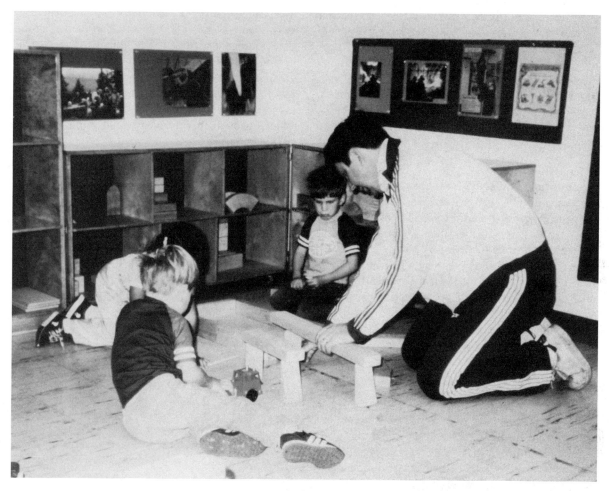

FIGURE 8.3 Children benefit when parents are involved.

involvement. Research shows examples of children's gains in academic skills, positive self-concept, and verbal intelligence when extensive parental participation is required (Honig, 1979). The family is the primary source from which the child develops and grows. Schools alone may not be able to provide all that is necessary. The family of the child is needed to reinforce the learning, the attitudes, and the motivation if children are to remain interested learners.

Prerequisites for a Good Parent Program

The quality of parent involvement and interest will depend on many factors. Some of the fundamental components of a good parent program are:

Support from School Personnel. School administrators must lend their full support to the concept of parental involvement, spending both time and energy to make it work. The endorsement of the school director or principal is critical, as are teacher interest and enthusiasm. Some teachers will gladly work with parents on any project; others will support their involvement by praising and promoting parental efforts. Teachers should have a choice in the ways in which they would like to get involved. They may volunteer to serve on parent committees, open their classes to parent aides, or coordinate the parent training.

Foundation of Needs, Concerns, and Interests of Parents. Offering a lecture series on "Child-Rearing Practices Around the World" will not meet the needs of parents when they are asking for help in coping with children fighting on the school bus. In order to sustain parent interest, the program must also use the skills and knowledge available within that group of parents. That means someone must take the time to find out what individual parents have to offer and are willing to share. Periodic evaluation of the total program is important. Regular assessment helps to develop programs that work well for parents and the school.

Variety. Parents have many needs in common, but they do not all have the same needs at the same time. A good program for parental involvement reflects those needs in the number, type, and kinds of opportunities it provides. It allows the individual parent to select where, when, and how to participate. A variety of times for participation—during school, evenings, weekends—allows parents many options.

Parents as Change Agents. Good parent programming means that the school has something of value to offer the parents and that parents have something to contribute to the school. This implies a willingness to learn from each other, a give-and-take relationship. School administrators and teachers show parents that they have influence and can bring about change. In one school this resulted in the development of day care and extended day facilities, inclusion of a toddler program, regularly scheduled parent support groups, and the beginning of a scholarship fund. Changes do not occur all at once and are the result of sympathetic school administrators and parents who are willing to work together in constructive ways. Parents should feel that what they have to say is important; school personnel who encourage and respond to parent feedback demonstrate a commitment to parent involvement.

Respect for Parents. A good parent program is based on mutual respect. Do not approach parents as though they are in need of being converted to new styles of parenting. Allow them freedom to accept what is useful and let them reject what they cannot, in good conscience, adopt for themselves. Parents will grow in self-confidence and security only if school personnel will respect their native intelligence and instincts about their own children.

Basic Guidelines for Working with Parents

Supporting and encouraging parents in their role is part of a teacher's responsibility. Good teachers are sensitive to parent concerns and understand their needs. To insure good parent–teacher relationships, review the following guidelines:

Prepare parents for what they can expect from their child's school experience. School policies and a yearly calendar should be clearly stated and thoroughly reviewed with parents as the child enters school. Then parents will know what their responsibilities are, where the school can be of assistance to them, and what expectations the school has of the parents.

Protect the parent–child relationship. Enhance the pride children naturally feel about their mothers and fathers. Tell Maggie her eyes are just like her Dad's or mention to Kevin that his Mom will be pleased to hear he slid down the big slide. Reinforce that unique place families have in children's lives. This is particularly critical for children who spend long hours in child care centers away from their parents. Parents need teachers to support them in raising their children and they like to hear when they have done well. They take pride in doing their best and appreciate teachers who acknowledge this.

Contact parents frequently and on a regular basis. Keep the lines of communication open and flowing between school and home. Be sure to know the parents by name. Take advantage of the daily contact as they bring their child to and from school. It may be brief and breezy, but it is a good way to stay in touch. Be sure to find ways to touch base with those parents who do not come to school every day.

Respect parents for the difficult job they have, the role they play, and the persons they are. Respect their religious, cultural, social, and ethnic backgrounds and heritage. Respect their privacy. Do not allow one parent to seek information about another. Respect the right of the parent to disagree. Above all, respect the unparalleled part they play in the growth and development of their child.

Listen to parents. Hear them out. They, too, have accumulated experiences to share, and their views are valid. Learn to listen to them with a degree of understanding; try to hear it from their point of view. Listen to parents without judging them or jumping to conclusions; that is the basis for open communication.

THE NATURE OF PARENTING

There is little preparation for the job of being a parent and most mothers and fathers feel inadequate in their role. Parents are pretty much alone as they strike out in unfamiliar territory. Due to our increasingly mobile society, most couples do not live around the corner from grandparents or other family members. There is no extended family to teach new mothers and fathers some of the traditional, time-honored child-rearing skills. There is no one with whom parents can share their worries, frustrations, and concerns. So the *pediatrician's* phone number is etched in their mind, and they proceed to do the best job of parenting they can.

More recently, an important change has taken place within young families. Parenting as a shared experience is becoming a commonly accepted way of life. Young men, influenced by changing values and attitudes toward traditional sex roles, are taking an active part in raising their families. Fathers seem aware of the critical role they play in the child's life and are making appropriate changes to see that they have the time to be with their children. Child rearing is no longer just the mother's responsibility, according to a new generation of fathers.

Child rearing is FUN!
Girls are harder to rear than boys.
Parents are mature and grown up.
Children can improve a marriage.
Good parents don't have bad kids.
All married couples should have children.
Parents are parents by choice.

Children are cute.
Boys are harder to rear than girls.
All children need two parents.
Parenthood is an American priority.
Child rearing today is easier.
Children appreciate their advantages.

FIGURE 8.4 Myths about parenthood. (Adapted from LeMasters, 1974)

Needs of Parents

The majority of parents today want to learn the best way to raise their children and want to improve their child-rearing skills. Honig (1979) has highlighted six basic needs of parents:

1. Parents need knowledge about how children develop.

2. Parents need to learn how to observe young children.

3. Parents need knowledge of alternative methods of discipline and of problem avoidance.

4. Parents need to learn how to take advantage of situations and activities at home to create learning opportunities for their children.

5. Parents need language tools to simplify explanations that will make sense to a preschool child.

6. Parents need to feel they are important and how much they make a difference in their child's life.

In their eagerness to do right by their child, parents grab for help whenever and however it is offered. They devour how-to books. Television talk shows where child-rearing methods are discussed and parenting issues are raised are popular. Magazines that feature articles by noted childhood specialists are in all corner grocery stores. Parents seem willing to listen to anyone, to try anything. That is surely some measure of how lonely and frightened they feel at times.

The Teacher's Role

The child care specialist is often one of the first people, outside the home, to whom parents turn for help. Parents come to the center looking for teachers who know about children and who will work with them. They arrive at school confused and discouraged; being a mommy or daddy is not at all like they thought it was going to be. Helping parents with their child-rearing problems is part of a teacher's role. The way in which teachers define

FIGURE 8.5 Parents like to know they make a difference.

that role and their response to parental concerns should be carefully thought through. The following are guidelines to consider in establishing a supportive atmosphere for parents:

Do not confuse the role of teacher and parent. While committed to meeting the needs of the individual children in the class, remember that teachers are not and cannot be *surrogate* mothers. Allow parents to do their part of the job to the best of their ability, and teachers their part without infringing on that relationship.

Support all parents, even those with differing opinions. Find ways to acknowledge them and what they are trying to do even though you may be at odds with some of their child-rearing philosophies. There is a greater chance to discuss differences and affect change if there are areas where teachers and parents find agreement. Children are sensitive to adult feelings, whether they are spoken or not. A teacher should not overtly disagree with a child's parents. Differences of opinions should be discussed out of the child's hearing, but teachers should also do nothing that would undermine that parent in the eyes of his or her child.

Respect the values of families. Social, cultural, and religious differences and a variety of life styles, child-rearing methods, and educational philosophies are reflected in every class. It is important that parents feel accepted. Capitalize on their differences by adding a multicultural aspect to the program.

Be friendly with parents, but do not be their friends. The temptation to move into a social relationship with some families in your class is one that every teacher faces. When a teacher develops close relationships with one family or another, this can complicate the teacher role. It makes a teacher feel good to know that friendship is desired, but it can be confusing to parents and children. The teacher maintains a more realistic, objective picture of the child if there is some detachment. The child and the family will probably benefit most if a close relationship is postponed until the child moves on to another class.

Ask parents instead of telling them. A teacher-tell approach should be used sparingly. Teachers are most helpful when they begin with the parents' concerns. Suggestions will be received more favorably if teachers avoid telling parents what to do. A teacher's role is one of helping parents clarify their own goals for their children and identifying the trouble spots. Teachers then encourage and support parents as they work together to solve the problem. Parents will feel overwhelmed and inadequate if they think they must change their whole child-rearing style. The sensitive teacher will observe parents and move toward reasonable solutions.

A little support goes a long way. Everyone likes to be reinforced for doing a good job. Parents respond positively to a comment, a phone call, or any brief acknowledgment of their efforts. As Alex's parents enter or leave school, the teacher could mention how Alex has relaxed since they began to insist on a reasonable bedtime. A quick note, sent home with Juanita, that commends her parents for getting her to school on time would be appreciated.

Help parents support each other. Any group of parents represents a multitude of resources. Each parent has accumulated experiences that might prove helpful to someone else. Parents have common concerns and a lot to share with one another. The teacher can provide an arena in which sharing happens. Introduce two families to each other by suggesting that their children play together outside of school. Parent meetings, work parties, and potluck dinners are methods for getting parents involved with each other. The teacher's role can be one of providing the setting, encouraging introductions, and then letting it happen.

Enhance parents' perception of their child. Parents want teachers who know their child, enjoy their child, and are an advocate for their child. According to Dr. Edith Dowley, teachers have a responsibility to make the children as attractive as possible to their parents. That means acknowledging the child's strengths and those personality traits that are particularly pleasing. Help parents to recognize the joys of parenthood, rather than focusing on the burdens.

Focus on the parent–child relationship. Help parents learn the "how to's" of their relationship with their child rather than the "how to's" of developing academic skills. Concentrate on the nature of the parent–child interaction—how they get along with each other and how they interact as a family. A major concern of parents may be how to get Rhoda to stop biting her nails; how to set limits that Joel will keep; how to stop Richard and Monica from fighting at the dinner table; how to get Timmy to stop wetting his bed; how to get Allie to take care of the puppy or how to get Frannie to clean up her room. These issues are the heart and soul of parent–child relationships. Teachers have a role to play in enhancing the quality of those relationships by helping parents focus on the real "how to's."

Accept parents for what they are. Their feelings get aroused by teachers, schools, children's behavior, being judged, being criticized, feeling inadequate, and being told what to do. Meantime, teachers have to face their feelings about parents. The important thing to keep in mind is that parents just want to be accepted for who and what they are. As teachers accept the individuality of each child, they must accept each parent as a unique combination of traits, personalities, strengths, problems, and concerns. Parents and teachers seem frightened of one another. This is especially true of inexperienced teachers and first-time parents. Each has anxieties about what the other one does—or does not do. They must work at putting the other at ease and come to some understanding and respect. Teachers who have a clear understanding of that role can help parents relax and set aside some of their fears.

Parents with Special Needs

Parents are parents the world over and have mutual problems and pleasures as they go about bringing up their young. Their shared experiences create an automatic bond whenever parents meet. There are some parents, however, who face additional challenges in child rearing, and who may need added teacher support. These are:

- parents of children with handicaps
- single parents
- parents who both work outside the home
- divorced parents
- teenage parents
- parents who are raising children in foreign cultures
- parents who do not speak English
- older first-time parents

Any one or combination of these situations can create complex challenges for parents. A teacher should become aware of the forces at work within these families and be sensitive to their needs. Teachers should treat these parents as they do any other; it is not necessary to single them out and, indeed, such an effort may be resented. For the most part, teachers can help these parents by focusing on the many interests and concerns they share with all other parents. In some cases, additional support for these parents is needed.

- Help parents locate community resources to assist them.
- Put them in touch with other parents who have similar parenting circumstances.
- Assist them in exploring school settings for the future.
- See that they are included in all school functions.
- Learn about their special needs.
- Seek their help and advice.
- Help them establish contact with other parents who may be willing to assist in translating, transporting, baby-sitting, and sharing friendship.

TEACHER–PARENT INTERACTIONS

The Separation Process

When parents leave a child at school, it is a time of stress for all concerned. Each time this process occurs, the child, parents, and teachers are entering into a new and unpredictable relationship.

The Child's Perspective

Each year, as school begins, a child enters a classroom and says good-bye to a parent. Each year this is, in some ways, a new experience for that child, no matter how long he or she might have been enrolled in school. Children returning to the same classroom will find some changes with which they must cope. There may be new teachers and new children together with some familiar faces. The room arrangement might be different enough to

FIGURE 8.6 Parents can help their child learn to say good-bye.

cause some anxiety. For most, school is a new and alien place. Each child will react differently to the situation, and it is difficult to predict how a child will respond. Some children will have had previous group experience to draw on; others will never have been part of a group of children before.

Here are some scenes of children entering school for the first time:

Paul, clinging to his Dad's trouser legs, hides his face from view. All efforts to talk with him are met with further withdrawal behind his father.

Sherry bounces in, runs from her mother over to the housekeeping area and begins to play with the dolls there. Her mother is left standing alone, just inside the classroom.

Boris is carried into the room by his grandmother. He sobs quietly into her shoulder.

Stacey and Virginia enter hand-in-hand. They are looking for Alejandro with whom they became acquainted in their gymnastic class. He sees them first, dashes over to where they are greeting the teacher, and beams at them. They grin at him and grab his hand.

Christine walks around the room, keeping a careful distance between her father and herself. She glances almost indifferently at the children, the toys, and the teachers as she circles the room. Her tense facial expression is relieved only when she sees something of momentary interest. Then her eyebrows shoot up and down several times.

The wide range of behavior these children exhibit is normal, predictable, and age-appropriate. Each child has a natural way of dealing with the anxieties of coming to school. Their behavior will be as varied as they are themselves.

The Teacher's Perspective

The separation process is one instance in which the teacher's role is to help the parents as much as the child. Parents and teachers must be especially clear with one another during this time. It is helpful to have written school policies and procedures so the teacher can go over the process step by step, on an individual basis, as each child enrolls, or at a general parent meeting held prior to the opening of school.

In some schools, teachers arrange to make a home visit to each child enrolled in the class before school begins. This helps the teacher know more about students before they enter school and gives children a chance to become acquainted with a teacher on their home ground.

The Parent's Perspective

Most parents want their children to make a smooth transition from home to school. Adjustment is a gradual process; parents need encouragement and guidance as their child moves toward independence. When parents are reassured their child is acting normally, and their own anxieties are common, they relax and begin to help the child feel more comfortable.

Parents encourage their child's participation in the program by asking questions and talking together about school activities. They communicate their interest in ways to help their child meet the challenge with a minimum of stress and a maximum of enjoyment.

The Partnership

In giving support and encouragement to both the parent and the child, the teacher helps them achieve independence from one another. Together, parents and teachers make a plan, going over the guidelines and ground rules. The teacher takes the lead, encouraging the child to move out from the parent. The teacher is there to make the decisions regarding the time of actual separation. The parent and teacher prepare children and tell them when it is time. The teacher supports the parents' exit and stands by the child, ready to give comfort, if needed. This is a time when a teacher needs to act with conviction. Parents appreciate firmness and confidence at a time when their own feelings may be *ambiguous*. Children are reassured by teachers whose attitudes express a belief in what they are doing.

Some parent–child relationships are difficult to assess, and it is not always easy or obvious for the teacher to know what to do. For most children, the separation process is a struggle between their natural desire to explore the world and their equally natural resistance to leaving what is "safe." It is during these years that the child is learning to move about under his own power and to trust himself. Coming to school can provide each child with the opportunity for growth, starting with the separation from parents. Through careful planning, close com-munication, and sensitivity to one another, parents and teachers will assure the child mastery of this task.

Parent Education

Almost any contact between the teacher and the parent can be perceived as parent education. Teachers interpret children's behavior to their parents, suggest alternative ways for dealing with problems, show them toys and games that are appropriate, mention books and articles of interest to parents, and reinforce parents' interest and skills. All of these activities are considered parent education. Some of it is planned, some of it is spontaneous.

FIGURE 8.7 Children reap the benefits of parental interest.

Parent education happens frequently, whether in a formal discussion about nightmares, or an informal chat about safe car seats. It happens as parents observe. They see how teachers respond to Kurt's name calling or the way teachers discuss plans for Kimmy's birthday celebration. They feel it when the teacher disagrees with them about cupcake and ice-cream treats at school.

Stevens and King (1976) view parent education as a type of parent involvement. They state the purpose of parent education as "the development of effective parenting skills, attitudes, and behaviors that optimize the development of young children. Parent education is most strictly those activities that are designed to enable adults to become better parents."

Communicating with Parents

There are many ways for parents and teachers to increase their communication with one another.

In doing so, teachers demonstrate that they value the role parents play in their children's lives. Parents are made aware of what their children are doing in school. Five of the most common ways teachers can involve and inform parents are:

1. *Newsletters from the classroom.* They give a general idea of what the children are doing and any special events taking place in class, personal information about new babies, vacations, or other important events in the lives of the children.

2. *Bulletin boards.* Posted where parents can see them, these boards contain notices about parent meetings, guest speakers, community resources, child care, baby-sitting, clothing and furniture exchanges, and library story hours. Information regarding health programs, automobile and toy safety, and immunization clinics are also publicized.

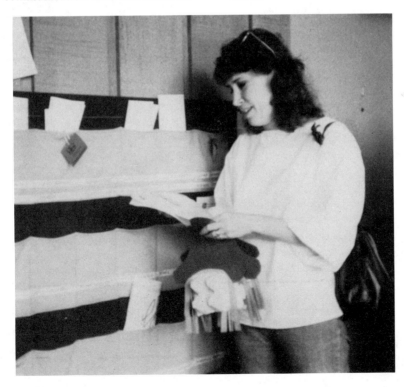

FIGURE 8.8 There are many avenues to parent–teacher communication.

3. *A place for parents.* An area or room at the school set aside for parent use can be an important step in letting parents know they are wanted and needed. Some schools provide space for a parent lounge, complete with a library of resource books on child rearing. If there is no available space, set up a coffee bar in the office or hall. The smallest amount of space—even a countertop with magazines—is a start.

4. *Informal contacts are the easiest and most useful lines of communication with parents.* All it takes is a phone call, a brief note, or a brief talk on a daily basis. For parents who have difficulty attending meetings or who do not accompany their child to and from school, teachers can send home a note along with a sample of artwork, or a story the child has dictated, or a photograph of the child with friends.

5. *Home visits.* Depending on its purpose, a home visit can be used to enhance communications. The visit might be set up to focus only on the relationship between the teacher and the child. Or, the visit might have a purely social function—a way for teachers to meet the whole family and for them to get acquainted with the teachers. In any event, the teacher can use this as a bridge to build a pleasant, casual beginning with this family.

Parent–Teacher Conferences

Parent conferences are the backbone of any good parent–teacher relationship. They provide a way of coming together to focus on the needs of the individual child. Conferencing can be a mutually supportive link established between the adults who are most concerned about an individual child, with the purpose of helping the child reach the fullest potential possible.

Too often, teachers are left to figure out for themselves how to have a conference that is satisfying and productive to both parties. Experience is the best teacher is an old saying that certainly has merit. The more new teachers work with parents and hold regular conferences, the more effective they become. The chart in Figure 8.9 might help the beginning teacher hold fulfilling parent conferences.

Parental Involvement

Parental *involvement* in education includes a wide range of activities. A school that is sensitive to parents will offer a number of ways for them to become involved. The term *involvement* has many meanings, ranging from observation to policy making (Stevens and King, 1976). Parents may choose to play a minor role, if they prefer. If they choose to take a more active part, the options are limited

---

1. *Schedule conferences on a regular basis.* Parents and teachers should share some of the positive aspects of child growth and development and not meet only in crisis. This promotes better feelings about one another, not to mention the child, if meetings are at times other than when a problem occurs.
2. *Be prepared.* Discuss with the staff ahead of time any points they want to include. Gather together any materials, notes, and samples of the child's work that might illustrate a point.

FIGURE 8.9 Twelve steps to successful parent–teacher conferences.

3. *Select a quiet place, free from interruption.* If necessary, sign up for use of a conference room. Make sure that someone is available to intercept phone calls and other appointments.
4. *Have a clear purpose.* Use a written format as a guide to keep focused on the intent of the conference. This gives a brief reminder of points to be covered and serves to keep parents on the track.
5. *Put parents at ease right away.* Offer them a cup of coffee or share an amusing anecdote that just took place in the classroom. Acknowledge the important part they played in the school fair. These light, positive comments will help relax both teacher and parent.
6. *Use up-to-date information and data.* Cite examples, from teacher's observations, that occurred that morning or a few days ago. Include examples of situations that occurred when they were present. "Timmy is very empathetic for a three-year-old, isn't he? That was so clear from the way you two were talking as you came through the door today."
7. *Give them a place to shine.* Tell them what they do well—their success with car-pool crowds or in mediating fights in the yard. If they have a special talent they have shared with the class, comment on its impact on the children.
8. *Ask—don't tell.* Get them talking by asking open-ended questions. "How is that new bedtime arrangement working?" "Tell me more about Katie's eating habits." Teachers will relate these to their own knowledge and experiences with the child and then share what has worked in school, but acknowledge the difference between school and home, teacher and parent.
9. *Learn how to listen.* Concentrate on what the parents are saying. Don't listen with half an ear while planning an appropriate response or comment.
10. *Avoid blaming parents.* Keep the conversation based on mutual concerns and how to help each other. Look at some alternatives together and make a plan of action. Discuss ways to check in with each other or provide for follow-through at school or home. This way the parent will have a feeling of working together rather than of being blamed.
11. *Know where and how to secure community resources and referrals.* Many parents do not know where to get a child's speech tested, or what an I.Q. test is, or where to secure family therapy. They may be unaware of play groups, gymnastic schools, library story hours, or children's museums. Be sure the school can provide this information for parents who need it.
12. *Find a good role model.* Ask experienced teachers to share their ingredients for success. When possible, attend a parent conference with one of them. Observe what works for them and learn from their experience. Ask them to critique your own performance after a conference.

FIGURE 8.9 Cont.

only by school policies and attitudes. A high degree of involvement might mean that parents are serving as salaried teacher aides or as members of governing boards who help define school policy and philosophy. Acting as classroom volunteer, fund raiser, or curriculum resource person are other ways parents get involved.

Maintaining Privacy and Confidentiality

The more involved parents are in the workings of the school, the more important it is to establish guidelines for protecting the privacy of all the families enrolled. When selecting parents for jobs, school administrators must be very clear about their expectations for ensuring such privacy. Parents who work in the office must be responsible enough not to carry tales out of school about any of the children, the teachers, the administration, or the other parents. They should not be expected to handle files that contain sensitive information regarding any of the children, their families, or the staff. Parents in the classroom, either as volunteers or paid aides, must come to understand the necessity for complete confidentiality. What goes on in the classroom must stay in the classroom. Whatever information teachers share with parents about a child is to be used in that classroom only. Teachers will have a responsibility here to uphold these professional standards where parents are concerned.

Classroom participation is the most direct way parents can contribute to the school program. There is always room for another pair of hands in the early childhood setting. Even parents who feel they have "nothing to contribute" soon realize how much they are needed. They often come in expecting to do very little. They leave exhausted, smiling, and saying how much they became involved—and how fast the time passed! The sensitive teacher will let parents know that when they tie a shoelace, go on a field trip, or organize a beanbag toss, they are providing valuable help. A calendar posted on the parent bulletin board is an obvious way of saying parents are welcome.

Not all parental participation takes place at

FIGURE 8.10 Families share the early childhood experience. (Courtesy of Stephanie Barry Agnew)

school. For parents who work and who are unable to volunteer, or for those with baby-sitting or transportation problems, other alternatives are available. Parents can work at home and still feel needed. Figure 8.11 shows some of the ways these parents can add to their child's school experience.

SUMMARY

The partnership in education between parent and teacher has a long and varied history. In current practice, parents and teachers have a growing awareness of the part each has to play in the child's life. Each has a separate but important function, and each has valuable information about the child that needs to be shared.

Parents in the Classroom Can	Parents at Home Can
Free teachers to give added attention to other children and situations.	Replace all the snaps on smocks with Velcro fasteners.
Give children a number of adults to work with; they are exposed to different personalities, values, and cultures.	Sew new paint smocks, doll clothes, and dress-up clothes, or make pillows.
Help children feel "special" on the day their parent participates.	Cut out materials for art projects.
Add depth to the curriculum; parents can share skills in music, art, drama; they can share their professional life as a doctor, fire fighter, nurse, dental assistant.	Purchase food for cooking projects. Type newsletters. Collect articles of interest for the parent bulletin board. Collect materials for the class. Gather wood for woodworking.
Give ethnic and religious celebrations new meaning when they share foods, clothing, toys, with which they celebrate Hannukah, Chinese New Year, or Thanksgiving.	Organize publishing projects, such as a class songbook or class cookbook. Build a rack to hold the scissors. Backhoe the vegetable garden before planting.
Allow for more cooking projects that require more adult supervision.	Help construct a rabbit hutch.
See first-hand what learning is all about with the preschool child; they see how their own child functions in a group and how teachers use a variety of techniques to deal with behavior problems.	

FIGURE 8.11 There are many ways to involve parents.

Parents have an intimate, subjective history of the child from birth. The teacher's perspective comes from an overall knowledge of child development principles, guidance techniques, observational skills, and objectivity. By pooling their information, each has a more complete picture of the whole child. Together they share some common goals for that child. As parents and teachers become more sensitive to each other, they grow in their understanding of their unique roles.

In order to have successful parent involvement, there must be mutual respect and strong support from the school administration. Programs that invite parent involvement must assess the needs of parents and offer a variety of ways to meet those needs. Parents want to know they are listened to and that they have the potential to effect change.

One of the first and most intensive ways parents and teacher work together is through the separation process that takes place when the child enters school. There are other basic skills teachers must have to work successfully with parents. Frequent communication and many levels of parent education are but two. Parent conferencing is a critical part of any parent effort, and the new teacher can be helped by guidelines that will ensure a good beginning.

Review Questions

1. What do you consider to be the most important reasons for teachers and parents to have good relationships? Why should parents be involved in their child's schooling?

2. Describe three ways you would encourage parents to participate in your classroom. Cite the advantages for the (a) children, (b) parents, and (c) teacher. Are there any disadvantages?

3. What are some of your own "Myths About Parenthood"? Make two lists, one headed "Myths Teachers Have About Parents" and another headed "Myths Parents Have About Teachers." Compare the two and then discuss them with both a parent and a teacher.

4. What are some of the key elements in a successful parent–child separation? What is the role of the teacher?

Learning Activities

1. Complete this sentence: "For me, the most difficult part of being a parent (is) would be _____." Discuss your response with another parent, a grandparent, a single person, and a teacher.

2. Interview three parents you know well. What do you see as their major concerns as they raise their children in today's world? What has surprised them the most about parenthood? Be sure to include fathers in your interview.

3. Write a newsletter for your classroom. Involve the children and let it be theirs to write.

4. On pages 180 and 181, look at the five "Basic Guidelines for Working with Parents." Give an example of how you would apply each of the five principles in your classroom. Look at another classroom setting and see if you can find any way in which these are being undermined.

5. The twelfth step in "Successful Parent–Teacher Conferences" suggests that you find a good role model. Look around at the teachers you know and select one. Go through the steps suggested in number 12 and write up your response.

Bibliography

Dowley, Dr. Edith. Personal conversations.

Honig, Alice S. *Parent Involvement in Early Childhood Education.* Washington, D.C.: National Association for the Education of Young Children, 1979.

Lane, Mary B. *Education for Parenting.* Washington, D.C.: National Association for the Education of Young Children, 1975.

LeMasters, E.E. *Parents in Modern America.* Homewood, Ill.: The Dorsey Press, 1974.

Spodek, Bernard. *Teaching in the Early Years.* Englewood Cliffs, N.J.: Prentice-Hall, 1972.

Stevens, Joseph H., Jr., and King, Edith W. *Administering Early Childhood Education Programs.* Boston: Little, Brown and Co., 1976.

Taylor, Katharine Whiteside. *Parents and Children Learn Together.* New York: Teachers College Press, 1967.

SECTION IV

CREATING ENVIRONMENTS FOR GROWTH AND LEARNING

Thelma Harms

The environment that adults create for children is a powerful tool for teaching. Through the way we structure children's surroundings, we communicate our values, provide guidance about how children are to behave in the environment, and influence the quality of their learning. Teachers of young children need to become aware of the constant influence the environment has on the children in their care. Preschool children are much more responsive to the here and now than older children and adults because they have not yet learned to screen out distractions and make sense of confusing messages. By creating an environment that young children understand easily and manage as independently as possible, the teacher can maximize the positive influence of this dependence on the here and now.

The important aspects of environment include arrangement of space, furnishings and equipment, activities to enhance development, the daily schedule, and supervision provided by staff. This broad definition of environment makes it possible for adults to take into consideration all the factors that together create the children's surroundings. For children, interpersonal interactions are interwoven with the physical features of the setting and contribute significantly to the impact made by the total environment. Similarly, the learning activities available to the children are an important part of what they react to in the setting. The term *environment*, then, includes a lot more than the physical features and equipment.

All settings for early childhood care and education have the same basic environmental components and the same basic goal—that of meeting the needs of children—despite the fact that programs vary in length of day, size of group, number of staff, and ages of children served. Consider each of the components listed below. I think you will agree that no program could meet the social, emotional, and intellectual needs of young children without doing a good job of providing environmental support for each of these areas:

1. Personal care routines
2. Appropriate furnishings and display space

What Is the Setting?

3. Language and reasoning experiences
4. Fine and gross motor activities
5. Creative activities
6. Social development experiences
7. Personal and professional needs of the adults in the program

The first six environmental components deal with the children's needs and the seventh with those of the teaching staff. It is painfully obvious that few people consider it important to include environmental provisions for the adults in early childhood settings. Yet, wherever there are children, there are, of necessity, key adults who are responsible for those children. Unless a facility provides proper space and time for the personal and professional needs of the staff, as well as providing opportunities for staff development and parent–staff interaction, teachers will not be able to reach their professional potential, and the program will suffer. Within each early childhood setting, it is important that the administration and teaching staff arrange the environment to meet their own needs, as well as those of the children entrusted to them.

As teachers of young children, we need to ask ourselves what sorts of goals we should have for early childhood settings. A primary goal is to avoid behavior problems by setting up a soft, responsive, clearly organized and supportive environment that keeps children relaxed, happy, and responding positively. An equally important goal is to set up a predictable environment that children can easily learn to manage independently. The more independent children become, the more teachers are free to provide language and cognitive stimulation through interaction instead of devoting time to the mechanics of running the room. The third goal for early childhood settings— namely, creating a stimulating environment with lots of active learning opportunities for children—can best be carried out if the first two goals are already met.

I believe there is no better tool than observation to help teachers improve their programs. Observation keeps a teacher in touch with what is really happening for children in the program. The challenge in using observation, however, is to remain as objective as possible, which is particularly hard for teachers to do in their own programs. An environment observation guide can help focus a teacher's attention on all the important aspects of the room, including some aspects that might be new areas of awareness for the teacher. Using such a guide periodically can not only increase one's objectivity, but can also help the teacher identify where improvements are taking place and which areas need work.

Teachers who want to be effective in creating quality care and teaching environments need to continue to learn and grow by:

- Trying out new spatial arrangements.
- Trying out new ideas for activities.
- Developing positive interaction skills with children.
- Communicating with parents about their children.
- Visiting other programs.
- Using their skills of observation to objectively evaluate their own programs.

The environment influences children and staff, whether or not we consciously harness this influence. Teachers need to assume responsibility for creating an attractive, functional, and stimulating environment for children and for themselves.

THELMA HARMS was formerly head teacher at the Harold E. Jones Child Study Center, University of California at Berkeley, in which capacity she served for 15 years. She has consulted extensively with a variety of early childhood programs, both in the United States and abroad, including day care, parent cooperatives, Head Start, public school, preschool, and kindergarten programs.

Dr. Harms is an active member of NAEYC and the author of a number of publications, including the Early Childhood Environment Rating Scale *(with R.M. Clifford) and* Cook and Learn *(with Bev Veitch). Her films,* My Art is Me *and* Growing up in a Scary World, *are used in teacher training, as are her many filmstrips. Much of her work has been focused on increasing parental involvement in education, and on clarifying the many underlying factors that have an impact on the quality of early childhood education, whatever the setting. She is presently Director of Curriculum Development, Frank Porter Graham Child Development Center, and Clinical Associate Professor, School of Education, both at the University of North Carolina at Chapel Hill.*

9

Creating Environments

Questions for Thought

- What does the term *environment* mean?
- What are routines and how do they affect planning?
- How do the philosophy and the environment affect one another?
- What criteria are used in planning an optimal environment?
- What health and safety measures must be considered when planning the total environment?
- How are the program goals reflected in the setting?
- What is a self-help environment?
- How are materials for a classroom selected?
- What adult needs must be considered in setting up an environment?

Outline

I. What Is the Environment?

II. General Considerations for Planning Environments
   A. Who Is in the Environment?
      1. Meeting Children's Needs
      2. Meeting Teachers' Needs
      3. Meeting Parents' Needs
   B. Health and Safety in the Environment
      1. Keeping Children Healthy
      2. Keeping Children Safe
   C. How Program Goals Are Reflected in the Environment
      1. Self-Help Environments
      2. General Principles of Self-Help Environments

III. Creating the Environment
   A. The Physical Environment
      1. General Requirements
      2. Bathrooms
      3. Room to Rest
      4. Out of Doors
      5. Food Service
      6. Materials and Equipment
      7. Organizing Space
   B. The Temporal Environment
   C. The Interpersonal Environment

IV. Summary

V. Review Questions

VI. Learning Activities

VII. Bibliography

WHAT IS THE ENVIRONMENT?

What does it mean to create an environment appropriate for young children? What makes up the environment? The environment is the stage on which children play out the themes of childhood: their interests, triumphs, problems, and concerns. An environment for children, therefore, includes all of the conditions that affect their surroundings and the people in it.

Each environment is unique. There is no such thing as a model or ideal setting for children. Each school has goals that reflect the values of its own program. When the goals and the setting mesh, the individual atmosphere of the school is created.

But just what does *environment* mean? What do teachers mean when they say they want to create:

- environments for learning?
- optimal growth environments?
- positive learning environments?
- child-centered environments?
- favorable classroom environments?

The environment is the sum total of the physical and human qualities that combine to create a space in which children and adults work and play together. Environment is the *content* teachers arrange; it is an *atmosphere* they create; it is a *feeling* they communicate. Environment is the total picture—from the traffic flow to the daily schedule, from the numbers of chairs at a table to the placement of the guinea pig cage. It is a means to an end. The choices teachers make concerning the *physical* setting (the equipment and materials, the room arrangement, and the facilities available), the *temporal* setting (timing for transitions, routines, activities), and the *interpersonal* setting (number and nature of teachers, ages and numbers of children), combine to support the program goals. The environments teachers create, if successful, are safe, effective, challenging, and in concert with the theoretical framework of the early childhood program. Figure 9.2 illustrates this.

FIGURE 9.1 Each environment is unique.

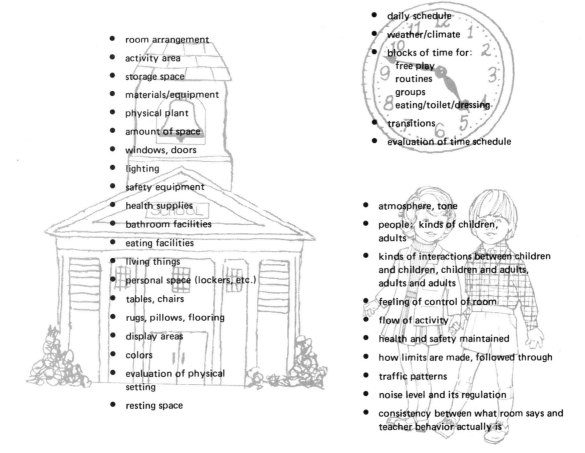

- room arrangement
- activity area
- storage space
- materials/equipment
- physical plant
- amount of space
- windows, doors
- lighting
- safety equipment
- health supplies
- bathroom facilities
- eating facilities
- living things
- personal space (lockers, etc.)
- tables, chairs
- rugs, pillows, flooring
- display areas
- colors
- evaluation of physical setting
- resting space

- daily schedule
- weather/climate
- blocks of time for:
  free play
  routines
  groups
  eating/toilet/dressing
- transitions
- evaluation of time schedule

- atmosphere, tone
- people: kinds of children, adults
- kinds of interactions between children and children, children and adults, adults and adults
- feeling of control of room
- flow of activity
- health and safety maintained
- how limits are made, followed through
- traffic patterns
- noise level and its regulation
- consistency between what room says and teacher behavior actually is

FIGURE 9.2 The environment is not only physical space and materials; it also includes aspects of time and interpersonal relationships.

GENERAL CONSIDERATIONS FOR PLANNING ENVIRONMENTS

Who Is in the Environment?

Many people live and work in the early childhood environment. Cooks, bus drivers, office personnel, yard and building maintenance people are but a few. Each of these persons has special demands on the environment in order to do the job they are hired to do.

Teachers, parents, and children have the greatest influence on the early childhood environment; their needs are outlined below.

Meeting Children's Needs

Children's needs are met through the environment. The physical, social, emotional, and intellectual requirements of children suggest the type of building, the size of the furniture, the choice of equipment, the size and age range of the group, the number of teachers who lead and supervise, and the budget allocations. Guided by child development principles, teachers match the setting to the children who will learn and play there. The individuality of a particular group of children, a school, and its philosophy is expressed by the arrangement of the environmental factors. First and foremost, though, is the question: Who are the children who will use this space? What are their needs?

How can those needs be met in this particular setting?

Routines. What is meant by a *routine?* Routines are the framework of programs for young children. A routine is a constant; each day, certain events are repeated, providing continuity and a sense of

Toileting Teaches Emotional Skills:
   Self-awareness: body functions, comparisons between boys and girls

   Self-identity: what girls/boys do

   Self-esteem: caring for one's own body

   Self-worth: through lack of guilt, fear, shame

   Human sexuality: in a natural setting, promotes healthy attitudes toward the body and its functions; that adults can be accepting, open, and reassuring about the body and its care

Eating Teaches Health:
   Introduction to new and different foods, good nutritional habits

Eating Teaches Social Skills:
   How to manage oneself in a group eating situation, focusing on eating *and* conversing; acceptable meal-time behavior and manners

Eating Teaches Small Motor Skills:
   Pouring; handling spoons, forks; serving self; drinking, eating without spilling

Eating Teaches Independence Skills:
   Serving self; making choices; sponging off the table

Eating Teaches Individual Differences:
   Likes/dislikes; choices of food; fast/slow pace of eating

Resting/Sleeping Teaches Health:
   Personal care skills; relaxation habits; internal balance and change of pace; alternating activity to allow body to rest

Resting/Sleeping Teaches Independence Skills:
   Preparing own rest place; selecting book/toy; clearing bed things after rest

FIGURE 9.3 Every routine can be used as a vehicle for meaningful learning within the environment.

order to the schedule. Routines are the pegs on which to hang the daily calendar. When should children eat? Sleep? Play? Be alone? Be together? These questions are answered by the placement of routines. The rest of the curriculum—art activities, field trips, woodworking—works around them. Routines in an early childhood environment setting include:

Self-care:	Group times
Eating	Task completion
Naps, sleeping	Making choices
Dressing	Transitions between activities
Toileting	Beginning and ending the day
	Room cleanup and yard restoration

Most routines are very personal and individual rituals in children's daily lives. Children bring to school a history firmly established around routines, one that is deeply embedded in their family and culture. Routines are reassuring to children, and they take pride in mastering them; they are also a highly emotional issue for some.

The self-care tasks—toileting, eating, sleeping, and dressing—can be difficult issues between adult and child, virtually from the moment of birth. Everyone can recall vivid memories associated with at least one routine. They seem to become battlegrounds on which children and adults often struggle. Many times this is where children choose to take their first stand on the road to independence.

The early childhood teacher must be able to deal with the issue of self-care routines in sensitive and understanding ways. Children adjust to routines when they are regularly scheduled in the daily program and when there are clear expectations.

Routines are an integral part of creating a good environment for children. All three environmental factors are influenced by routines:

1. *Physical:* Child-sized bathroom and eating facilities; storage of cots, blankets, and sleeping accessories; equipment for food storage and preparation.

2. *Temporal:* Amount of time in daily schedule for eating, resting, toileting, cleanup

3. *Interpersonal:* Attitudes toward body functions; willingness to plan for self-care tasks, expectations of staff, parents, and children.

As teachers plan for children's basic needs, they are aware of the learning potential of ordinary, everyday routines. Figure 9.3 illustrates what three particular routines teach the young child.

Meeting Teachers' Needs

What about the needs of the teachers who work in the setting? Do they have an office? A teachers' room? A place to hold conferences? Where do they keep their personal belongings—or the materials they bring to use at school? Do they have a place to park? All teachers need a room in which to create curriculum materials, or evaluate their programs, to review other educational materials, to meet with their peers. How well teachers are provided for helps to determine the atmosphere they will establish in their classrooms for children.

Meeting Parents' Needs

The needs of parents will differ, depending upon whom the program serves. Parents who drive

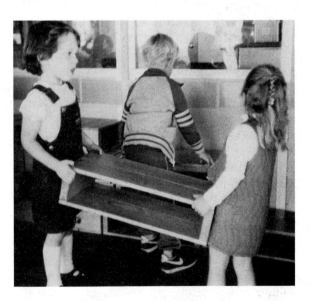

FIGURE 9.4 Cleanup is a routine part of the day.

their children to child care or school need adequate and safe parking facilities. In settings where parents are free to stay, a reading room, resource library, and a comfortable place to talk with other parents is desirable.

There are many reasons parents may need to contact the school or center. Are there ways for parents to reach teachers and children in emergencies? How welcoming is the environment to parents as they enter the building? The office? The classroom? What does the environment say about parent involvement and interest?

Health and Safety in the Environment

Regardless of how many children are in the setting and for how long, the first priority is to provide for their health and safety. Government regulations vary, but all establish some kind of standards to ensure good health and safety practices.

Keeping Children Healthy

Sanitation. When groups of people live in close quarters, proper sanitary conditions are imperative to prevent the spread of disease. For an early childhood center, the physical plant must have adequate washing and toileting facilities for both children and adults. The number and size of toilets and wash basins are usually prescribed by local health or other regulatory agencies. The classrooms require daily cleaning, and equipment that is used regularly should be sanitized on a periodic basis. Nontoxic paint must be used in all circumstances, including on outdoor equipment, cribs, and for art activities with children. Classroom dress-up clothing, pillows, nap blankets, and cuddle toys all need regular laundering, either at school or at home.

Temperature, Ventilation, and Lighting. Heating and ventilation should be comfortable for the activity level of the children and should change when weather conditions do. Adequate, nonglare lighting is a necessity. Rooms should have some means of controlling light (shades, blinds). Cross-

ventilation is necessary in all rooms where children eat, sleep, or play. Proper heating and insulation are important.

Nutrition. What children eat is also important for proper health. Places where food is prepared and stored must be kept especially clean. The child who has regular, nutritious meals and snacks will likely be healthier and less susceptible to disease. Many children do not have the benefits of healthy meals and snacks. Some do not receive adequate food at home; others are used to sugar-laden treats and "fast foods." Education about nutrition becomes the responsibility of a school that is concerned with children's health and physical development. The need

FIGURE 9.5 Good eating habits are established early in life. (Courtesy of Stride Rite Children's Centers, Cambridge, Mass.)

for educating parents regarding child nutrition exists in virtually all early childhood programs, regardless of social or economic status. Some centers establish food regulations in an attempt to ensure that nutritionally sound meals are served to children. Most schools attempt to provide a relaxed atmosphere at meal and snack time. Children are asked to sit and eat, sharing conversation as well as food. Since lifelong eating patterns are established early in life, teachers of young children have a responsibility to understand the critical role nutrition plays in the child's total development.

Communicable Disease. This is an important issue when dealing with young children in group care. Some people question the advisability of early group care on the grounds that it exposes children to too much illness. Others claim that such exposure at an early age helps children build up resistance and that they are actually stronger and healthier by the time they enter primary grades.

Parents should be notified when normal childhood diseases (such as chicken pox) or common problems (such as head lice) occur in the classroom. A description of the symptoms and the dates of exposure and incubation period may be helpful to parents. They can then assist the school in controlling the spread of the disease in question.

In group care, children can contract a fair number of colds and viruses, especially when they are eating and sleeping in close proximity. The school and its staff have a responsibility to ensure that good health standards are instituted and maintained to keep illness to a minimum.

Health Assessment and School Policies. Every early childhood center should establish clear health policies and make them known to parents. A daily inspection of each child will help adults spot nasal discharge, inflamed eyes, and throat and skin conditions of a questionable nature. This daily check will screen out more serious cases of children too ill to remain at school, and may be done by a teacher, nurse or administrator.

It is very important for the school to inform parents about what happens when children are refused admittance or become ill during the school day. Every school should provide a place for sick children where they can be isolated from others, kept under supervision, and be made comfortable until they are picked up. For their part, parents must arrange to have sick children cared for elsewhere if they are unable to take them home. School policies on these issues must be *explicit* and upheld consistently, for the sake of all the children.

Most schools require, under state or local laws, a doctor's examination and permission to participate in an early childhood education program before a child can enter the program. This includes a record of immunizations and the child's general health. Parents, too, should submit a history of the child, highlighting eating, sleeping, and elimination habits. It is critical to note any dietary restrictions or allergies and then post them in the classrooms for a reminder.

Clothing. The health and safety of children is affected by the clothing they wear. A simple way to

FIGURE 9.6 Clothing should allow children freedom to move.

be sure children stay healthy is to encourage them to dress properly for play and for varying weather conditions. Children need clothing in which they can be active—clothing that is not binding, and is easy to remove and easy to clean. Pants are a good choice for both boys and girls; long dresses can become a hazard when climbing, running, or going up and down stairs. The safest shoes for active play should have composition or rubber soles. Whenever possible, it helps to keep changes of clothes at school.

Health of the Staff. A responsible early childhood center is one that supports and maintains a healthy staff. Teachers should be in good physical and mental health to be at their best with children. It is wise to check the health regulations and benefits of the individual school when employed there. Many states require annual chest X rays as a condition of employment. Sick leave policies should be clearly stated in print.

Keeping Children Safe

Everything is planned with the children's safety in mind. Creating a hazard-free environment for children takes careful observation and attention to detail. A quick walk around the room and yard will reveal potential problems:

- Are there any sharp corners at children's height?
- Are rug edges snagged or loose?
- Are absorbent surfaces used wherever there is water? Are mops and towels available for spillage?
- Is hot water out of the reach of children?
- Are children allowed to run inside?
- Are there rules governing the children's use of scissors, hammers, and knives?
- Are safety rules explained to children and upheld by adults?
- Are electrical outlets covered when not in use?
- Do open stairwells have gates?
- Do adults monitor the use of extension cords and appliances?
- Is broken equipment removed promptly?
- Are fences high enough to protect and safe to touch?

FIGURE 9.7 Teachers create safe environments.

FIGURE 9.8 The handyman tests out his repairs.

- Are there areas where wheel toys can move freely without fear of collision?
- Are swings placed away from traffic areas and set apart by bushes or fences?
- Can a child's foot or ankle be caught on equipment; under a chain-link fence?
- Does traffic flow easily?
- Are the toys safe for children's use?

First Aid. Every school should establish procedures for dealing with children who are injured on the property. First aid instructions should be required of all teachers and made available as part of their in-service training. Teachers should know how to treat bumps and bruises, minor cuts and abrasions, bleeding, splinters, bites and stings, seizures, sprains, broken bones, and minor burns. Each classroom should be equipped with two first aid kits. One is for use in the classroom and yard, the other should be suitable for taking on field trips. The kit should be readily available to adults, but out of children's reach, and supplies should be replenished regularly.

Emergency numbers to be posted near the telepone in each room include those of the ambulance squad, fire department, police, health department, nearest hospital, and a consulting physician (if any). All families enrolled at the school should be aware of school policy regarding injuries at school and provide the school with emergency information for each child: the name of their physician, how to locate the parents, and who else might be responsible for the injured child if the parents cannot be reached. The school in turn must make sure they notify parents of any injuries the child has incurred during the school day.

Fire Safety. Most local fire regulations require that fire extinguishers be in working order and placed in all classrooms and the kitchen area. Fire exits, fire alarms, and fire escapes should be well marked and functioning properly. Children and teachers should participate in fire drills regularly and, in some areas of the country, earthquake and

tornado drills. These experiences can reinforce in parents the need for establishing similar procedures at home.

Automobile Safety. Automobile safety is a related concern when considering potential hazards for preschool children. The use of approved car seats and restraints for children riding in automobiles has received national attention in recent years. Some states have passed legislation requiring the use of specific devices to ensure safer travel for young children. Whether or not they walk to school, children should also be aware of basic rules for crossing streets. The school parking lot can be a source of danger unless the school articulates policies to parents regarding the safety needs of children. There are potential risks when cars and children occupy the same space. Children should not be left unattended in parking lots.

How Program Goals Are Reflected in the Environment

In creating an environment, teachers plan a program directed toward their goals:

1. They take care to arrange the daily schedule in ways that provide the time blocks needed to teach content when and how they want to teach it.

2. The room and yard are arranged to give maximum exposure to the materials and equipment they want children to use.

3. They see that a warm relationship exists among the teachers and in their interactions with children.

It is essential that teachers have a clear idea of their program goals before they begin to arrange the environment for children. When they invite children in to work, play, and learn, teachers must be sure that the way they have expressed goals through room arrangements, daily schedules, and personal styles, matches what they believe. Blending all the factors that create an environment for children uses the environment to its fullest and demonstrates a belief in how and what children need for learning to take place.

If a goal of the program is to have children practice cognitive skills by using puzzles, table games, prereading and writing materials, then the area where that is to take place should have an appropriate number of tables and chairs to accommodate all the children, and little room for larger motor activity. Larger amounts of time in the daily calendar should be made available for children to work on these activities and teachers should be involved to reinforce and encourage children as they play.

When children walk into a classroom, the environment should communicate how they are to live and work in that setting. Children should receive clear messages about what they can and cannot do there as well as cues that tell them:

- Where they are free to move to and where they cannot go.
- How they will be treated.
- Who will be there with them.
- What material and equipment they can use.
- How long they have to play.

- That they are safe there.
- What is expected of them.

Good environmental principles are not dependent upon numerous or expensive equipment, materials, or buildings. A creative child-centered environment can happen in any setting, regardless of the lack of financial resources. Some equipment can be made, borrowed, or purchased second-hand. In church-based schools, annual rummage sales at the church provide a wealth of dress-up clothes, books, toys, and some appliances. A few church organizations even assist with scholarship funds or by financing playground equipment.

The teacher is the key element in making a creative environment. It is not the facility itself that counts as much as the teacher's understanding of the use of all the environmental factors and how they relate to one another. A room is just a room and a yard is just a yard until a teacher makes them environments for learning. The teachers themselves are the most responsive part of the environment; it is they who converse, hug, appreciate, give information, and see the individuality of each child. They are the ones who create the space, the time, and the atmosphere that will engage children's curiosity and involvement. Figure 9.9 summarizes these environmental goals.

Children Need to	So the Environment Should
Have an opportunity to make choices and participate in independent learning.	Be arranged to encourage free exploration and a clear view of what is available. Offer a variety of activity centers so children can explore, manipulate, probe. Allow large blocks of time for free play so children can make more than one choice. Provide an adequate number of trained teachers to support self-discovery.
Be treated as individuals, with unique strengths and developmental goals.	Ensure that the teacher–child ratio supports one-to-one interactions. Provide private as well as public spaces so children can experience group and solitary play. Ensure that children have ready access to teachers and materials.

FIGURE 9.9 The environment mirrors the goals of the program.

	Be staffed by teachers who will set goals for each child based on observation and assessment. Be equipped with materials that will match the developmental level of the group.
Learn to be part of a group.	Be set up for group play with four to six chairs around the tables, easels adjacent to one another, more than one telephone, carriage, wagon. Facilitate regular scheduling of small and large group times, which children are expected to attend and participate in. Include trained staff who select appropriate group activities for the age range. Allow children to use each other as resources. Provide activities that will stress cooperation and social interaction.
Become responsible for the setting and take care of the equipment and materials.	Schedule cleanup times as part of the daily routine. Include teachers and children working together to restore order. Allow time for children to be instructed in the proper use of materials and be made aware of their general care.
Be aware of the behavioral limits of the school setting.	Ensure that the teachers and the daily schedule reflect the important rules of behavior. Include teachers who deal with behavior problems in a fair and consistent way. Allow plenty of time during transitions so that children can move from one activity to another without stress. Be arranged to avoid runways and dead ends created by furniture.
Be with adults who will supervise and facilitate play, and encourage learning throughout the day.	Be set up before children arrive so teachers are free to greet them. Encourage teacher–child interactions through the use of small groups, and a time schedule that allows for in-depth interactions.

FIGURE 9.9 Cont.

Self-Help Environments

There is one common goal in most early education programs which can be demonstrated through the careful use of environmental factors. Promoting *self-help* and independent behavior in children is a widespread practice. As they plan their environ-ments, teachers attempt to create situations and setting where this is likely to happen.

A self-help environment has as one of its fun-damental goals the development of children's own skills—fostering their mastery of basic abilities that will allow them to become responsible for their own personal care, their own learning, their own emotional controls, their own problem solving, and their own choices and decisions. A self-help environment tries to give children the feeling that they are capable, competent, and successful. It allows children to do for themselves, to meet the challenge of growing up. A self-help environment reflects the belief that autonomy and independence are the birthright of every child.

Nothing renders people more helpless than not being able to maintain their own needs or to take care of themselves in basic ways. Children are still in the process of learning about what they can and cannot do. They need many different kinds of experiences to help them learn the extent of their capabilities. Most of all, they need adults who understand their tremendous drive to become self-reliant, adults who will not only encourage their abilities and provide the time for them to practice skills, but adults who understand that it is the nature of the child to develop this way.

Self-concepts are based on what we know about ourselves, which includes the ability to take care of one's own needs. To care for oneself, to feel capable of learning, to solve problems, are all related to feelings of *self-esteem*. Self-esteem is the value we place upon ourselves; how much we like or dislike who we are. Helping children achieve positive self-concepts and self-esteem is the most important part of teaching. The development of a strong sense of self-esteem is a lifelong process; its origins are in the early years.

For all of these reasons, teachers establish settings that promote self-help. They want children to feel good about themselves and they want to foster that growing sense of self-esteem. This happens in classrooms which allow children to do what they are capable of doing. For the teacher, the reward comes from each child who says, "I can do it by myself."

Planning an environment designed to promote self-help skills is the teachers' responsibility. Every aspect of the environment, from the room arrangement to the attitudes of the teachers, supports children in doing all they can for themselves. Each

FIGURE 9.10 Through self-help environments, children become independent.

FIGURE 9.11 "I can do this by myself."

activity is designed to foster self-reliance, thereby building self-esteem. It takes preparation and thought to produce space that says to children, "Do me. Master me. You are capable." Teachers want to communicate to children that they value self-help skills as much as they appreciate an art project or science experiment. The ultimate goal is for children to see self-reliance as valuable. If Claudia feels that learning to tie her shoes is worth doing just because of the pleasure it gives her to manipulate the strings, weave them through the holes, and bring them together in a knot, then that becomes her reward. She becomes capable of reinforcing herself and leaves the way open for adults to praise her for other important learnings.

General Principles of Self-Help Environments

- *Give children ways to identify their own space.* Label their cubbies with their names, a photo, or a familiar picture so that they can see where to put up their wraps, artwork, and other personal belongings.

FIGURE 9.12 "That's my cubby."

- *Give children an opportunity to make choices.* Both indoors and out, children should be given an abundance of materials and a range of activities from which to choose so that they will decide how they spend their time. Choosing to play with the hamster rather than in the block corner helps children practice self-direction. Children should also be able to decide with whom they would like to play and with which teachers they would like to establish close relationships.

- *See that children are responsible for caring for the equipment and materials.* Establish a cleanup time in the daily schedule and allow children time to help restore the room and yard. Label shelves and cupboards with pictures or symbols of what is stored there so that children can readily find where things belong. Outlining block cabinets with the specific shape of the blocks that are stored on each shelf will encourage children's self-help skills. Outdoor areas, clearly marked for wheel toys, help children function independently. A drying rack with large clothespins that is accessible to children tells children that they are expected to care for their own artwork.

- *Provide children with enough time.* One of the ways children learn is to repeat an activity over and over again. They explore, manipulate, experiment, and come to master an 18-piece puzzle, a lump of clay, or how to brush their teeth. Large blocks of time in the daily schedule—especially for routines—let children proceed to learn at an unhurried pace.

- *Allow children to solve their own problems without adult interference whenever possible.* See how far a child can go in discovering how to manipulate a pin so that it will close, or work out with another child who will use the red paint first. In solving social or mechanical problems, young children can begin to find out for themselves what is or is not successful. One mark of a good teacher is a person who can let a child struggle sufficiently with a problem before stepping in to help.

- *Accept children's efforts.* To support children in their quest for independence, the adult must be

FIGURE 9.13 Allow children to do as much for themselves as possible.

satisfied with children's efforts, and be ready to accept the way Tom made his sandwich or Shelley's boots on the wrong feet.

- *Communicate expectations.* Let children know what they are expected to do. Tell them in both verbal and nonverbal ways. "You don't have to hurry; we have plenty of time for cleanup" lets children know they can do a job without pressure. Prompt children by giving them clues that indicate how to proceed: "If you pull up your under-

pants first, it will be easier to get your trousers up," can be said to Raymond who is waiting for an adult to dress him. Give him feedback on what is working. "Good. You've got the back up. Now reach around the front." Focus on how Raymond is succeeding and communicate your confidence in his ability to finish the task.

- *Be sure staff expectations are consistent.* The teaching team should set common goals for each child and reinforce them consistently. Janice will become confused if one teacher tells her to get her cot ready for nap and another teacher does it for her.

- *Consider the developmental level of the child.* Recognize that there are many things young children will not be able to do for themselves, but allow them the chance to do all they can. Be developmentally aware—know what children in the class are capable of, where they are now in their development, and what the next step should be. Perhaps two-year-old Sophie can zip her jacket now. Soon she will be able to put the zipper in the housing by herself. Recognize her readiness for taking the next step.

- *Make it safe to make a mistake.* Children learn from their own actions and their own experiences. Let them know it is perfectly acceptable, indeed inevitable, that they will at times make mistakes. Children need to be accepted for who and what they are, and this includes when they are in error. Help them deal with the consequences of their mistakes. Adults in the preschool can provide models for children in coping with unexpected results and how to bring forth a positive resolution. When Chelo spills her juice, she is encouraged to find a sponge and clean up the table. The teacher reinforces Chelo's efforts and comments on her scrubbing ability or her swift action in preventing the juice from going on the floor.

- *Give credit where it is due.* Provide feedback so that children will know when they have been successful. Compliment Chaz on the length of time he took sorting through the nails to find the one he wanted. Tell Ellen she worked hard at opening

FIGURE 9.14 Children feel successful when they are able to help themselves.

her own thermos bottle. Let children take some credit for their own accomplishments.

- *Be sure children have access to enough toys and materials.* Show children respect by giving them the option to take care of themselves. Make sure that supplies are stored in such a way that adults do not have to hand them to children each time they will be used. Equipment placed at a child's height on open, low shelving permits children to proceed at their own pace and select materials without depending upon adults to serve them.

- *Let children teach one another.* Encourage children to share the skills they have mastered with their peers. Those who can tie shoes enjoy helping their friends with stubborn laces or slippery knots. Whether reading or telling stories to one another, or showing a friend a fast way to put on a jacket, children benefit from helping each other.

Adults who work with children should remember to interact with children in ways that will help them grow toward independence. To perceive children as helpless is to rob them of the satisfaction of achievement. A well-planned environment opens up infinite possibilities for children to achieve a feeling of self-satisfaction while they explore the boundaries of their own beings.

FIGURE 9.15 Help yourself!

CREATING THE ENVIRONMENT

The Physical Environment

Every school setting is organized fundamentally around physical space. This means teachers work with the size and limitations of the facility, both inside and out-of-doors. The building itself may be new and designed specifically for young children. More than likely, it is a converted house or store, a church basement, a parish hall, or an elementary classroom. Sometimes a program will share space with another group so that mobile furniture is moved daily or weekly. There may be a large yard or none at all. Some playgrounds are on the roof of the building, or a park across the street may serve as the only available play space.

Restraints also come in the form of weather conditions. Outside play—and therefore large-muscle equipment—may be unavailable during the winter months. This may suggest that a room for active, vigorous play is needed inside during that time. Hot summer months can make some types of play difficult if there is little or no shade outdoors. Weather conditions must be taken into consideration when planning programs for children.

Early childhood programs have specific needs that must be met by the buildings they occupy. Although the choice of building is generally deter-

FIGURE 9.16 The early childhood playground is found in many environments. (Courtesy of Stride Rite Children's Centers, Cambridge, Mass.)

mined by what is available, at a minimum the setting should provide facilities for:

playing/working	food preparation
eating	storage
washing/toileting	office
sleeping/resting	clothing and wraps

Ideally, the setting should have enough rooms to house these various activities separately. In practice, however, rooms are multipurpose and more than one event takes place in the same space. A play room doubles as an eating area, since both require the use of tables and chairs. When a school room serves many functions (playing, eating, sleeping), convenient and adequate storage space is a necessity. The amount of teacher time needed to prepare the room for each change of activity is worth consideration when planning the daily schedule.

General Requirements

Ground floor classrooms are preferable for young children to ensure that they can enter and leave with relative ease and safety. For noise reduction, the walls and ceilings should be soundproofed. Carpeting, draperies, and other fireproof fabrics in the room will help absorb sound. Floors must be durable, sanitary, and easily cleaned. They should be free from drafts. Rugs should be vacuumed each day. Room size should be sufficient to allow for freedom of movement and the opportunity to play without interference. Some licensing agencies may suggest minimum room and yard size standards.

Many local and state agencies have regulations regarding the use of space for children in group care settings. The fire marshall, health department, and similar agencies must be consulted and their regulations observed. It is wise to consider their requirement when arranging space.

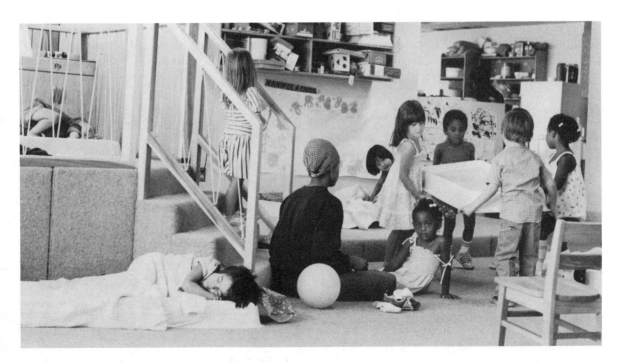

FIGURE 9.17 The classroom serves many functions. (Courtesy of Stride Rite Children's Centers, Cambridge, Mass.)

Bathrooms

These should be adjacent to the play and sleeping areas and easily reached from outdoors. Child-sized toilets and wash basins are preferable, but if unavailable, a step or platform may be built. In most early childhood settings, the bathrooms are without doors, for ease of supervision. Toileting facilities for children should be light, airy, attractive, and large enough to serve several children at a time. An exhaust fan is desirable. Paper towel holders should be at child height and waste baskets placed nearby.

Room to Rest

Schools that provide nap and sleeping facilities require adequate storage space for cots and bedding. Movable screens set up throughout the classroom allow for privacy and help reduce the noise level.

Out of Doors

A wide porch or covered patio is ideal for rainy days or days when the sun is too severe. Many activities can be extended to the outside area with this type of protection. The physical plant should include adequate playground space adjacent to the building. A variety of playground surfaces makes for more interesting play and provides suitable cov-

ering for outdoor activities. Tanbark can be used in the swing area, cement for wheel toys, and grass for under climbers. Sand is used for play, but can also cushion falls from climbing equipment. No matter what the surface, the yard should be constructed with a good drainage system. Trees, bushes, and other plantings will allow for both sunshine and shade. Fences are *mandatory*. They must be durable, an appropriate height, with no opportunity for a child to gain a foothold.

Food Service

All schools for young children serve some sort of refreshment during the daily session. In an infant program, formula and milk storage is a necessity. Whether involved in a light snack or full meal program, the center must adhere to the most rigid standards of health protection and safety provisions. Every precaution must be taken to ensure maximum hygienic food service. Daily cleaning of equipment, counters, floors, and appliances is a necessity.

Materials and Equipment

Selection of materials and equipment is based on a number of criteria. Out of necessity, most school budgets limit the amount of dollars available

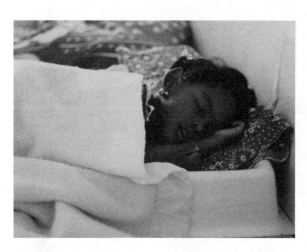

FIGURE 9.18 Time to rest. (Courtesy of Stride Rite Children's Centers, Cambridge, Mass.)

FIGURE 9.19 Snacks are a favorite part of the day.

for such purchases. To make every dollar count, teachers select materials that:

- Reflect the age-level characteristics of the group.
- Relate to the school's philosophy and curriculum.
- Reflect quality design and workmanship.
- Are durable.
- Offer flexibility and versatility in their uses.
- Have safety features (for instance, nontoxic paints, rounded corners).
- Are attractive and appealing to children.
- Are easy to maintain and repair.
- Reflect the cultural makeup of the group.
- Are nonsexist and nonstereotypical.

Materials should be appropriate for a wide range of skills since children within the same age group develop at individual rates. Many of the materials can be *"open-ended,"* that is, they can be used in their most basic form or they can be developed in a variety of ways. Unit blocks, clay, and Lego® are examples of materials that children can use in a simple fashion; as skills develop these materials can be manipulated in a more complex manner.

Children are active learners, and their materials should provide them with ways to explore, manipulate, and become involved. Teachers encourage the use of fine and gross motor skills by providing equipment that involves their use. Children learn through all their senses, so the materials should be appealing to many of the senses.

Organizing Space

There are many different ways to arrange and organize the living space in an early childhood setting; the final result expresses the diversity of the program. Most early childhood centers are arranged by *interest areas,* *learning centers,* or *activity areas.* These will most likely include:

Indoors	*Outdoors*
Blocks	Sand
Manipulatives/table toys	Water play/sensory play
Art	Woodworking
Science	Wheel toys
Music	Climbers
Math	Swings
Dramatic play	Ball games
Books/language/listening center	Art
Water play/sensory play	Science/nature
Housekeeping	Dramatic play

The room arrangement and the choice of activity centers show what is being emphasized in the program. The amount of space devoted to any one activity says a great deal about its value to the staff. A housekeeping area with plenty of space encourages active use by a number of children. Social play is promoted when two or more items are available. Four telephones, three doll buggies, or two easels can be tools for social interaction.

Some activities are noisier than others, so the placement of the interest centers is important. Balance the number of noisy and quiet activities, both indoors and out. Quieter activities, such as puzzles, language games, story telling, take place in areas away from blocks, water play, or dramatic play, since the last three tend to kindle animated, active, and sometimes noisy behavior.

FIGURE 9.20 Duplicate equipment encourages social interaction.

When arranging environments, there must be enough play spaces for the number of children in the group. Kritchevsky and Prescott (1969) analyzed the number of play opportunities in school settings, both indoors and out. Areas and activities were assigned a value.

- A simple area (swings, climbers) counts as one play space.
- A complex area (housekeeping/dramatic play) counts as four play spaces.
- A super area (sand and water play combined) counts as eight play spaces.

The value assigned to the three areas generally coincides with the number of children who might be accommodated in that space. When the total is figured, it is matched against the actual number of children in the group to see if there is a place for everyone to play.

Adult needs are also met through proper organization of classroom and yard. Are there barriers that prevent teachers from supervising the entire classroom? Are the teachers on the staff deployed evenly throughout all the space? Can all areas be supervised? Is the storage integrated so that equipment is always located near the place where it will be used?

Clearly defined boundaries and obvious pathways make it easy for children to live and work in the space. There should be enough space for larger groups to gather together as well as small groups.

A good environment for children reflects the teachers' knowledge of how children play, what skills they possess, what they know, and what they need to learn. The settings are arranged to promote those aspects of child growth and development.

The Temporal Environment

The daily schedule defines the structure of each program. It creates the format for how children will experience the events of the day—in what order and for what length of time.

No two schedules are alike, since each reflects the program it represents. The amount of time devoted to specific activities communicates clearly what value the school places on them. The amount of time given to certain aspects of the curriculum, the variety of events, and the flexibility tell children and adults what is important in this particular setting.

In developing a schedule by which to function on a daily basis, teachers first decide what is important for children to learn, how that learning should take place, and how much time to allow in the daily program. If small-group work and individual attention are program goals, enough time will have to be set aside to ensure its success. More time is needed to allow children a number of curriculum choices than if they only had one or two activities from which to select. Three-year-olds need more time for toileting activities than do five-year-olds, who are considerably more self-sufficient.

The physical plant itself may dictate a portion of the daily schedule. If toilet facilities are not located adjacent to the classroom, then more time must be scheduled to travel to and from the bathrooms. If the building or space is shared with other groups, some portion of the program may be modified. Many schools housed in church buildings schedule field trips during the annual church rummage sale in order to free up the space for the church's use.

The daily schedule is important for everyone in the setting. When the time sequence is clear to all, then everyone can go about the business of learning and teaching. Children are more secure in a place that has a consistent schedule; they can begin to anticipate the regularity of what comes next and count on it. In that way they are then free to move, explore, and learn without hesitation. Children can freely involve themselves without fear of being interrupted. Adults, too, enjoy the predictability of a daily schedule. By knowing the sequence of events, they are then free to flex the timing when unforeseen circumstances arise.

There are common elements in all schedules, whether they are designed for toddler groups or

Toddler Program

9:00-9:30 Greet Children
Inside Activities
- playdough and art/easel
- housekeeping
- blocks and manipulatives
- books

9:40 "Time to Put Our Toys Away" song
- all participating in cleanup

9:45-10:20 Outdoor Play
- large motor
- social play

10:20 Music/movement outdoors

10:30 Snack/"Here We Are Together" song
- washing hands
- eating/pouring/cleanup

10:45-11:15 Outside

11:20 Closure
- parent-child together
- story or flannelboard

Kindergarten Plan

8:15-8:30 Arrival:
Getting ready to start
- checking in library books, lunch money, etc.

8:30 Newstelling
- "anything you want to tell for news"
- newsletter written weekly

9:00 Work assignment
- write a story about your news *or*
- make a page in your book (topic assigned)

9:30-10:00 Choice of indoors (paints, blocks, computer, table toys) *or*
second grade tutors read books to children

10:00 Recess

10:30 Language: phonics lesson *or* chapter in novel read

11:00 Dance *or* game *or* visitor and snack

11:50 Closure

12:00-1:30 for part of group each day:
Lunch, then:
- field trips
- writing lesson
- math or science lab

Day Care Program for Preschoolers

7:00 Arrival, breakfast

8:00 Inside free play
- arts/easels
- table toys/games/blocks
- dramatic play center: house, grocery store, etc.

9:30 Cleanup

9:40 Group time: Songs/fingerplays and small-group choices

9:40 Choice Time/small groups
- math lab
- cooking for morning or afternoon snack
- language art/prereading choice

10:30 Snack

10:45 Outside free play
- climbing, swinging; sand and water, wheel toys, group games

12:00 Handwash and lunch

12:45 Get ready: toileting, handwashing, toothbrushing, prepare beds

1:15 Bedtime story

1:30 Naptime for the whole group

2:30 Outdoors for those awake

3:30 Cleanup outdoors and singing time

4:00 Snacktime

4:15 Free play: some outdoor/indoor choices, fieldtrips, story teller

5:30 Cleanup and read books until going home

FIGURE 9.21 Daily schedules reflect the children's needs and ages while meeting the program's goals.

five-year-olds, all-day programs or half-day nurseries. Sound child development principles provide the framework on which the daily schedule is structured. The individual schools then adapt these requirements to their own philosophy as they work out their individual daily schedule. All schedules must:

- Include time for routines (to eat, rest, wash, toilet) as well as time for *transitions* (what happens when there is a change from one activity to another).
- Alternate quiet and active play and work to help children pace themselves.
- Provide opportunities for both inside and outside play.
- Allow children to participate in structured activities as well as those of their own choosing.
- Make it possible for children to work individually, in small groups, or in larger ones.
- Gear the time to the age and developmental levels of the group.
- Provide for flexibility so that children's interests can be maintained and emergencies met.
- Have a beginning and an end. Some provisions must be made for children to be met and greeted when they enter. The day is brought to closure with a review of the day's activities and anticipation of what will come tomorrow. Allow time for dismissal.
- Include time for cleanup and room restoration.
- Incorporate the teachers' roles and assignments so that they will know their area of responsibility.
- Be posted in an obvious place in the classroom for all to see.

The Interpersonal Environment

A child responds to everything in school: the color of the room, the way the furniture is arranged, how much time there is to play, and how people treat one another. To the child, everything is a stimulus. The *feeling* in a room is as real as the blocks or the books. Thus, the interpersonal or social aspects of an early childhood setting are powerful components of the environment.

Children are the most important people in the setting; they should feel safe and comfortable. A warm, interpersonal environment invites children to participate and to learn. When children feel secure with one another and with the setting, they will be able to engage more fully in the total program.

Parents are an important part of school, especially in the early years. The interpersonal connection between parent and teacher can bolster what happens to the child within the classroom and can offer the child a smooth transition between school and home. Learning is enhanced when parents and teachers come to communicate in supportive, nonthreatening ways.

Teachers are the most critical element in creating environments with positive interpersonal goals. What teachers do—and how they do it—determines the learning that takes place in the class. The attitudes and behaviors of teachers affect children's behaviors. Questions teachers can ask themselves as they evaluate the quality of the environment are:

- Is there a feeling of mutual respect between children and adults?
- How do children treat one another?
- Do teachers model cooperative behavior with other adults and children? Do they show by example how to work through a disagreement or problem?
- Does the physical setup allow the teacher to focus on the children?
- Do housekeeping details keep teachers disconnected from children?
- Do teachers encourage children to use one another as resources?
- Do teachers take time to show children how to accomplish a task by themselves?
- Do teachers use reasoning and follow-through?
- How and when do teachers interact with children?

- What is the teacher's posture and facial expression when involved in a problem situation?
- If I were a child, would I like to come to school here?

The answers to these questions provide teachers with a barometer of how well they are maintaining an atmosphere of positive social interaction. The most important thing to remember is that the way people feel about each other and how they express it has an impact on children. Teachers must focus as much attention on the interpersonal part of the environment as they do on buying equipment or arranging the room.

SUMMARY

A good environment for young children is a combination of many factors. Teachers must take into consideration the needs of the children, teachers, and parents as well as the program goals and objectives.

The physical environment includes the buildings and yard, the equipment and materials, and the way the space is organized and used. The setting is organized to support the program's goals and must meet necessary health and safety standards.

The daily schedule outlines the timetable of events. Time blocks are arranged around the daily routines of food, rest, and toileting. The temporal environment is balanced so that children alternate indoor and outdoor play, quiet and active play, and self-selected activities with teacher-directed learning. It is the interpersonal relationships that set the tone in each environment. The size of the group, the number of teachers per child, and the quality of relationships affect the interpersonal environment.

It is essential to have a clear idea of program goals before arranging the environment. The environment mirrors those goals in the way the room is arranged, teachers are deployed, and the time schedule is framed. In early childhood settings where children's independence and self-reliance is valued, the environment is created to enhance the child's budding sense of autonomy. Self-help environments reflect the goals through careful application of the environmental factors.

Creating good environments for young children does not require great sums of money or newly designed buildings. In most settings, teachers can adapt general principles of environments to create challenging, safe, and effective group settings for children.

Review Questions

1. Why is there no standard or ideal environment for early childhood schools?

2. What are the three different types of environments?

3. Why is self-help a common goal in most early childhood settings?

4. Discuss three school health and safety policies that help keep illness and injury to a minimum.

5. What messages should the total environment communicate to children?

6. How do routines affect the daily schedule?

Learning Activities

1. Hunch down on your knees and look at an early childhood classroom from the child's perspective. Describe what you see in terms of the principles of a self-help environment as described on pages 209 to 211.

2. Examine a daily schedule from an early childhood center. What do you think are the program goals of the school? How can you tell? Compare this to a daily schedule of a family day care home. How are they alike? How are they different?

3. Below are listed some common problems that can be remedied by changing the environment.

List at least one solution for each problem.
a. Too many children crowding into one area
b. Overcrowded shelves
c. Arguments over the same toy
d. Hoarding of materials
e. Lack of cooperation during cleanup
f. Wheel toy collisions

4. Visit a toddler program, a four-year-old program, and a kindergarten. How are the learning centers defined? Name the centers of interest and indicate which of them are for quiet play and which are for active play and work.

Bibliography

Cherry, Clare; Harkness, Barbara; and Kuzma, Kay. *Nursery School Management Guide.* Belmont, Calif.: Fearon Publishers, 1973.

Criteria for Selecting Play Equipment for Early Childhood Education. Rifton, N.Y.: Community Playthings, 1981.

Found Spaces and Equipment for Children's Centers. New York: Educational Facilities Laboratory, Inc., 1971.

Harms, Thelma. "Evaluating Settings for Learning." In Baker, Katherine Read (ed.), *Ideas That Work with Young Children.* Washington, D.C.: National Association for the Education of Young Children, 1972.

Harms, Thelma, and Clifford, Richard M. *Early Childhood Environment Rating Scale.* New York: Teachers College Press, 1980.

Kritchevsky, Sybil, and Prescott, Elizabeth. *Planning Environments for Young Children—Physical Space.* Washington, D.C.: National Association for the Education of Young Children, 1969.

Mattick, Ilse, and Perkins, Frances J. *Guidelines for Observation and Assessment: An Approach to Evaluating the Learning Environment of a Day Care Center.* Washington, D.C.: The Day Care and Child Development Council of America, 1972.

Osmon, Fred Linn. *Patterns for Designing Children's Centers.* New York: Educational Facilities Laboratory, Inc., 1971.

Sunderlin, Sylvia, *Equipment and Supplies.* Washington, D.C.: Association for Childhood Education International, Bulletin #39, 1967.

10

Evaluating for Effectiveness

Questions for Thought

- What is evaluation?
- Why is evaluation important?
- What are the components of good evaluations?
- What are the areas of concern when using evaluations?

- Who is evaluated in the early childhood setting?
- How does evaluating children, teacher, and program increase effectiveness in the early childhood setting?

Outline

INTRODUCTION

Evaluations are a part of everyday life. We look out the window and assess the weather situation, then decide if we want to carry an umbrella. Before making a purchase, we read the label on the box of crackers. We size up a person we have just met. We check the newspapers to find out where our favorite football team is ranked.

We are constantly evaluating, judging, and rating. In education, we evaluate:

- *Curriculum.* Will this language game help develop the listening skills of three-year-olds?

- *Materials and equipment.* If we order the terrarium, will there be enough money for the math lab?

- *Organizing the classroom.* Should the children begin school with free play or a group time? Where can we store the nap cots? Do the cubbies create a hazard out in the hallway?

- *Behavior management.* Evan and Francie interrupt each other too much. Perhaps they should be placed in separate work groups.

- *Teacher effectiveness.* Sandra has a knack for making parents comfortable in her classroom. Audrey finds leading large groups difficult. Karl supervises student teachers with great skill.

What Is Evaluation?

Definition

Evaluation is a process. It is at once a definition, an assessment, and a plan. Defining the kind

FIGURE 10.1 Evaluations are a part of everyday life in an early childhood setting. Can these children handle animals safely? How will having a pet chicken affect the program?

of weather outside helps a person evaluate what to wear. Assessing a person's manner and style determines whether or not to talk with that person at a party. Planning a meal involves evaluating who will be eating and what their food preferences may be. Evaluation involves making decisions, choices, and selections.

In educational circles, evaluations involve materials, people, and processes. Programs may be evaluated by taking an inventory of a school's curriculum and educational materials. Classroom organization may require mapping the environment, counting the number of play spaces in a room or yard, and evaluating the daily schedule. Observing and recording children's behavior could effectively evaluate behavior management techniques. Assessing teacher effectiveness requires gathering information about what teachers do and how they work. Feedback about performance is based on specific information concerning teacher behavior. Program evaluation might involve analyzing children, teachers, parents, and administration, and how they all work together to meet the goals of the program.

Premises

All evaluation procedures are based on three important premises:

1. *Evaluation must be part of the goal-setting process.* Without evaluation, goals are meaningless. Evaluation helps shape a goal into a meaningful plan of action. For instance, a family who wants to go weekend camping will have to decide what they need in order to pack their suitcases. In the classroom, teachers decide what they want their children to learn before ordering equipment for the program.

2. *Goals are based on expectations.* Everyone has standards for themselves and others. Standards are used to anticipate performance and behavior. Should the office buy a block of tickets to the upcoming football game? Many people would consider the team ranking and likelihood of a victory before making the decision. Teachers think about how two-year-olds will use Tin-

kertoys® or what use the four-year-olds will make of wheel toys before purchasing equipment.

In every early childhood setting, more than one set of expectations is at work. The director has job expectations of all the teachers. Teachers have standards of performance for themselves, the children, and parents. Parents have some expectations about what their children will do in school and about the role of the teachers. Children develop expectations regarding themselves, their parents, teachers, and the school.

3. *Evaluations determine the degree to which expectations are met.* By evaluating, people check to see if their goals have been realized. This can be as simple as listening for the doorbell after hearing a car stop outside. It can be as complex as analyzing questionnaires for parents. A good evaluation tool outlines clearly and specifically how expectations have been met. Evaluation is a system of mutual accountability. It is a way of stating expectations and defining how they are being met.

Why Evaluate?

In early childhood education, evaluations are used for several reasons. Teachers are aware that *evaluation* and *education* must be linked when creating good programs for children. To evaluate is to test the quality of the educational endeavor. Evaluation of children, teachers, and programs monitors growth, progress, and planning.

Evaluation is a way to look at where and how improvements can be made; to challenge methods, assumptions, and purposes. Teachers and children are rated for their level of development and areas of growth. Environments are assessed to see if they foster behavior and learning according to their stated goals. Total programs are evaluated to see if they accomplish their objectives. In fact, evaluations provide information by which to rate performance, define areas of difficulty, and look for possible solutions.

Setting goals is a third reason for evaluating. In order to be useful, an evaluation must include suggestions for improving the performance or behavior. The assessment tool that only describes a situation is an unfinished evaluation; goals for improvement must be established.

Components of a Good Evaluation

Certain elements are common to all evaluations. The following criteria serve as a guideline to good evaluations:

1. *Select who or what will be evaluated.* Decide how often and under what circumstances the evaluation will take place.

2. *Have a clear purpose or motive.* Know the reasons you are making an evaluation and consider who or what will benefit from the process. State what you expect to gain from it.

3. *Decide how the data will be collected.* Have a good understanding of the process or format that will be used. For a report, discover what tools you might need and what is available to you. Outline who will collect the data and make the report. If more than one person is reporting, check for consistency among the evaluators.

4. *Know what use will be made of the evaluation.* Be aware of what decisions will be made from the results. Know who receives this information and how they will interpret it.

5. *State goals clearly.* Make sure goals and objectives are outlined in ways that can be measured and observed easily. State behavioral goals in terms of what the person will *do.*

6. *Make a plan.* Be prepared to act. Use the results to motivate people to put into action what they learned from the evaluation. Set new goals. Continue the process for another stated period of time. Set up a timetable to check progress on a regular basis.

Evaluations are deliberate and systematic ways to judge effectiveness. Since they are based on goals

FIGURE 10.2 Some evaluations take into consideration children's use of materials. (Courtesy of Stephanie Barry Agnew)

and expectations, all evaluations need some kind of *feedback loop* to recycle what is perceived (Steps 1–4) into action for improvement (Steps 5 and 6). The important point to remember is that evaluation should be an ongoing process, clearly outlined and established on a regular basis.

Cautions

A number of concerns have been voiced about assessment procedures. Anyone involved in evaluation should avoid:

1. *Unfair comparisons.* Evaluations should be used to identify and understand the person or program

involved, not to compare one to another in a competitive manner.

2. *Typecasting.* Evaluations can label unfairly or prematurely the very people they are intended to help. Insufficient data and overemphasis on the results are two areas that need close monitoring.

3. *Overemphasis on norms.* Most evaluation tools imply some level of normal behavior or performance, acceptable levels of interaction, or quantities of materials and space. People involved in an evaluation must remember to individualize the process, rather than try to fit a person or program into the mold created by the assessment tool.

4. *Interpretation.* There is sometimes a tendency to overinterpret or misinterpret results. Whether the evaluation assesses a child's skill, a teacher's performance, or an educational program, it must be clear *what* is being evaluated and *how* the information will be used.

5. *Too narrow a perspective.* An evaluation tool may focus too much on one area and not enough on others. An imbalanced assessment gives an incomplete picture.

6. *Too wide a range.* An evaluation should be designed for a single level or age group and not cover too wide a range. It is appropriate to measure a child's ability to print at age six but not at age two. A teacher's aide should not be evaluated with the same method used to rate head or supervising teachers. The expectations of the person or task should be taken into account and the evaluation method modified accordingly.

7. *Too little or too much time.* The amount of time necessary to complete an evaluation must be weighed. The evaluation that is too lengthy loses its effectiveness in the time it takes. Time for interpretation and reflection must be included in the overall process.

For evaluations to be most productive, teachers must use caution in selecting an assessment method.

Often, they will rework a common technique to meet their needs better. For instance, a testing tool could be used to describe children's skills, but the averages that accompany the test could be discarded. In this way, teachers would avoid overemphasizing norms (Caution 3), making unfair comparisons (Caution 1) or typecasting the children according to the results (Caution 2).

Sometimes a staff or administrator will design an instrument, rather than using one already devised. Individualizing the evaluation process can thus balance an assessment, giving a perspective that is more in tune with the individual or program in a particular setting (Caution 5). Periodic evaluation checks give more than one set of results, so that early childhood personnel are less likely to misinterpret or overemphasize the data (Caution 4). A comprehensive evaluation done semiannually is more time efficient than a lengthy, detailed one done only once every year or so (Caution 7). In all evaluations, it is important to keep in mind that

FIGURE 10.3 Evaluations in programs with a wide age range may need to be individualized to adequately record children's skills.

children and teachers are at various stages of development and skill; an assessment that is individualized or one in which a range of scores is acceptable allows for these variations (Caution 6).

Evaluations in the Early Childhood Setting

In the educational setting, the process of evaluation is separate from the teaching or instructing process (Spodek, 1978). Judging an activity, a child's growth, or a teacher's performance is something "extra," apart from the everyday routine of the class. But evaluation is also related to teaching since it is a way of rating how effective are the teaching methods. Teaching and evaluating are closely integrated. As teachers examine how they work, they look at the effect this has on the children, the curriculum, the program, and themselves. Evaluating is a tool for improvement as well as a method of seeing what works well.

The teacher plays a critical role in the evaluation process. Through evaluation, teachers link specific goals to larger, more encompassing objectives, such as those illustrated in Figure 10.4.

These goals focus on the relationship between teaching in the classroom and the overriding educational objectives. The teacher sees the broad picture and keeps a perspective on education that includes the children, the program, and the teaching staff. The three areas of evaluations we will discuss in this chapter are: (1) evaluating children; (2) evaluating teachers; and (3) evaluating programs. The purposes underlying each type of evaluation will be examined, followed by specific techniques for effective evaluations.

EVALUATING CHILDREN

How do we evaluate children? What do we look for? How do we document growth and difficulties? How do we communicate our findings to parents? These questions focus our attention on children's issues and the evaluation process.

Why Evaluate?

Children are evaluated because teachers and parents want to know what the children are learning. The process of evaluating children attempts to answer several questions: Are children gaining appropriate skills and behaviors? In what activities does learning take place? What part of the program supports specific learning? Is the school philosophy being met? Are educational goals being met?

In evaluating children, teachers first decide what it is they want to know about each child, and why. With an understanding of children in general, teachers then concentrate on individual children and their unique development. Goals for children stem from program objectives. For instance, if the school philosophy is, "Our program is designed to help children grow toward increasing physical, so-

Educational Aims	Behavioral Goals
To achieve independence and autonomy.	Children separate from their parents successfully; can manage their own clothing needs; initiate own activities.
To become a functional part of a larger society.	Children participate actively in small and large groups.
To learn to live effectively with others.	Children develop social skills with peers and adults.
To learn basic tools for acquiring knowledge.	Children show signs of curiosity, memory, and symbol recognition.

FIGURE 10.4 Teachers relate what happens in the classroom (behavioral goals) to traditional educational goals.

cial, and intellectual competencies," an evaluation will measure children's progress in those three areas. One that claims to teach specific academic skills will want to assess how learning the alphabet or counting to one hundred is being accomplished.

Evaluations provide teachers with an opportunity to distance themselves from the daily contact with children and look at them in a more detached, professional way. Teachers can use the results to share their opinions and concerns about children with each other and with parents. This concentrated effort expands everyone's vision on who and what the child can be, highlights patterns of the child's behavior, and helps in understanding the meaning of that behavior. It gives teachers the chance to chart growth and acknowledge progress and, in doing so, sets the child apart as an individual and unique human being. Evaluations are a reminder to all that they work with *individuals* and not just a group.

In general, evaluations are made to:

1. Establish a baseline of information about each child by which to judge future progress.

2. Monitor the growth of individual children.

3. Have a systematic plan for intervention and guidance.

4. Plan curriculum.

5. Provide parents with updated information on their child.

6. Provide information for making administrative decisions.

To Establish a Baseline

One purpose of evaluating children is to establish a starting point of their skills and behavior. This is the beginning of a collection over a period of time of important information on each child. Through this cumulative record, teachers learn a great deal about the children: whom they play with, how they spend their time, how they handle problems, what fears and stress they show. In other words, they learn a lot about how children live their lives.

A *baseline* is a picture of the status of each child; an overview of individual development. It shows where the child is in relation to the school's objectives since the child is being measured according to program expectations. Baseline data give a realistic picture of a child at that moment in time, but there is a presumption that the picture will change.

A Baseline Tool. The beginning of the school term is an obvious time to start collecting information. Records of a child are established in the context of the child's history and family background. Parents frequently submit this information with an application to the school. Teachers can gather the data by visiting the child at home or holding a parent conference and speaking directly with the parents about the child's development.

An *entry-level assessment* made during the first few weeks of school can be informative, particularly

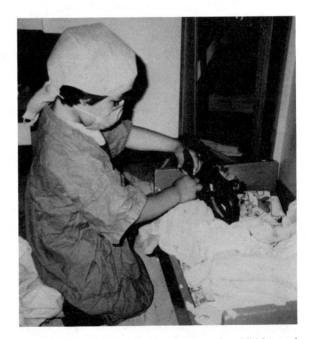

FIGURE 10.5 A baseline is a picture of a child framed at a particular moment.

when added to the child's family history. The evaluation itself can be done informally. A few notes jotted during the first month of school can serve as a beginning collection of pertinent data about the child. Or the format can be more structured, such as in Figure 10.6.

ENTRY-LEVEL ASSESSMENT

1. Child's name _____ Teacher _____
   Age _____ Sex _____ Class _____
   Major language_____ Fluency in English? _____
   Any previous school experiences? _____
   Siblings/others in household _____
   Family situation (one/two parents, other adults, etc.) _____

2. Separation from parent:
   Smooth_____ Some anxiety _____ Mild difficulty __ Unable to separate _____
   Did parent have trouble separating? _____
   Comments: _____

3. How does child come to and leave from school?
   Parent _____ Carpool _____ Babysitter _____ Bus _____

4. Physical appearance:
   General health _____
   Expression _____
   Dress _____
   Body posture _____

5. Self-care:
   Dressing: Alone _____ Needs assistance _____
   Toileting: By self _____ Needs help _____
   Eating: _____
   Toothbrushing: _____
   Sleeping/resting: _____
   Allergies/other health-related problems: _____

6. Child's Interests:
   Indoors:
   Clay __ Books __ Puzzles __ Water play __ Easels __
   Language __ Table/rug toys __ Sensory choices __
   Art __ Science __ Blocks __

   Outdoors:
   Swings __ Climbers __ Sandbox __ Water play __
   Wheel toys __ Animals __ Group games __ Woodworking __
   Group times (level of participation): _____

FIGURE 10.6 A good way to collect baseline information is through an entry-level assessment. (Developed by Bing Nursery School, Stanford University, 1975 to present)

7. Social-emotional development:
   a. Initiates activities ___ Plays alone ___ Seems happy ___
      Has to be invited ___ Brings security object ___
      Seems tense ___
   b. Plays mostly with children of: Same age ___ Younger ___
      Older ___
   c. Moves into environment: Easily ___ Hesitantly ___
      Not at all ___ Wanders ___
   d. Special friends: _____
   e. Does the child follow teachers? ___ Anyone in particular? _____

8. Cognitive development:
   Use of language: Follows directions ___ Clear pronunciation ___
   Memory ___ Curiosity ___ Holds conversations ___
   Words/Phrases _____

9. Physical development:
   Climbs safely ___ Uses scissors ___ Hand preference ___
   Runs smoothly ___ Uses pens, brushes ___ Foot preference ___
   Handles body well ___

10. Goals: _____
    _____
    _____
    _____
    _____

FIGURE 10.6 Cont.

Application. Teachers then use this information to understand children and their various levels of development. They can see children's strengths and weaknesses and where future growth is likely to occur. When the information is shared with parents, they feel more relaxed about their child and even laugh when they recall those first few days of school. So much happens in that short period of time; the rich information we gain from documenting this growth is invaluable.

Goals and Plans. Teachers use baseline data to set realistic goals for individual children. They tailor the curriculum to the needs and interests they have observed. An entry-level assessment is a vehicle for watching children's growth throughout the year. For instance, after setting a baseline of Mariko's language ability in English, teachers plan activities to increase her understanding and use of language. Then, they make periodic checks on her increased vocabulary as the school year progresses.

To Monitor Children's Progress

Teachers use evaluations to document children's growth. Data collected provide evidence of children's growth or lack of progress. A careful evaluation of each child furnishes the teaching staff with the necessary foundation from which they can plan the next steps.

Cathy has mastered the brushes at the easel. Now we can encourage her to try the smaller brushes in table painting.

Enrico has been asking how to spell simple words. Let's see that he gets some time away from the blocks to work with him.

It looks like all the children are fairly competent with scissors now; let's add them to the self-help art shelf.

A Progress Tool. Figure 10.8 is a sample *midyear evaluation*. Criteria for each area of development are included to build a profile of the whole child. Teachers note the intervention and guidance steps they plan, where appropriate. While a general form is outlined here, early education teachers individualize their assessments to specify the skills of their group; an infant/toddler group would have different age-appropriate skills than those of a preschool or primary-age class. Such a revised form should include what the child will do to show a suitable level of behavior in each developmental level.

Application. Information about a child will be used to assess growth and change. How often this happens can vary. Although many changes occur in rapid succession in these early years, it takes

FIGURE   10.7 Evaluations monitor children's progress and assess how individual children use materials and activities.

A TOOL FOR MONITORING CHILDREN'S PROGRESS

Check one of the evaluations below for each skill area; for those that need work, document with specific examples.

Developmental Area	Age Appropriate	Highly Skilled	Needs Work
Self-Management Personal care Making choices Following routines			
Physical/Motor 1. Fine Motor Art materials Woodworking tools Manipulatives			

FIGURE 10.8 A midyear evaluation is a more detailed description of the child. It highlights areas of concern and progress. (Developed by Bing Nursery School, Stanford University, 1975 to present)

2. Gross Motor
   Ball handling
   Balancing
   Jump/hop/skip

Communication and Language
Vocabulary
Articulation
Comprehension
English as a second language
Converses with children
Converses with adults
Listens
Expresses self (needs,
   ideas, feelings)

Cognitive Development
Sees cause and effect
Processes and uses
   information
Solves problems with:
   objects
   peers
   adults
Premath (sequencing,
   measuring, numbers)
Prereading concepts (size,
   colors, shapes, letters,
   position)

Social-Emotional
Independence/initiative
Positive self-concept
Recognizes/accepts own
   feelings
Deals with frustration
Flexibility
Leadership
Initiates social contacts
Prosocial behaviors (friendly,
   sharing, inclusive,
   cooperative, empathetic)
Child–child interactions
Child–adult interactions

OVERALL STRENGTHS: GOALS:

FIGURE 10.8 Cont.

time for a child to integrate life experiences and for teachers to see them expresssed as a permanent part of behavior. Evaluating too frequently does not reveal sufficient change to make it worthwhile and places an added burden on the teaching staff as well.

Once the initial baseline data has been gathered, a progress evaluation approximately every three months seems reasonable. In a normal school year, this would mean establishing a baseline in the fall and checking progress in the winter and the spring. For centers operating on a year-round basis, a brief summer report would be in order. These need not be time consuming. Many evaluations take the form of a checklist and can be accomplished while the class is in session.

Goals and Plans. Goals are established for children as a result of an assessment. These goals are changed as growth takes place. A good assessment tool monitors progress in each developmental area so that plans can be made to challenge the child physically, socially, emotionally, creatively, and intellectually.

At the same time, theory reminds us that the child develops as a whole, with each area of growth influencing and being influenced by what changes take place in other areas. Evaluations that document growth include information so that all teachers see the interrelationships among areas of development. By assessing growth in individual areas, teachers relate that development to the child's collective abilities, as in this example:

> Dylan's midyear report shows that he lacks dexterity in running and climbing. This influences his development in the following areas:
>
> *Emotionally.* He lacks self-confidence, and his self-esteem deteriorates the longer he feels inept at physical skills. He may even be afraid to master the art of climbing and running for fear he will fail.
> *Socially.* Children tease Dylan because he cannot possibly keep up with them while playing outside. He often ends up playing alone or

watching the other children in more active pursuits.
Intellectually. There is a lack of risk taking in Dylan's whole approach to play. Because of his slow physical development, he seems unlikely to challenge himself in other ways.

Dylan's progress report thus sets a primary goal in physical/motor skills, with the knowledge that such growth can positively affect learning in other areas.

To Plan for Guidance and Intervention

A third purpose for evaluation is to help teachers determine guidance procedures. These are based on insights and perceptions brought into focus through the evaluation. This process serves as a primary tool on which guidance and planning are based.

FIGURE 10.9 What does this child need from the program? From teachers? From his parents? Child evaluation can help teachers assess what guidance and intervention may be needed.

A Guidance Tool. Evaluations help in behavior management. Once a need has been pinpointed, the teaching staff decides how to proceed. Individual problems are highlighted when teachers make a point of concentrating on the child's behavior. Figure 10.10 illustrates a form used to determine intervention. Used at a team meeting, this form demonstrates what steps are to be taken in addressing the concern directly.

Application. The following case studies demonstrate how information from evaluations are used for guidance and intervention:

Elizabeth's recent evaluation revealed an increase in the number of toilet accidents she has had. The staff noted a higher incidence during midmorning snacks, but came to no conclusion as to the cause. They agree to continue to treat her behavior in a relaxed manner, and have one teacher remind Elizabeth to use the toilet before she washes her hands for snack. At the same time, they make plans to contact the parents for further information and insights. They will confer again afterwards and agree upon an approach.

Trevor says he has no friends at school. The staff plans to contact his parents and suggest

---

CHILD-STAFFING FORM

Presentation of Problems (In behavioral terms)

What behaviors are causing the staff concern? Be specific. Limit to three problems or concerns.

1.
2.
3.

Family History (Information from family, medical info if needed)

School History (Child's relations to adults, children, materials, activities)

Intervention (Procedures that have been taken so far. What has and has not worked?)

Future Plans (What is going to happen as a result?)

1. In classroom

2. With parents

3. Date for reviewing results

FIGURE 10.10 One purpose of evaluating children is to plan for guidance and behavior management. A good evaluation form will include how to follow through on the plans made for intervention. (Courtesy of K. McLaughlin and S. Sugarman)

they invite Ryan and Brooke over to play with Trevor at home. Teachers have seen both children approach him but he didn't seem to know how to respond. At school, the teachers will give Trevor verbal cues when children make attempts to play with him.

Goals and Plans. An evaluation tool, such as the *child staffing form* in Figure 10.10, helps teachers set goals for children. By narrowing the focus to include only those behaviors that concern the staff, the needs of many children can be reviewed quickly.

To Plan Curriculum

Teachers plan curriculum based on children's evaluations. Translating the assessment to actual classroom practice is an important part of the teacher's role. A thorough evaluation helps teachers plan appropriate activities to meet children's needs.

A Planning Tool. All three of the previous evaluation tools can be used to plan curriculum. The entry-level assessment and midyear report are often summarized in a group chart, such as in Figure 10.11. One such chart, made at the end of the first semester of a prekindergarten class, revealed this pattern:

At least one third of the class was having trouble listening at group time, as evidenced by the group chart that identified "Group Time" and "Language Listening Skills" as areas for growth for nearly half the children. The staff centered their attention on the group time content. It was concluded that a story made the group times too long; the children were restless throughout most of the reading. It was agreed to move storytime to just before nap and shorten the group time temporarily.

Summary of Development/Fall Progress Reports (see forms for details)
Developmental Area: + = fine; − = needs work; ? = don't know

Child	Physical	Language	Cognitive	Social	Emotional	Creative
Greg	−	+	+	+	−	?
Anwar	?	−	+	−	−	+
San-Joo	+	?	?	−	+	+
Reva	+	+	+	+	+	+
Katy	−	+	?	?	?	−

Group Goals for Winter:
 • Emphasize social and emotional areas of curriculum.
 • Plan physical games (indoor games because of weather).
Individual Goals for Winter:
 Greg: Encourage some creative arts, games. Observe creativity in intellectual activities.
 Anwar: Needs to be helped to feel confident and express himself; don't push too hard on physical risks yet.
 San-Joo: Need assessment of language and cognitive skills; observe use of table toys, receptive language at group time.
 Reva: What is the next step? Is she ready for helping the others? Involve her with 100-piece puzzles and the computer.
 Katy: Need to focus on her overall development; too many unknowns— is she getting enough individual attention?

FIGURE 10.11 Teachers can use individual assessment tools to plan for the entire group and for each child in the class.

Application. Evaluation results assist teachers in seeing more clearly the strengths and abilities of each child in the class. Curriculum activities are then planned that will continue to enhance the growth of that child. Also, areas of difficulty will be identified:

Jolene has trouble mastering even the simplest puzzle. Provide her with common shapes found in attribute blocks (small plastic shapes of varying color, thickness, size) and do some matching exercises with her.

The younger children in the class are reluctant to try the climbing structures designed by the older ones. Build an obstacle course with the youngest children, beginning with very simple challenges and involving the children in the actual planning and building as well as rehearsing climbing techniques with them.

Goals and Plans. Each of the previous case studies demonstrates how evaluation tools can be used to plan curriculum. By analyzing both group and individual skills through periodic assessment, teachers maintain a secure and challenging environment.

To Communicate with Parents

Plans for evaluating children should include the means by which parents are to be informed of the results. Once the teachers have identified a

FIGURE 10.12 Assessing group skills is one reason to evaluate children. These children are ready for curriculum challenges in group time.

child's needs and capabilities, parents are entitled to hear the conclusions. The teaching staff has an obligation to provide a realistic overview of the child's progress and alert the parents to any possible concerns. (See Chapter 8 for details about parents and teachers working together.)

Using the child staffing form (page 233), teachers define problem behavior for a child and work closely with the parents to reach a solution:

Yum-Tong refuses to let his mother leave. The teachers agree that there are two issues: (1) Y.-T.'s screaming and crying as his mother leaves, and (2) his inability to focus on an activity while she attempts to go (though she stays as soon as he starts screaming). The family has told them that their other two children had separation problems as preschoolers. The previous school asked the parents to stay until the children stopped protesting, although the parents report that this took nearly six months and so was a hardship for them in their work places.

The teachers choose to intervene by asking Yum-Tong's mother to plan ahead with Y.-T. and spend five minutes each morning playing with him and helping him to settle in. She will then say good-bye and leave Y.-T. with Pete, his favorite teacher. Pete will be prepared to be with him at the departure and stay with him until he calms down. They also plan to have a conference date after two weeks of this intervention plan.

A Tool with Parents. Teachers and parents need to talk together, especially when problems are revealed by the evaluation. As parents and teachers share knowledge and insights, a fuller picture of the child emerges for both. Each can then assume a role in the resolution of the problem. The role of the teacher will be defined in the context of the parents' role, and the parents will be guided by the teacher's attitudes and actions.

Evaluation tools can help parents target areas in which their child may need special help. A child staffing form such as the one described earlier is an effective tool for parent–teacher conferences and

as a method for forming intervention plans. The tool that works best is one that summarizes the school's concerns and solicits high parent involvement.

Application. Aside from identifying normal behavior problems, evaluations may raise questions concerning a child's physical development, hearing and visual acuity, or language problems. Potentially serious problems may emerge from the evaluation, and parents can be encouraged to seek further professional guidance.

Goals and Plans. Since evaluation is an ongoing process, reevaluation and goal-setting are done regularly. Communicating to parents both progress and new goals is critical for the *feedback loop* of an evaluation form to be effective.

To Make Administrative Decisions

Evaluation results can help a school make administrative decisions. They can lead to changes in the overall program or in the school's philosophy. For example, a day care component might be added to the half-day program after learning that most children are enrolled in another child care situation after nursery school. Or an evaluation might conclude that there is too little emphasis on developing large motor skills and coordination. To invite more active play, the administration might decide to remodel the play yard and purchase new equipment.

In the early childhood setting, both *informal* and *formal methods* are used for evaluating children. *Informal methods* (such as in Figures 10.2–10.4) include observation, note taking, self-assessments, parent interviews and surveys, samples of children's work, and teacher-designed forms. More *formal* kinds of *evaluations* are used also, although somewhat less frequently in the early years. These include standardized tests and various "screening" instruments. The yearly tests taken in school, using a Number 2 pencil, are an example of such procedures. Those and other standardized forms are examples of formal methods of evaluation. Commercially developed, these tests usually compare the individual child's performance to a predetermined norm.

An Administrative Tool. Many kindergartens and some nursery schools use various kinds of "screening" tests, before children begin school in the fall. The usual purpose of these evaluations is to determine readiness; that is, to verify that the child will be able to cope with and succeed in school. Figure 10.13 shows one type of *screening evaluation*.

Some teachers conclude the year with a summary report. This evaluation serves as an overview of what a child has accomplished, what areas of strength are present, and what future growth might occur. These records are useful to parents as a summary of their child's learning experiences. Teachers may use them as references should they ever be consulted by another school about the child.

SKILLS INVENTORY

Teacher _____

Child _____ Age _____ Date _____

Task	Teacher Comments

Cognitive Skills

1. Can you say the alphabet?

2. Can you tell me what these letters are?

3. Can you count for me?

4. Please point to the number.

5. Can you put these in order from smallest to biggest?
   Which is the largest?
   Smallest?
   First?
   Last?

6. What color is this?
   If child cannot, then ask to "Point to the red one," etc.

7. What shapes are these?
   If child cannot, then ask to "Point to the circle," etc.

8. Can you find your shoulders? Elbow? Thumb? Neck? Lips?

9. Name all the animals you can think of.

10. Please put these animals into two groups. One has the animals that live in water, and the other the ones that live on the land.

1. Sequence correct? Yes __ No __
   Length:

2. Number of letters correct __
   Comments:

3. Note how far:
   Sequence correct how far? __

4. 3–1–6–4–8–2–9–7–5
   How many correct? __

5. Three sizes of triangles.
   Comments:

6. Point to red, blue, yellow, black, green, orange, brown, purple.
   Comments:

7. Point to circle, square, triangle, rectangle.
   Comments:

8. Comments:

9. Comments:

10. Giraffe, deer, cat, frog, alligator, shark, goldfish

FIGURE 10.13 By creating effective tools for assessment, we are able to evaluate children's readiness for the next educational step. (Developed by Bing Nursery School, Stanford University, 1975 to present) (cont. on pp. 238 and 239)

Task	Teacher Comments

11. Here is a bear and a cube. Put the cube on top of the bear.
    Under the bear.
    Behind the bear.
    Beside the bear.
    In front of the bear.
	11. Check correct responses:

12. Here are three pictures. Can you put them in order so that they tell a story?	12. Tree with green leaves.
	    Tree with orange/red leaves, falling.
	    Bare tree.
	    Comments:

Auditory-Perceptual Listening Skills

Task	Teacher Comments

1. Please repeat these numbers after I say them (Practice with 6–3–1–4):
    5–3–8–2
    2–7–9–3
	1. Sequence correct? Numbers correct?

2. Tell me the sentence in the same order as I say. (Practice with "The dog ran to the park.") The mother pointed to the airplane in the sky.	2. Sequence correct? Words correct?
3. Listen to what I say, and then do what my words tell you. (Practice with "Put your hands on your head.") Stand up, go to the door, and walk back to me.	3. Comments:

Fine Motor Skills

Task	Teacher Comments
1. Print your name.	1. Note grasp, hand preference.
2. Draw a circle, square, triangle, rectangle.	2. Comments:
3. Write the letters: O E P A J	3. Comments:
4. Write the numbers: 1 3 7 2 5	4. Comments:
5. Cut out a circle.	5. Note scissor grasp, hand preference.
6. Draw the best person that you can. Have you left anything out?	6. Comments:

Gross Motor Skills

Task	Teacher Comments
1. Jump on two feet from A to B.	1. Note balance.
2. Hop on one foot from B to A.	2. Note balance.
3. Skip from A to B.	3. Comments:
4. Walk backwards from B to A.	4. Comments:
5. Stand on one foot while I count to three.	5. Note balance.
6. Walk across this balance board.	6. Note balance.
7. Can you jump over these poles with your feet together?	7. Comments:
8. How high can you climb our climber? Go up our slide?	8. Comments:

FIGURE 10.13 Cont.

9. Now run from the climber to the fence and back to me as fast as you can!	9. Note gait and balance.
10. Please throw the ball to me. Catch it. Kick it.	10. Comments:

FIGURE 10.13 Cont.

Application. Making administrative decisions based on evaluation results is a sound idea. Assessments give administrators specific and verifiable information on which to base decisions.

The issue of readiness or placement of children is difficult and complex. Whether or not a child is ready to succeed in a program affects parents and children personally. Having a good evaluation tool helps in making such decisions equitably and in communicating results in a clear and kind manner.

Goals and Plans. The evaluation tool that gives a specific profile of a child's skills will allow an administrator to share information with a family clearly and honestly. By choosing a tool with goals for children's further growth, administrators give the parents information they can use to plan for the child's development.

EVALUATING TEACHERS

Teachers are the *single most important* factor related to program quality (Grotberg, 1971). What makes "the effective teacher" has no one simple answer. However, there are ways to evaluate teachers that guide them toward more effective teaching, in their work with children, coworkers, parents, and administrators.

Think of teachers as conductors of a symphony orchestra. They do not compose the music. They do not design or build the instruments, nor do they decide which ones will be played in the orchestra pit. They may even have limited choice of the music that will be played. Yet, it is their job to lead a group of musicians through a medley of songs, bringing out the best in each. And all under the intense scrutiny of a critical audience. Teachers must do this with care and expertise under the

FIGURE 10.14 Assessing a child's readiness must consider all developmental areas. Motor skills are one indicator of an ability to succeed in kindergarten.

watchful eyes of parents, boards, and funding agencies.

Many teachers do this well, often with little training except direct experience. As teachers' effectiveness is measured, they can learn better techniques for working with children, for planning environments and programs. The process for establishing and meeting these goals is evaluation.

Why Evaluate?

Teachers are evaluated for several reasons. The end result of an assessment may be setting guidelines for what kinds of teaching are expected. Or the intent of an evaluation might be to set clear goals for job improvement. The first part of any effective evaluation procedure is a statement of purpose.

To Describe Job Responsibilities

It is essential for teachers to understand their job to do it well. A good job description outlines what is expected. One purpose of an evaluation is to see how those expectations are being met.

In an infant/toddler center, for example, teachers try to help children learn to separate comfortably from their parents. Evaluation in this setting could focus on the exact skills needed to implement this goal. How does a teacher help a parent separate from a young child? What environmental cues does the teacher prepare? How is the child in distress comforted? What teaching strategies are important?

Evaluation for specifying job responsibilities is a part of one's professional self-definition as well as a clarification of actual duties. Studying ourselves helps us know who we are and what we do. Assessing job responsibilities aids in this process.

To Monitor Job Effectiveness

Once clear guidelines are set for teaching expectations, a method is needed to monitor actual teaching. Most evaluation systems attempt to check teacher effectiveness. It is important to establish a process for analyzing how teachers are doing their job.

FIGURE 10.15 Evaluating teachers includes assessing their work with children.

FIGURE 10.16 Evaluations help teachers set goals for themselves that focus on their work with children. (Courtesy of St. Thomas' Episcopal School, New Haven, Conn.)

This process may vary from school to school. In some schools, teaching effectiveness is measured, in part, by child achievement, such as how children score on tests. Other centers may solicit parent opinion. A teacher's coworkers may be part of an assessment team. For the most part, an evaluation for job effectiveness will include an observation of teaching time with children.

To Clarify Strengths and Weaknesses

An evaluation procedure preferred by many teachers is one that identifies specific areas of strength and weakness. Feedback about actual teaching and other job responsibilities is helpful to all teachers, whether beginners or experienced personnel. As assessment that offers teachers information about how to perform their job better contributes to job competence and satisfaction. By recognizing strengths, teachers receive positive feedback for high-quality work. By identifying weaknesses, they can begin to set realistic goals for improvement.

To Set Professional Growth Goals

One function of teacher evaluation is "to foster professional development, which aids the teacher in establishing and attaining goals" (Hatfield, 1981). Teachers do not become "good" and then stay that way for life. Regardless of their stage of development, teachers need goals in order to continually improve.

Regular feedback to staff can help in setting goals for continual professional growth. Beginning teachers will need to work on skills that apply their educational training or background to the classroom and children. A professional with 15 years of experience might need to polish skills acquired a decade or more ago, or try another educational challenge, such as developing curriculum or planning a workshop.

To Determine Employment

An evaluation can also be used to decide whether teachers should be "retained, promoted, or released" (Stoops et al. *in* Hatfield, 1981). Assessment procedures are an administrator's most valuable tools in performing these tasks. With a clear and effective evaluation tool, a teacher's performance can be monitored and specific areas targeted for improvement. The administrator then has a fair and equitable way to determine promotional status of each employee.

Critical Issues in Teacher Evaluation

How to evaluate is an important issue in teacher assessment. A system for evaluating employees can be one of trust and mutual respect or of anxiety and tension. The method often determines how successful the entire evaluation will be.

Preliminary Steps

To begin with, a school follows the same guidelines for developing a teacher evaluation as for child assessment. That is, the process includes determining a purpose, establishing who will collect the data and how, and clarifying how the evaluation will be used. When assessing teachers, the important components are: purpose (as described earlier in the chapter), evaluators, process, and follow-through.

Evaluators

Several models have been developed around the issue of who will assess teacher performance.

Self-Evaluation. This can be an effective starting point. Self-assessment is used in the Child Development Associate's evaluation system, for these reasons (Ward and CDA staff, 1976):

- The candidate is a valid source of information for use in assessment. Certain information is available only from the candidate's perspective.
- The candidate is able to clarify information or his or her performance, thereby adding to the assessment team's evidence for a valid decision.

- The candidate is better able to identify strengths and weaknesses and to receive recommendations for continued professional growth.

Figure 10.17 illustrates one type of systematic self-assessment. Another self-assessment technique, somewhat less formal, is to ask questions about yourself and your job, such as:

- What aspects of my work give me the greatest sense of satisfaction and achievement?

- What changes in my work assignment would increase my contribution to the school and my own personal satisfaction?

- What additional development activities would help me do a more effective job or prepare me for the next step on my career path?

- What would improve the effectiveness and quality of my relationship with my supervisor? (Young-Holt et al., 1983)

SAMPLE SELF-EVALUATION

Rate the following items on the scale below, based on your performance in the classroom. (Note: This form allows for a yes/no response if desired. Supervisors may use this same form to rate the student following the self-evaluation.)

Superior Perf. 3	Acceptable Perf. 2	Unacceptable Perf. 1	Not Applicable 0

Relationship to Children

_____ I am able to understand and accept a child as he/she is and recognize individual needs.

_____ I use knowledge and understanding of child development principles to understand children.

_____ I use information regarding home, family, and sociocultural background to understand children.

_____ I am able to forestall situations before negative behavior occurs.

_____ I use positive suggestions and choices to redirect behavior.

_____ I use prescribed limits and follow-through.

_____ I adapt methods of guidance to the individual and adjust guidance measures to fit the situation.

_____ I avoid the use of threats.

_____ I express positive reinforcement when appropriate.

_____ I can verbalize my own feelings in an honest, open, and humane manner when interacting with children.

_____ I avoid using baby talk.

_____ I relate to individual children.

_____ I relate to children in small groups.

_____ I relate to children in large groups.

Developing the Program

_____ I permit the children to explore materials in a variety of ways.

FIGURE 10.17 Self-evaluation can be an insightful and useful process. (Adapted from Young-Holt et al. [1983] and Hatfield [1981])

_____ I recognize and use spontaneous happenings to help children's learning.

_____ I make use of child development principles to plan curriculum for children.

_____ I offer a wide range of experiences so children can make choices according to their interests and needs.

_____ I allow for various levels of ability among children.

_____ I utilize a variety of media when developing instructional materials.

_____ I use a note-taking system to assist in planning and evaluating experiences for children.

_____ I maintain equipment and materials in good order and consider health and safety factors.

Relating to Parents

_____ I recognize parents by name.

_____ I converse with parents at appropriate times.

_____ I incorporate the cultural backgrounds of families into the program.

_____ I facilitate a free flow of information between staff and parents.

_____ I communicate concerns to parents in both written and verbal forms.

_____ I recognize and appreciate parental values and priorities for their children.

_____ I communicate children's school experiences with parents.

Administration and Professional Development

_____ I recognize and use policies and procedures of the program.

_____ I attend and participate in staff meetings.

_____ I inform the administrative staff correctly of illness, time off, vacation, etc.

_____ I am a member of at least one professional organization in the field of early childhood.

_____ I attend meetings conducted by professional groups.

_____ I make use of professional resources and contacts.

_____ I maintain professional confidentiality and discretion.

Working with Other Staff Members

_____ I show positive attitudes toward other staff members.

_____ I give directions carefully.

_____ I take directions from others.

_____ I participate as a team member.

_____ I coordinate my efforts with those of my coworkers.

_____ I share my time, interest, and resources with other staff members.

_____ I listen and hear staff feedback regarding my teaching.

_____ I act on suggestions.

_____ I communicate my perceptions of my teaching in an honest and clear manner.

FIGURE 10.17 Cont.

The answers to these few questions can provide a solid base for discussion between teacher and supervisor or assessment team.

One drawback of self-assessment is its subjectivity. We see ourselves too closely, too personally, to be able to be entirely objective about our teaching. Therefore, self-assessment must be accompanied by other evaluating feedback.

Supervisory Evaluation. Supervisors, or head teachers, are usually part of the evaluation process. Job performance is an administrator's responsibility; therefore, teachers can expect their supervisors to be involved in their evaluation.

Coevaluation. Evaluation by others associated with the teachers is a welcome addition to the evaluation process. Often a system includes more than a teacher's supervisor. Possible combinations are:

- Teacher (self-evaluation) and supervisor
- Teacher, supervisor, and parent
- Teacher, supervisor, and another team member (coteacher, aide, student teacher)

A team evaluation is a more collaborative approach. More information is collected on the teacher's performance. A team approach may be more valid and balanced, since a decision about teaching will be made by consensus and discussion rather than individual, perhaps arbitrary, methods. And the evaluation will have a wider perspective, evaluating a teacher's job performance from several viewpoints.

Coevaluation does have its disadvantages, however. It is a time-consuming process since more than one person is asked to evaluate a teacher. Feedback may be contradictory; what one evaluator sees as a strength, another may view as a shortcoming. The system can be complicated to implement. For instance, how do teachers work in a classroom and evaluate another team member at the same time? Can funds be found to bring in substitutes? Do fellow teachers have the time to devote to evaluating each other? How and when does a parent evaluate a teacher? Clearly, a school must weigh these issues carefully as evaluation systems are devised.

The Process

The evaluation tools used determine the information gathered. Informal techniques often use information that is gathered sporadically, and conclusions may be unreliable or based on opinions. A process that is formalized and systematic has a greater chance of success. Such evaluations will be based on observable, specific information on what the teacher actually does. This is known as *performance-based assessment.* When paired with specific goals and expectations, this system is known as competency-based assessment.

Competency-based assessments outline exactly what teachers must do to demonstrate their competency, or skill, in their job assignment. Criteria are set as a teacher begins working (or a student starts a class or teacher education program). Areas are targeted that pinpoint what knowledge, skills, and behaviors the teacher must acquire. Figure 10.18 is an example of an evaluation based on defined areas of competency.

Competency Area:
1. Establishes and maintains a safe and healthy learning environment.
2. Advances physical and intellectual competence.
3. Builds positive self-concept and individual strength.
4. Promotes positive functioning of children and adults in a group.
5. Brings about optimal coordination of home and center child-rearing practices and expectations.
6. Carries out supplemental responsibilities related to children's programs.

FIGURE 10.18 One type of competency-based assessment has been developed by the Child Development Associate Consortium. Competency areas are further elaborated with specific examples of teacher behavior. (Adapted from Ward and CDA Staff, 1976)

Follow-Through

What happens after the evaluation is critical to the overall success of an evaluation system. For instance, after gathering information for an evaluation session, a supervisor and teacher might discuss and evaluate concrete examples and live performance. Together they can establish goals for changing what may be ineffective or problematic.

Follow-through is the final part of a continuous *feedback loop* in a good evaluation system. Data is collected on teacher behavior and given to the teacher in person. Goals are set to improve teaching. A follow-up check is done periodically, to see how— and if—goals are being met. Teaching improves as recommendations are put into practice. The *feedback loop* is complete as information about improvement is communicated. Figure 10.19 illustrates this cycle.

Evaluation takes hard work, time, and dedication to a higher quality of teaching. It is also a shared responsibility. The supervisor must be explicit about a teacher's performance and be able to identify for the teacher what is effective and what

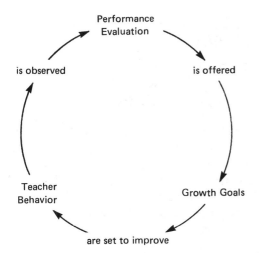

FIGURE 10.19 A "feedback loop" is a continuous cycle in which teacher behavior is observed for a performance evaluation. The evaluation is offered through growth goals, which are set to affect teacher behavior. Thus, the circle is continuous, with each part helping the next.

is problematic. The teacher is responsible for participating in the evaluation.

Techniques for Productive Evaluation Sessions

Teachers must value the process itself. They need to analyze and take seriously the substance of the evaluation and understand its implications for their teaching. To further their professional growth, they must use this opportunity to improve the tools of their trade.

Certain techniques help make evaluation sessions productive for teachers:

1. Become involved from the beginning as the evaluation procedure is established. Know what is expected and how you will be evaluated.

2. Set a specific meeting time for your evaluation. Ask your supervisor for a time that works for you both.

3. Set some goals for yourself before meeting with your supervisor. If you know what you want to work on, you are more likely to get help achieving your goals.

4. Develop a plan for action. Be prepared to set a timeline for when and how you will work on your goals.

5. Establish a feedback loop. Make a follow-up date and make copies of your goal sheet for both you and your supervisor.

6. Approach the meeting with a sense of trust, respect, and openness. Planning ahead promotes these attitudes.

What results from productive feedback sessions is better teaching and continued professional growth. Teacher evaluations help recognize strengths and build upon them. They identify areas where growth is needed. They individualize the process itself. No two teachers are identical; each evaluation must be interpreted in terms of the behavior and stage of development of the individual person. As teachers become more effective in their work with children, the quality of the entire program is improved.

EVALUATING PROGRAMS

Why Evaluate?

To Gain an Overview

Evaluating a program gives an overview of how all the various components function together. Looking at children, teachers, and the total environment reveals the entire system as an integrated whole. Program evaluations add an awareness of how one area relates to another and how the parts mesh in a particular setting. To a great extent, evaluating a program amounts to asking, "What is a good program for children?"

To answer that question, a program evaluation looks at several issues:

- children's progress
- teacher performance
- curriculum development
- the financial structure
- the parents
- the community at large
- the governing organization of the school

In evaluating programs, each of these is assessed for how it functions alone and how each works in concert with the others.

To Establish Accountability

Besides providing an overview, a program evaluation establishes *accountability*. This refers to a program's being answerable to a controlling group or agency, for instance the school board or the government office. These groups want to know how their funds are being spent and how their philosophy is being expressed through the overall program. Just as a teacher's evaluation is sometimes linked to salary increases, a program evaluation may be related to future finding. This can add stress to the evalua-

tion process since teachers and administrators must justify their worth in dollars and cents.

To Make Improvements

A third purpose of a program evaluation is to determine where and how improvements can be made. Program evaluations are an opportunity to take an objective look at how the goals of the school are being met. A good evaluation will support the strengths of the existing program and suggest where changes might improve overall effectiveness. An indepth assessment increases the likelihood that program goals and visions will be realized. The evaluation helps determine the direction the program may take in the future.

To Acquire Accreditation

Finally, evaluations are a necessary step for some schools who wish to be approved for certification or accreditation by various organizations. Such groups require that a school meet certain evaluation standards before the necessary permits are issued or membership granted.

Guidelines for Program Evaluation

Defining the Objectives

A program evaluation begins with a definition of the program's objectives. Knowing why a program is to be evaluated indicates how to tailor the procedure to the needs and characteristics of an individual school. With the objectives defined, the choice of evaluation instrument becomes clear. If, for example, a program objective is to provide a healthy environment for children, the evaluation tool used must address the issues of health, safety, and nutrition.

Choosing a Tool

Evaluation instruments vary with the purpose of the program evaluation. Moreover, a survey of various program evaluations shows that many are designed to be program-specific; that is, the evaluation itself is devised to examine one program only.

FIGURE 10.20 Program evaluations should be designed to fit the needs of the individual school, for example by analyzing the outdoor space.

Individualized assessments are difficult to generalize. However, it appears that most program evaluations assess several, if not all, of the following areas:

The Physical Environment
Are the facilities clean, comfortable, safe?
Are room arrangements orderly and attractive?
Are materials and equipment in good repair and maintained?
Is there a variety of materials, appropriate to age levels?
Are activity areas well-defined?
Is cleanup and room restoration a part of the daily schedule?
Are samples of children's work on display?
Is play space adequate, both inside and out?

Is personal space (e.g., cubby) provided for each child?

The Staff
Are there enough teachers for the number of children? How is this determined?
Are the teachers qualified? What criteria are used?
Is the staff evaluated periodically? By whom and how?
Does the school provide/encourage in-service training and continuing education?
Do the teachers encourage the children to be independent and self-sufficient?
Are the teachers genuinely interested in children?

Are teachers aware of individual abilities and limitations?

What guidance and disciplinary techniques are used?

Do teachers observe, record, and write reports on children's progress?

Are teachers skilled in working with individual children, small groups, and large groups?

Does the teaching staff give the children a feeling of stability and belonging?

Do teachers provide curriculum that is age-appropriate and challenging?

How would you describe the teachers' relationships with other adults in the setting? Who does this include, and how?

Can the teaching staff articulate good early education principles and relate them to their teaching?

Parent Relationships

How does the classroom include parents?

Are parents welcome to observe, discuss policies, make suggestions, help in the class?

Are different needs of parents taken into account?

Where and how do parents have a voice in the school?

Are parent–teacher conferences scheduled?

Does the school attempt to use community resources and social service agencies in meeting parents' needs?

The Organization and Administration

Does the school maintain and keep records?

Are there scholarships or subsidies available?

What socioeconomic, cultural, religious groups does the school serve?

What is the funding agency, and what role does it play?

Is there a school board and how is it chosen?

Does the school serve children with special needs or handicaps?

Are the classroom groups homo- or heterogeneous?

What hours is the school open?

What age range is served?

Are there both full- and part-day options?

Is after-school care available?

Does the school conduct research or train teachers?

What is the teacher–child ratio?

The Overall Program

Does the school have a written, stated educational philosophy?

Are there developmental goals for the children's physical, social, intellectual, and emotional growth?

Are the children evaluated periodically?

Is the program capable of being individualized to fit the needs of all the children?

Does the program include time for a variety of free, spontaneous activities?

Is the curriculum varied to include music, art, science, nature, math, language, social studies, motor skills, etc.?

Are there ample opportunities to learn through a variety of media and types of equipment and materials?

Is there ample outdoor activity?

Is there a daily provision for routines: eating, sleeping, toileting, play?

Is the major emphasis in activities on concrete experiences?

Are the materials and equipment capable of stimulating and sustaining interest?

Are field trips offered?

Do children have a chance to be alone? In small groups? In large groups?

Tools for program evaluation, then, include criteria about the teacher, the child, and the environment. They are woven together to give a more comprehensive look at the total program. The result is that the whole is greater than the sum of its parts. More is learned about the program than if teachers, children, and the environment were measured by themselves.

HOW EVALUATIONS AFFECT AN EARLY CHILDHOOD SETTING

A useful assessment encourages positive change. It is easy to continue the same program, the same teaching techniques, even the same assessment techniques, year after year when a school is operating smoothly. Sometimes it is not clear what—or how—improvements could be made. A regular evaluation keeps a system alive and fresh.

Evaluations help give meaning and perspective to children, teachers, and programs. An assessment that helps clarify these processes brings renewed dedication and inspiration.

Assessments of children, teachers, and pro-

FIGURE 10.21 A program evaluation can determine if the curriculum materials are varied enough to provide opportunities for children to use a wide range of equipment that fits their developmental skills. (Courtesy of St. Thomas' Episcopal School, New Haven, Conn.)

FIGURE 10.22 Evaluations give an overview of how children, teachers, and the environment interrelate.

grams can blend together for positive results. Children and program evaluations often work in tandem, as program goals must be defined in terms of children and their growth. How well the children are doing is a measure of program success.

Teacher evaluations may relate to program assessment when they include an *upward evaluation,* or teacher evaluation of administrators. The program effectiveness is checked by the people who are responsible for its implementation.

A teacher's effectiveness is evaluated everyday by how the children respond to the environment, the schedule, teaching techniques and relationships, and each other. No more effective test exists than the dynamics of the children at work and play in a class.

As teachers, we learn to accept evaluation as a process, rather than a series of static endpoints. In doing so, we see that there can be continuity and consistency in how evaluations of the people and programs in early childhood education work together to enhance learning and growth at all levels.

SUMMARY

Evaluation is a way of taking stock; it is an opportunity to look at how things are going. We can assess where we are now and where we want to be. A good evaluation instrument may even suggest ways to achieve our goals. A good evaluation process includes a clear purpose, knowing who and what will be evaluated, and what use will be made of the results.

Any program designed to meet the needs of children must be evaluated on a regular basis. Teachers, children, and the program must be assessed individually and then evaluated as a whole. Each supports and depends upon the other; an evaluation is a way to look at how those relationships are working. It can identify specific concerns and determine the areas of growth and potential development.

Setting goals is an important part of the evaluation process. Evaluating goals is a measure of success or lack of it. We judge whether or not we have met our goals effectively and whether or not the goals are reflective of the program.

Evaluations serve many purposes. Assessing individual children highlights their growth and potential more clearly. Evaluation gives teachers information about their own performance and ways to strengthen their teaching style. Examining the total program reveals a better picture of how all these factors work in unison.

The process of evaluation can be positive and can encourage growth for all involved. The choice of evaluation instruments is important, as is the use made of the data collected. Programs will keep pace with their children and professional teachers if evaluation is considered an integral part of the program structure.

Review Questions

1. List three reasons for evaluation in the early childhood setting.

2. What are the components of all good evaluations?

3. Name several problems in evaluation.

4. What are the reasons for assessing children's progress?

5. Who can be involved in evaluating teachers?

6. How can teachers help to make their evaluation sessions productive?

7. Name three purposes of program evaluations.

Learning Activities

1. Does your own setting have an evaluation plan? Which of the evaluation criteria does it include?

2. Develop an informal assessment tool to evaluate children's skills in a toddler class. Discuss how this would differ from one for a preschool, and from a school-age day care program.

3. Try to establish goals for your own growth as a professional in the following areas:

	Goal	Objectives/ Implementation	Timeline
Programmatic			
Administrative			
Staff Relations			
Professional Growth			

Ask your supervisor or a colleague to help you make a realistic timeline for each goal.

Bibliography

Decker, Celia A., and Decker, John R. *Planning and Administering Early Childhood Programs.* Columbus, Ohio: Charles E. Merrill, 1976.

Grotberg, E.; Chapmen, J.; and Lazar, J. *A Review of the Present Status and Future Needs in Day Care Research.* Washington, D.C.: Office of Child Development, 1971.

Harms, Thelma. "Evaluating Settings for Learning." In Baker, Katherine Read (ed.), *Ideas That Work Well with Young Children.* Washington, D.C.: National Association for the Education of Young Children, 1972.

Hatfield, L.M. "Inservice Evaluation in Early Childhood Education." *Young Children,* November 1981, pp. 59–65.

Hoestetler, Lana, and Klugman, Edgar. "Early Childhood Job Titles: One Step Toward Professional Status." *Young Children,* September 1982, pp. 13–22.

Popham, W. J. *Educational Evaluation.* Englewood Cliffs, N.J.: Prentice-Hall, 1975.

Smith, Marilyn, and Giesy, Rosemary. "A Guide for Collecting and Organizing Information on Early Childhood Programs." *Young Children,* June 1972, pp. 264–271.

Spodek, Bernard. *Teaching in the Early Years,* 2nd Ed. Englewood Cliffs, N.J.: Prentice-Hall, 1978.

Stevens, Joseph H., Jr., and King, Edith W. *Administering Early Childhood Education Programs.* Boston: Little, Brown and Co., 1976.

Ward, E.H., and CDA Staff. "The Child Development Associate Consortium's Assessment System." *Young Children,* May 1976, pp. 244–255.

Young-Holt, C.; Spitz, Gay; and Heffron, M.C. *A Model for Staff Evaluation, Validation, and Growth.* Palo Alto, Calif.: Center for the Study of Self-Esteem, 1983.

SECTION V

CURRICULUM FOR YOUNG CHILDREN

David Elkind

Any subject matter that is to be taught must take the capacities and limitations of the learner into account. While that axiom may seem straightforward and so obvious that it does not require articulation, the facts are otherwise. Bruner's famous dictum that any subject can be taught to any child at any age in an intellectually responsible way has embedded itself in our consciousness. So, too, has the idea offered by Margaret Mead that we are in a prefigurative culture where the young are wiser than their parents.

Both positions were and are dead wrong. But the idea that children can learn and understand anything we throw at them permeates the contemporary scene. It is found not only among the avaricious who are eager to sell parents materials and workshops for teaching babies to read, do math, and learn foreign languages. It also appears among those who desire to teach sex education, dangers of nuclear war, and much, much more to young children, regardless of their capacity to comprehend or to assimilate it. The idea that the young can cope better than the mature and that "earlier is better" is a rampant theme in our society.

Children are, in fact, the young of the species. And like the young of any species, their survival depends upon the nurturance, guidance, direction, and support of the adult members of the society. There is no animal species in which the young teach their parents or other adults, or in which the young give guidance and direction to the mature. One has only to watch a mother duck look after her ducklings in a pond to see how dependent the young of a species are upon the adult generation for their survival.

What we impart to young people should grow out of their developmental needs for adaptation. In the human infant, these needs, beyond the nutritional ones, are intellectual, social, and emotional. In addition, these needs are not separate and distinguishable as they are in older children and in adults. Rather, the young child functions as a totality, such that an activity that furthers intellectual growth serves to further social and emotional growth as well. A child playing with blocks learns size, weight, relations (on top of, below) and so has the emotional satisfaction of building and learns cooperation with other children who are playing with or beside him or her.

Furthermore, a curriculum for young children must recognize their limitations. Children before the age of six need a gradual entrance into the world of printed symbols and general rules. Certainly, young children can learn to recognize single words in functional settings—"go, stop, cold, hot, on, off" and so on. And children

What Is Being Taught?

should be read to and have a chance to dictate their own stories. But early childhood is not a time for formal instruction (work books, phonic rules) in reading and math. Young children learn best, most efficiently, and most comprehensively through direct interaction with the materials in their environment. This interaction can be playful—an attempt to express personal feelings, needs, and impulses—or it can be work-oriented—directed at learning skills of social adaptation. Whether the young child is engaged in play or in work, it is important that the materials be concrete rather than symbolic. Symbols take their meaning from concrete experience. Without the concepts acquired from concrete experience, the learning of symbols to represent those concepts becomes an unproductive learning experience for young children. Children need to learn about things and relations before they learn the names for those things and relations.

DAVID ELKIND is currently Professor of Child Study and Visiting University Professor and Scholar at the Lincoln Filene Center at Tufts University. He was formerly Professor of Psychology, Psychiatry and Education at the University of Rochester. After taking his doctorate at UCLA, Dr. Elkind spent a year as a postdoctoral fellow with David Rapaport at the Austen Riggs Center. In 1964–65 he spent a year at Piaget's Center D'Epistemologie Genetique in Geneva. He has attempted to build upon the research of Jean Piaget in the areas of cognitive and perceptual development.

Dr. Elkind has authored three hundred items, including research studies, review and theoretical articles, book chapters, books, and articles and children's stories for popular magazines. Among his most recent books are Children and Adolescents: Interpretive Essays on Jean Piaget, 3rd Ed., *and* The Hurried Child: Growing Up Too Fast Too Soon. *Forthcoming is a book titled* All Grown Up and No Place to Go. *Dr. Elkind is a consulting editor to many psychological journals, a member of ten professional organizations, and a consultant to government agencies, private foundations, state education departments, clinics, and mental health centers. He lectures extensively and has made several television appearances.*

11

Play: The Curriculum of the Child

Questions for Thought

- What is curriculum in the early childhood setting?
- What is the process of developing curriculum for young children?
- What is the value of play?
- How are play and curriculum related?
- How do children learn through play?
- Why is dramatic play important to the young child?
- What is the role of the teacher?
- How do teachers support the play process?

Outline

CURRICULUM

What Is Curriculum?

Curriculum is considered to be one individual course of study or many courses. In elementary and secondary schools, social studies, geography, math, English, and art are part of curriculum. In an early childhood setting, curriculum consists of the art activity and language game; it is also the spontaneous gymnastics on the climbers and the song that accompanies digging in the sand. It can become, literally, everything that happens in the course of a school day.

Curriculum is the planned and the unplanned. Young children are like sponges; they absorb everything going on about them. Since they are young, the whole world is new and fresh. Therefore, children do not discriminate between what is prepared and structured for them to learn and whatever else happens to them at school. It is *all* learning.

The group of two-year-olds is more interested in the process of pouring milk (especially what happens after the cup is filled) than in eating and conversing at snack time.

Three kindergarteners become absorbed in watching a snail make its way across the sidewalk, ignoring for the moment the lesson on running relays.

Creating a good curriculum for young children is not simply a matter of practicing curriculum planning. It is a matter of understanding the process on which the practice is based. The basis of curricu-

FIGURE 11.1 Curriculum happens when children and materials meet.

lum planning is an understanding of how children interact with people and materials to learn. Teachers apply what they know about children when they plan classroom activities; that is curriculum planning. It is the sum of a teacher's knowledge about children's needs, materials, and equipment, and what happens when they meet. Curriculum translates theories of education into practice.

Two Approaches

There are two general approaches to curriculum that are common in early childhood settings. The first is based on the premise that curriculum is everything that happens throughout the course of a day; it is all of the children's experiences as they interact with people and materials. The emphasis is on children's interests and involvement in their learning and in their ability to make constructive choices. Teachers set up the room and the yard, sometimes planning one or two activities that will invite children to participate. For the most part, teachers respond by watching and evaluating what children do and support what use children make of their experience. This is a process-oriented approach; curriculum content is apparent, but an end product or result is not the major focus.

A second approach to curriculum development requires more formal, organized planning. Comprehensive lesson plans are developed and usually include *teaching objectives*, the stated concepts that children will learn through this experience. A lesson plan may also include a detailed outline of activities and events. In some cases, as with Montessori programs, the curriculum will convey one specific theory.

Planning Curriculum

Written Plans

When using either approach to curriculum, written plans are helpful, especially for the beginning teacher. A written plan is an organized agenda, an outline to follow, a framework for the curriculum. It may include a list of activities, goals for children's learning experiences, the process or

method of instruction, the teacher's responsibilities, the time of day, and other special notations. A curriculum may be developed for a day, a week, a month, or for a specific unit or theme. Figure 11.2 illustrates a weekly curriculum based on the theme of the five senses.

Setting lesson plans to paper has many advantages. Doing so:

- Helps teachers focus on the nature of the children they teach—their interests, their needs, their capabilities, their potential.
- Encourages thorough, in-depth planning of curriculum in a logical progression; provides a direction.
- Helps teachers clarify thoughts and articulate a rationale for what they do.
- Stimulates teamwork when teachers plan together, sharing their ideas and resources.
- Allows everyone to know what is happening; in case of absences, a substitute teacher can carry out the plans.
- Gives a foundation from which changes can be made; allows for flexibility, adaptation, and on-the-spot decisions.
- Allows for time to prepare materials, to see what is needed and what resources to gather or contact.
- Provides a concrete format from which evaluation and assessment can be made.
- Serves as a communication tool for the teaching staff, for parents, and for the governing agency.

Teacher Considerations

The aim of curriculum is to help children acquire the skills and behaviors that will promote their optimal growth physically, socially, emotionally, and intellectually. Teachers consider a number of factors in developing a curriculum to provide maximum learning opportunities.

Among these are the educational philosophy and goals of the program. A family day care provider plans activities for a few children in an intimate setting while the kindergarten teacher arranges

Curriculum Planning for Week of _____ May 17–21 _____

Theme: _____ My Senses and Me _____

Day	Art	Science	Group Time	Other
Monday: Sense of smell	Printing with fresh fruits and vegetables Make scented play dough: peppermint	Identify mystery food by smells: onion, garlic, lemon, cinnamon, clove, peppers	Read: *Arthur's Nose;* discuss animal noses, which ones have strong sense of smell and why	Add scent to water table Make popcorn Take a Smell Walk: outside
Tuesday: Sense of touch	Collage of various seeds and pods, legumes, assorted sizes and shapes	Texture walk with hands: bins of fabric, feathers, styrofoam, yarn, paper, popcorn	Read: *Going Barefoot;* touching game: touch parts of body that are soft, hairy, fat, thin, hard, soft, cool, warm	Texture puzzles Fingerpainting Make oobleck (cornstarch and water): outside
Wednesday: Sense of sound	Make a sound mobile: a hanger with metal products	Explore variety of musical instruments: drums, bells of varying sizes and shapes	Read: *Too Much Noise;* sing *John Jacob Jingleheimer Schmidt* Learn to sing a round *Row, Row, Row Your Boat*	Children play musical instruments Parent volunteer plays instrument Parade of sounds: outside
Thursday: Sense of sight	Shrink art Crayon melt Ink blot butterflies	Use color paddles Mix colors with water and food coloring Use magnifying glasses with variety of objects	Read: *Little Blue and Little Yellow* Discuss eyebrows, eyelashes, tears Use braille sample, talk about being blind	Display of items that help us see in the dark Mix two colors of dough Shadow games: outside
Friday: Sense of taste	Collage of food products: popcorn, dry macaroni, peas, legumes	Make ice cream Make fruit salad Make vegetable salad	Read: *The Very Hungry Caterpillar;* show pictures of pig, chicken, cow; identify where milk, eggs, meat come from	Identify tastes: salty, sweet, sour, bitter, no taste

FIGURE 11.2 Curriculum planning can focus on a theme.

small working groups so that the large group will not seem overwhelming. The activities should support the goals of the program and result in the goals being accomplished.

Probably the single most important determinant the teacher must consider is the children themselves. Their ages, developmental levels, individuality, and learning styles are barometers of what will be successful and stimulating curriculum. The number of children in the class will affect the teacher's planning, as will their ethnic and cultural backgrounds. Teachers like to plan curriculum experiences that draw on children's prior knowledge and experience, but which also extend their thinking.

Effective curriculum planning stems from a knowledge of young children. Teachers ask themselves what concepts children should learn and how they will teach those concepts. What does the child already know, and how can the teacher build on that? What is the most effective way to teach a particular concept to this group of children—through sensory exploration or large-motor practice? In many ways, teachers start at the end: they look at what they want the child to accomplish or to learn as a result of this experience and then plan the curriculum to lead toward those results.

A *prerequisite* for planning is the availability of people and material resources and ways to use them. What are the strengths of the teaching staff? Are there enough supplies and equipment available? Are there enough adults to supervise the activities?

The amount of time available in the daily schedule and the amount of space in the room or yard affect a teacher's planning. Fingerpainting requires time for children to get involved, a proximity to water for cleanup, and an area in which to store wet paintings. All of these elements must be considered when teachers plan to include fingerpainting in the curriculum.

Guidelines for Planning Curriculum

The process of developing curriculum is the process of teaching children who and what they are. It begins with understanding what goals are set for learning and then choosing the most pressing

ones for attention. Using available resources, teachers plan effective curriculum for young children. The five steps below are guidelines to sound curriculum planning.

1. *Set goals.* Decide what it is you want children to learn. What do you want them to know about themselves? Others? The world? State goals clearly, preferably in behavioral terms so results can be measured.

2. *Establish priorities.* Make a list of three to five goals or objectives you consider most important. State the reasons for your choices; your own values and educational priorities will emerge more clearly.

3. *Know the resources.* A rich, successful, and creative curriculum relies on a vast number of resources. To create a health clinic in the dramatic play area, for instance, you might need the following resources:
   - *Materials:* Props, such as stethoscopes, X rays, tongue depressors, band aids, medical gowns, and masks.
   - *People:* Parents and/or community people in the health care professions to visit the class.
   - *Community:* Field trips to nearby clinics, hospitals, dentist's office.

4. *Plan ahead.* Set aside a regular time to meet for curriculum planning. This may be on a weekly, monthly, or seasonal basis. Discuss the curriculum activities as well as the daily routines in order to integrate the two.

5. *Evaluate.* Reflect on the outcome of your planning. Consider what worked and what did not, why it was successful or not. Look at the part of the experience that did not work as well as you would have liked. How can it be improved? What can you change about it? An evaluation should be immediate, precise, and supportive. Teachers need feedback about their planning and implementing skills. By refining and improving the curriculum, the needs of children are better served.

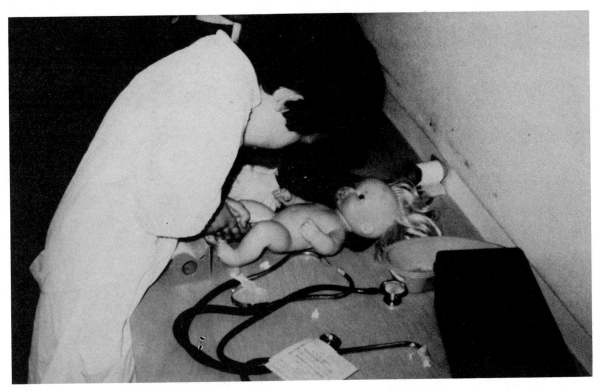

FIGURE 11.3 A rich curriculum provides many resources.

Curriculum Focus

Curriculum, as defined here, is all-encompassing. How then do teachers select from all the possibilities that afford the potential for learning? How do teachers begin to focus on projects and activities in a balanced, integrated way? Three common approaches are to look at (1) the activity or learning centers in the classroom; (2) the skills of the children; and (3) themes.

Classroom Activity Centers

The activity centers in most early childhood programs consist of:

Indoors	Outdoors
Creative arts	Climbing equipment
Blocks	Swings
Table toys/manipulatives	Sand/mud/water
Science/discovery	Wheel toys
Dramatic play	Woodworking
Language arts/books	Hollow blocks
Math	Music
Music	Nature/science

Activities and materials are available in all of these areas. Some will be teacher-directed and others will be self-initiating and child-centered.

Whatever the area, it needs attention and planning. Wherever children are present, learning and playing will take place. Since each play space will make a contribution to children's experiences, teachers should develop appropriate curriculum for

Activity _____
    1. Brief description _____
       _____

    2. What will the teacher's role be? _____
       _____

    3. What will the children do? _____
       _____

Where in the room/yard will this be set up? _____
_____

How many children will participate at once? _____
_____

How will the activity be limited to the desired number of children? _____
_____

What equipment and materials are needed? _____
_____
_____

How much time will this activity require? Where in the daily schedule will
it take place? _____
_____

Why was this activity selected? What are the learning objectives? _____
_____
_____

List comments and questions that will help involve children in the activity
and enrich their experience. _____
_____

List any related projects that might expand this as a learning experience
(activities, books, accessories, etc.) _____
_____
_____
_____

What are the clean-up provisions? Will children be involved? _____
_____
_____

FIGURE 11.4 Sample form for curriculum planning: one activity. (Adapted from Vassar College Nursery School)

Activity _____
How many children participated? _____ Did any avoid the activity? _____
How involved did children become? Very ___ Briefly ___ Watched only ____
What were children's reactions? Describe what they said and did. _____
_____
_____
_____
_____

What did you do to attract children? To maintain their interest? _____
_____
_____
_____

How would you rate the success of this activity? Poor ___
Adequate ___ Good ___ Great ___ Why? _____
What skills/abilities were needed? Did the children exhibit the skills? ____
_____
_____

What parts of the activity were most successful? Why? _____
_____

Describe any difficulty you encountered. Give reasons and tell how you
would handle it if it happened again. _____
_____
_____

If you did this activity again, what would you change? _____
_____

In light of your evaluation, what would you plan for a follow-up activity?
_____

How did this activity compare with your goals and expectations? _____
_____
_____

FIGURE 11.5 Sample form for activity evaluation. (Adapted from Vassar College Nursery School)

that learning area. Figure 11.6 demonstrates curriculum potential, both indoors and out.

Children's Skills

Just as curriculum can be developed by focusing on the activity or learning centers, so, too, can an early childhood program be planned around the skill levels of the children in the class.

The first decision teachers must make concerns what particular skill they wish to help children develop. The skill can be in the area of physical, cognitive, language, creative, social, or emotional development. The nature of the individual class and the program philosophy will help teachers establish priorities for these skills. Teachers then select the activities and materials that will enhance the development of any one or more of those particular skills. Figure 11.7 shows how the cognitive skill of classification can be implemented in the classroom, making it the focus of the entire curriculum.

Themes

A common method of developing curriculum is to focus on themes. This mode of planning is used in many early childhood and elementary settings; it is often a way to emphasize holidays. Focusing on themes, however, can and should be much more than that.

Themes that are of great interest to young children are those that directly concern themselves. The body as a theme suggests many avenues for development: body parts may be emphasized; exploration using the senses may be stressed; measuring and weighing children may be used to demonstrate growth of the body. Another subject to which children readily respond is that of home and family. Animals, especially pets, are appealing to young children and can lead into further curriculum areas of wild animals, prehistoric animals, and so on.

The more in touch with children the teachers are, the more their classroom themes should reflect the children's interests and abilities. Children who live in Silicon Valley in California, in Houston, Texas, or in central Florida will have a local interest in space shuttles and computers. The urban child of New York, Detroit, or Washington, D.C., will relate more readily to themes about subways, taxis, and tall buildings. Children's interests often focus on, but are not necessarily limited to, what they have experienced. By choosing themes that coincide with children's daily lives, teachers promote connected and relevant learning.

Television, travel, and older brothers and sisters enlarge a child's vision so that the themes a teacher chooses do not have to reflect only the world in which the child lives. With appropriate visual aids and manipulative materials, a child in the sunbelt can experience snow and ice *vicariously* or enjoy learning a song and dance from Spain.

Some themes in an early childhood setting can address children's own issues. All young children share similar fears and curiosity about the world they do not know but imagine so vividly. The cues children give, particularly about their concerns, suggest to the observant teacher some important themes of childhood. During Halloween, for example, it can be helpful and reassuring to children if the theme of masks is developed. Select some masks that have a function, such as hospital masks, ski masks, safety glasses, sun glasses, snorkel masks, or wrestling and football helmets. Children can try them on and become comfortable with the way their appearance changes. They can laugh with friends as they look in the mirror to see how a mask changes the appearance but does not change the person.

Prehistoric animals are another theme that calls attention to the natural world and deals with issues of monsters, both real and imaginary. Learning about sea animals and the ocean can give young children an opportunity to talk about the wild and noisy waves, sharks, and just getting their faces wet in salty water.

Through holiday themes, teachers can reinforce the multicultural nature of the curriculum. Ethnic, national, and religious holidays from all over the world help children celebrate the differences and similarities in people and their heritage.

Area	Activity	Learning Objectives
	OUTDOORS	
Art	Use nature material for collage	Observing/finding materials; experimenting (Why does the leaf stick and not the pine cone?)
Small toys/ manipulatives	Woodworking	Counting nails, hammers, C-clamps; classifying (Which nail will go into the redwood, the pine, the plywood?)
Science	Wet or dry sand	Locomotion; force/physics; change in matter (What happens when the sand is wet? Can I carry, pull, slide, push it the same as when it is dry?)
Language arts	Discovering birds' nests	Communication/observation; reasoning and problem solving (What is the nest made of? Where do birds find the materials for it? How do young birds learn how to fly?)
Dramatic play	"Camping out" dramatic play accessories	Social conflict resolution; acting out people, places; symbolic representation (using a map)
	INDOORS	
Art	Painting with corn cobs	Tactile stimulation; awareness of textural design, small-motor coordination; use of imagination
Small toys/ manipulatives	Flannel board cutouts in adult and children's shapes with clothes to dress them	Creating an awareness of body parts and their use; small-muscle coordination, awareness of body and clothing; identification of body parts, self, clothing
Science	Making butter	Learning about cause/effect relationship; small-muscle development; language development; awareness of milk by-products
Language arts	Read *Katy and the Big Snow, The Snowy Day*	To stimulate discussion about weather and seasons; differences between hot and cold climates; to compare and contrast seasons; vocabulary words related to temperature
Dramatic play	Post office and office dramatic play accessories	To experiment with other roles; to reinforce letter concepts; to encourage social interaction; to learn about the mail process

FIGURE 11.6 Curriculum happens indoors and out.

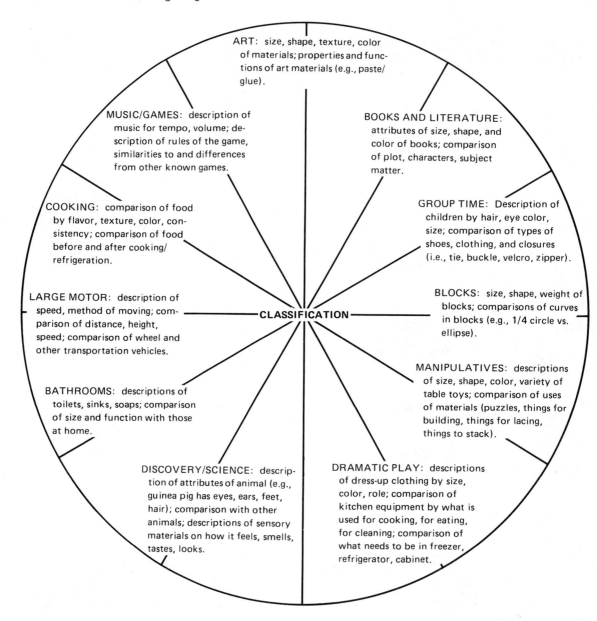

FIGURE 11.7 Curriculum can be developed with a focus on a particular skill.

FIGURE 11.8 Physical skills are included in curriculum development.

CURRICULUM EXPRESSED THROUGH PLAY

What Is Play?

Play! What a wonderful word! It calls up images from the past, those childhood years when playing was the focus of our waking hours. "Will you play with me?" is one of the most expressive, expectant questions known. It carries with it hope and anticipation about a world of fun and make-believe, a world of adventure and exploration, a world of the young child.

Play is the essence of creativity. Children play in cultures where creativity and imagination are valued (Sutton-Smith, 1978). City streets, parks and fields, tenements, huts, empty rooms, and backyards are all settings for play. Play is a way of life for

FIGURE 11.9 Play: the essence of childhood.

children; it is their natural response. It is what children *do* and it is serious business to them. Any activity children choose to engage in is play; it is neverending.

What is play? Educators and psychologists have called play the work of childhood and the mirror of the child's growth (Hartley, Frank, and Goldenson, 1952). It is a window into the child's world—a self-satisfying activity through which children gain control and come to understand life. Play teaches children about themselves; they learn how tall—or short—they are, what words to use to get a turn on the swing, and where to put their hands when climbing a ladder. Through play, children learn about the world: what the color purple is, how to make matzoh balls, and how to be a friend. Play helps children define who they are.

Play takes many forms. Children play when they sing, dig in the mud, build a block tower, or dress up. Play can be purely physical (running, climbing, ball throwing) or highly intellectual (solving an intricate puzzle, remembering the words to a song). Play is creative when crayons, clay, and fingerpaint are used. Its emotional form is expressed when children pretend to be mommies, daddies, or babies. Skipping rope with a friend, playing jacks, and sharing a book are examples of the social side of play.

Types of Play

There is a general sequence to the development of social play. Toddlers begin by playing alone (*solitary play*) or with adults. Playing with parents decreases as interest in other children increases. During the toddler years, children become aware of one another. They begin to play side by side, without interacting (*parallel play*). They are aware of and pleased about the other person, but are not directly involved with them. The preschool years bring many changes for children in relation to social development. The number and quality of relationships outside the home increases as does the ability to play with other children. At first, this is accomplished just by a child's presence in a group: playing at the water table with four other children or joining a circle for fingerplays (*associative play*). When children join forces with one another in an active way, when they verbalize, plan, and carry out play, *cooperative play* is established. This is the most common type of peer interaction during these preschool years. Figure 11.10 shows a timeline of social play development.

Most play is unstructured and happens naturally when the curriculum is designed for play. *Spontaneous play* is the unplanned, self-selected activity in which children freely participate. Children's natural inclinations are toward play materials and experiences that are developmentally appropriate. Therefore, when they are allowed to make choices in a free play situation, children will choose activities that express their individual interests, needs, and readiness levels.

Dramatic play—or imaginative play—is a common form of spontaneous play. Three- and four-year-olds are at the peak of their interest in this type of activity. In dramatic play, children assume

Infant and toddler play is solitary. (Courtesy of Stephanie Barry Agnew)

Parallel play: side by side.

Associative play: nearby but alone.

Joining forces in cooperative play.

FIGURE 11.10 A timeline of social play.

FIGURE 11.11 Dramatic play reaches its peak in the preschool years.

the roles of different characters, both animate and inanimate. Children identify themselves with another person or thing, playing out situations that interest or frighten them. Dramatic play reveals children's attitudes and concepts toward people and things in their environment. Much of the play is wishful thinking, pretending great strength and deeds. This is the way children cope with their smallness or lack of strength. Superhero play is appealing, since it so readily addresses a child's sense of helplessness and inferiority. Pretending to be Wonder Woman makes it easier to understand and accept the limitations of the real world. Dramatic play provides the means for children to work out their difficulties by themselves. By doing so, they become free to pursue other tasks and more formal learning. For all these reasons, play is invaluable for young children.

Values of Play

In their classic book, *Understanding Children's Play* (1952), Hartley, Frank, and Goldenson define eight functions of play:

1. To imitate adults.
2. To play out real-life roles in intensive ways.
3. To reflect home relationships and real-life experiences.
4. To express pressing needs.
5. To release unacceptable impulses.
6. To reverse roles usually taken.
7. To mirror growth.
8. To work out problems and experiment with solutions.

The main theme of these functions is the emotional release they provide children. Play becomes a suitable outlet for expressing negative feelings, hostility, and aggression. Clay can be pounded, balls can be kicked and thrown, dolls can be spanked. Young children give free expression to a wide range of emotions, playing them out and releasing tension. The early childhood curriculum is developed with this in mind.

But play is more than an avenue for emotional growth. Play promotes learning for the whole child. There are a wide range of learning opportunities inherent in any one play activity. Water play is a popular curriculum offering in most early childhood settings. What specific learnings take place as children explore the properties of water? How are their developmental needs challenged?

Water play promotes:	*By teaching children:*
Emotional growth	The soothing effect of water; the pleasure of playing with a messy, sometimes forbidden medium; sensory pleasure in splashing, trickling, swirling water through fingers, hands, and feet.
Language development	Play with words of alliteration (swish, swirl, splish, splash); new words: funnel, eyedropper, siphon, float.
Creativity	New ways to store, move, and pour water.
Social growth	To share space at a water table as well as to share some of the equipment; to be next to or across from a friend; to have fun with others; to wait for a turn.

Water play promotes:	*By teaching children:*
Cognitive development	Problem solving with tubes, sieves, pipes; experimenting with measurement, float and sink properties, volume, quantity, fractions, weight, comparisons, numbers, temperature.
Physical coordination	Eye–hand coordination; small-motor control in learning to pour, squeeze, balance.

All play activity holds this potential for growth and learning. Blocks, easel painting, woodworking, and clay could also be analyzed for how they contribute to the development of the child as a whole. Figure 11.13 demonstrates further the learning possibilities in all play activity.

Play as a Cornerstone of Learning

Play is the cornerstone of learning, the foundation from which children venture forth to investigate, to test out. Curriculum takes on expression through play; teachers plan curriculum that uses play as the medium for learning. As they mature, children integrate and assimilate their play experiences. What started out as play—the sheer fun of it—is transformed into learning experiences. Curiosity about magnets at age five nourishes a scientific attitude for the later years, as well as a foundation for studying gravity, planetary movements, and the like. Feeling free to sing out at group time at age three can prepare a child to be an active participant in the kindergarten classroom at age six.

Teachers want children to learn about *themselves,* to learn about the *world around them,* and to learn how to *solve problems.* A childhood filled with play opportunities should culminate in these three types of learning.

1. *Learning about themselves* includes developing a positive self-image and a sense of competence. Children should know and feel good about them-

FIGURE 11.12 Water play is fun—and promotes learning.

COGNITIVE/LANGUAGE

Distinguishes between reality and fantasy
Encourages creative thought and curiosity
Allows for problem solving
Encourages thinking, planning
Develops memory, perceptual skills, and concept
  formation
Learns to try on other roles
Takes initiative
Acquires knowledge and integrates learning
Learns communication skills
Develops listening and oral language skills

PHYSICAL

Releases energy
Builds fine and gross motor skills
Gains control over body
Provides challenges
Requires active use of body
Allows for repetition and practice
Refines eye–hand coordination
Develops self-awareness
Encourages health and fitness

SOCIAL

Tries on other personalities, roles
Learns cooperation and taking turns
Learns to lead, follow
Builds a repertoire of social language
Learns to verbalize needs
Reflects own culture, heritage, values
Learns society's rules and group responsibility
Shows respect for other's property, rights
Teaches an awareness of others
Learns how to join a group
Builds awareness of self as member of a group
Gives sense of identification
Promotes self-image, self-esteem
Experiences joy, fun

EMOTIONAL

Develops self-confidence and self-esteem
Learns to take a different viewpoint
Resolves inner fears, conflicts
Builds trust in self and others
Reveals child's personality
Encourages autonomy
Learns to take risks
Acts out anger, hostility, frustration, joy
Gains self-control
Becomes competent in several areas
Takes initiative

FIGURE 11.13 Play is the cornerstone of learning. (Photo courtesy of Stride Rite Children's Centers, Cambridge, Mass.)

selves as learners. They should develop a sense of independence, a measure of self-discipline, and knowledge based on full use of their sensory skills.

2. *To learn about others and the world around them* means developing an awareness of other people. Teachers want children to perfect their communication and social skills so that they will be more sensitive participants in the world in which they live. This means that children learn and appreciate some of the values of their parents, the community, and society at large. When children become aware of the demands of living in today's society, it can help them become more responsible citizens. The emphasis on social interaction and group relationships in the early childhood setting underscores this goal.

3. *To learn to solve problems,* children need to be accomplished in observation and investigation. When exploring a puzzle, for example, children need to know how to manipulate it, take it apart, and put it back together, to see how other people solve puzzles, and to know how to get help when the pieces just do not seem to fit together. They should know how to predict and experiment. What will happen, wonders a kindergartener, when a glass is placed over a glowing candle? How will that change if the glass is large or small? What is the effect if the glass is left over the candle for a long time or for a second? Young children also need to learn how to negotiate, discuss, compromise, and stand their ground, particularly when they encounter and solve problems socially. "I want the red cart and someone already has it," thinks the preschooler. "Now what? How can I get it? What if the other person says no? Will the plan that works with my best friend work with someone else? When do I ask for help? Will crying make a difference?" In order to be effective problem-solvers, children must know and experience themselves and others.

Teacher Considerations

Play is a window to the child's world and the adult who knows the value of play is committed to learning about children while they play. The vast knowledge of human development and behavior comes from researchers who spent countless hours observing and recording children playing. Classroom teachers continue to learn about children by listening to and observing spontaneous play activity and planning curriculum that encourages play. They discover each child's individual personality, learning style, and preferred mode of play.

Genuine interest is one way teachers show their approval of the play process. Creating a safe environment where children feel physically and emotionally secure is another. To establish play as an important part of the curriculum, teachers must:

- *Understand,* appreciate, and value play experiences for young children.
- *Focus* on the process of learning rather than on the process of teaching.
- *Reflect* on their observations in order to know what activities, concepts, or learning should be encouraged or extended.

The two major roles of teachers in promoting spontaneous play environments are (1) as facilitators or supervisors of play, and (2) by setting the stage and creating an atmosphere for play.

The Teacher as Facilitator

One of the most difficult tasks teachers face is knowing when to join children at play and when to remain outside the activity. They must ask themselves whether their presence will support what is happening or whether it will *inhibit* the play. Sometimes teachers are tempted to correct children's misconceptions during play. Abby and Salina, deeply involved in their grocery store drama, are making change incorrectly. A teacher must judge whether or not to explain the difference between nickels and quarters at that time or create an opportunity at a later date. Teachers must be aware of what happens

FIGURE 11.14 Teachers learn about children by watching them play. (Courtesy of Stride Rite Children's Centers, Cambridge, Mass.)

if they interrupt the flow of play and how they influence the direction it takes. If Abby and Salina begin to talk about their coins, showing an interest in learning how to compute their change, the teacher can move into the discussion without seeming to interfere.

When do teachers interact and intervene? Many adults enjoy playing with the children in their class. Others feel more comfortable as active observers. Every teaching situation will demand the teachers' involvement at some level. The hesitant child may need help entering a play situation; children may become too embroiled in an argument to settle it alone; play may become inappropriate, exploitative, or dominated by a particular child.

The following guidelines are ways teachers facilitate play. A good teacher:

- Guides the play, but does not direct or dominate the situation or overwhelm children by participation.
- Capitalizes on the children's thoughts and ideas; does not enforce a point of view on them.
- Models play when necessary. Shows children how a specific character might act, how to ask for a turn, how to hold a hammer when hammering.

Models ways to solve problems that involve children interacting on their own behalf.
- Asks questions; clarifies with children what is happening.
- Helps children start, end, and begin again. Gives them verbal cues to enable them to follow through on an idea.
- Focuses the children's attention on one another. Encourages them to interact with each other.
- Interprets children's behavior aloud, when necessary; helps them verbalize their feelings as they work through conflicts.
- Expands the play potential by making statements and asking questions that lead to discovery and exploration.

Creating the Environment for Play

To structure the environment for play, teachers include uninterrupted time blocks in the daily schedule (at least one half-hour to forty-five minutes) for free-play time. This allows children to explore many avenues of the curriculum free from time restraints. It is frustrating to young children to have their play cut off just as they are getting deeply involved.

A variety of activity areas and learning centers set up with specific play and learning materials provides children with choices for play. There should be enough to do so that each child has a choice between at least two play options. Established routines in the schedule add to the framework of a day planned for play. The raw materials of play—toys, games, equipment—are changed periodically so that new ones may be introduced for further challenge.

In choosing materials, teachers select dress-up clothes and accessories that appeal to all children's needs, interests, and emotions. Props are required for a variety of roles: men, women, babies, doctors, nurses, grocers, mail carriers, teachers, and fire fighters. Hats for many occupations help a child establish the role of an airline pilot, tractor driver, construction worker, police officer, or baseball player. Large purses are used for carrying mail and babies' diapers; they also double as a briefcase or luggage. Simple jackets or capes transform a child for many roles. Things that represent aspects of the child's daily life are important; children need many opportunities to act out their life stories.

For young children, teachers make sure there are duplicates of popular materials. Group play is more likely to occur with three telephones, four carriages, eight hats, and five wagons. Social interaction is enhanced when three space shuttle drivers can be at the controls.

Play is further enlarged by materials that are open-ended. These are materials that will expand the children's learning opportunities because they can be used in more than one way. Blocks, a staple of the early childhood curriculum, are a case in point. Children explore and manipulate blocks in many ways. The youngest children carry and stack blocks and also enjoy wheeling them around in wagons or trucks. They also enjoy the repetitious action of making small columns of blocks. As children learn to make enclosures, they add animals, people, and transportation toys to their block play. Older preschoolers build multistoried structures as part of their dramatic play—offices, firehouses, garages, and the like.

Play is the way curriculum is expressed in the early childhood setting. The function of play in the life of a young child is more than sheer enjoyment. Play provides an avenue for growth in social, emotional, intellectual, and physical development. Teachers, aware of play as a foundation for learning, provide an atmosphere that supports the play process. They provide a setting in which play is recognized as the curriculum of the child, the primary process through which children learn. Curriculum comes alive as children discover and take pleasure in learning.

OTHER CURRICULUM PERSPECTIVES

A sound curriculum is the *linchpin* of a quality program for children. Curriculum planning and development is a creative act, one that is rewarding for teachers. In the next three chapters, curriculum implementations will be explored from another perspective, that of the major areas of development in the child's growth. In Chapter 12, the focus will be on how curriculum affects the growing body. Chapter 13 will emphasize the curricular role in developing the mind, and Chapter 14 will explore the curricular issues surrounding social and emotional growth.

SUMMARY

Curriculum encompasses the planned and unplanned events children experience in group settings. Curriculum can include whatever happens to a child while in school or day care, or it can be a syllabus with detailed lesson plans.

Developing curriculum includes setting goals, establishing priorities, knowing what resources are available, planning ahead, and then evaluating the process. As teachers develop their curriculum plans, they may focus on the classroom activity or learning centers, the skills of the children, or a particular theme. All three lend themselves to a basis for curriculum planning, and all are important vehicles for creative and effective curriculum for young children.

Review Questions

1. What are the two common approaches to curriculum in the early childhood setting? Give an example of each.

2. Name five steps to effective curriculum planning.

3. How are written curriculum plans useful to the beginning teacher?

4. How is play beneficial to the child's development?

5. Define four stages of play.

6. How are number concepts learned when children play (a) in the sand area; (b) easel painting; (c) on the climbers; (d) during housekeeping dramatic play?

Learning Activities

1. How is curriculum developed in an early childhood setting in your area? Are all five steps used? What would you change (and why) in planning activities for a group?

2. Develop a curriculum for a week-long celebration of a major holiday: (a) for three-year-olds in a half-day nursery school; (b) for six-year-olds in an after-school extended day program; (c) for a family day care home.

3. Make up your own definition of play.

4. Observe a class of children at play. What is the difference between a teacher who interacts with them as they play and one who intervenes?

5. Develop a dramatic play kit for your school. Select a theme and collect appropriate props and accessories. Describe why you chose this theme and what you expect children to gain from this experience.

Bibliography

Bjorklund, Gail. *Planning for Play: A Developmental Approach.* Columbus, Ohio: Charles E. Merrill Publishing Co., 1978.

Brown, Janet F., ed. *Curriculum Planning for Young Children.* Washington, D.C.: National Association for the Education of Young Children, 1982.

Hartley, Ruth E.; Frank, Lawrence K.; and Goldenson, Robert M. *Understanding Children's Play.* New York: Columbia University Press, 1952.

Read, Katherine, and Patterson, June. *The Nursery School and Kindergarten.* New York: Holt, Rinehart and Winston, 1980.

Schwartz, Sydney L., and Robison, Helen F. *Designing Curriculum for Early Childhood.* Boston: Allyn and Bacon, 1982.

Sponseller, Doris, ed. *Play as a Learning Medium.* Washington, D.C.: National Association for the Education of Young Children, 1978.

Sutton-Smith, Brian. "Play Isn't Just Kids' Stuff." *Parents,* August 1978, pp. 48–49.

12

Planning for the Body: Physical/Motor Development

Questions for Thought

- What is physical/motor development?
- Does physical growth differ from motor development in young children?
- What are the physical and motor skills children learn in an early childhood setting?

- What should the teacher of young children consider when planning for physical/motor development?
- In what ways can physical/motor curriculum be developed?

Outline

Portions of this chapter were developed with the assistance of Gay Spitz, Hartnell College, Salinas, Calif.

INTRODUCTION

Teachers often characterize children through their movements. Movements are one of the most notable features of young children's behavior. Pregnant mothers are aware of fetal motions and often assign personality traits to their children by these movements. What is striking about newborns is the extent of their full-bodied, random movements when they cry, roll over, follow, and reach for a crib mobile. Learning to walk is a major milestone in a child's development. Holding a pencil, cutting with scissors, tying a shoe are further illustrations of how motor development signifies growth. Motor skills are a good indication of how the child is progressing.

As teachers and parents concentrate on the child in motion, they see two categories of physical and motor development: "learning to move and learning through movement" (Halverson, 1971).

Learning to Move

Basic motor skills develop in the early childhood years. As in other areas of development, by six or seven years of age, most motor skill development has been accomplished. These years form the foundation for movement and motor proficiency. Though skills will improve throughout a lifetime, it is generally believed that after the early years, no new basic skills will be added to children's movement repertoire (Malina, 1982).

Learning Through Movement

Motor abilities affect other areas of development. Recent research reinforces this notion. Malina (1982) claims that motor development greatly affects "the child's cognitive development, the child's own self-discovery, and the child's ability to communicate." There is evidence of such interrelationships in children.

Tim is reluctant to climb outside. He is easily frightened when he—or anyone else—is up in a tree or on any climber. Because he cannot

risk using his body in space, he stops himself from playing with anyone who invites him to try these activities. Thus, Tim's lack of gross-motor development is affecting his social skills.

Samantha loves to draw and cut. She chooses the art area every day she attends the two-year-old class. Not only are her fine motor skills well developed for her age, she takes great pride in her creations. Her motor skills enhance her self-confidence in school. In turn, she receives praise and attention from others as she communicates with both adults and children through her work.

The greatest portion of the young child's day is spent in physical activity. Quality early childhood programs recognize this, providing for a full range of physical and motor experiences. Indoors, children use puzzles, scissors, and dressing frames as they practice fine motor skills. They dance with scarves and streamers to music. *Perceptual–motor development*, as with body awareness, occurs when children learn songs and games ("Head and Shoulders, Knees and Toes" or "Mother May I Take Two Giant Steps?") or while fingerpainting. Outdoors, gross motor skills are refined by the use of climbers, swings, hopscotch, and ring-toss.

Throughout the program, physical/motor development is emphasized as an important part of children's learning. Children will need time as well as equipment and activities to practice their skills. The value teachers place on physical/motor development is directly related to the time allotted in the daily schedule for children to pursue them.

For years, early childhood programs have made an outdoor environment available to children, assuming a great need for physical activity and that children will find ways to fill that need themselves. However, many school outdoor areas contain few challenges, perhaps only a blacktop for bouncing balls and a small, metal climber for hanging and climbing. Moreover, American children are exposed to a value system in which physical/motor fitness is not always a high priority. Children live with adults whose primary sport is as spectator only, and they are often encouraged toward *sedentary* activi-

FIGURE 12.1 Children are the picture of movement, spending the greatest portion of their day in physical activity.

ties themselves at an early age, such as watching TV and using computers.

Physical/motor development is the central focus of the needs and interests of young children; it should play a central role in planning the curriculum. Teachers must recognize that children have different needs from adults; they are growing, developing, emerging beings with a set of physical needs and interests that are quite different. Too often, adults try to develop miniathletes without first de-

veloping the child's fundamental movement activities.

PHYSICAL GROWTH/ MOTOR DEVELOPMENT

Physical Growth

Physical growth refers to increases in size and changes in body proportions (Stone and Church,

1979). Physical growth follows several basic principles. Early childhood is the time of most rapid growth, though development does not take place at an even pace, but in starts and spurts. A child will tend to grow rapidly in infancy and as a toddler, with the growth rate beginning to taper off during preschool and middle childhood years. While there are individual differences in the rate of maturation among children, growth follows a sequential pattern. Development seems to follow a directional pattern as well:

- *Gross to fine.* Large muscles develop before smaller ones. The gross motor skill of walking develops before that of handling scissors and pencils, both fine motor activities.

- *Proximal to distal.* Growth starts at the center of the body and moves outward. To reach an object, a child will use shoulders and elbows be-

fore the fingers and wrist. Toddlers walk first with the whole leg, then develop refined use of the knees and ankles.

- *Cephalocaudal.* Children develop physically in a head-to-toe pattern. First, babies will move their eyes, head, and hands. Later, they learn to stand, creep, and climb.

Growth is influenced by a variety of factors. Genetics, disease, and injury all play a part in how children grow. Environmental influences, such as nutrition and experience, are greatest during the early years. Figure 12.3 shows an overview of growth from infancy through early childhood.

Motor Development

Motor development is the process through which a child acquires movement patterns and skills. It is a process of continuous modification based upon the interaction of (1) *maturation* (i.e., the genetically controlled rate of growth); (2) *prior experiences;* and (3) *new motor activities.* Like physical growth, motor development is a sequence of stages that is universal but still allows for individual differences. Each stage is different from, yet grows out of, the preceding level. Figure 12.4 charts motor development through the early years.

FIGURE 12.2 Children's growth follows a predictable pattern: large muscles develop before smaller ones.

PHYSICAL/MOTOR SKILLS IN EARLY CHILDHOOD EDUCATION

Types of Movement

Physical/motor skills involve three types of movement: gross motor, fine motor, and perceptual–motor.

Gross Motor Activity

Gross motor activity involves movements of the entire body, or large parts of the body. Using various

Age	Weight	Height	Proportion	Teeth
Newborn	7 pounds	20 inches	Head = ¼ of length	None
Infancy (up to 18 mos.)	Gains 15 pounds (now 20–25 lbs.)	Adds 8 inches (now 28–29″)	About the same	6
Toddler (18 mos. to 2½ yrs.)	Gains 5 pounds (now 28–30 lbs.)	Adds another inch or two (now 29–33″)	Legs = 34% of body	20
Preschool (2½ to 5 yrs.)	About 5 pounds/yr. (now 30–40 lbs.)	Adds 14–15 inches from birth; at age 3 = ½ of adult height (now 35–40″)	Head growth slows; legs at age 5 = 44% of body	20
Early– middle childhood (5–8 yrs.)	Doubles before adolescence; (age 6 = 45–50 lbs.)	Adds 9–10 inches (age 6 = 44–48″)	Continues to move slowly towards adult proportions	Begins to lose baby teeth; replaced by permanent teeth (age 6 = 20–24)

FIGURE 12.3   An overview of growth shows how rapid is physical growth in early childhood.

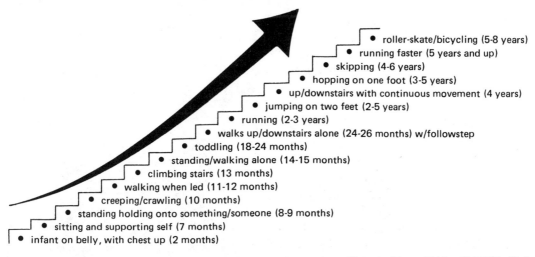

FIGURE 12.4   Motor development follows a developmental sequence. (Adapted from Shirley [1931] in Roberton and from Shirley [1933] in Teeple [both in Ridenour, 1978])

muscle groups, children try to crawl, throw, or hop. Activities that include balance, agility, coordination, flexibility, strength, speed, and endurance foster gross motor development.

Fine Motor Activity

Fine motor activity uses the small muscles of the body and its extremities (the hands and feet). Such movement requires dexterity, precision, and manipulative skill. Grasping, spinning, and turning are all activities that refine these skills.

Perceptual–Motor Activity

Perceptual–motor activity involves both how children move (motor) and what they perceive (perceptual). As Gallahue (1976) puts it:

> The dash that appears in the term "perceptual–motor" signifies the interdependence of one on the other. This becomes apparent when we recognize that efficient and effective movement is dependent upon accurate perceptions of ourselves and our world and that development of one's perceptual abilities is dependent, in part, on movement.

In a sense, every movement is perceptual–motor activity, since the body and mind must work together to complete all motor tasks. The perceptual task is to process information; the motor response activates what is received in a physical way. The complex nature of perceptual–motor development can be seen when examining its three elements, those of spatial, temporal, and sensory awareness.

Spatial Awareness. For children, spatial awareness means a sense of their own bodies and the body's relationship to space, as well as a knowledge of what the body parts can do. This includes *laterality* and a sense of direction. Laterality is a map of the child's internal space; *directionality* is one of external space (Radler, 1960). Specifically, spatial awareness refers to left and right, up and down, front and behind. To illustrate, let us look at 2½-year-old Tamara. She demonstrates her awareness of spatial relationships as she moves herself up to a table (without bumping into it), reaches to her

FIGURE 12.5 Gross motor activity uses the various large-muscle groups so that children can move their entire bodies.

FIGURE 12.6 Fine motor activity requires using the smaller muscles of the body with dexterity and precision. (Courtesy of Stephanie Barry Agnew)

left to pick up a ball of clay, and turns around behind her to choose a rolling pin.

Temporal Awareness. Temporal awareness is the child's inner clock, a time structure that lets the child coordinate body parts. Dancing to a rhythmic beat develops this kind of skill. For instance, seven-year-old Luis and Aref ask if it is time to clean up as they finish their game of soccer. The after-school center has sports time for about an hour before cleaning up for snack; the children have an inner sense of time that parallels their knowledge of the daily schedule.

Sensory Awareness. Sensory awareness refers to use of the senses. It is another way the body gives the mind information. Vision is the dominant sense for young children. Auditory (hearing) skills help children process information about language. Babies seem to put everything in their mouths to learn. When four-year-old Stephanie picks up each object at the display table, she is using her sense of touch to discover size, shape, and volume.

Learning Motor Skills

Children must use their bodies in order to learn motor skills. They acquire these skills by making comparisons between their past experience and new actions. Such comparisons use memory and experience.

Memory and Experience

Memory plays an important part in learning motor movements, since children need to recall what they just did in order to make corrections or refinements. In the short term, the ball that does not reach the basket is tossed further on the next shot. To get the puzzle piece to fit, a child remembers other ways to manipulate the pieces. A long-term memory of movement is one that may go unrehearsed for longer periods of time. The experience of swimming, for example, may be recalled only in the summer. Whether using short-term or long-term memory, children learn motor skills by remembering what they have already learned and by practice.

The experiences children have and the ability to recall those experiences are necessary to the process of gaining motor skill. Rehearsal is as important to the young child as it is to the actors in a play. "Overt practice, repeating a specific movement over and over again, provides a motor rehearsal young children display everyday." (Clark *in* Ridenour, 1978)

Practicing Basic Skills

Children learning motor skills need experience in basic skills; they must learn simple skills before combining them into complex activities. To gain mastery over a skill, there must be an opportunity for practice. Children must have time to try, refine, and try again.

FIGURE 12.7 To learn a motor skill, children must combine memory with experience, taking advantage of opportunities to try something new and to practice what has already been learned. (Courtesy of Stride Rite Children's Centers, Cambridge, Mass.)

Feedback

Children modify and improve their motor skills as they receive information about their movements, both *intrinsic* (the paintbrush makes marks when it is pushed across the paper) and *extrinsic* ("I notice that your legs are very far apart as you try the somersault; how about holding them together as you roll next time?").

A Range of Developmental Levels

Any group of young children will have various levels of motor growth and physical development. An individual child may have different abilities and skills in gross, fine, and perceptual–motor areas; activities should, therefore, be offered on several developmental levels. Climbing boards put on several levels and puzzles ranging from six to sixty pieces are two examples of how teachers can meet the need for success and challenge.

ROLE OF THE TEACHER

Considerations

As teachers plan programs for physical/motor development, they reflect on several important issues.

Sex-Role Stereotyping

Is motor behavior different for boys and girls? If so, why? Research indicates that there are differences between girls and boys in these areas. For example, behavioral differences in motor development are apparent in early life: one-year-old girls already spend more time in fine motor tasks, while baby boys are more engaged in gross motor activity. Preschool boys, on the average, are better in activities requiring speed or strength, while girls excel in jumping, hopping, and balancing. Yet by five or six, boys have begun to do better in most gross motor tasks (Malina, 1982).

Why does this happen? Probably some sex differences are the result of genetics. At the same time, sex role expectations profoundly affect the motor

and physical development of young children. This is the crucial issue for teachers, for their attitudes can either encourage or discourage children from developing to their fullest potential. Teachers must acknowledge the differences that exist, and then ask themselves:

- What messages do I give children about physical activity? Do I value it for myself? For children? Do I value physical expression for girls as well as boys?

- Do I emphasize sports as a way to have fun? A way to be healthy? Do I only praise the "winner"?

- Can I provide male and female role models for physical activities?

FIGURE 12.8 Teachers must consider sex-role stereotyping in their classrooms as they model for children participation in indoor, fine motor tasks as well as outdoor, gross motor activities.

- Do I encourage children to wear clothing that allows them the freedom to run, climb, tumble? What do I do when girls arrive in long dresses and party shoes? What do I wear?

- Are all physical/motor activities made equally available and attractive to boys and girls? What happens if some children dominate these activities, while others never choose them?

- How do I actively engage all children in every form of physical activity? Do I let them know I think it is important?

A Safe and Challenging Environment

Teachers ensure the safety of the children. To maintain a safe physical environment, they see to it that materials and equipment are in usable condition, and that overall traffic patterns are hazard-free. For example, to make a gymnastic activity safe, teachers would provide mats and make sure that only one child is tumbling at a time.

Psychological safety requires an even finer sensitivity on the part of the teaching staff. Fear is a learned response and teachers must be careful not to discourage children from using their full range of abilities, creating overly anxious and fearful children. The new teacher is often concerned about children's safety, particularly when they are climbing. It helps to remember that children generally climb to heights that are comfortable for them; in other words, they set their own limits.

The practice of picking children up and placing them on equipment, often at their own request, is often questioned. If teachers comply with children's wishes to be lifted and set somewhere high, they are placing those children in situations outside of their natural limits. The children may see this as saying, "You are incapable of climbing up there yourself," or "It is too dangerous for you to try that alone." Also, this does not allow children to gain experience in basic skills first, but puts them in a situation that calls for skills more complex than they have at the time. This denies the child the opportunity to practice those skills. Children learn their capabilities by being held responsible for what

they do. When they must seek solutions to getting up, out, in, or down, they learn to handle realistically their current level of physical and motor development. Teachers lend encouragement and confidence to children by saying, "I can't put you up there, but I will help you try."

When creating and maintaining a challenging environment, teachers consider both variety and level of challenge. A variety of surfaces encourages a variety of movements. Cement may be appropriate for transportation toys, but climbing/hanging/dropping are more likely to occur with tanbark or rubber mats. Varying the equipment also stimulates motor activity. Equipment that is mobile allows for greater range of uses, and allows children to manipulate their own environment. By creating their own physical challenges with wooden crates, children make platforms, caves, and houses to crawl in, over, and through. Another way to provide variety is to focus on the less-developed skills, such as catching and throwing, rolling, latching, snapping, or zipping. When children are encouraged to discover their own physical capabilities, they learn to solve problems of movement defined by the limits of their own abilities rather than by performance. This kind of learning encourages self-confidence as children find success through their own challenges.

A Child's Self-Concept

The image of physical self is an important part of self-concept. How people feel about themselves is rooted in the way they feel about their bodies and what they can or cannot do with them. Attitudes about the body and its abilities directly affect the types of activities children will try. Studies show that skill in games appears tied to peer-group acceptance (Gallahue, 1976). Psychologists and teachers often notice a link between learning problems and clumsiness. Children with problems seem to have motor difficulties more often than those who do well in the classroom (Cratty, 1971).

Physical activity, then, contributes to a child's self-concept. With practice comes a sense of competence. Children can learn to relax as they gain experience in physical activities, and thus reduce the stress of anticipating failure. Competence breeds self-confidence, and a willingness to try greater challenges. As children try new activities, they learn more about themselves. And physical activity increases awareness of what fun it is to move—to run through a field or pump a swing just for the sheer joy of it!

Teachers support positive self-concept through physical and motor development in several ways. They let children discover their own physical limits, rather than warning or stopping them from trying out an activity for themselves. "I'm stuck!" a child shouts across the yard. Rather than rushing to lift down the child, the teacher might reply, "Where can you put your foot next? How can you find a way to get across?" To the child afraid to climb, the teacher might stand close by, responding to the fear by saying, "I'll stand close to the climbing ropes so you will feel safe." Using positive reinforcement encourages children in physical and motor endeavors. Teachers notice children who try something new: "Greg, it's good to see you cutting out the pumpkin yourself." They congratulate efforts for the achievements they really are: "Your hands reached the top this time, Shannon! I'll bet you are feeling proud of yourself."

It is often not so much what teachers say to children that influences their feelings about themselves as it is the way in which children are treated. Children value themselves to the degree they are valued by others. The way teachers show how they feel about children actually builds their self-confidence and sense of self-worth. Children create a picture of themselves from the words, attitudes, body language, and judgment of those around them.

Behaviors to Encourage

Teachers encourage both positive self-concept and skill level in the realm of physical and motor development by:

- Showing children ways to find personal satisfaction and achievement through physical activity.
- Helping children practice goal-oriented activities so that they learn to make realistic and challenging tasks for themselves in all physical and motor areas.
- Providing all children with the opportunity to try a variety of movements, to dance as well as race, to use hammers as well as paintbrushes.
- Encouraging children to work together, take turns, create ways to interact socially while using their bodies.
- Supporting individual responses and various levels of movement skill, so that children have the freedom to try new and unique activities and accept others' ways of moving.
- Letting children imitate each other as well as imitate adults or a set of directed steps. This shows children that their physical movements and attempts are worthy as well as those of adults.

When children develop their physical and motor skills under this kind of encouragement, their skills and sense of competence grow.

Recognizing Possible Problems

The perceptive teacher notices what children do with their bodies, and keeps records in order to spot possible problems early. A checklist for motor development will outline norms of development for a specific age level of the group and focus on what the child can do. At the same time, teachers must know what behaviors indicate potential problems. Figure 12.9 lists what to look for when observing children. If one or more of these problems is noticed, a teacher should then get additional information from the family or physician and through more evaluation procedures such as diagnostic testing of whatever motor skill is in question.

Curriculum Planning for Physical/Motor Development

Teachers plan activities that promote physical/motor skills in the areas of gross motor, fine motor, and perceptual–motor development. They look at the environment, both indoors and out, to see that all three areas of physical growth are encouraged.

Motor Problem	Evidence (cite exactly what and when the child did this)
☐ 1. Has trouble holding or maintaining balance	
☐ 2. Appears clumsy	
☐ 3. Cannot carry self well in motion	
☐ 4. Appears generally awkward in activities requiring coordination	
☐ 5. Has difficulty making changes in movement	
☐ 6. Has difficulty performing combinations of simple movements	
☐ 7. Has difficulty in gauging space with respect to own body; bumps and collides with objects and other children	
☐ 8. Tends to be accident-prone	
☐ 9. Has poor eye–hand coordination	
☐ 10. Has difficulty handling the simple tools of physical activity (beanbags, balls, other objects that require visual–motor coordination).	

FIGURE 12.9 A checklist of possible problems in physical/motor development serves as a guideline when devising a developmentally specific profile for spotting problems.

In the Classroom Setting

When thinking of physical/motor development in the classroom and yard, teachers tend to focus on the fine motor (or small-muscle) tasks for the classroom, and gross motor (or large-muscle) tasks for the outdoor play space. The indoor area lends itself more readily to activities with less movement, and the outdoor area encourages whole-body play. Yet children can have a wider variety of activities if teachers remember that both gross and fine motor projects can happen everywhere in the environment.

Indoor Areas. Indoors, the art area is stocked with pens, crayons, scissors, and hole punches that develop the fine motor skills. Add large brushes or rollers to the easel, or plan fingerpainting, and the art area now includes gross motor development. When children use templates to trace both inside and outside spaces, they develop perceptual–motor skill. In the science area, getting "just a pinch" of fish food is a fine motor activity; cleaning out the turtle house requires larger muscles to move rocks and sand. Perceptual–motor development occurs as children use pitchers to fill the fish tank or turtle tub and learn about water levels. When a child puts pegs into a pegboard, fine motor skills are used in

FIGURE 12.10 Teachers are encouraged to keep an open mind when developing curriculum. Both gross and fine motor skills can happen everywhere in the environment.

the manipulative area. Removing puzzles from a shelf and carrying them to a table brings in gross motor skills. Add nuts and bolts and the child's perceptual–motor skills are called into play. The block area has endless possibilities, from lifting and carrying (gross motor), to balancing and stacking (fine motor), to building a space so that an animal or car will fit through (perceptual–motor). The language and library areas are places for turning pages or looking at words and pictures (fine motor). They also involve taking books off shelves and replacing them, and trying out the movements and activities read about in books. For instance, Tana Hoban's *Is It Hard? Is It Easy?* encourages children to act out the scenes pictured in the story, all gross motor tasks. With a listening post nearby, children listen for the "beep," and coordinate what they hear (perceptual) with turning the pages (motor).

Outdoor Areas. Outdoors, children develop motor skills of all kinds. In the sand, children dig, a gross

motor activity. As they judge how big a hole is, or how much water will fill it, they are practicing and improving their perceptual–motor skills. Turning on a faucet, planting seeds, and making mudpies are for fine motor development.

Wheel toys offer children opportunities in all motor areas. Pushing someone in a wagon develops arm and leg strength—gross motor development. Guiding tricycles and carts on a path and around obstacles requires perceptual–motor skill. Trying to "repair" or "paint" a wheel toy with tools or with large brushes, tying wagons together, or weaving streamers through the spokes of a bicycle all use fine motor skills. By looking at the classroom and yard with an eye to physical and motor development, teachers can plan activities that support growth in all skill areas.

Transitions and Group Times. Every part of the daily schedule can be planned to use all physical/motor skills. For instance, getting in and out of coats and snowsuits is a large-muscle activity. Children learn perceptual–motor skills as they try to get their arms in the correct sleeves. Buttoning, zipping, and tying are fine motor activities. As children get ready for group time, often a difficult transition, they might practice drawing faces in the air, or making their bodies into the shape of letters, both perceptual–motor tasks.

Group times also include activities for motor development. When there are balloons, scarves, or a parachute at music time, children practice gross motor skills. Fingerplays at group time are a fine motor task. Activities for developing the senses of hearing and sight are two areas of sensory growth that can be utilized as content for group times.

Focus on Skills

The physical/motor skills include those that use large muscles, the smaller muscles, and the coordination of perception and motor response. Teachers planning activities for children can focus on any one of these as a basis for curriculum planning. For example, the skills of eye–hand coordination (perceptual–motor) and of walking on a balance

Physical/Motor Task	Activity
Gross motor	Lifting wood, sawing, using a brace and bit, a C-clamp. Carrying wood and tools; moving the carpentry table.
Fine motor	Screwing in a screw, tightening a vise. Bending wrist, arm in sawing. Hammering, drilling with a hand drill.
Perceptual–motor	Eye–hand coordination of hitting a nail on the head. Spatial: knowing where one's body ends and the wood begins. Temporal: finding the sequence of placing a nail in position, holding it, then moving the hammer through the air to pound it in. Sensory: following a line visually when sawing; listening to the sound of the drill; feeling the wood, or the comparative roughness of sandpaper.

FIGURE 12.11 The classroom carpentry area can include activities that develop all physical and motor skills.

FIGURE 12.12 The outdoor sand area has great potential for developing gross motor, fine motor, and perceptual–motor skills.

beam (gross motor) are elaborated below. They show how teachers can focus on a single skill and develop a rich curriculum for children.

Eye–Hand Coordination. Developing stitchery skills uses the perceptual–motor skill of eye–hand coordination. A series of activities can be planned to help children learn these skills. Stringing large wooden beads is a first step and leads to using pieces of straw and punched paper, with somewhat smaller holes. Macaroni can be strung on shoe laces or stiff string, then onto yarn, which is softer and more challenging. Sewing cards made by punching holes in styrofoam trays can be introduced as the next activity. Large, plastic needles can be used with the lacing cards or with styrofoam trays; large embroidery needles with big eyes can be used for stitching yarn onto burlap. Children may be ready to use embroidery hoops, with which they can make a design on burlap first and then stitch over the outlines. Buttons can be sewn on burlap or other fabric. Popcorn can be strung using a needle. A final project might be to make a group wall hanging, with squares of children's stitchery sewn together. Simple backpacks and coin purses might be made, with the children sewing most of it themselves.

Walking on a Balance Beam. Teachers might want to focus on the skill of walking on a balance beam, a gross motor activity. Using any kind of beam requires more balance and slower movements than regular walking. Teachers place tape on the floor and ask children to walk forward and backward. Use a rope on the floor and everyone can pretend to be a tightrope walker. Place a wide board flat on the floor, then substitute a narrow one (still on the floor itself). Next, place the wide board at a minimal height (perhaps 2 inches off the ground). Once children have mastered walking on this board, they are ready to try a narrower board at the same height. Set some boards at a slant, from the ground level up, providing a challenge that allows children to move their bodies off the ground as gradually as they wish. By planning activities for walking on wide and narrow boards of various heights, teachers

help children of all levels acquire the gross motor skills necessary to master these tasks.

Use of Themes

When beginning teachers plan activities, they often have a theme or unit as their focus. Themes can be used to encourage physical and motor involvement. A unit of "Outerspace" involves gross motor skills (jumping around on the moon, taking a space walk, getting in and out of the rocketship, building a spaceship with large blocks). Fine motor skills are needed to manipulate knobs on the instrument panel, to draw maps of the stars or write out a countdown on a chalkboard. Perceptual–motor skills are needed to work out how to get ready for a trip to Mars, what happens on the trip, and when and how to get back to Earth.

Once teachers realize which physical/motor skills the children possess and what the group is ready to learn, they can plan activities around a classroom unit. Figure 12.14 outlines a theme familiar to Mexican-American children that will encourage physical/motor skills as well as an appreciation for cultural diversity.

Curriculum planning for motor and movement skills requires teachers to know principles of physical growth and motor development. They then can

FIGURE 12.13 When planning curriculum, teachers can focus on a particular skill, such as dressing, both a self-help and a motor skill.

CINCO DE MAYO

Activity	Skill
1. Make a piñata	
a. make strips of newspapers for paper maché; cut and paste colored tissue paper	Fine motor
b. feel the flour paste; choose the colors that go together	Perceptual–motor (sensory)
c. organize the children by height	Perceptual–motor (spatial)
d. try to break it with a bat; clap and jump each time someone swings at the piñata	Gross motor and perceptual–motor
2. Cook corn tortillas	
a. mix the masa with water	Perceptual–motor (measuring) Fine motor (mixing)
b. roll the masa into balls; put into tortilla press	Fine motor and gross motor
c. put onto griddle, flip, eat!	Perceptual–motor (sensory) Fine motor
3. Using music	
a. dancing "La Raspa":	
hearing the rhythm	Perceptual–motor (sensory)
learning the steps	Perceptual–motor (temporal) and gross motor
using costumes	Gross motor (getting in and out) Fine motor (doing fastenings)
dancing the steps	All three
b. making and playing maracas	
using shakers/hearing sounds,	Fine motor/perceptual–motor
making shakers	Fine motor
4. Learning Spanish words and stories	
hearing and trying new words	Perceptual–motor (sensory, both hearing and speaking)

FIGURE 12.14 When teachers use a theme to develop physical/motor activities, they are matching children's interests and cultural awareness with activities to practice the skills they need to learn.

use this knowledge to plan activities that encourage children to master their own movements and to learn other skills through movement. In the early childhood setting, curriculum can be planned by concentrating on activity areas, focusing on a specific motor skill, or using a classroom theme.

SUMMARY

Children are in motion virtually from conception and develop their abilities to move their bodies as they grow. Young children spend most of the day in physical activity; therefore, the development of physical and motor skills must take a high priority in early childhood programs. Physical growth, that which pertains to the body, is for teachers an issue of fitness and health. They need to have an overview of growth in order to help children develop functional and flexible bodies. Motor development means learning to move with control and efficiency. Development involves maturation and experience. Teachers must know the sequence of development and what part they play in providing physical and motor experiences for the young child.

Muscular movements can be categorized as gross motor, fine motor, and perceptual–motor. Gross motor movements use the entire body or large parts of it, such as the legs for running or the arms and torso for throwing. Fine motor movements, such as manipulating objects, are those that use smaller muscles and that require precision and dexterity. Perceptual–motor movements are those that combine what is perceived with a body movement. Spatial, temporal, and sensory awareness all play an important part in the development of perceptual–motor skills.

In the early childhood years, children need exposure to many motor activities. They need a chance to practice, to get feedback, and to have a broad range of experiences of variety and challenge. Since children acquire motor skills through short- and long-term memory, rehearsal plays an important role as well.

When planning curriculum, teachers must have an awareness of sex-role stereotyping and must consider safety as well as challenge. A child's self-concept is linked with the concept of physical self and skill, so teachers keep in mind which behaviors should be encouraged, and which behaviors may indicate potential problems. As they plan activities for children, teachers use classroom and yard areas, focus on a specific skill, or use a theme to develop curriculum for physical/motor skills.

Review Questions

1. How does physical growth differ from motor development in young children?

2. What factors influence motor development in young children?

3. What physical/motor skills are appropriate for young children to develop?

4. How can the teacher of young children support motor development in classroom areas?

5. How can the teacher support acquisition of specific motor skills in young children?

Learning Activities

1. Map the classroom in which you are currently working. List at least one activity in each area that develops physical motor skills. Add one more activity of your own that widens such development.

2. In what ways does a school program you know reinforce sex-role stereotyping in motor activities? What could be done to change this?

3. Try to develop the theme of "at the beach" or "camping" in your setting in such a way that physical/motor skills are used. Be sure to include gross motor, fine motor, and perceptual–motor activities.

Bibliography

Ames, Louise Bates, et al. *The Gesell Institute's Child from One to Six.* New York: Harper and Row, 1979.

Cratty, Bryant J. *Active Learning: Games to Enhance Academic Abilities.* Englewood Cliffs, N.J.: Prentice-Hall, 1971.

Drowatzky, John N. *Motor Learning: Principles and Practices.* Minneapolis: Burgess Publishing Company, 1975.

Flinchum, Betty M. *Motor Development in Early Childhood.* St. Louis: C.V. Mosby Co., 1975.

Gallahue, David L. *Motor Development and Movement Experience for Young Children.* New York: John Wiley & Sons, 1976.

Halverson, L.E. "The Significance of Motor Development." In Angstrom, Georgeanne (ed.), *The Significance of the Young Child's Motor Development.* Washington, D.C.: National Association for the Education of Young Children, 1971.

Malina, Robert M. "Motor Development in the Early Years." In Moore, Shirley G., and Cooper, Catherine R. (eds.), *The Young Child: Reviews of Research,* Vol. 3. Washington, D.C.: National Association for the Education of Young Children, 1982.

Mussen, P.H.; Conger, J.J.; and Kagan, J. *Child Development and Personality,* 3rd Ed. New York: Harper and Row, 1969.

Radler, D.H., with Kephart, Newell C. *Success Through Play.* New York: Harper and Brothers, 1960.

Ridenour, Marcella V., ed. (Contributing Authors: Clark, Herkowitz, Roberton, Teeple) *Motor Development: Issues and Applications.* Princeton, N.J.: Princeton Book Company, 1978.

Riggs, Maida L. *Jump to Joy: Helping Children Grow Through Active Play.* Englewood Cliffs, N.J.: Prentice-Hall, 1980.

Sprung, Barbara. *Non-Sexist Education for Young Children.* New York: Citation Press, 1975.

Stone, Jeannette Galambos. *Play and Playgrounds.* Washington, D.C.: National Association for the Education of Young Children, 1970.

Stone, L. Joseph, and Church, Joseph. *Childhood and Adolescence.* New York: Random House, 1979.

13

Planning for the Mind: Cognitive and Language Development

Questions for Thought

- What is the relationship between cognitive and language development?
- What is meant by cognitive development?
- How can the teacher support cognitive development?
- What language skills are developed in an early childhood setting?

- What is the teacher's role in supporting and extending language development in young children?
- How does the teacher introduce and develop reading and writing in the early childhood setting?
- What can children's literature offer young children?

Outline

Portions of this chapter were developed with the assistance of Gay Spitz, Hartnell College, Salinas, Calif.

PREFACE

The relationship between language and thought cannot be overemphasized. Thoughts are produced when people internalize what they experience. Language is the powerful tool that turns actions and events into thought. Language also shapes the way thoughts are produced and stored; language brings a semblance of order to the thought processes. It is, according to Bruner, a "logical and analytical tool in thinking" (Vygotsky, 1962).

Psychologists and educators today acknowledge the interdependent nature of cognition and language. People are molded by the tools they use; language and thought are the instruments people use to interact with the world.

For these reasons, this chapter contains curriculum planning units for both cognition and language rather than treating them in separate chapters. Inclusion in the same chapter emphasizes their close relationships.

Graphic language—reading and writing—is a major avenue for creating curriculum that stimulates and encourages language and cognitive skills. A third unit addresses these special topics as vehicles for language and intellectual development in the young child.

INTRODUCTION

Ah, to be a child again! The world is a place of wonder and promise. There are worlds and people to discover, explore, and understand. Childhood is a time:

- Of self . . . a baby plays with his hands and feet for hours, and rolls over just for the sake of doing it.
- Of things everywhere . . . a toddler invades the kitchen cabinets to see what treasures can be found.
- Of people . . . a preschooler learns the teachers' names and then makes a first "friend."
- Of faraway places . . . a kindergartener packs for the first "sleepover."

The amount of learning that takes place in early childhood is staggering. How do children manage to absorb the sheer quantity of information and experience they accumulate in their first few years of life?

Every child accomplishes this mighty feat by *thinking*. To think is to be able to acquire and apply knowledge. By using conscious thought and memory, children think about themselves, the world, and others. Educating the thinking child is a critical function of every teacher and parent. Curriculum in the early years of school must address the skill of *cognition,* the mental process or faculty children use to acquire knowledge.

Language is the primary form of expression through which people communicate their knowledge and thoughts. A baby does not start life with language, but always communicates. In fact, oral language begins early, as infants learn to express themselves with sounds if not words. The growing child communicates needs, thoughts, and feelings through meaningful language. Thus, language and thought are intertwined.

Yet, the two are also separate. Cognition can occur without the language to express it. For example, when the infant laughs during a game of peek-a-boo, it indicates the child's knowledge that the hidden face will reappear. Conversely, the use of language can occur without cognition (i.e., without knowing the meaning). A child counting from one to twenty (". . . 11,13,17,19,20!") is a case in point.

Cognition and language generally become more interdependent as development progresses. Children expand their knowledge base through language. They listen, question, tell. The child with good language skills can thus apply them to widen the horizons of knowledge.

Cognition and language relate not only to the developing mind, but also to all areas of the child's growth. Young thinkers are at work no matter what they are doing. For example, physical/motor development is also a cognitive process. Learning to roller-skate involves skinned knees and learning to balance (motor tasks), along with analyzing, predicting, generalizing, evaluating, and practicing the art of locomotion on wheels (cognitive skills). When

FIGURE 13.1 As children investigate the world of people and places, they ask themselves and others what they want to know. (Courtesy of Vassar College Nursery School)

trying to enter into group play (a social task), children will think of strategies for how to get started (cognitive skill).

Children use language in developing emotionally. They listen, label, describe, elaborate, and question (language skills) as they learn to tell themselves and others how they feel (emotional tasks). And anyone who has heard a child mumbling instructions on how to get down from a tree knows that language can be of great help in using physical skills.

This chapter will explore in depth the framework for planning curriculum for the mind. For the purposes of clarity, cognition and language will be separated into units. However, teachers must remember that these work together constantly in the

minds and lives of young children. Planned programs for early childhood will be more successful if that link is recognized.

UNIT 13–1 COGNITION

THE DEVELOPMENT OF COGNITION: A PERSPECTIVE

An Eclectic Point of View

In trying to enhance cognitive development, early childhood educators draw upon developmental and learning theories and their direct experiences with children. By combining theoretical and practical viewpoints, teachers take a blended, or *eclectic*, perspective on the development of the thinking process. They work with children to encourage their ability to formulate ideas and to think rationally and logically.

Most important, the early childhood professional works toward helping children acquire skills that will lead to the development of:

Concepts: labeling or naming an idea, moving from the specific to the abstract.

"What is a grape?"

Relationships: What is the association between two or more things? How are they similar or different? What are their functions, characteristics, attributes?

"How many colors of grapes are there? Do all of them have seeds? Are they different sizes? Do they taste alike?"

Generalizations: Drawing conclusions from relationships and concepts/ ideas. This means grouping into classes and finding common elements.

"Are grapes a fruit or meat? How do grapes grow?"

A Piagetian Perspective

Developmental psychology, particularly through the works of Jean Piaget, has provided a deeper understanding of cognitive development. Piaget's view of cognition is twofold: First, learning is a process of discovery, of finding out what one needs to know to solve a particular problem. Second, knowledge results from active thought, from making mental connections among objects, from constructing a meaningful reality for understanding.

Piaget divided knowledge into three types:

- *Meaningful knowledge* is what children learn gradually, adding new concepts and ideas to what they already know. For example, being able to explore magnetism with horseshoe and bar magnets gives the child the opportunity to connect objects to thoughts.

- *Rote knowledge* is just what it implies: information with no particular meaning to the learner. In this case, an explanation of magnetism might be given to a class without a chance to handle or explore magnets.

- *Social knowledge* comes from our culture, the rules of the game, the right vocabulary, the moral codes. Value-laden and often arbitrary, this knowledge can rarely be constructed logically. Still, social knowledge is learnable and a crucial part of children's cognitive development. A new set of magnets is brought to school. Who gets to play with them? When is it someone else's turn?

In developing cognitive curriculum, teachers plan experiences that enhance those types of knowledge they feel are most important for children.

COGNITIVE SKILLS IN EARLY CHILDHOOD EDUCATION

The actual skills children acquire as they learn to think are considerable. Most skills fall into the

FIGURE 13.2 Being able to explore actual materials and objects encourages children to use and assimilate new knowledge.

nine categories below. The list, while long, is a comprehensive one; what children learn in the thinking realm of their development will fall into one of these categories. The teacher plans activities for all cognitive skills to ensure challenging children's thinking.

Basic Skills of Inquiry

Young children are curious, watching the world carefully. Through exploration and examination, they increase their attention span. Inquisitive children begin to organize what they see, analyzing and identifying confusions or obstacles for themselves. The next step is communication; the child asks questions, listens, gets ideas, and makes suggestions. This includes interpreting what others communicate. Then children are ready to use resources, seeking assistance from other people and materials.

Reasoning and problem solving are also inquiry skills. As children examine alternatives, they choose a course of action, revising their plans as needed.

Young children thrill in making educated guesses, then checking their *hypotheses* by experimenting and taking risks. In doing so, they learn to evaluate, to use judgments and opinions, and to distinguish between fact and opinion, reality and fantasy.

Knowledge of the Physical World

How do children learn about the physical world? First, they use objects, spending plenty of time exploring, manipulating, choosing, using toys and natural materials. They observe how objects react, discovering relationships and trying to predict what will happen. As they learn the properties of objects, they understand better the idea of cause and effect.

Knowledge of the Social World

Learning about others is hard work, since the social world is not concrete and is often illogical. The child needs an awareness of self before developing an awareness of others and how to interact socially. The next step is to expand their knowledge of roles to include those of family, school, and the community. Then they can learn what is appropriate conduct in various situations—indoors or out, happy or sad, at the grocery store or dinner table.

Classification

Knowledge of the physical world teaches children to have different responses to different objects. *Classifying* this knowledge is a lengthy process. To clarify this process, consider how two-year-old Tisa learns to classify:

What can Tisa do to the stuffed bear *and* the pet dog? What can she do with one and *not* the other? Which are her toys? Rover's? Which ones have fur? What is different about them?

Tisa learns the *attributes* of objects by exploring, learning the class names of "toy" and "pet."

She makes collections, sorting by similarity those that are Rover's toys and those that are her own. She uses class relationships to understand that both animals have fur, but she can tug on only one animal's ears without encountering a problem.

Seriation

How do children learn to seriate, or to arrange items according to a graduated scale? Like classification, *seriation* can appear confusing at first glance. To illustrate its development, look at some of the materials designed by Dr. Maria Montessori. These toys were developed to make clear to children exactly what seriation is and how it can be learned. Many of these toys distinguish grades of intensity by size, color, weight, number. Children build pyramid towers, fit nesting blocks together, and use the counting rods. By noting differences, often through trial and error, children learn seriation systematically. For instance, the pyramid tower is ordered from largest piece to smallest as it is built. Boxes are nested, one inside the other, by their graduated size or volume. The counting rods can be put into a staircase array, the units building on each other from one to ten. Children can arrange several things in order and fit one ordered set of objects to another.

Numbers

To learn about numbers, one begins with their sound. Settings for children under five have plenty of songs, chants, and fingerplays that include numbers ("One Potato, Two" or "Five Speckled Frogs"). Beyond these rote experiences, children learn that numbers represent things. They are an expression of amount, of degree or position, and once children know this, they are ready to use mathematical expressions and terminology. For instance, after singing about the frog that jumped in the pool in the song "Five Speckled Frogs," Chantel is ready to hear that four is one less than five. Knowledge of numbers also means comparing amounts, arranging two sets of objects in one-to-one correspondence ("Each person needs one and only one napkin for snack, Tyler"). Children can also count objects and begin computation ("Parvin, you have three shovels. Here is one more; now how many do you have?").

Symbols

A symbol stands for something else; it is not what it appears to be! Young children have to think hard and long in order to symbolize. It is a task of some skill to imitate or use one object to represent something else.

Children begin by using their bodies. Youngsters love to play peek-a-boo, reacting to "Boo!" with full-bodied excitement each time it is said. Preschoolers revel in playing favorite characters. Primary school children make up plays and puppet shows. Make-believe helps in the process of symbolizing, as does making sound to represent objects ("Choo-choo" is a train, for example). Using and making two- and three-dimensional models are other ways children symbolize, when they transfer what they see to the easel or to the clay table. Children are also symbolizing when they dress up in costumes and uniforms. Teachers add to the symbolizing process when they use descriptive words. Description games encourage children to do the same. For example, "It is round and red and you eat it. What is it?" (An apple!) After all these skills have been mastered, children are ready for written symbols, when they can use the written word to label, take dictation, or write notes.

Spatial Relationships

Spatial relationships develop early. Infants visually track what they see, trying to reach and grasp. As they experience one object's position in relation to another, they begin to have a mental picture of spatial relationships. Toddlers find this out as they learn to steer themselves around tables and seat themselves on the potty. The concept of "close" (the chair) and "far away" (the cookies cooling on the counter) give clues to length and distance ("How far do I have to reach to get the cookies?"). As spatial skills develop, children learn to fit things

FIGURE 13.3 Small animals and blocks symbolize a farm: cognitive skills at work. (Courtesy of Stride Rite Children's Centers, Cambridge, Mass.)

together and take them apart. They rearrange and shape objects. They observe and describe things from different spatial viewpoints. This perspective is learned only through experience. The child under five needs to describe and then try out the notion that what one sees from the side of the hill is *not* what can be seen from the top.

Adults help children learn such skills by letting them locate things at home, in the classroom, in the department store. They encourage children to represent such spatial relationships in their drawings, with pictures, and in photographs.

Time

Understanding time is a complicated affair, since time is composed of at least three dimensions:

time as the present, time as a *continuum*, and time as a sequence of events. Children must learn each of these to fully understand the concept of time. In some settings children learn to stop and start an activity on a signal (when the teacher strikes a chord on the piano for cleanup time). They try to move their bodies at different speeds, indoors and out. Older children begin to observe that clocks and calendars are used to mark the passage of time. Specifically, children come to know the sequencing of events in time: which comes first, next, last? Having an order of events through a consistent daily schedule helps children learn this aspect of time. They also benefit from anticipating future events and making the appropriate preparations. Planning a course of action and completing that plan gives meaning to the idea of time (Furth, 1970; Ginsburg & Opper, 1969; and Piaget, 1969).

What children learn intellectually in the early years is massive in quantity and quality. Yet young children are ready—eager, in fact—to engage themselves with the world around them in order to acquire these cognitive skills. By remaining aware of how much is to be learned, educators keep a realistic—and humble—appreciation for the "work" of children.

THE TEACHER'S ROLE

Considerations

When considering children's intellectual development, teachers should keep in mind:

- *Education is exploration.* The process of education is more than its products. Teachers enhance learning by allowing children to interact with the environment. The teacher is a source of information and support rather than one who gives answers or commands. The goal is to have children ask their own questions and create their own challenges.

- *Children do not think like adults.* Children think and perceive in their own ways. They think in concrete terms and come to conclusions based on what they see and touch.

- *Children's thinking is legitimate and should be valued.* Their thought processes and perceptions are as valid as adults'. Teachers support those processes by asking questions to stimulate further thought and by providing materials for exploration.

- *The language of the teacher should support cognitive development.* Throughout their interactions with children, teachers help children use words, terms, and concepts correctly:

Mariko (at water table): I need that suck-up.
Teacher: The baster really does suck up water, doesn't it?

Teachers' questions are open-ended; they cannot be answered with a simple yes or no. For example, Tony asks his kindergarteners what will happen if they do not count the cups of flour while making bread. What he is really asking them to do is to predict what will happen and consider the results. The goal is to use language to help children to *think.*

Sometimes teachers use their own language skills to define a problem, help children figure out what they are doing, and decide what they need to do next. They leave the child with something to ponder:

Teacher: I wonder why the turtle's head went back in its shell when you put your finger close by.
Teacher: If you want to play with José, how can you let him know?
Teacher: What *do* we need from the woodworking shelf to make a spaceship?

Figure 13.4 shows further how teachers' use of language helps children think and develop cognitive skills as part of their early childhood experience.

Skill	Teachers Can
Inquiry	• Ask questions so children make statements about their conversations. *Example:* "What do you notice about the guinea pig?" • Try to be more specific if such questions seem overwhelming or if they elicit little response. *Example:* "What sounds do you hear? What can you find out by touching her?" • Ask how children arrived at their answers. *Example:* "How did you know that the marble wouldn't roll *up* the ramp?" • Ask questions that expand the process. *Example:* "Can you tell me anything else about your doll?"
Social Knowledge	• Try not to respond to unstated needs. *Example:* "Do you want something? Can I help you?" • Help children define what they want or need, so that they learn how to ask for it. *Example:* Marie: I wonder who is going to tie my shoes? Teacher: So do I. When you want someone to tie your shoe, you can say, "Would you tie my shoe?" Marie: Would you tie my shoe? Teacher: I'd be glad to.
Classification	• Ask questions that will help children focus on objects and see differences and details. *Example:* While cooking and using measuring cups, ask, "Can you think of anything else used for measuring? What do the red lines on the cup mean?"
Spatial Relationships	• Ask for the precise location of an object the child asks for or is interested in. *Examples:* "Where did you say you saw the bird's nest?" "You can find another stapler in the cabinet underneath the fish tank."
Concept of Time	• Use accurate time sequences with children. *Example:* Teacher: Just a minute. Milo: Is this a real minute, or a "wait a minute"? Teacher: You're right. I'm with Phoebe now. I'll help you next.

FIGURE 13.4 Teachers' use of language affects how children develop cognitive skills. The more children are allowed and encouraged to think for themselves, the more their cognitive skills will develop.

Curriculum Planning for Cognitive Development

In the Class Setting

Teachers can plan cognitive curriculum for their children by considering the class setting, both indoors and out, throughout the daily schedule. Each activity center can be used to encourage intellectual development with a variety of curriculum materials and methods.

Indoor Areas. The indoor areas might have some of the following materials and activities:

Art: Include a shelf for self-chosen projects. A variety of paper, drawing implements, and tools encourages children to re-create their own reality, using representational art forms that show how children see the physical and social worlds.

Blocks: Have paper models of each block shape to help children with classification by shape and size. Accessories, such as animals and homemade trees and lakes, help children symbolize.

Discovery/Science: Rotate a display of "touch me" materials. This gives children first-hand experience with plants, seeds, animals, magnets, seashells, foods, etc.

Dramatic play: Stock this area with materials for role playing, puppet making, and acting out of adult activities. Children learn to understand the world of people as they pretend to be adults with adult occupations and responsibilities.

Language/Library: Choose books that focus on both the physical and social worlds. Children's interests in numbers, symbols, and time can also be extended by selecting literature that reflects their level of understanding. Be sure to listen to the group's interests, and make a point to place books that respond to those interests in the library.

Manipulatives (table toys): The manipulatives area is an ideal place for materials that encourage cognitive development; highlight this area with both favorites (Lego® or Crystal Climbers®) and new items (Construx® or sewing cards). Counting cubes aid in classification and seriation, while puzzles or nesting blocks focus on spatial relationships.

Figure 13.5 shows how an indoor activity contributes to the development of children's thought processes across the curriculum areas.

Outdoor Areas. The outdoor area provides opportunities for children to plan and organize their own thoughts. Playing a group game requires inquiry skill. Predicting how sand will change when wet uses knowledge of the physical world. Children learn to classify water table and wheel toys; they learn seriation when they select sand buckets by size. Counting shovels to see that there are enough to go around, building with large, hollow blocks, and watching the seasons change are all cognitive skills children gain as they play outside.

Groups, transitions, and routines all play a part in developing children's knowledge base of the social world. As children learn to conduct themselves in school, they learn:

- To enter a class and start to play (transition).
- To take care of their own belongings and those of their school (routines).
- To concentrate on an activity with others around (group times).
- To interact with others while at the same time pay attention to a leader or task (group times).
- To end an activity, an interaction, a school day (transition).

Teachers plan environments, activities, and grouping of children to give the class experience in all these cognitive challenges.

Focus on Skills

After choosing a specific skill, teachers identify the process, the concepts, and the vocabulary involved. Any skill can be the focus of curriculum development. The skill of inquiry is one that teachers can develop throughout the classroom and yard.

They ask children to observe what others are doing, to see how children play and work. They

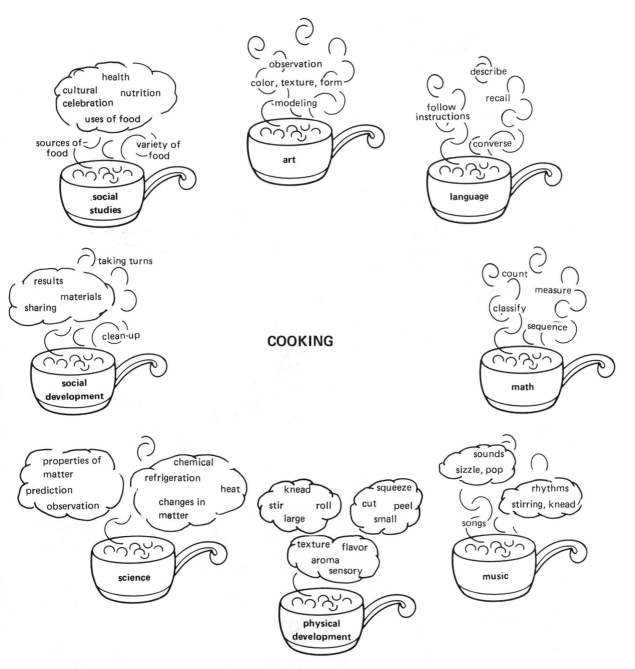

FIGURE 13.5 The activity of cooking enhances cognitive development throughout the curriculum.

FIGURE 13.6 A small-group time allows teachers to plan curriculum that meets cognitive needs of a select group of children.

ask questions to model such a technique, showing their own curiosity about process:

> Teacher: I wonder which piece of wood you'll choose to glue on your board next?
>
> Teacher: What part do you want to play in our grocery store?
>
> Teacher: How can we find out how long your road of blocks is?

When children see that it is all right to ask "Why?", they feel encouraged to ask questions themselves. *Brainstorming* is a technique that helps children get ideas and use resources to find out how many ways there are to make a kite or build a castle.

Outdoors, inquisitive children explore their environment. Children ask questions: "Can we turn on the water? What if we bury all the toy bears in the cornmeal?! Could we use the ladder to see over the fence? Let's all hide from the teachers?!" The way teachers handle inquiries from children about what they want to do sends a message that supports—or discourages—this cognitive skill. When there is no harm in *asking* (though the answer may be "No"), children are encouraged to develop further the skill of inquiry. Figure 13.8 illustrates how another cognitive skill can be the focus of curriculum development.

Use of Themes

A specific theme can be chosen for cognitive development. Units based on current events, seasonal changes, holidays, or the special interests of children are particularly appealing.

Current events must be chosen carefully, as young children may have only passing knowledge or interest in most of them. Meaningful events might be a space shuttle mission or a solar eclipse. More

FIGURE 13.7 The skill of inquiry: "How does this lock work?"

The Concepts: Selecting a course of action
                Making educated guesses
                Making and revising a plan
                Risking and evaluating the results

The Vocabulary: Guess
                  Plan
                  Problem
                  Solution/solve
                  What? why? how?

The Process:

Activity area	Process question
Art	How many ways can you use the brush (pen, squirt bottle) to make a mark on the paper?
	Why is it dripping? How can you stop it when you're ready?
Bathrooms/ cubbies	You found Paul's sweater . . . How can you find where it goes?
	Where did the water come from? How can you clean it up?
Blocks	What makes the tower of blocks fall over?
	How can a block be used to connect two others?
Cooking	How do we mix these ingredients together?
	What will happen when it is put in the oven?
Discovery/ science	Why did the magnet pick up the nail and not the pen?
	What is the difference between the rabbit and the guinea pig? How are they alike?
Dramatic play	Who will be the dad? What happens when these other children want to play?
	How can you get to wear the costume you want?
Language/ library	What happens next in the story? Why do you think so?
	Why did the child feel unhappy at first? Then what happened?
Large group	Why can't you see/hear the leader?
	What can you do about feeling too crowded?
	What can you do when your friend keeps whispering to you during storytime?

FIGURE 13.8 Teachers who focus on the skills of reasoning and problem solving have a wealth of curriculum plans at their fingertips. (cont. on p. 304)

Large motor	How do you jump rope?
	What do you use to pump yourself on a swing?
	How will you find a ball?
Manipulatives	How do you figure out what puzzle piece fits?
	Do you see a pattern on the peg board? What is it?
Sensory	How do you get the water from the large pitcher to the small cup?
	How will you get the wet sand through the funnel?

FIGURE 13.8 Cont.

Area	Cognitive Skill(s)	Activity
	Indoors	
Art	Organization	Papier mâché model of a dinosaur; use templates to trace/cut. Dinosaur cookie cutters in clay/playdough.
Blocks	Seriation	Use blocks to compare relative sizes of dinosaurs.
Cooking	Relationships	Prepare vegetarian snack (herbivores), then meatballs for the carnivores.
Discovery	Observation	Get fossils, other skeletons. Collect books on how scientists learn about dinosaurs. Compare relationships (size, stature, etc.) of prehistoric to common animals.
Dramatic play	Symbols	Dinosaur puppets. Masks of dinosaurs.
Library	Label/recall; use of resources	Provide books about dinosaurs.
Manipulatives	Reasoning; problem solving	Individual and floor dinosaur puzzles.
	Outdoors	
Sensory	Symbols	Rubber dinosaurs in cornmeal, pebbles, etc.
Large motor	Symbols	Measure children's bodies with a rope the length of various dinosaurs.

FIGURE 13.9 Using a theme of special interest, such as "Dinosaurs," teachers can develop children's cognitive skills in many classroom areas.

| Sand | Symbols | Act out digging up dinosaur bones. |
| Games | Social world | "Tyrannosaurus, May I?" game, naming and taking steps of various dinosaurs. |

Groups

Large	Label/recall; educated guessing	"Who Am I?", verbally describing dinosaur. Mystery Pictures, showing parts of dinosaurs and having children guess.
Music	Symbols	Acting out dinosaurs to the record, or to music of various tones.
Small	Label/communicate	Draw your favorite dinosaur; dictate what you like about it and what you know. Dinosaur sheet, folded in quarters, with a sentence to fill in and space to draw: The dinosaurs laid . . ./ Some dinosaurs lived . . ./ Dinosaurs ate . . ./ Dinosaurs died because . . ./

FIGURE 13.9 Cont.

likely, the event will be a local one, such as a children's fair or circus in town. Units based on these happenings might be named "Space and Travel" or "Circuses and Celebrations."

Themes can change with the seasons. Fall is the time for a unit on "Harvest Time," "Corn," or "Masks and Hats." Winter may mean a unit on how water changes with the seasons, since snow, sleet, hail, and rain are a regular part of most winter months. Spring is a time for green and growing things, and a unit could focus on the physical world of growing plants from seeds, hatching chicks, visiting a farm. Summer weather on the coasts sends everyone to "The Seashore," or at least the local lake or river.

The theme of friendship during Valentine's Day expands children's knowledge of the social world, as they increase their awareness of others through the giving and receiving of letters and cards.

A unit can also focus on symbolizing through use of names, letters on a "post box," or the numbers and location of people's houses and apartments.

One special interest of young children is dinosaurs. Figure 13.9 outlines how a unit on this topic can be used to encourage cognitive skills throughout the curriculum.

Unit 13–1 Checkpoint

Cognition is the ability to learn, remember, and think abstractly. Children's cognitive development relates to learning in all other skill areas. Early childhood educators see cognitive development from an eclectic point of view and draw heavily from the works of Jean Piaget.

Cognitive skills in the early years can be put into several categories. The teacher's role is to understand how cognition develops in children and to put that knowledge to work in the classroom. While creating curriculum, teachers keep certain attitudes and ideas in mind. Then, they set about planning for their programs.

The methods of developing children's cognitive skills are as varied and creative as the teachers—and children—can be. By focusing on the class setting, a specific skill, or a theme, teachers help children acquire and use the skills of thinking to understand themselves and the world around them.

Ask yourself:

- What perspective do early childhood teachers have on the development of cognition?
- What are nine cognitive skills of the early years?
- What should teachers consider when defining their role in cognitive development?
- How can cognitive curriculum be developed in the class setting?
- What skills could be the focus for curriculum planning?
- What are three themes that encourage the development of cognitive skills?

UNIT 13–2 LANGUAGE

Alexis:	Laleña, will you help me full this pitcher up?
Laleña:	No, because my ponytail is keeping me in bothers.
Veronique:	Hey, come here! I accidently dropped a piece of bread and the birds yummed it right up!
Abhi:	I know, that's what the tooth fairy did to my tooth.
Marty:	I'm going to keep *all* my baby teeth in a jar and the next time a baby comes along, I'll give him my baby teeth.

Language is the aspect of human behavior that involves the use of sounds in meaningful patterns. This includes the corresponding symbols that are used to form, express, and communicate thoughts and feelings. Any system of signs used for communication is language. For the developing child, language is the ability to express oneself. Language is both *receptive*—listening, understanding, and responding—and *expressive*—pronunciation, vocabulary, and grammar. In other words, as illustrated above, language has meaning.

THE DEVELOPMENT OF LANGUAGE

Language seems to be an innate characteristic of humankind. Wherever people live together, language of some form has developed. Languages worldwide vary remarkably in their sounds, words, and grammatical structure. Nonetheless, young children around the world acquire language.

What Research Tells Us

Research into language development and expression reveals several interesting characteristics. First, the language of children is different from adult language (deVilliers and Jill, 1981). Children's language deals with the present and is egocentric, taking into account only the child's own knowledge. There appears to be a lack of awareness on the child's part of language form and structure. In other words, children use language to communicate but seem to have no understanding of language as an entity itself.

Language is not learned simply by imitating adult speech (Beck, 1979). Child language is not garbled adult language, but rather unique to the child's age and linguistic level. Children are not just trying to imitate others and making mistakes, but are trying to come to terms with language themselves. A child will try out theories about language in attempts to understand its patterns. In language, as in so many areas of cognition, children are involved as active participants in their own learning. The use of speech is not merely imitative but productive and creative.

Moreover, language development is a process of maturation. Just as in the development of cognitive skills, there are stages of language growth that follow a specific sequence. There are also variations in timing that are important to remember.

Stages of Language Development

Children follow a six-step sequence in language development, one that seems *invariable* regardless of what language is being learned.

1. *Infant's Response to Language.* Babies begin by attending to speech, changes in sound, rhythm, and intonation. These are the *precursors* of speech, and young infants are especially sensitive to some sound differences. Infants need to hear speech, and plenty of it, to develop the foundations of sound.

2. *Vocalization.* By three to four months of age, infants begin cooing and babbling. Babbling increases with age and seems to peak around nine to 12 months. This is a matter of physical maturation, not just experience; deaf children do it at the same time as those whose hearing is normal. Furthermore, there are similar patterns across different languages.

3. *Word Development.* According to deVilliers and Jill (1981), the child must first separate the noises heard into speech and nonspeech. The speech noises must be further separated into words and the sounds that form them. The growing infant starts to shift from practice to playing with sounds. The end result is planned, controlled speech.

Children begin playing with sounds around 10 to 15 months of age. From this point, the development of speech is determined as much by control of motor movements as by the ability to match sounds with objects.

Most children can understand and respond to a number of words before they can produce any. Their first words include names of objects and events in their world (people, food, toys, animals). Then the child begins to overextend words, perhaps using "doggy" to refer to all animals. Finally, single words can be used as sentences: "Bye-bye" can refer to someone leaving, a meal the child thinks is finished, the child going away, a door closing.

4. *Sentences.* Children's sentences usually begin with two words, describing an action ("Me go"), a possession ("My ball"), or a location ("Baby outside"). These sentences get expanded by adding adjectives ("My big ball"), changing the verb tense ("Me jumped down"), or using negatives ("No go outside"). Children learn grammar not by being taught the rules, but as they listen to others' speech and put together the regularities they hear.

Child language, while not identical to that of adults, does draw upon language heard to build a language base. Children incorporate and imitate what they hear to refine their own language structures.

5. *Elaboration.* Vocabulary begins to increase at an amazing rate. Sentences get longer, and communication begins to work into social interaction. In the hospital corner of a nursery school, this conversation takes place:

Chip: I'm a nurse.
Brooke: I'm going to try to get some patients for you.
Megan: Do I need an operation?
Chip: Yeah, if you don't want to be sick anymore.

6. *Graphic Representation.* By five or six years of age, reading and writing emerge as children be-

FIGURE 13.10 Children's language skills reach their peak when they begin to represent language graphically.

come aware of language as an entity itself and of the written word as a way of documenting what is spoken. Figure 13.10 is a sample of a child's beginning writing skills.

LANGUAGE SKILLS IN EARLY CHILDHOOD EDUCATION

Teachers translate language development theory into practice as they work with children. Language skills in the early childhood setting include articulation, receptive language, expressive language, and enjoyment.

Articulation

Articulation is how children actually say the sounds and words. Children's ability to produce sound is a critical link in their connecting the sounds to form speech. As children talk, teachers listen for their ability to hear and reproduce sounds in daily conversation. Can they hear and produce sounds that differ widely, such as "sit" and "blocks"? Can they produce sounds that differ in small ways, such as in "man" and "mat"?

Receptive Language

Receptive language is what children acquire when they learn to listen and understand. It is what

FIGURE 13.11 Children learn receptive language when they hear people share with them important and interesting facts.

they hear. With this skill children are able to understand directions, to answer a question, and to follow a sequence of events. They can understand relationships and begin to predict the outcome of their behavior and that of others. They develop some mental pictures as they listen.

Children begin early and can become experts in reacting to words, voice, emphasis, and inflection. How many times does the child understand by the *way* the words are spoken?

"You finally *finished* your lunch." (Hooray for you)
"You *finally* finished your lunch." (You slow-poke)

Children learn to listen for enjoyment, for the way the wind sounds in the trees, the rhythm of a storytelling, or the sound of the car as it brings Mom or Dad home.

Expressive Language

Expressive language in the early years includes words, grammar, and elaboration.

Words

Expressive language is the spoken word. Children's first words are of what is most important to them (Mama, Da-Da). Adults help children extend their knowledge and vocabulary by using the names of objects and words of action (walk, run, jump) and feelings (happy, sad, mad). By describing objects in greater and greater detail, teachers give children new words that increase their skills. Children are then ready to learn that some words have more than one meaning (the word "orange," for example, is both a color and a fruit) and that different words can have the same meaning (such as "ship" and "boat").

Grammar

Basic grammatical structure is learned as children generalize what they hear. They listen to adult speech patterns and use these patterns to organize their own language. It helps to hear simple sentences at a young age, with the words in the correct order. Next, children can grasp past tense as well as present, plural nouns along with the singular. Finally, the use of more complex structures is understood (prepositions, comparatives, various conjugations of verbs).

Elaboration of Language

Elaboration of language takes many, many forms. It is the act of expanding the language. Through description, narration, explanation, and communication, adults elaborate their own speech to encourage children to do the same. For instance, communication for children includes talking to oneself and to others. When a teacher verbalizes a process aloud, children see how language helps them work through a problem. ("I am trying to get the plant out of its pot, but when I turn it upside-down, it doesn't fall out by itself. Now I'll use this shovel to loosen the dirt from the sides of the pot, and hope that helps.") Communicating with others involves giving and following directions. ("It's time to make a choice for cleanup time. You find something to do and I'll watch you.") It means asking and answering questions. ("How do you feel when she says she won't play with you? What can you say? What can you do?") Sticking to the subject keeps communication flowing: "I know you want to play kickball, but first let's solve this problem between you and Conor about the wagon." Children are encouraged to communicate verbally with others as they see teachers using speech to get involved in play themselves. ("What a great house you have built. How do you get inside? Do you need any dishes?")

Enjoyment

To encourage language is to promote enjoyment in using it. Teachers converse with children, parents, and other adults, modeling for children how useful and fun language can be. Children learn to enjoy language by participating in group discussions and being encouraged to ask questions. Reading and

FIGURE 13.12 Teachers and children can share intimate moments when they enjoy using language together.

listening to stories and poems everyday is an essential part of any program. The program should also include children's literature and stories children dictate or write themselves.

Word play and rhyming are fun as well as educational. Group language games are useful, such as asking the question, "Did you ever see a bat with a hat? a bun having fun? a bee with . . .?" and letting the children add the rest. Begin a song, for instance, "Do You Know the Muffin Man?", and add the children's names. Whatever contributes to the enjoyment of language supports its growth, from varying voice and tone to fit the situation (in storytelling, dramatic play, and ordinary activity periods) to spontaneous rhyming songs.

THE TEACHER'S ROLE

Considerations

When considering how to work with young children in language development, teachers should keep several things in mind.

Children Must Use Language to Learn It. Adults who are unaware of this sometimes spend a lot of their time with children talking to, at, and about them. Children need the time, place, and support for practicing language. Practice must include time with peers and adults, and in both structured (group time) and nonstructured (free play) situations.

The Most Verbal Children Tend to Monopolize Language Interactions. Research shows that teachers interact verbally with the children who are most skilled verbally (Cazden, 1979). Seek out and support language development in those with fewer skills, generally by drawing them out individually through (1) reading the unspoken (body) language that communicates their ideas, needs, and feelings, and (2) helping them express verbally those ideas, needs, and feelings.

Adults Should Know the Individual Child. Consistency in adult–child relationships may be as important for language as for affective development during the early years (Cazden, 1979). If so, teachers must have a meaningful relationship with each child. This includes knowing the parent(s) and how they communicate with their child.

Bilingualism. In early childhood terms, *bilingualism* is the acquisition of two languages during the first years of life. The bilingual child must learn to comprehend and produce aspects of each language and then develop two systems of communication. Bilingualism in early childhood also occurs under these general conditions:

1. Children can comprehend and produce some aspects of both languages.

2. Through natural exposure, such as in a classroom, children get experience in both languages.

3. Development occurs simultaneously in both languages (Garcia, 1983).

The preschool setting is an excellent laboratory for studying exactly how children meet these conditions. Unfortunately, little systematic research has been done of children who acquire two languages at the same time. The challenge to a young child is enormous, particularly since acquiring a second language is more than linguistics. The issue of bilingualism must include cognitive and social considerations as well as linguistic ones.

What can be concluded at this time, however tentatively, is that:

- Children can and do learn two languages at an early age.

- Two languages can be learned at the same time in a parallel manner. The depth of knowledge of one language may be different from the other, or the two may develop equally.

- The acquisition of languages may mean a "mixing" of the two, as heard in children's speech when they use words or a sentence structure of both languages.

- Learning two languages does not hurt the acquisition of either language (Garcia, 1983).

Teachers must understand the increased workload bilingualism creates, and they must keep in mind that learning another language affects cognitive and social development.

Speech and Language Disorders. Early childhood professionals should have knowledge of speech and language disorders. Disorders of both receptive and expressive language can be detected early. The perceptive teacher does a great service to children and parents by discovering potential problems.

The Language of the Teacher. What teachers say—and how they say it—is important. Moreover, it is often what they do *not* say that communicates the most to children in their struggle to gain mastery of the language. For instance, when a child is stumbling over a word or phrase, teachers must give the child the time to work through the difficulty, rather than correcting or "helping" by finishing the sentence themselves. Teachers provide a rich environment and a high quality of interaction with the child that encourages articulation, receptive language, expressive language, and graphic language (the written word).

To *articulate* means to speak distinctly and with moderate speed. Teachers reinforce clear speech by giving frequent opportunities for children to practice speech.

Receptive language can be developed by using several strategies.

1. Give clear directions: "Please go and sit on the rug next to the chairs," instead of "Go sit over there."

2. Let children ask questions, and give them acceptable answers. For example, repeat a phrase from the child's last sentence that asks the child to try again: "You want *what?*" or "You ate *what?*". Or cast the question back to a child by changing the phrase "Where did you put it?" into "You put it *where?*".

3. Give instructions in a sequence: "Put your lunch on your desk, then wash your hands. Then you are ready to go to lunch." It often helps to ask the children what they think they are to do: "How do you get ready for lunch? What comes first? Next?"

4. Try to understand what the child means, regardless of the actual verbal language. Look for the purpose and intent beyond what the child may have said.

5. Ask children to state their thoughts out loud. "Tell me what you think is going to happen to the eggs in the incubator. Why do you think some hatched and some didn't?"

6. Use literature, poetry, and your own descriptions to give children an idea of how words can be used to paint verbal and mental pictures. Ask questions about children's own images and dreams. Read aloud from books without pictures.

When teachers focus on the spoken word, they are encouraging *expressive language.* They use short, concise sentences to frame or highlight a word. If a child says, "Look at that!", teachers reply, "That's a butterfly," or "I see; do you think it's a butterfly or a bee?"

One way children gain a greater awareness of themselves is by describing their own actions in words. Ask them to say what they are doing. Make a statement describing the child's behavior or actions. This is particularly helpful when dealing with feelings, such as the statement "It looks like you are feeling angry" (when confronted with a frown and clenched fists).

Teachers help children by directing their attention to objects, events, and relationships.

Michelle:	I have something to show you.
Teacher:	Can you give us some clues?
Michelle:	It's not a record and it's not a book, and you can't play with it.
Teacher:	Can you hold it in your hand?
Michelle:	No, silly; it's a kiss!

Give children opportunities to describe what they are going to do and what they have done. Through this, teachers discover what is meaningful to children and what they remember, and it gives them the chance to plan and review. When the class celebrates a birthday, children will want to discuss when their birthday is, what they will do, or how they feel. The answers may range from "July thirty-last" to "We're going to the moon" to "On my birthday my heart is filling me with lightening."

"Why do you think that happened?" is a thought-provoking question for children. Questions that encourage children to expand on their thoughts include those that ask for classification ("Who has short-sleeved shirts on today?"), seriation ("If the blue ball is the smallest, which one comes next?"), and other concepts of cognition.

An interesting and revealing aspect of working with children is listening to how they communicate and to the kinds of confusions that arise. "I can see you are really thinking about . . ." supports children's self-talk and concentration.

Developing communication skills with others is particularly important for children in the early years. Encouraging active listening and repeating one child's words to another ("Bahrain, did you hear what Joanna said about the sandtruck?") give children support. Expressing thoughts and feelings in words offers a model. By telling a child what

Description
- Use nouns for people, places, events: "We are going to visit Grandma now. That means we need to get dressed and walk to her apartment."
- Use modifiers: "That is your uncle's truck outside" or "Can you find your sister's teddy bear?"
- Use relational terms: "You are taller than the chair; the wagon is wider than the bed."
- Try more differentiated words to express differences: Instead of just "big/little," try "fat/thin" and "tall/short."

Narration
- Describe simple relationships of time: "Yesterday you stayed at home. Today is a school day. Tomorrow is Saturday, a stay-home day."
- Clarify a sequence of events: "When you come to school, first you put your things in your cubby, then you make an inside choice."
- Use words to describe repetition, continuation, and completion: "We are going to the store again, to buy food for dinner" or "I see that you and Juana are still playing together today" or "You finished building the box last time; now you are ready to paint it."

Explanation
- Point out similarities and differences: "Both Cathi and I have brown hair, but what is different about us? Yes, she has on shorts and I am wearing overalls."
- Try classifying what you see as well as asking children to do so: "I notice that all these shells have ridges on the outside; what do you see that is different about them?"

FIGURE 13.13 Several aspects of language development affect how teachers speak to children in the early years.

works for you ("I like it when you listen to my words"), a teacher provides a good example of how to communicate. Helping children stick to the subject shows that there is a topic at hand: "Stevie, now we're talking about our field trip to the track. You can tell us about your new dog next."

Curriculum Planning for Language Development

Teachers who plan curriculum for language skills, just as for cognitive development, focus on the class setting, specific skills, and themes. They organize the environment and activities to help children acquire linguistic skills of their own.

In the Class Setting

Indoors. Teachers arrange space so that children will practice speaking and listening and, in programs for older children, reading and writing. For example, a restaurant in the dramatic play area encourages the use of language. There are many signs: the name of the restaurant, OPEN and CLOSED, and COME AND GET IT! The children help create what is written on the menu. They can suggest "daily specials," and how to advertise them. Stories are written as a group-time project. A follow-up activity to encourage graphic language might be a newsletter about the restaurant corner, signed by the children themselves.

There is new vocabulary to learn in the restaurant unit: names of objects (menu, waiter, customer), action (serving, eating, paying), and feelings (waiting, impatient, hungry, finished). Children describe to one another where things are located, how much food to serve, how to pay for the meal.

The following dialogue shows expressive and receptive language as overheard in the restaurant:

Jean: I'm the cooker! Torrey, you make the money.

Frankie: What's goin' on around here?

Jean: We're the rest'rant. Whadda you want to eat?

Frankie: I'm thirsty. Where's my coffee?

Teacher, who is watching nearby: What happens when someone comes into a restaurant?

Torrey: We need a waitress, man. Emily, come here!

Emily: Tell me what you want to eat.

Frankie: Don't give me rabies; I'm allergic to them but my mom makes me eat them all the time.

Teacher: What's rabies?

Frankie: Oh, that's meatloaf and other yucky stuff.

Emily: All we have is scrambled eggs.

Jean: Here's your eggs.

Frankie: Hey, my eggs are gooder than these. Yuck.

Torrey: Come back here! You haveta pay me! He's a robber!

Other indoor areas can also be arranged to enhance language development:

Art
- Offer templates for tracing letters.
- Have signs and pictures that show where things are kept.
- Ask children to describe the materials they use.

Blocks
- Ask children to give each other directions for where blocks go and what they are used for.
- Label block shelves with shapes and words.

- Sketch children's structures and then write their word descriptions.

Cooking
- Label utensils.
- Describe actions (pour, measure, stir).
- Use recipe cards with both pictures and words.

Discovery/Science
- Label all materials.
- Ask questions about what is displayed.
- Encourage children's displays, with their dictated words nearby.
- Graph growth and changes of plants, animals, children, and experiments.

Language
- Label the bookshelf, record player, other equipment.
- Help children make their own books that involve description (My family is . . .), narration (It is winter when . . .), and recall (Yesterday I . . .).

Manipulatives
- Recognize this area as a place for self-communication, as children talk and sing to themselves while they work.
- Explain similarities and differences of materials and structures.

Outdoors. Outdoors, motor skills can be described and pointed out by teachers and children, as both use words of action and of feeling. For example, what actions does it take to get a wagon up the hill? How does a child's face feel when swinging up high?

Transitions and routines are more manageable if the children understand what is happening and exactly what they are to do. Teacher language helps talk children through the process so that they can internalize what they are asked to do. A teacher can write a note to "Please save" for the child who does not have time to finish a project, or they can write children's dictated notes to parents.

Group times, with fingerplays, songs, and stories, are language-intensive activities. Children's articulation skills are strengthened, as is receptive language through listening to others. Group times are also opportunities for children to express themselves. When children discuss daily news and important events, brainstorm ideas about a subject, or report on what they did earlier in the day, they gain experience in listening and speaking. Children can also dramatize familiar stories and fingerplays.

Using visual aids or name cards gives children experience in *graphic language*. These might include having felt letters for the song "B–I–N–G–O," numbers for the fingerplay "One, Two, Buckle My Shoe," or name cards for the activity "I'm Thinking of Someone . . ." And children enjoy the cadence and rhythm of language spoken or chanted.

Focus on Skills

Language development involves five different skills. Teachers can plan a curriculum focusing on a single skill, be it articulation, receptive, expressive, or graphic language, or the enjoyment of language. After choosing one of the skills, they look at the environment to see how that skill can be developed.

To focus on expressive language, teachers remember that children learn to express themselves by practicing words and grammatical structure, and by elaborating on their own expressions. A teacher asks Ceva to describe what she is doing with the art materials. "I'm dripping my paint," she replies. Outdoors, Hadar describes her actions: "Teacher, look at me! I'm taller than you!" The teacher responds, "You climbed up the ladder to the top of the tunnel. Now, when you stand up, your head is above mine." At group time, the whole class makes a group story about "The Mystery of Space." Then they separate into small groups to write their own books in story form, complete with illustrations.

Use of Themes

How could using themes for curriculum planning be used to develop language skills? One unit with universal appeal is "Babies," charted in Figure

---

Art: Limit the art materials to just what toddlers and infants can use.
Cooking: Make baby food.
Discovery/science: Display baby materials, then bring in baby animals.
Dramatic play area: "The Baby Corner" with dolls, cribs, diapers.
Manipulatives: Bring in several infant and toddler toys.
Large motor/games: Make a "crawling route," an obstacle course that requires crawling *only.*
Field trip/guest: A mom brings her baby to school.
Large-group time: Sing lullabies ("Rock-a-Bye-Baby").
Small/large group: Children discuss "What can babies do?"
   Joshua: Babies sleep in cribs. They wear diapers. Babies can't talk.
   Becky: They sometimes suck their thumbs. Babies cry when they are hungry.
   Dennis: Babies go pee in their diapers.
   Stevie: Babies sit in highchairs. Babies eat baby food that looks like squished bananas.
   Corey: Babies sleep in a basinette. Then they crawl and bite your finger.

FIGURE 13.14 Teachers plan a unit to promote the skills they are focusing on in the class. To encourage language, a "babies" theme brings out the "expert" in all children.

13.14. Other units that elicit an extensive use of language are:

- *Thanksgiving.* Activity area: Make a display of food from a Thanksgiving in the past, and then of food today.

  Group time: Begin a group story using the sentence "I am thankful for . . ."

  Special project: Plan a feast, with the children creating the menu and preparing both the food and the table.

- *Summertime.* Activity area: Children bring a piece of summer clothing for a display and "try-on" corner.

  Group time: Children respond to the phrase, "One summer morning . . ." with stories and pictures.

  Special project: A trip to the beach, or a treasure hunt for buried shells in the sand area outside.

- *Holidays.* Activity area: Decorate each corner of the room with materials from different countries or ethnic groups.

  Group time: "Holidays are when . . ."

  Special project: Children make a gift for someone they love.

- *Favorite Foods.* Activity area: Make a salad from everyone's favorite vegetable, or follow the story-line of *Stone Soup.*

  Group time: Discussion topic: "My favorite fruit is . . ." (Example: "An apple because it is crunchy and is big enough to share.")

  Special project: Make recipe cards to send home. (Example: Chicken—"First you get seven pounds of skin. Then you get flat pieces of roast chicken. Then you put some bones in. Then you get one pound of pickle seeds and put them on the chicken. Then cook it in the oven for about five hours!")

Any theme can be developed, as long as it brings out oral and graphic language experiences.

Unit 13–2 Checkpoint

Children develop language in their own ways, following patterns consistent over different cultures and countries. In the early years, language consists of several skills. The teacher's role is one of knowing how language develops and what skills to encourage in a class setting.

Then, teachers plan curriculum for language development. They organize the environment and schedule by focusing on the various areas and activities, a specific skill, or a unit.

Ask yourself:

- What does research tell us about child language and its development?
- What are the six stages of language development?
- What are the five language skills in early childhood education?
- What are six teacher considerations in planning for language development?
- How can teachers plan a curriculum that uses language skills?
- What themes promote language skill in the classroom?

UNIT 13–3   SPECIAL TOPICS IN COGNITION AND LANGUAGE

READING AND WRITING

Graphic language is the written word. For the young child, what once looked like dots and lines becomes letters and words. How does the early childhood teacher help children in this process?

The ability to read and write does not just happen when children reach a certain age. Their readiness for graphic language must be nurtured. A child's language proficiency will determine readiness for reading. Teachers identify this readiness by knowing how well a child understands the structure and vocabulary of the language. Therefore, a program to encourage beginning reading will offer experiences in oral language. Research shows that successful readers see a relationship between spoken language and the written word. They are aware that sounds are how language is put together (Nurss, 1980). So teachers plan activities that make connections between what is said and what is written.

There is an important role, then, for teachers of young children in the early stages of reading and writing. Teachers can influence positive attitudes toward reading and writing. Supporting children's interest in learning to read and write is a part of this role. Teachers encourage children to talk and converse with others about what they see and do; this gives them increasing experience in using and attaching experiences to words. When adults take the time to write down what children say and then read it back, it gives a sense of importance to children's language and their ability to express themselves. In these ways, teachers can help children get involved with print in natural and unpressured ways.

Children and Reading

The role of the adult is one of engaging children with print in ways that make sense to them. By creating an environment that provides rich opportunities to use the printed word, teachers help

When is your birthday?
- Where is your name?
- How many children have birthdays in April? February? December?
- How many children have birthdays on the 10th? the 2nd? of the month?

JAN.	FEB.	MAR.	APRIL	MAY	JUNE	JULY	AUG.	SEPT.	OCT.	NOV.	DEC.
13	1	3	2	16	11	5	2	8	21	7	13
Ann	Joey	Leon	Mrs. K.	Brian	Katie	Mr. W.	Carrie	Jim	Chris	Nick	Kay
19	3	7	10	27		9		29	30		25
Bill	Mary	Kirk	Peter	Adele		Patty		Danny	Jay		Carol
26	6	15	11			12					30
Judy	Sue	Bob	Jon			Kevin					Mrs. M.
24	11		18								
Tom	Andy		Jill								
	19		23								
	Sean		Libby								
			30								
			Mia								

FIGURE 13.15 A language experience chart involves children through the subject matter and through the way the information is displayed.

motivate children toward reading. Research tells us that children who are successful readers in elementary school are typically those who have a history of successful reading in their early years (Schickedanz, 1983).

At the preschool level, we often find a stereotypical concept of reading. Both children and adults associate the ability to read with the literal translation of signs and symbols on a printed page (called *decoding*). But for the young child, learning to read is not merely decoding the symbols. It is attaching experiences and knowledge to those words and understanding the use of the written word in their daily lives. Many parents and teachers believe that reading instruction begins in elementary school, so little is done to expand a child's simplified concept of reading before first or second grade.

In the early childhood setting, there is an opportunity to teach a broader concept of reading that goes beyond decoding and permeates children's lives. To do this, reading should not be taught as "basal reading," but instead should be treated as part of a child's immediate and ongoing life. This can help create positive attitudes about reading before the decoding process begins.

It is up to adults to provide children with opportunities that will enlarge their concepts of the power of the written word. Teachers and parents can wield a great deal of influence in communicating positive feelings about reading. One way to do this is by providing real and valid prereading experiences.

Children can learn to recognize, read, and write their names when given interesting ways to do it. A popular technique in many early childhood centers is to use a waiting list for highly desirable activities. By learning to read or print their names, children receive a tangible benefit: they can sign up for the activities they want and check the list to see where their names are. Some computer programs now allow children to manipulate letters for making their names, then print them. Through these experiential activities in reading and writing, children learn that words are useful and can be fun.

The child's readiness to read is related to the development of certain skills (see Figure 13.16). Readiness skills can be acquired through planned experiences in the school program that:

- Promote meaningful interaction with words.
  Example: Writing children's names on their drawings; labeling cubbies with children's names and pictures.
- Are age-level appropriate.
  Example: Lotto games for 2½-year-olds have pictures of familiar objects; those for four-year-olds have alphabet letters.
- Are fun and enjoyable for children.
  Example: Creating a class newspaper to take home.
- Take a gradual approach through the use of non-reading materials.
  Example: Labeling toy storage boxes with pictures instead of words.
- Acknowledge the child's ability to read the environment, to read events, to read other people.
  Example: Clark, looking out the window at the darkening sky, says, "Looks like it's gonna rain." Margo "reads" her painting as she describes the vivid monster to the teacher.
- Involve the use of children's senses.
  Example: Display baskets of vegetables and foods along with the book *Stone Soup*.

The school will have many activities in the area of "reading readiness." Recent research implies that an early childhood program promotes an awareness of the graphic aspects of language by:

1. Developing children's speaking and listening proficiencies through the use of conversation, descriptive language, oral feedback, and meaningful listening comprehension activities.

2. Helping children hear phonemes (language sounds) through oral language activities such as

Reading Readiness Is	Teachers
1. Oral vocabulary	1. Encourage talking, learning new words and phrases, singing, fingerplays, remembering and reflecting verbally.
2. Curiosity about/for reading	2. Provide a separate area for books (and are available to read to children), language games (lotto), dictation from children ("If I could fly I would . . ."), notes about children that the children deliver themselves to other adults.
3. Auditory discrimination (the ability to detect sound differences)	3. Create sound discrimination boxes in the science area, a "listen-to-the-sound" walk, guessing games with musical instruments, activities that teach letter sounds by using the children's names.
4. Visual discrimination	4. Support directionality: left and right (in the "Hokey-Pokey" dance and labeled on shoes and mittens), up and down, top and bottom, likeness and differences.

FIGURE 13.16 Children gain reading readiness skills through activities for oral vocabulary, curiosity about reading, and auditory and visual discrimination.

rhyming, initial consonant substitution, and the use of alliterations in jingles and language play.

3. Providing many opportunities for children to make the connection between spoken and written language.

4. Emphasizing children's own language in beginning reading activities.

5. Filling the environment with printed words and phrases, so children become familiar with meaningful print.

6. Highlighting the language used in beginning reading instruction; for example, the terms, "letter," "sound," and "word" (Nurss, 1980).

Children and Writing

Children learn about words in print much the same as they learn about reading and other aspects of language; that is, by seeing it used and having plenty of opportunities to use it themselves. Writing can be as natural for children as walking and talking. Children begin to write when they first take a pencil in hand and start to scribble. Later, they can write a story by drawing pictures or by dictating the words and having someone else write them down.

The early childhood classroom heightens an interest in writing through a writing center. It can be part of a language area or a self-help art center. Wherever it is located, this center will include a variety of things to write with and write on, and "writing helpers." Children write with pencils (fat and thin, with and without erasers), colored pencils, narrow and wide marking pens, and crayons. They enjoy having many kinds of paper products, including computer paper, old calendars, data-punch cards, and colored paper. Children also enjoy simple books, a few blank pages stapled together. Carbon paper, dittos, and lined paper will add variety. "Writing helpers" might be a picture dictionary, a set of alphabet letters, a print set, an alphabet chart, chalkboard, or magnetic letter board. All of these serve to help children practice writing skills.

Writing materials can be available throughout the room and yard. Paper and pencils come in handy in the dramatic play area. Menus, shopping lists, prescriptions, and money are but a few uses children will find for writing equipment. The block corner may need traffic signs; the computer, a waiting list. Outdoors, pictures can label the location of the vegetables in the garden; markers indicate where children have hidden "treasures," or where the dead bird is buried.

The "language experience" approach involves taking dictation, writing down and reading back to children their own spoken language. It is important to use the child's exact words so they can make the connection between their speech and the letters on the page. This is true for group stories, for children's self-made books, or for descriptions of their own paintings. A useful technique in taking dictation is to say the words while writing them, allowing the child to watch the letters and words being formed. When the content is read back, the child has a sense of completion. Figure 13.17 is an example of this kind of language experience in a classroom of five-year-olds.

The early childhood setting encourages an awareness of and interest in writing by having the printed word displayed regularly. Storage units are labeled with pictures and words of what belongs where (scissors, turtle food, blocks). Areas of the room are named, and stories, poems, or familiar fingerplays are hung on charts. Written signs remind children of the rules, such as "Inside Voices Here"

in the book corner or "Wear an Apron" near the easels. Primary classes may add calendars and helper charts, visual cues for children to read and prepare for the next event. In these ways, teachers help raise awareness of the use and enjoyment of the printed word.

CHILDREN'S LITERATURE

From the beginnings of education on this continent, literature has had a place in the curriculum. To be sure, from era to era, the emphases in the literary experiences of children . . . have changed; but the basic commitment to literature as a valuable . . . enterprise has been maintained. And today the potential of literature for children is greater than ever before. For we have more . . . beautiful books . . . more children who are capable of reading on their own . . . more good aids to teachers for selecting and utilizing literature in the education of youngsters. There is, indeed, little reason why any child . . . in these times should not be amply provided with . . . contact with literature throughout his entire . . . life.

(Jacobs *in* Rasmussen, 1961)

Literature does indeed have an important place in the curriculum today. It is especially valuable as a vehicle for cognitive and language development. Books help to acquaint children with new words, ideas, facts, and adventures. Planned and spontaneous reading experiences are a vital part of the young child's day.

Reading books to children introduces them to the reading concept, to a different form of communication from spoken language. It is a symbol system with which they will become familiar as they learn that words and pictures have meaning.

Literature and Cognitive Development

Literature can perform several functions in aiding cognitive development. Through the use of good

If I were a musical instrument:

Dennis: I would be a violin. Someone would play me with a bow and I would make a beautiful sound.

Janette: I would be a drum. I would be hit and I wouldn't be happy because they would make me hurt.

Corey: I would be a flute and someone would play my keys and it would craze me out. I would feel funny and I would play with my keys so hard that my wits would jump out and then my feet would jump out.

Michelle: I would be a piano with strings and lots of sparklies on top. And, you could play me even if you were blind.

Stevie: I would be a guitar because my friend is a guitar player.

Sara: I would be a flute. I would go whistle, whistle, whistle. And if I was a triangle I would go dong, dong, ding, ding. If I was a triangle they would use me for dinner so everybody would come.

Matthew: I would be a flute. I would make noise. I would make music.

Joshua: I would play the trombone 'cuz I would play songs. It has buttons. I would put it away up high where my sister couldn't reach it.

Matt: I would be a rattle and I would sound like a rattlesnake when somebody shakes me. I would be happy.

Johnny: I would be a drum and somebody would hit me with a stick. I would go pum, pum, pum.

Jocelyn: I would be a triangle so I could hit myself. It would make a ding-dong, a ding, ding. If I was, I knew that if I hit myself it would hurt; if I hit myself, it would hurt real badly.

Gregory: I would be a trumpet. I would play and everyone would be happy.

Becky: I would be a flute. I would make all different kinds of sounds.

FIGURE 13.17 Dictation, as a language experience approach, gives children a meaningful way to learn about the printed word.

books, teachers can help children broaden their interests and concepts. Books that are primarily used for transmitting information expand the child's knowledge base. Thoughtful books that draw on children's everyday experiences widen their understanding of themselves and others. Through books, children can learn to see things in an endless variety of ways. Six different books will describe and illustrate the behavior of cats in six different ways. Exposure to *Millions of Cats* (Gag), *Angus and the Cats* (Flack), and *The Cat in the Hat* (Dr. Seuss), as well as to the cats portrayed in *Peter Rabbit* (Potter) or *Frog Went A-Courtin'* (Langstaff), will enlarge the child's concepts of cats. Different cultures are also represented in any number of children's books, teaching a greater awareness of all of humankind.

Teachers have an opportunity to encourage divergent thinking through the use of children's literature. Children gain more than facts from books; they learn all matter of things, providing they can interpret the story rather than just hear the individual words. Quizzing children about whether the dinosaur was a meat- or plant-eater will bring about responses that are predictable and pat, but comprehension does not have to be joyless. Zingy questions will provide not only thought but also interest. "Would a brontosaurus fit in your living room?" will get children to think about *Danny and the Dinosaur* (Hoff) in a new way. "Is the troll bigger or smaller than your brother?" might be a point of discussion after reading *The Three Billy Goats Gruff.* The point is not to have children feed back straight factual information, but to get them involved in the story.

Selection of books obviously plays a part in using literature to stimulate thought and conversation about what was read. The wise teacher will choose books that invite participation. Everyone can "roar a terrible roar, gnash their terrible teeth, and show their terrible claws" during a rendition of *Where the Wild Things Are* (Sendak). Meaning for children lies more in action than in words. Children will be more apt to talk about stories that have in some way touched them and stimulated their involvement.

Questions for thought and children's participation must be related to children's experiences and knowledge, yet lead them toward discovery. Books provide a pleasurable avenue for this type of intellectual growth.

Literature and Language Development

A great many language skills are learned when children are exposed to good literature in the classroom. The value lies in the use of language by the author and the use the teacher makes of the language potential.

If language development is the goal, auditory appeal is one of the best reasons for choosing a book. The actual sounds of the words catch children's attention and imagination. Familiar sounds

of animals or objects reinforce and provide new ways to express thoughts. "Buzz" and "humm" are playful words that have great appeal to children. Sensory words, such as cold, soft, and slippery, capture children's attention.

Building and extending vocabulary is another function of literature in the language arts curriculum. Old familiar words take on new meaning as they reflect the content of each different story. Children love new words, especially big ones, and they do not necessarily need them defined. If used correctly in the context of the storyline, the words will be self-explanatory. Many children memorize phrases from favorite books, sometimes unaware of their meaning, but fitting the rhythm and pattern into their play.

> When Andrea was struggling to find the words to describe a large amount, Colin began to recite: "Hundreds of cats, thousands of cats, millions and billions and trillions of cats!" (*Millions of Cats,* Gag)

> Riding home in the car after school one day, Parker chanted: "Tik-ki tik-ki tem-bo no sa rembo, chari bari ru-chi, pip peri pembo." (*Tikki Tikki Tembo,* Mosel)

> Derek and Sylvia were playing grocery store. In order to attract customers they called out: "Caps for sale! Fifty cents a cap." (*Caps for Sale,* Slobodkina)

Language—and vocabulary—come alive with such repetition, as children integrate the words into their play. This demonstrates another benefit of books and literature in language development: that of learning the skill of listening. Teachers could ask for no better activity to promote good listening habits than a wealth of good children's books.

Creating a Rich Literary Environment

The comics of yesterday are far outdistanced by the television and video games of today. How

SCIENCE: SEA LIFE

Swimmy (Lionni)
One Morning in Maine (McCloskey)
Houses from the Sea (Gaudy)
I Saw the Sea Come In (Tressault)
What Does the Tide Do? (Kinney)
Ranger Rick magazine (National Wildlife
   Federation)
My Big Backyard magazine (National Geographic)
Little Tim and the Brave Sea (Ardizzone)
The Sand The Sea and Me (Craig)

MUSIC

Hush Little Baby (Aliki)
I Know an Old Lady (Bonne)
Drummer Hoff (Emberley)
Frog Went A-Courtin' (Langstaff)
One Wide River to Cross (Emberley)
Over in the Meadow (Wadsworth)
Fox Went Out on a Chilly Night (Spier)

SOCIAL STUDIES: OTHER CULTURES

Mei Li (Handforth)
Crow Boy (Yashima)
Tikki Tikki Tembo (Mosel)
Umbrella (Yashima)
The Story of Ping (Flack)
The Fish from Japan (Cooper)
The Trip (Keats)
First Pink Light (Greenfield)
On Mother's Lap (Scott)
Why Mosquitoes Buzz in People's Ears (Aardena)
Stevie (Steptoe)
Arrow to the Sun (McDermott)
Gilberto and the Wind (Ets)

TO READ ALONE: WORDLESS BOOKS

Gobble Growl and Grunt (Spier)
A Boy, a Dog, and a Frog (Mayer)
Rosie's Walk (Hutchins)
Out! Out! Out! (Alexander)
Look What I Can Do (Aruego)
Apples (Hogrogian)

BLOCKS

Changes Changes (Hutchins)
The Big Builders (Dreany)
Boxes (Craig)
Shapes (Schlein)
Who Built the Bridge? (Bate)
The Giant Nursery Book of Things That Work
   (Zaffo)

MATH: PASSAGE OF TIME

The Very Hungry Caterpillar (Carle)
Goodnight, Moon (Brown)
Carrot Seed (Krauss)
Inch by Inch (Lionni)
The Little House (Burton)
The Growing Story (Krauss)
Annie and the Old One (Miles)
Fast Is Not a Ladybug (Schlein)

ART

Start with a Dot (Roberts)
I Like Red (Bright)
Little Blue and Little Yellow (Lionni)
The Color Kittens (Brown)
Red Light, Green Light (MacDonald)
Hailstones and Halibut Bones (O'Neill)
A Color of His Own (Lionni)
My Very First Book of Colors (Carle)
The Great Blueness and Other Predicaments
   (Lobel)
Black Is Brown Is Tan (Adoff)

DRAMATIC PLAY

Curious George Goes to the Hospital (Rey)
Madeline (Bemelmans)
My Doctor (Rockwell)
What Happens When You Go to the Hospital
   (Shay)
A Visit to the Doctor (Berger et al.)
Tommy Goes to the Doctor (Wolde)

FIGURE 13.18 Reading around the curriculum. When good literature is a natural part of the environment, children learn to appreciate and use it.

can teachers give children experiences in literature in the face of such competition?

The field of children's literature is rich in its variety, including both great classic stories and those of present-day situations and concerns. Fiction and informational books, children's magazines, and poetry add balance to the literary curriculum. Every classroom should contain representative works from each of these areas.

Provide plenty of time for using books and other materials. Children need time to browse, to flip through a book at their own pace, to let their thoughts wander as they reflect on the storyline. They also enjoy retelling the tale to others. Be sure to plan enough time for children to be read to every day.

Make a space that is quiet and comfortable. In addition to soft pillows or seats, locate the reading area where there is privacy. Crashing blocks and messy fingerpainting will intrude on the bookreader. A place to sprawl or cuddle up with a friend is preferable.

Have plenty of books and supporting materials. The language arts center might contain a listening post, with headsets for a record or tape player. Perhaps there is even a place where books can be created, a place supplied with paper and crayons. There may even be a typewriter, puppet stage, or flannel board nearby so that stories can be created in new ways.

Display children's literary creations. The efforts of children's stories and bookmaking should be honored by establishing a place in the room where they can be seen and read. Children then see how adults value the process of literary creation and the final product.

Teachers must model how to care for a book and keep classroom books in good repair. Children can come to realize that a book is like a good friend and should be given the same kind of care and consideration.

Fostering children's reading at home is one of the important contributions a teacher can make to the reading process. Attitudes about reading are communicated to children from the important peo-ple in their lives. Because teachers do not have a direct influence on the home environment, their route to the home is through the children. A child who is enthusiastic about books and carries them home is likely to involve parents in the quest for good books and stories. Teachers encourage this in a number of ways. Posting the local library hours, establishing a lending library, and providing parents with lists of favorites will reinforce the child's interest in literature.

Use books around the room. Don't confine them to just the book corner or the book shelf. Demonstrate their adaptability to all curriculum areas by displaying a variety of books in the activity centers. Figure 13.18 shows how books can enhance play and learning throughout the school room.

Extending Literary Experiences

Good literature comes in many forms and can be presented in a variety of ways. A creative teacher uses books and literature to develop other curriculum materials. Translating words from a book into an activity helps a child remember them. Books and stories can be adapted to the flannel board, storytelling, dramatizations, puppets, book games, and audiovisual resources.

Storytelling

Storytelling is as old as humanity. The first time a human being returned to the cave with an adventure to tell, the story was born. Storytelling is the means by which cultural heritage is passed down from one generation to another.

Children's involvement with a story being told is almost instantaneous. The storyteller is the medium through which a story comes to life, adding a unique flavor through voice, choice of words, body language, and pacing.

The beginning teacher will want to start with a familiar story, perhaps a classic like *The Three Little Pigs*. Props can be added to draw attention to the story. Flannel board adaptations of stories are helpful; they give the storyteller a sense of security and a method for remembering the story. Children can be involved in the action by placing the characters on the felt board at the appropriate time. Puppets or an assortment of hats can be used as props. Good storytellers enjoy telling the story and communicate their enthusiasm to children.

Dramatizing Stories

Acting out characters from a favorite story has universal appeal. Young preschoolers are introduced to this activity as they act out the motions to fingerplays and songs. "The Eensy-Weensy Spider" and its accompanying motions is the precursor for dramatization.

Stories such as *Caps for Sale* (Slobodkina) and *Swimmy* (Lionni), as well as fairy tales, are popular choices for reenactment by four- and five-year-olds. They need plenty of time to rehearse, and simple props help them focus on their role. A red scarf helps Jeannada become *Little Red Riding Hood;* an old pair of sunglasses transforms Jack into a character from *Goggles* (Keats).

Puppet Shows

Puppet shows can involve a large number of children as participants and audience. Children of all ages enjoy watching and putting on a puppet show. Teachers can support their efforts by helping them to take turns, suggesting questions and dialogue to them, and involving the audience. The project of puppet making can be quite elaborate and very engaging for older children.

Book Games

Book games are a good way to extend the literary experience. Buy two copies of an inexpensive book with readable pictures, such as *The Carrot Seed* (Krauss). Tear out the pages and cover with clear plastic. Children must then read the pictures in order to put the book into proper sequence. A book of rhymes, *Did You Ever See?* (Einsel), lends itself to rhyming games. Children can act out the rhymes from the storyline or match rhyming phrasing from cards the teacher has made.

Audiovisual Resources

Records, cassettes, and filmstrips enlarge the child's experience with books. The auditory and the visual media reinforce one another. The pictures can show children new aspects of the words; sometimes the music or the voices bring the book to life. Often both happen. Hundreds of children's stories—classics and modern day—have been translated to these media.

Unit 13–3 Checkpoint

Children and books belong together. Good literature gives insight into human behavior. Children learn from books, "not just the less important though entertaining things such as how to escape a cat or tease a dog, but matters of character that are both subtle and humanistic" (Sebesta and Iverson, 1975). The preschool years should lay a concrete foundation in literature upon which children themselves can build.

> Books are no substitute for living, but they can add immeasurably to its richness. When life is absorbing, books can enhance our sense of its significance. When life is difficult, they can give a momentary relief from trouble, afford a new insight into our problems or those of others, or provide the rest and refreshment we need. Books have always been a source of information, comfort, and pleasure for people who know how to use them. This is as true for children as for adults.
> (Arbuthnot and Sutherland, 1972)

Ask yourself:

- How do teachers help children become ready to read?
- What should a writing center in an early education classroom look like?
- How does literature support cognitive development? Language development?

- What are the guidelines for creating a rich literary environment?
- What are five ways to extend literary experiences?

SUMMARY

People entering early childhood education as a profession are challenged to develop children's minds and language. This chapter begins with the premise that intellectual development and language are interrelated. As teachers help children learn how to think, they learn about children's thinking processes by listening to what they say, and observing how they respond to others' words, thoughts, and actions.

Much of cognitive development theory has its roots in the work of Jean Piaget. Cognitive development includes the areas of inquiry, knowledge of the physical and social worlds, classification, seriation, numbers, symbols, spatial relationships, and time. Language development, on the other hand, takes into consideration how children learn articulation, receptive and expressive language, graphic representation, and enjoyment of language.

Teachers plan curriculum to develop these skills in several ways. Many class settings offer children an opportunity to refine cognitive and language skills. At times, teachers focus on a specific skill, such as reasoning or conversation, and adapt the curriculum to emphasize those areas.

The teacher's role also requires an understanding of bilingualism and a working knowledge of speech and language disorders. Early childhood teachers use their own language abilities to stress and support the language development of their students.

Reading and writing are part of the language and thought processes. Adults in early childhood seek ways to involve children with the printed word in ways that have meaning to the here-and-now in children's lives. Books and literature further the development of reading and writing skills and provide an enjoyable tool for the enhancement of cognition and language.

Review Questions

1. How are cognition and language related?
2. Match the cognitive skill with the appropriate activity:

inquiry	being aware of others
physical world	learning to locate things
social knowledge	pretending to be a puppet
classification	asking questions
seriation	sequencing events
numbers	using nesting blocks
symbols	expressing amounts
spatial relationships	sorting objects
time	manipulating materials

3. What kinds of questions does the teacher ask to help children to think?
4. How does the teacher help children develop speech and language skills in planning curriculum?
5. The way teachers use language is critical in encouraging children's own language. Name the four areas of language and what a teacher can say to encourage growth in those areas.

Learning Activities

1. Look at the program in which you now teach, or recall your own first classrooms. Find at least one example of rote knowledge, social knowledge, and meaningful knowledge.
2. Take one cognitive skill and trace how it could be developed in each curriculum area of the program.

3. How does teacher language affect how children develop cognitive skills? Give several examples of what discourages such growth; counter that with how what a teacher says encourages skills.

4. Make a list of the classroom areas. Beside each, name one activity that would foster cognitive development and one that calls for language skills.

5. One theme often used in early childhood programs is that of the changing season in the fall. How can that theme develop language and thinking skills in preschoolers?

6. Teaching reading readiness involves trying to develop oral language and listening skills. What could a teacher of toddlers plan for each? A kindergarten teacher?

7. Describe three ways children's books and literature help to develop intellectual skills and language proficiency. Through what techniques can literary experiences be extended in the curriculum?

Bibliography

GENERAL

Bloom, Benjamin S.; Hastings, J.T.; and Madaus, G.F. *Handbook on Formative and Summative Evaluation of Student Learning.* New York: McGraw-Hill, 1971.

Brown, Janet F., ed. *Curriculum Planning for Young Children.* Washington, D.C.: National Association for the Education of Young Children, 1982.

McCarthy, Jan, and May, C.R., eds. *Providing the Best for Young Children.* Washington, D.C.: National Association for the Education of Young Children, 1974.

Piaget, Jean. *The Language and Thought of the Child.* Cleveland: World Publishing Co., 1969.

Schickedanz, Judith A.; York, M.E.; Stewart, I.D.; and White, D.A. *Strategies for Teaching Young Children,* 2nd ed. Englewood Cliffs, N.J.: Prentice-Hall, 1983.

Stone, Joseph L., and Church, Joseph. *Childhood and Adolescence.* New York: Random House, 1979.

Vygotsky, L.S. *Thought and Language.* New York: M.I.T. Press and John Wiley and Sons, 1962.

COGNITION

Furth, H.G. *Piaget for Teachers.* Englewood Cliffs, N.J.: Prentice-Hall, 1970.

Ginsburg, H., and Opper, S. *Piaget's Theory of Intellectual Development.* Englewood Cliffs, N.J.: Prentice-Hall, 1969.

Hohlmann, Mary; Banet, B.; and Weikart, D.P. *Young Children in Action.* Ypsilanti, Mich.: The High/Scope Press, 1979.

Hunt, J. McVicker. *Human Intelligence.* New Brunswick, N.J.: Transaction Books, 1972.

Moore, Shirley G., and Kilmer, Sally. *Contemporary Preschool Education.* New York: John Wiley and Sons, 1973.

Weikart, David P., et al. *The Cognitively-Oriented Curriculum.* Washington, D.C.: National Association for the Education of Young Children, 1974.

LANGUAGE

Beck, M. Susan. *Baby Talk: How Your Child Learns to Speak.* New York: New American Library, 1979.

Cazden, Courtney B., ed. *Language in Early Childhood Education.* Cambridge, Mass.: Harvard University Press, 1979.

deVilliers, Peter A., and Jill, G. *Early Language.* Washington, D.C.: National Association for the Education of Young Children, 1981.

Garcia, Eugene. "Bilingualism in Early Childhood." In Brown, Janet S. (ed.), *Curriculum Planning for Young Children.* Washington, D.C.: National Association for the Education of Young Children, 1983.

MacIntosh, Helen K., ed. *Children and Oral Language.* Washington, D.C.: Association for Childhood Education International, 1964.

Nurss, J.R. "Research in Review: Linguistic Awareness and Learning to Read." *Young Children,* March 1980, pp. 57–66.

Smith, J.S. *Creative Teaching of the Language Arts in the Elementary School,* 2nd ed. Boston: Allyn and Bacon, 1973.

LITERATURE

Arbuthnot, May Hill, and Sutherland, Zena. *Children and Books,* 4th ed. London: Scott, Foresman and Co., 1972.

Rasmussen, Marjorie, ed. *Literature with Children.* Washington, D.C.: Association for Childhood Education International, 1961.

Sebesta, Sam, and Iverson, William. *Literature for Thursday's Child.* Chicago: Science Research Inc., 1975.

Trelease, Jim. *The Read-Aloud Handbook.* New York: Penguin Books, 1982.

14

Planning for the Heart and Soul: Emotional, Social, and Creative Growth

Questions for Thought

- What is emotional growth in the early childhood years?
- How do teachers handle the expression of feelings in the class setting?
- What is social growth in the early childhood years?
- What social skills are developed in young children?
- What is creativity?
- How is creativity expressed in the early years?
- How can teachers encourage creative growth in the classroom?

Outline

Portions of this chapter were developed with the assistance of Gay Spitz, Hartnell College, Salinas, Calif.

PREFACE

The heart and soul of any good program for young children is a commitment to help children as they struggle with (1) the reality of emotions; (2) the awareness of the need for social skills; and (3) the creative urge. The foundation must be laid in these early years for children to understand themselves and others.

Emotional, social, and creative development are related to the child's self-concept and self-esteem; the child must have an understanding of self before seeing that self in relation to others. It is primarily through emotional, social, and creative growth that children learn who they are, and they must have self-confidence to experience and learn the necessary skills.

This chapter contains three separate units. Each area—emotional, social, and creative growth—is explored individually to give a greater understanding of its importance to the developing child. An overview of development is followed by a discussion of the skills children learn in the preschool years. The crucial role of the teacher is emphasized next, followed by curriculum planning to reinforce each developmental area. At the end of each unit, a checkpoint and review serve as a short summary.

INTRODUCTION

The first thing one notices upon entering an early childhood classroom is the children at play. A quick survey of the area shows who is playing together, whether or not there is crying and fighting, and how happy or sad the children look. This overview gives an immediate sense of the emotional, social, and creative climate in that early childhood setting.

Emotional: Abier cries after she splashes soapy water in her eyes and needs to be comforted.

Social: Danny wants his favorite red wagon so Pat, the student teacher, helps him negotiate a turn with Christa.

Creative: Fabio, Erika, and Benjy work steadily to build a tall, intricate block structure. When it is finished, the three children stand back and marvel at their creation.

Together these three factors—emotional mood, social dynamics, and creative tone—define the overall atmosphere in which children play and work.

Emotional, social, and creative well-being are woven together in the developing child. Children who are sensitive to their own feelings and moods are able to begin understanding other people and thus become more socially effective and successful. Children with experience in many creative endeavors have the self-confidence that comes from having an outlet for self-expression.

These three areas are also linked to other aspects of the child's growth:

- *Creative/Physical:* Physical skills can define and limit children's creative abilities. Two-year-old Andrea, whose physical skills do not yet include balancing objects, plays with blocks by piling them on top of one another, filling her wagon with blocks, and dumping them or lugging them from place to place.

- *Social/Cognitive:* It is hard for five-year-old Karena to share her best friend Luther with other children. Her intellectual abilities do not yet allow her to consider more than one idea at a time, so she cannot understand that Luther can be her friend and Dana's at the same time.

- *Emotional/Language:* Tyler is upset at his mother's refusal to let him play outside. "I hate you!" he screams, "I want a new mommy!" Children learn to label and express their emotions through words.

It is difficult to observe and measure the child's growth in creative, social, and emotional areas; it is easier to determine a child's progress in physical, cognitive, and language development. After all, a child counts or doesn't count, is either 40 inches tall or not, and speaks in full sentences or short phrases. Emotional, social, and creative expressions are more subtle and subjective. A child usually gets immediate and concrete feedback when playing lotto, calling for a teacher, or riding a tricycle. That does not always happen when children express their feelings, encounter others, and create something important. Talbot may feel rejected and sad if no one greets him as he enters the playhouse. He may mistake the children's busyness as an act of exclusion. In reality, the children did not even know he was there. Teachers can play a critical role helping children interpret their emotion, social, and creative interactions.

FIGURE 14.1 The emotional, social, and creative growth of children is the heart and soul of an early childhood education program. (Courtesy of Stephanie Barry Agnew)

Traditionally, early childhood educators have concerned themselves with children's well-being, knowing that in the early years the foundations must be laid for children to understand themselves and others. Social growth, creative expression, and experience with a wide range of emotional behaviors also help children develop a strong self-concept and positive self-esteem.

Self-esteem (the way children feel about themselves) is expressed through children's behavior. They make judgments about themselves as they confront the world. To the extent that children feel worthy and capable, they are ready to succeed. If children disapprove of themselves, they may feel like failures and expect to do poorly.

Self-esteem develops as a reflection of experiences: the way people respond to you gives you some indication of your importance or value. Newborn infants have no concept of self and no past experience to judge their own worth. A young child who has positive experiences with others will more likely have a high sense of self-esteem than one who has felt unloved or unnoticed. Eventually, the child becomes independent of others' opinions, but early in life self-esteem is tied to family, friends, and other important people. There appear to be four components of self-esteem (Clemes and Bean, 1980; Brophy and Willis, 1981):

1. A sense of one's own identity.

2. A sense of belonging.

3. A sense of one's uniqueness is recognized and respected.

4. A sense of self through the use of the power of self-definition.

Children with these characteristics are ready to meet the emotional, social, and creative challenges of the early years. They will have the self-confidence to deal with the reality of their emotions, the adaptability of their social learnings, and the risk of creativity.

UNIT 14–1 EMOTIONAL GROWTH

THE DEVELOPMENT OF EMOTIONS

Emotions are the feelings a person has—joy and sorrow, love and hate, confidence and fear, loneliness and belonging, anger and contentment, frustration and satisfaction. They are responses to

FIGURE 14.2 Young children feel their emotions strongly.

events, people, and circumstances. Feelings are an outgrowth of what a person perceives is happening. Emotionally healthy people learn to give expression to their feelings in appropriate ways. They do not allow their feelings to overshadow the rest of their behavior. The optimal time to learn these skills is in the early years.

Early childhood teachers encourage children to identify and express their emotional nature so that they can learn to live with these powerful forces. When a child begins to understand and communicate feelings, the emotions are no longer in control of the child; the child is becoming the master of the emotions.

Infants respond in agitated emotion whether wet, hungry, hurt, or bored. Gradually, the expression of the emotion becomes more refined and varies with the situation. A toddler's cry of distress is different from the cry of discomfort or hunger. As children get older, their emotional expressions change as they gain control over some of their feelings and learn new ways to express them.

Strong external forces are also at work. Parents, family members, teachers, and friends are social influences, helping the young child learn socially acceptable behavior. Much of what children learn is by example; therefore, children learn more from adult models than from simply being told how to behave (Clemes and Bean, 1980; Jensen and Wells, 1979).

EMOTIONAL SKILLS IN EARLY CHILDHOOD EDUCATION

The emotional skills children learn in their early years are substantial. Young children are not yet limited by *social mores* and standards of conduct that prevent them from sincere and truthful self-expression. Teachers observe children and learn how youngsters feel about facing their own feelings, the feelings of others, and the range of skills categorized as emotional growth.

Ability to Deal with Feelings

Dealing with feelings involves four steps. Each builds upon the other so that they follow a developmental sequence; the learning that takes place at one level affects the development of what follows.

To Notice and Label Feelings

This is the first step. The sobbing one- or two-year-old may have many reasons for feeling in distress. As parents recognize the cries of hunger, hurt, and fear, they name these feelings. The child will learn to notice what the feeling is and recognize it. Preschoolers are quite verbal and curious about language and ready to learn words that describe a wider range of feelings. They can learn "lonely," "scared," "silly," "sad," and "happy." Labeling what one feels inside is a critical skill to learn. It is a healthy first-grader who can say, "I have tried to cut this string three times and the scissors aren't working. I am frustrated. I need some help!"

To Accept Feelings

Teachers recognize that children are capable of strong feelings. Children can feel overwhelmed by the very strength and intensity of a feeling, be it one of anger or of love. As children come to accept feelings, they learn how to handle the depth of the feeling and not let it overpower them. The changing nature of feelings is also part of accepting the feeling. It can be a source of comfort and relief for young children to discover that the strong emotion they experience now will pass. Adults who work with young children help them work through those feelings safely. The sadness Carlos felt as his mother left is over in a few minutes; the teacher can point this out once Carlos has recovered his composure.

FIGURE 14.3 Teachers and children explore emotions together.

Acknowledgment of the feeling and his ability to accept it help give Carlos the confidence to move on.

To Express Feelings in an Appropriate Way

This is a two-part process. First, children must feel free to express their feelings; second, they must learn ways of expression that are suitable to their age and to the situation. Many beginning teachers are uncomfortable because children express themselves so strongly (and often aggressively). Yet the child who is passive and unable to express feelings freely should be of equal concern and should be encouraged in self-expression.

As children grow, they acquire the modes of expression that are developmentally appropriate for their age. Two-year-olds express their displeasure by pushes and shoves, while four-year-olds use their verbal power and argue. By six or seven, children learn to tell others—clearly and with reasons—what they are feeling. The ability to express feelings is intact, but the methods of expression change as children grow.

To Deal with the Feelings of Others

This is the culminating step in the development of emotional skills. Feelings are the spark of life in people: the flash of anger, the "ah-hah" of discovery, the thrill of accomplishment, the hug of excitement. Helping children to tolerate and appreciate how different people express their emotions leads to understanding and cooperation.

Ability to Deal with Change

Change is inevitable. Many people fear or reject change. Children can learn that change is a constant part of their lives and to cope with the challenges changes present. Fear, insecurity, and uncertainty are some of the emotions felt when people experience changes in their lives or routines. Many times, these feelings arise from not knowing what to expect or how to behave or from not understanding different sets of values. Teachers can help

children accept change in several ways. Anticipating changes that are likely to occur and identifying the process for children is very important. "Junko, your mother will be leaving soon. We'll go looking for that favorite puzzle after you say good-bye to her." If the daily routine is altered, children should be notified. "We won't be having snacks inside today; let's use the patio table instead." When children are informed that change is anticipated, accepted, and not necessarily disrupting, they become more relaxed about handling the unpredictable.

Ability to Exercise Judgment

The ability to exercise judgment is an important skill, for it helps children make decisions and

FIGURE 14.4 The ability to exercise judgment is an emotional skill related to self-knowledge.

figure out what to do in new situations. On entering school, a child faces many decisions: Where shall I play? Who shall I play with? What if my friend wants to do something I know is wrong? Who will I turn to for help when I need it? Judgment is selecting what to do, when to do it, with whom to do it, and when to stop.

There is no easy way to teach children how to make decisions since each situation must be dealt with on an individual basis. The judgment a child exercises in choosing a friend to play with today may have other factors to consider tomorrow. Instead, teachers help children base their decisions on the best judgment they are capable of in each instance. As they mature, children are able to sort out what judgments might be made here, what factors need to be considered there.

Enjoying One's Self and One's Power

Teachers want children to feel powerful—to know that they can master their lives and feel confident in their own abilities. This feeling of power is particularly important in the early years when so much in a child's eyes is out of reach, both literally and figuratively.

Responsibility and limits, however, go hand in hand with power. The child who is strong enough to hit someone has to learn not to use that strength unnecessarily. The child who shouts with glee also finds out that noise is unacceptable indoors. By holding children responsible for their own actions, teachers can help children enjoy their power and accept its limitations.

Teachers can help children learn to appreciate and enjoy themselves. Each time a child is acknowledged, a teacher fosters that sense of uniqueness. "Carrie, you have a great sense of humor!" "Freddie, I love the way you sing so clearly." Saying it aloud reinforces in children the feeling that they are enjoyable to themselves and to others.

FIGURE 14.5 With an awareness of their own power comes the need for children to act responsibly with their new-found abilities.

THE TEACHER'S ROLE
Considerations

The first step in helping children develop healthy emotional patterns is for adults to acquire and use a "feeling" vocabulary. Words of an emotional nature can be used to label and identify feelings as teachers talk with young children.

There are many ways to develop a list of words related to emotions. Figure 14.6 illustrates one way. Identify some of the feelings children express; then describe how the children look and act when experiencing those emotions. This helps to build a vocabulary and an understanding of children's emotional expressions.

Teachers can also become more attuned to the emotional climate in the classroom by knowing

Feeling	Behavioral Definition
1. Fear	Pale face, alert eyes, tense mouth, rigid body.
2. Surprise	Wide eyes, eyebrows uplifted, involuntary cry or scream, quick inhale of breath.
3. Anger	Red face, eyes staring, face taut, fists and jaw clenched, voice harsh or yelling, large gestures.
4. Joy	Smiling face, shining eyes, free and easy body movements, laughing.
5. Pride	Head held high, smiling face, jaunty walk or strut, tendency to announce or point out.
6. Embarrassment	Red face, glazed and downcast eyes, tight mouth, tense body, small and jerky movements, soft voice.
7. Sadness	Unsmiling face, downturned mouth, glazed and teary eyes, crying or rubbing eyes, limp body, movements are slow or small, voice is soft, trembly.
8. Anxiety	Puckered brow, pale face, tight mouth, whiny voice, jerky movements, lack of or difficulty in concentration.
9. Curiosity	Raised brow, shining eyes, perhaps tense body in absorption of the object of curiosity, often hand movements to touch and pick up object, sometimes mouth agape.

FIGURE 14.6 As we observe children's behavior, we understand how their feelings are expressed.

when and how feelings are expressed. To gain insights, teachers might ask themselves:

- What causes children in the class to become excited? Frightened? Calm? Loud?
- How do I anticipate children's emotional behavior?
- What can teachers do to handle children's emotional outbursts and crises?
- What happens to the rest of the class when one teacher is occupied in an emotional incident with one or more children?
- What do I do when a child shows emotion? How do I feel when a child displays emotion?
- What types of emotions are most common with the young child?

In the early childhood setting, teachers help children come to grips with their strong feelings by discussing these feelings openly. They take the time to help children find names for feelings, to speak of their own feelings, and begin to be aware of the feelings of others.

When teachers perceive that children are ready to talk about their feelings, small group discussions or individual conversations can be helpful. Good books that touch upon sensitive issues (being excluded, being blamed, caring for others) offer possibilities for teachers and children to talk about feelings. Classroom problems (not sharing materials, pushing on the climbers) offer topics for discussion. The ability to express emotions verbally gives children the power to deal with them without resorting to inappropriate behavior.

When adults show an understanding of feelings, children come to believe that adults are able to help them with their emotions, and the children become more at ease with their own feelings. When something painful happens to a child, adults can express what the child is feeling. "It really hurts to bend your knees now that you have scraped them." "You look so sad now that Gabi is playing with someone else." Children then become familiar with ways to express how they feel in a variety of emotional situations.

Adults can also help children become aware of the emotional states of others. "Look! Paul is crying. Let's go over and see if we can comfort him." Teachers can encourage children to help care for each other's hurts and needs. A child can ease the pain of a friend by sitting nearby as a wound is cleansed or by giving a hug when an achievement is made. Teachers must be sure to allow children to express their concern and to help them learn ways to respond to the emotional needs of others.

FIGURE 14.7 Teachers who reflect children's feelings show they understand.

Curriculum Planning for Emotional Growth

In the Class Setting

Teachers set up their classrooms and yards to promote emotional growth. Materials and activities enhance self-esteem and self-expression. How activities are presented and carried out is also a factor. In looking at the class setting, it is important to remember that the "how" is as critical as the "what" in curriculum planning for emotional development.

Select materials that enhance self-expression. Indoors, children's inner thoughts and feelings are best expressed through:

- *The Arts.* Clay or dough lets children ventilate feelings, since it can be pounded, pinched, poked, slapped, and manipulated. Fingerpainting and painting on broad surfaces with large brushes encourage a freedom of movement that permits children to express themselves more fully.

- *Blocks/Manipulatives.* Vary the materials regularly to help children adjust to change and to allow them to exercise judgment about playing with different materials. A variety of props—motor vehicles, animals, people, furniture—gives children the opportunity to reenact what they see of the world.

- *Discovery/Science.* Often science projects are geared toward cognitive and language development. This need not always be so; some activities can focus on feelings. Caring for pets, for instance, brings out feelings of nurturing and protectiveness. Making "feeling clocks" can emphasize emotions. Blank clock faces are used as a base upon which children draw or paste pictures of people showing various emotional states. Display these at children's eye level so they can be changed frequently.

- *Dramatic Play.* Home-life materials give children the props they need to express how they see their own world of family, parents, siblings. Mirrors, telephones, and dress-up clothes encourage children to try out their emotional interests on themselves as well as each other.

- *Language/Library,* Stories and books in which characters and situations reflect a wide range of emotions are readily available (see Figure 13.19 and Figure 14.9 for some suggested titles). Children enjoy looking at photographs of people and guessing what the person in the photo is feeling. This encourages children to find words that label feelings; their responses can be recorded and posted nearby. Once children seem at ease in using feeling words, the discussion can continue when the teacher poses the question, "Why do you think this person is sad/happy/angry?"

Outdoors, the environment itself encourages self-expression. Whether in the sand or on a swing, children seem to open up emotionally as they relax in the physical freedom the out-of-doors fosters. Outdoor games are usually highly emotionally charged. Running, chasing, and the dramatic play of superheroes provide emotional release for children.

The outdoor area is an ideal place for large, noisy, and messy activities. It is ideal for tracing body outlines, for instance. These life-size portraits of each child reinforce self-concepts and encourage a feeling of pride in one's self. Woodworking is an outdoor activity that allows children to vent anger and tension. Nails won't be hurt no matter how hard they are pounded; there is satisfaction in sawing a piece of wood into two pieces. Music offers numerous opportunities for self-expression. Children can dance with scarves or streamers, march through the yard with drums pounding, imitate Wild Things, make a maypole around the tree, and create a Chinese dragon for a parade. A rich musical repertoire of band instruments, phonograph records, tapes, and voices can stimulate children to pretend to be elephants, tigers, and dinosaurs, as well as circus performers and ballet artists. Even a simple project such as water painting becomes an avenue for self-expression as children use paint brushes and buckets of water on trees, cement, and buildings, giving them all a fresh coat of "paint."

Figure 14.8 outlines how curriculum can be developed for emotional growth. Using the senses and sensory activities, teachers can promote an atmosphere in which emotions can be explored.

Focus on Skills

Emotional development is a lifelong process, requiring experience with one's own feelings. Each child has a unique emotional foundation, which the knowledgeable teacher assesses. Only then can teachers plan curriculum with realistic goals in mind for the children in that class. The goals teachers set for children will determine which emotional skills will be the focus as they individualize the curriculum. Maggie has difficulty with changes in the routine, Caroline never cries, no matter how she hurts, and Clyde screams when he is frustrated. To help children like these learn to express and control their emotions, teachers plan programs like the one illustrated in Figure 14.9.

Use of Themes

One particular theme, that of "Who Am I?", is useful when developing curriculum for emotional growth. Figure 14.10 outlines how this theme can be incorporated in many ways, both indoors and out. A number of other units can be developed to extend the theme of "Who Am I?" Some of these are: "My Body," "The Senses," "The Community Where I Live," and so on.

Unit 14–1 Checkpoint

Emotional growth is a crucial part of children's development in the early years. Emotions develop as children respond to life experiences with a full range of feelings. An undifferentiated state of emotions during infancy evolves into a more refined array of feelings in childhood. Children gain control of their emotions through maturation and experience.

Emotional skills learned in the early years are: the ability to deal with feelings and with change,

Emotion/Skill Developed	Sensory Activity (Senses Used)
Self-Esteem	
1. Identity: "Look at what I can do, the noise I can make, the weight I can pick up and move!"	Use rocks of various sizes with balances, so that children can touch and hear when they move things around.
2. Connectedness: "I can make the same snakes as you, we can all make cakes."	A malleable material such as playdough can be used first alone, then with tools.
3. Uniqueness: "I'm pouring mine; you're dripping yours, and she is squeezing her stuff out her fingers!"	Make "oobleck," a mixture of cornstarch and water, in separate tubs for each child. Children can manipulate it in their own ways.
4. Power: "I can make this water go anywhere I want; look out for the tidal waves!"	Water play offers the child choices: pour into any of several containers, fill or empty the jug, use a funnel or a baster to squirt the water, make waves or splash hands.
Feelings	
1. Identification: "Does it feel very smooth, slippery, slidy? Is it soft and soothing?"	When fingerpainting, the teacher can describe what it appears the child is feeling. Children can identify their feelings as the teacher describes them while they use the materials.
2. Acceptance/Mastery: "She took your baker's dough and that made you angry. You can tell her you don't like it when she grabs what you are using."	Whether the sensory material is clay, cornmeal, soapy water, or fine sand, the issues of ownership and use of materials arise. Then, teachers reflect children's feelings and help them take responsibility for their own feelings.
3. Appropriate Expression: Child: "Tami has all the big pitchers." Teacher: "How can you let her know you want one?" Child: "And she splashed me two times!" Teacher: "If you feel too crowded, you need to tell her so."	As children begin to use the sensory materials, they need to communicate to others. Usually the issues are about wanting more material and personal space.
4. Appreciation of Feelings: "Whee! Yuk! Mmm! Ha!"	When children share in a sensory activity, such as a feeling walk through tubs of cornmeal, lentils, flour, and soapsuds, they have the delightful experience of enjoying their own feelings with another.

FIGURE 14.8 Sensory materials offer a sensorimotor opportunity to deal with materials in a nonstructured way. Because they are sensory oriented themselves, children like to manipulate and will often share their feelings in the comfortable atmosphere surrounding the sensory area.

to be able to exercise judgment, to know and enjoy one's power. Teachers help children develop these skills by building a vocabulary of feeling words, by an awareness of the emotional climate in the classroom, by talking with children about their feelings, and by helping children sense the emotional framework of others. Self-esteem and self-concepts are enhanced by positive emotional growth.

Curriculum planning for emotional development involves an emphasis on many avenues for

1. IN-CLASS SETTINGS
Art:
a. "You look like you're enjoying yourself." "Your face tells me that it feels funny to you." Such statements reflect children's expressions and help them become aware of how they are feeling.
b. Write the words children use at work and at play. This can be at the bottom of their individual artwork, or on a sheet of paper you post alongside several examples as a display.

Blocks:
As children play in this area, be aware of what they do, and ask them how it feels when:

- you make a structure all by yourself
- it falls down
- someone knocks it over (accidentally and on purpose)
- someone laughs

Discovery/Science:
Use the words "curious" and "proud" to describe what children do as they explore and experiment with materials. Ask them to describe both their feelings and the objects.

Dramatic Play:
a. Have a full-length mirror so children can try on expressions with their roles.
b. Provide a variety of role-play materials.
c. Include in the wall display pictures of a variety of expressions, with mirrors nearby to aid imitiation.

Language/Library:
a. Have books that reflect a variety of feelings and ways to deal with them, such as:
Fear: *There's a Nightmare in My Closet* (Mayer)
Self-Esteem: *The Growing Story* (Krauss)
Loss: *The Maggie B* (Keats); *Amos and Boris* (Steig)
Change: *Changes, Changes* (Hutchins)
Friendship: *Two Is a Team* (Bemelman); *That's What Friends Are For* (Kidd)
Security: *One Step, Two* (Zolotow); *The Bundle Book* (Zolotow); *Big Sister, Little Sister* (Zolotow)
b. Include books on themes, particularly when a child or group is dealing with an emotional issue:
Death: *Death and Dying* (Open Family Series, by Sara Bonnet Stein); *The Dead Bird* (Brown); *Nana Upstairs, Nana Downstairs* (de Paoli)
Divorce: *Two Places to Sleep* (Schuchman)

FIGURE 14.9 Teachers plan programs that help children express their feelings.

Doctor/Dentist: *Curious George Goes to the Hospital* (H.A. Rey); *Your Turn, Doctor* (Robison and Perez); *My Doctor* (Harlow)

Moving: *Mitchell Is Moving* (Sharmat); *Jamie* (Zolotow)

New Baby: *Baby Sister for Frances* (Hoban); *I Want to Tell You About My Baby* (Banish); *Peter's Chair* (Keats)

Nightmares: *Where the Wild Things Are* (Sendak); *In the Night Kitchen* (Sendak); *There's a Nightmare in My Closet* (Mayer)

Spending the Night: *Ira Sleeps Over* (Waber)

c. When reading stories, stop and ask how a particular character is feeling.

d. Tie in children's lives to books. For example, have children bring a special object or toy to share. A warm cuddly can be tied into the stories of *Goodnight Moon* (Brown) or *Teddy Bear's Picnic* (Kennedy).

Movement:

a. "How would you walk if you were glad?" (sad, mad, worried, giggly?)

b. "A Tiger Hunt" (this game is known by many names). Go on a "hunt" with children, using their bodies to describe such movements as opening/shutting a gate, swishing through tall grass, climbing a tree, swimming in water, going through mud, looking in a cave, running home so that the "tiger" doesn't catch us.

Music:

a. Choose several cuts of music that differ in tone and type. Ask children how each makes them feel, then have them show you with their bodies.

b. Write songs/chants about feelings.

2. AT GROUP TIMES

a. Use children's faces as a focus: Practice facial expressions with mirrors; have them draw facial expressions; have them tell you how they are feeling and show you on their faces; show photographs of children's faces and expressions and ask the group how the child in the picture is feeling, and why.

b. Try idea completions:
"I feel glad when . . ." (also mad, sad, bad, safe, excited, scared, silly)
"I like school when . . ." (also don't like; also my friend, mom, it)

c. Use situations to elicit feelings:
1. "Here's a picture of a family. What are they doing? How does the child feel? The grown-ups? What happened?"
2. "I'm going to cover part of the picture of the face to see if you can guess what expression it's going to be."
3. "These are cards of situations that the teachers have seen happen in our class. Let's read them and then ask ourselves, 'How do I feel? What can I say? What can I do?' "

FIGURE 14.9 Cont. (continues on p. 342)

    d. Using circles already drawn with various facial expressions and labels, the teacher can ask each child to assess the state of feelings at that time, and even try to give some reason.

    e. Use songs and fingerplays that reflect expressions.

3. ROUTINES AND TRANSITIONS

    a. Respect children's feelings of anticipation. Have a chart of the daily schedule; discuss upcoming field trips or visitors ahead of time when possible.

    b. When unexpected changes occur, discuss them with individuals and the group. "Andy isn't here today. He has a sore throat, so he is staying home. Esther will be the teacher in his group today."

    c. When possible, let children set the stage for themselves by encouraging them to take responsibility for known sequences. Let them use the toilet without you there, set their own snack table, get flowers for the table, help clean a place for the next children.

    d. Self-help: Provide time for children to do things for themselves, such as dressing, putting on a name tag, washing hands and drying them without too much hurrying. Reflect their pride in being able to do it "all by myself."

FIGURE 14.9 Cont.

WHO AM I?

1. *Art:* Body outlines
   Facial expressions pictures—variations: (a) look in a mirror, (b) have a blank face and you draw in the features, (c) have a face partly done and you complete, (d) magazine cut-outs
   Face painting
   Fingerprinting (hand and foot)
2. *Blocks:* People, furniture, structures people live in
   Pictures of same
3. *Cooking:* Share ethnic dishes (tortillas, pasta, things you like to cook at home)
4. *Discovery/science:* Height–weight charts
   Drawing around hands and feet and comparing sizes
   Doing body outlines of a large group of children, each with a different color, and comparing sizes
   Mapping—where people live, charts of phone numbers
   Put out a globe
   Weather–homes connections
5. *Dramatic play:* Lots of mirrors
   A variety of dress-up play for taking on a variety of roles and seeing how they feel
6. *Language/library:* Have children write books about themselves—variations: (a) use *Is This You?* (Krauss) as model, (b) loose-leaf binder of their own books they can add to themselves,

FIGURE 14.10 Many themes can be developed to stimulate emotional expression.

(c) "My house is me" as title, (d) families
Books on families of various sorts; books about other children and what they are like (Corduroy lives in an apt.)
Where animals live
Feelings about where children live

7. *Manipulatives:* Puzzles with body parts, with people and clothing
Self-help skills with dressing frames
Encourage children to build a structure that things could live in; i.e., lincoln logs.

8. *Sand and water play:* Bubble-blowing
Using your bodies to build—digging with hands and feet, encouraging sensory exploration
Use body parts to help you, like using your foot on the shovel.

9. *Swinging/climbing:* All these activities use body parts; teachers emphasize this when watching children at play.

10. *Games:* Rolling the barrel, rolling yourself
Mother May I?
Hide and Seek and Tag
Dramatic play games with family members

11. *Large block-building:* Making house-like structures
Using vehicles that need your body's force to move

12. *Woodworking:* Using body parts
Make a map board of school, neighborhood, a city.

13. *Routines:* Self-help: Awareness of what you can do by yourself; by definition all "Who Am I?" tasks; teachers use verbal and musical reinforcement.

14. *Transitions:* Use physical characteristics of children for transitions—"Everyone who has brown eyes . . . freckles . . . blue jeans can go outside . . ."

15. *Group times:* "Head and shoulders"
Description games—describe someone and guess who it is as a game "I'm thinking of someone" or with song "Mary Has a Red Dress"
"Little Tommy (Tina) Tiddlemouse," voice recognition
"Good morning little Teddy Bear," with bear going around circle and saying names

16. *Snacktime/bedtime:* Mark places with names and pictures, such as beds or placemats
Try to coordinate the nametag, bed, or placemat with symbol on cubby.

FIGURE 14.10 Cont.

self-expression in the class setting, sometimes focusing on one particular emotional skill or theme that emphasizes emotional expression.

Ask yourself:

- What are the principles of emotional development?

- What emotional skills are learned in early childhood?

- What is the role of the teacher in emotional development?

- What are three ways to plan curriculum that will enhance emotional growth?

UNIT 14–2 SOCIAL GROWTH

THE DEVELOPMENT OF SOCIALIZATION

Social development is the process through which children learn what behavior is acceptable and expected. A set of standards is imposed on the child at birth that reflects the values of the family and the society in which the child lives.

Social development begins in the crib. Within the first few months of life, the infant smiles, coos, and plays in response to a human voice, face, or physical contact. Young children are influenced from birth by a conscious attempt on the part of adults to guide them in ways that society expects. Parents attempt to transmit behavior patterns that are characteristic of their culture, religion, gender, educational, and ethnic backgrounds. Children imitate what they see; they adapt social expectations to their own individual personality.

This process—called *socialization*—includes learning appropriate behavior in a number of different settings. Children learn very early to discriminate between the expectations of each environment. At school, free exploration of play materials is encouraged, but in a church pew it is not. Grocery stores, circuses, libraries, and Grandma's home call for a repertoire of fitting behaviors.

In general, the socialization process in a school setting revolves around a child's relationships with other people. During this time of their lives, children work out a separate set of relationships with adults other than their parents. They also establish different relationships with adults than they do with other children.

Through socialization, the customary roles that boys and girls play are also transmitted. Children come to understand how teachers, mommies, daddies, grandparents, males, and females are expected to act.

Children also learn social attitudes at an early age. They learn to enjoy being with people and participating in social activities. Favorable attitudes toward people and a strong desire to be part of the social world, to be with others, are established in the early years.

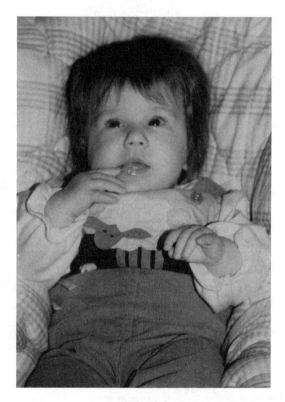

FIGURE 14.11 Infancy: the beginning of socialization (Courtesy of Michael Neilan)

The child's social development is an integral part of the total growth process. Cognitive and social growth are related. In order to consider the consequences of one's actions, for instance, there must be a certain level of intellectual understanding. According to Smith (1982), the manner in which children define their appearance influences their attitudes toward themselves and their relationships with others. Emotional development is affected also. When children conform to the behavior expected of them, they have a greater self-acceptance and like themselves better. Language, of course, is what allows the socially developing child to communicate with others as part of the social process.

There are four basic social expectations of preschool children: (1) that they will show affection and interest in family members; (2) that they will learn right from wrong and act accordingly; (3) that they will learn to get along with other children; and (4) that they will learn to play an appropriate sex role (Hurlock, 1972).

It is through play (as discussed in Chapter 11) that children learn much of their social repertoire. Dramatizations, role playing, and dramatic play provide opportunities to act out many roles and help children deal with some of the demands placed upon them. In play, the child experiments with options: finding out what it feels like to be the boss, to be the baby, to behave in ways that might otherwise be unacceptable. Carla was the oldest of three children and had many "big girl" expectations placed on her within the family setting. At school, Carla enjoyed being the baby, acting out a helpless infant role whenever she could. Under the guise of play, children, like Carla, rehearse for life without suffering the real-life consequences.

Peer Relationships

For the young child, social development means moving away from adults toward people of one's own age. During the early years, the child learns to socialize outside the family; social contacts outside the home reinforce the enjoyment of social attitudes and prepare the child for future group activity.

FIGURE 14.12 Social attitudes are established in the preschool years. (Courtesy of Stride Rite Children's Centers, Cambridge, Mass.)

FIGURE 14.13 Being friends means sharing secrets.

Peer interactions, that is, associating with friends of the same age group, become important to the child once infancy and early toddlerhood are past. Through peer interactions, children can identify with models who are like themselves and can learn from each other's behavior. Friends provide models for imitation, for comparison, for confirmation of themselves, and are a source of support.

Playing with other children begins with solitary or parallel play at around two years of age, where two or more children are in the same area with each other but do not initiate social interaction. By the ages of three and four, more interaction takes place: there is conversation as well as cooperation in playing together.

A peer group is important for a number of reasons. Social development is enhanced because a child learns to conform to established social standards outside of his home setting. The expectations of the larger society are reinforced. In order to become autonomous, the child must also learn to achieve independence from the family, especially parents. Young children must also come to understand themselves as part of society. Their self-concepts are enlarged by a group of peers as they see how others respond to them and treat them.

Smith (1982) states that three trends emerge in the way children relate to each other. First, children become more sensitive to their play partners; then they begin to use language more effectively in their interactions. Finally, cooperative play increases as parallel play decreases. Rubin (1980) defines three stages of social understanding through which children pass: (1) they shift from a preoccupation with self to an awareness of the thoughts and feelings of another; (2) they shift from the observable, physical qualities of the play partner to an awareness of their friend's less obvious characteristics; and (3) they begin to perceive the friendship as long lasting (Smith, 1982).

SOCIAL SKILLS IN EARLY CHILDHOOD EDUCATION

Social skills are strategies children learn that enable them to behave appropriately in many environments. They help children learn to initiate or manage social interaction in a variety of settings and with a number of people.

Social cognition plays a part in the development of social skills. It is the application of thinking to personal and social behavior; it is giving meaning to social experience (Smith, 1982). Nadia used her cognitive skills in memory when she wanted to play with Paul, a very popular four-year-old. She remembered Paul's interest in the rope swing and challenged him to swing higher than she did. Bruno, on the other hand, is well known throughout the group for his inability to share materials. When Sandy wanted to play with the small fire trucks (Bruno's favorite toys), she used cognitive skills to negotiate the use of one truck. Social cognition requires children to interpret events and make decisions, to consider the impact of their behavior on others, and to consider the cause as well as the consequence of an action. Cognitive skills are necessary when we ask children to seek alternative solu-

FIGURE 14.14 Peer relationships: a source of pleasure and support.

tions to social problems: "How else could you ask him for a turn, Pete?" These are all social cognition skills, and they serve as the basis for the acquisition of other skills.

In an early childhood setting, children learn a great deal about social behavior and expectations. They develop many skills as they learn to interact with adults other than their parents and children other than their siblings. Social skills emerge as children learn to function as members of a group and as they come to understand themselves as social beings. The following are some of the specific skills and values young children learn.

In their relationship with adults, they learn:

- They can stay at school without parents.
- They can enjoy adults other than parents and respond to new adults.
- Adults will help in times of trouble or need.
- Adults will assist in learning social protocol.
- Adults will keep children from being hurt and from hurting others.
- Adults will not always take a side or solve the problem.
- Adults will work with them to solve problems.
- Adults believe that every child has a right to a satisfying social experience at school.

In their relationships with other children, they learn:

- There are different approaches to others; some work, some don't.
- Interactive skills, and how to sustain the relationship.
- How to solve conflicts in ways other than retreat or force.
- How to share materials, equipment, other children, friends, teachers, and ideas.
- How to achieve mutually satisfying play.
- Self-defense, and how to assert their rights in socially acceptable ways.

- How to take turns and how to communicate desires.
- Negotiating skills.
- How to be helpful to peers with shoelaces, information, and by modeling behavior.
- To anticipate/avoid problems.
- Realistic expectations of how other children behave and respond toward self.

FIGURE 14.15 Quarreling is a common form of social behavior in young children. (Courtesy of Stephanie Barry Agnew)

FIGURE 14.16 "You push me—then I'll push you!"

In a group, they learn:

- How to take part as a member and not as an individual.
- That there are activities that promote group association (stories, music).
- A group identity (center room class, Mrs. T's group, four-year-old group).
- To follow a daily schedule and pattern.
- To adapt to school routines.
- School rules and expectations.
- Interaction and participatory skills: how to enter and exit from play.
- To respect the rights, feelings, and property of others.
- How to work together as a group, during clean-up time, in preparation for an event, etc.
- How to deal with delay of gratification: how to wait.

As an individual, they learn:

- To take responsibility for self-help, self-care.
- To initiate their own activities and to make choices.

FIGURE 14.17 Learning how to work together is a social skill.

- To work alone in close proximity to other children.
- To negotiate.
- To cope with rejection, hurt feelings, disappointment.
- To communicate in verbal and nonverbal ways, and when to use communication skills.
- To test limits other people set.
- Their own personal style of peer interaction: degree, intensity, frequency, quality.

- To express strong feelings in socially acceptable ways.
- To manage social freedom.

THE TEACHER'S ROLE

Considerations

A major role for the early childhood teacher is to see that children have enjoyable social contacts and to help motivate children toward a desire to be with others. The early childhood setting affords children numerous learning opportunities for social development.

The teacher has an important role to play as children learn the give-and-take of social interaction. In the role of social organizer, the teacher creates a physical and interpersonal environment that promotes the development of children's social skills.

A first consideration is to *plan and arrange a social environment* to enhance appropriate social behaviors. To stimulate child-initiated activities, self-care, and group responsibility, the use of low, open shelves and furniture scaled to size is a necessary ingredient. Group activities, toys, materials, and placement of furniture should be structured in ways that allow children to play alone or with someone. Many areas lend themselves to group play, such as dramatic play corners or blocks. Books, puzzles, and easels, on the other hand, can be a singular experience or can generate associative play. Cooperative play is suggested in the environment when there is more than one piece of equipment. The placement of two telephones, three wagons, and eight fire fighter hats fosters child–child interactions. The teacher must also allow enough time in the daily schedule for children to get thoroughly involved in playing with one another.

The teacher's role in social development is also one of *facilitating children's interactions and interpreting their behavior.* In order to help young children understand each other and to pave the way for continued cooperation, the teacher reports and

FIGURE 14.18 Young children learn the social skill of initiating their own activities. (Courtesy of Stephanie Barry Agnew)

reflects on what is happening. In the classroom setting, during an active, free-play period, the teacher might:

Reflect the Action:	*Say:*
Call attention to the effect one child's behavior is having on another.	"Randy, when you scream like that, other children become frightened and afraid to play with you."
Show approval and reinforce positive social behavior.	"I like the way you carefully stepped over their block building, Dannetta."
Support a child in asserting her rights.	"Chrystal is hanging on to the doll because she isn't finished playing yet, Wilbur."
Support a child's desire to be independent.	"I know you want to help, Keyetta, but Sammy is trying to put his coat on by himself."
Acknowledge and help children establish contact with others.	"Omar would like to play, too. That's why he brought you another bucket of water. Is there a place where he can help?"
Reflect back to a child the depth of his feelings and what form those feelings might take.	"I know George made you very angry when he took your sponge, but I can't let you throw water at him. What can you tell him? What words can you use to say you didn't like what he did?"

Curriculum Planning for Social Growth

In the Class Setting

Teaching social behavior in most classrooms usually occurs in response to spontaneous situations. The teacher's direct involvement in children's social interactions is the most frequent method used.

Occasionally, teachers will approach the acquisition of social skills in a more formalized way through planned curriculum activities. The way the environment is arranged has a profound effect on social interaction among children. Most indoor activities are planned and set up to encourage participation by more than one child at a time. Specific areas that enhance social relationships indoors are:

• *The Arts.* At the art table, four or more children will share collage materials, paste, and sponges that have been placed in the center of the table. When easels are placed side by side, conversation occurs spontaneously among children. A small table, placed between the easels, on which a tray of paint cups is placed, also encourages children's interactions. If there is only one of each color, the children will have to negotiate with one another for the color they want to use.

• *Blocks/Manipulatives.* A large space for block cabinets gives children a visual cue that there is plenty of room for more than one child. Puzzle tables set with three or four puzzles also tell children that social interaction is expected. Many times children will talk, play, and plan with one another as they share a large bin full of Lego® or plastic building towers. A floor puzzle always requires a group: some to put the picture together, others to watch and make suggestions. As children build with blocks next to one another, they soon share comments about their work; many times this leads to a mutual effort on a single building.

• *Discovery/Science.* Many science projects can be arranged to involve more than one child. A display of magnets with a tray of assorted objects can become the focus of several children as they decide which ones will be attracted to the magnets. Cooking together, weighing and measuring one another, and caring for classroom pets can be times when teachers reinforce social skills.

• *Dramatic Play.* This area more than any other seems to draw children into contact with one another. Provide an assortment of family life accessories, dress-up clothes, kitchen equipment and utensils, and children have little trouble getting involved. A shoe needs to be tied, or a dress zippered up. Someone must come eat the delicious meal just cooked or put the baby to bed. A medical theme in this classroom area also enhances children's social skills. They learn to take each other's temperature, listen to heartbeats, and plan operations, all of which require one or more people.

- *Language/Library.* Children enjoy reading books and stories to one another, whether or not they know the words. Favorite books are often shared by two children who enjoy turning the pages and talking over the story together. Lotto games encourage children to become aware of one another, to look at each person's card in order to identify who has the picture to match. Name songs and games, especially early in the year, help children learn to call each other by name.

Outdoors, the environment can be structured in ways to support group play. Painting or pasting on murals or drawing chalk designs on the cement are art activities that promote social interaction. Planning and planting a garden is a long-range activity that involves many children. Decisions must be made by the group about what to plant, where to locate the garden, how to prepare the soil, and about the shared responsibilities of caring for the garden.

Most gross motor activities stimulate group interactions. Seesaws, jump ropes, and hide-and-seek require at least two people to participate. A-frames, boards, and boxes, as well as other moveable equipment, need the cooperative effort of several children in order to be rearranged. Sand play, when accompanied by water, shovels and, other accessories, draws a number of children together to create rivers, dams, and floods. Ball games and relay races also encourage social relationships.

As a directed learning experience, small-group times afford an opportunity to focus on social skills in a more structured way. Small groups provide a setting for children and teachers to participate in more relaxed, uninterrupted dialogue. The intimacy of the small group sets the stage for many social interactions.

Group-time discussions can focus on problems that children can solve, for instance. Too many children crowding the water table, a child's fear of fire drills, or the noise level on a rainy day are subjects children will talk about in small groups. Solutions may emerge when the teacher supports active and involved participation. Teachers pose the problem and ask children to respond in several ways: "How does it make you feel when that happens? What can you do about it? What can you say? What are some alternatives?" The problems must be real, and they must be about something that is important to children. Figure 14.19 is an example of a sequentially planned curriculum that fosters the development of social skills in small group settings.

Day	Skill	Activities
Monday	Developing a positive self-image	Do thumb print art. Make foot and hand prints. Compare children's baby pictures to current photos. Play with mirrors: make faces, emotional expressions. Dress felt dolls in clothing. Sing name songs: "Mary Wore Her Red Dress." Make a list: "What I like to do best is . . ." Post in classroom. Do a self-portrait in any art medium. Make a silhouette picture of each child.

FIGURE 14.19 Building social skills through small-group experiences (continues on p. 352)

Tuesday	Becoming a member of a group	Take attendance together: Who is missing? Play picture lotto with photographs of children. Play "Farmer in the Dell." Share a favorite toy from home with other children. Tape record children's voices; guess who they are. Have a "friendly feast": each child brings favorite food from home to share.
Wednesday	Forming a friendship within the group	Provide one puzzle (toy, game, book) for every two children. Take a "Buddy Walk"; return and tell a story together of what you saw. Play "Telephone Talk": pretend to invite your friend over to play. Play "copy cat": imitate your friend's laugh, walk, cry, words. Practice throwing and catching balls with one another. Form letter together with two children's bodies: A, T, C, L, etc. Play tug-of-war with your friend. Build a house out of blocks together. Make "mirror image" movements with your friend.
Thursday	Working together as a group	Play with a parachute; keep the ball bouncing. Make snacks for the rest of the class. Plan and plant a garden. Make a mural together to decorate the hallways. Play "Follow the Leader." Celebrate a holiday with a piñata. Sing a round: "Row, Row, Row Your Boat."
Friday	Learning a group identity	Make a map of the town and have children place their houses on it. Take a field trip together. Print a newspaper with articles by/about each child. Select and perform a favorite story for the rest of the class. Take a group snapshot. Make a "family tree" of photos of children in group. Learn a group folk dance. Make a mural of handprints joined in a circle.

FIGURE 14.19 Cont.

Focus on Skills

Social development for the preschool child includes gaining an awareness of the larger community in which the child lives. The early childhood curriculum contains elements of what is often in the later grades called social studies. Visits from police officers, mail carriers, fire fighters, and other community helpers are common in many programs. Learning about children from other cultures, exploring the neighborhood around the center, and making maps are other ways children learn social studies skills.

Learning how to cooperate with others is one primary social skill in which young children need plenty of practice. The opportunity for children to learn and rehearse this skill takes place in many areas of the classroom. Figure 14.20 illustrates this.

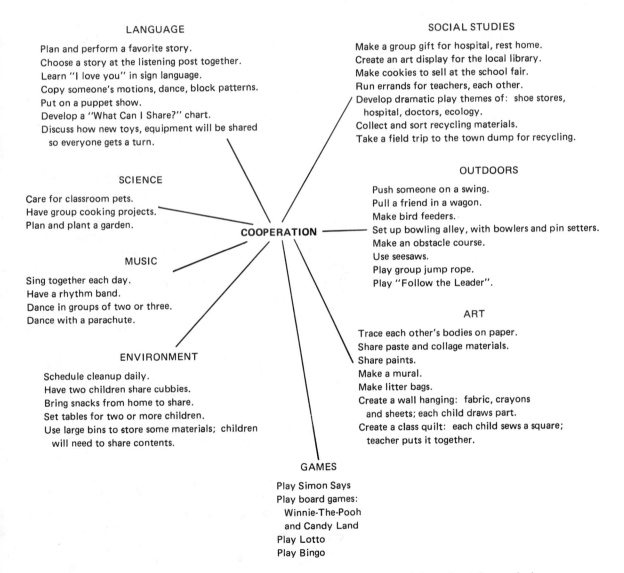

LANGUAGE

Plan and perform a favorite story.
Choose a story at the listening post together.
Learn "I love you" in sign language.
Copy someone's motions, dance, block patterns.
Put on a puppet show.
Develop a "What Can I Share?" chart.
Discuss how new toys, equipment will be shared
    so everyone gets a turn.

SCIENCE

Care for classroom pets.
Have group cooking projects.
Plan and plant a garden.

MUSIC

Sing together each day.
Have a rhythm band.
Dance in groups of two or three.
Dance with a parachute.

ENVIRONMENT

Schedule cleanup daily.
Have two children share cubbies.
Bring snacks from home to share.
Set tables for two or more children.
Use large bins to store some materials; children
    will need to share contents.

COOPERATION

SOCIAL STUDIES

Make a group gift for hospital, rest home.
Create an art display for the local library.
Make cookies to sell at the school fair.
Run errands for teachers, each other.
Develop dramatic play themes of: shoe stores,
    hospital, doctors, ecology.
Collect and sort recycling materials.
Take a field trip to the town dump for recycling.

OUTDOORS

Push someone on a swing.
Pull a friend in a wagon.
Make bird feeders.
Set up bowling alley, with bowlers and pin setters.
Make an obstacle course.
Use seesaws.
Play group jump rope.
Play "Follow the Leader".

ART

Trace each other's bodies on paper.
Share paste and collage materials.
Share paints.
Make a mural.
Make litter bags.
Create a wall hanging: fabric, crayons
    and sheets; each child draws part.
Create a class quilt: each child sews a square;
    teacher puts it together.

GAMES

Play Simon Says
Play board games:
    Winnie-The-Pooh
    and Candy Land
Play Lotto
Play Bingo

FIGURE 14.20 The social skill of cooperation can be fostered throughout the curriculum.

Use of Themes

A popular theme that lends itself to social growth is that of friendship. This has particular appeal during the month of February when the meaning of friendship is enhanced by the celebration of Valentine's Day. At other times, relay races and noncompetitive games (those in which everyone is a winner) promote working with friends to achieve a goal. Teachers who encourage children to help each other read, tie shoes, pour milk, fasten a smock, or sponge a table reinforce what friendship can be in the early years. Many books and songs can be found that emphasize friendship. Group discussions can help children define what is a friend. Figure 14.21 illustrates how a friendship unit can be developed for an early childhood setting.

Dusty, a four-year-old, is clear about what quality he has that makes him a good friend:

Dusty (to Nathan): Be my friend?
Nathan: No!
Dusty (thoughtfully): You really should, you
    know, because I'm FUNNY!
Nathan (appreciatively): Okay.

Concepts Children Will Learn	Activity
Everyone has a name and likes to have it used.	Friendship songs, using children's names
Each person is something special and unique.	Make a "Friend Puppet" with paper plates, tongue depressor handles. Child decorates it with felt pieces and yarn to look like a friend.
Friends are different; they do not all look the same.	Children respond to: "Tell me about your friend Alice. She . . ." (Child describes a friend as teacher writes the words.)
Having friends is fun.	Make a friendship ring: each child traces own hands on mural, making a circle.
Friends enjoy doing things together.	Go on a scavenger hunt with a friend.
Adults can be your friends.	Teacher helps child solve conflict or gives comfort when child is hurt.
Animals and pets can be your friends.	Children have an opportunity to bring small house pets to school to share with rest of class.
To have a friend is to be a friend.	Children respond to: "A Friend Is Someone Who . . ." (They describe their impressions while teacher writes down their words.)
Friends enjoy doing things for one another.	Children respond to: "Being A Friend With Someone Means . . ." (Teacher writes down children's dictation.)
Everyone can have a friend.	Teacher reads stories about friendships: *Will I Have A Friend?* (Cohen), *Corduroy* (Freeman), *Play With Me* (Ets), *Little Bear's Friend* (Minarik), *A Letter To Amy* (Keats), *Hold My Hand* (Zolotow).
You can show someone you want to be friends.	Write a letter to a friend; invite a friend over to play.
Friends will help you.	Form a relay team and have a race.

FIGURE 14.21 Making friends. When objectives are clear, the activities reinforce the concepts children will learn.

UNIT 14–2   CHECKPOINT

Early in life children become aware of their social nature. The socialization process begins under the guidance of parents and family members. When children enter group settings, they are further exposed to behavior, social roles, and attitudes that foster social development. Much of a child's social repertoire is learned by playing with other children.

Children learn a great many social skills in these early years. They learn to enjoy and trust adults other than their parents. In their relationships with others, children learn ways to cooperate, disagree, share, communicate, and assert themselves effectively.

Children also learn how to be a member of a group—to take part in group activities, adapt to school expectations, and to respect the rights and feelings of others. The young child also learns to express feelings in appropriate ways and to begin self-care tasks.

Teachers plan and arrange the early childhood environment in ways that will promote social growth and interaction. The adults help children understand each other's actions and motivations by interpreting the behavior to children as they play.

Curriculum to develop social skills in young children can be spontaneous as well as planned. Much of the focus in an early childhood setting is on social interactions throughout the day. At other times, social growth is enhanced by group-time discussions, awareness of the community and society at large, and an emphasis on specific social skills.

Ask yourself:

- What are the four social expectations of the preschooler?
- Why is peer group experience important?
- What social skills do children develop with adults? With other children? In a group? As individuals?
- How do teachers help children develop social skills?
- How are social skills fostered in the curriculum?

UNIT 14–3   CREATIVE GROWTH

THE DEVELOPMENT OF CREATIVITY

Creativity is the ability to have new ideas, to be original and imaginative, and to make new adap-

FIGURE 14.22 Teachers are creative when they design equipment and plan activities for children's creative growth.

tations on old ideas. Inventors, composers, and designers are creative people, as are those who paint and dance, write speeches, or create curriculum for children. The more teachers realize they are a part of a creative act, the more sensitive they become in helping young children develop creatively.

Creativity is a process; as such, it is hard to define. As one becomes involved in creative activity, the process and the product merge.

> . . . It is probably best to think of creativity as a continual process for which the best preparation is creativity itself . . . there is real joy in discovery—which not only is its own reward, but provides the urge for continuing exploration and discovery.
>
> (Lowenfeld and Brittain, 1975)

The young child is open to experience, exploring materials with curiosity and eagerness. For young children, developing the senses is part of acquiring creative skills. Children are also quick to question, wonder, and see things that do not quite match up. These are traits of creative children.

CREATIVE SKILLS IN EARLY CHILDHOOD EDUCATION

There are characteristics common to creative people. For the teacher interested in fostering creative growth in children, these are the skills they should help children learn.

Flexibility

Flexibility, or fluency, is the ability to produce many ideas and the capacity to shift from one idea to another. Children who are flexible in their thinking have original ideas and usually demonstrate a unique perspective on issues. This is a natural trait and can be encouraged by teachers who are aware of its relationship to creative growth. Children are challenged, for instance, if they must think of another way to share the wagons when taking turns doesn't work.

Sensitivity

Being creative involves a high degree of sensitivity to one's self and one's mental images. Creative people, from an early age, seem to be aware of the world around them: how things smell, feel, and taste. They are sensitive to mood, texture, and how they feel about someone or something. Seeing detail, noticing how a pine cone is attached to the branch, is a detail the creative person does not overlook.

Creative children take delight and satisfaction in making these images come to life. Their creative response is in the way they paint a picture, dance with streamers, or find a solution to a problem. Figure 14.23 shows how a 5½-year-old's sensitivity to perspective and detail comes out through a drawing.

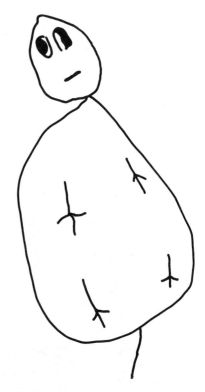

FIGURE 14.23 Sensitivity to one's own mental images, such as perceiving direction and movement, are part of creativity in the young child. A 5½-year-old sketched how a rat looked from below after picking it up often and watching it run on its exercise wheel.

Use of Imagination

Imagination is a natural part of the creative process. Children use their imagination to develop their creativity in several ways.

Role Playing. In taking on another role, children combine their knowledge of the real world with their internal images. The child becomes a new character, and that role comes to life.

Image-Making. When children create a rainbow with a hose or with paints, they are adding something of their own to their understanding of that visual image. In dance, children use their imagination as they pretend to be objects or feelings, images brought to life.

Constructing. In building and constructing activities, children seem to be re-creating an image they have about tall buildings, garages, or farms. In the process of construction, however, children do not intend that the end product resemble the building itself. Their imagination allows them to experiment with size, shape, and relationships.

A Willingness to Take Risks

People who are willing to break the ordinary mental set and push the boundaries in defining and using ordinary objects, materials, and ideas are creative people. They take risks. Being open to thinking differently or seeing things differently is essential to creativity.

Self-esteem is a factor in risk-taking since people who are tied to what others think of them are more likely to conform rather than follow their own intuitive and creative impulses. People usually do not like to make mistakes or be ridiculed; therefore, they avoid taking risks.

A teacher concerned about creative growth in children realizes that it will surface if allowed and encouraged. When a child is relaxed and not anxious about being judged by others, creativity will more likely be expressed. With support, children can be encouraged to risk themselves.

Using Self as a Resource

Creative people who are aware of themselves and confident in their abilities draw upon their own perceptions, questions, and feelings. They know they are their own richest source of inspiration. MacKinnon found that those who excelled in creative productivity had a great deal of respect for self, that they used the self as a resource (Shallcross and Sisk, 1982).

Experience

Children need experience in order to gain skills in using materials creatively. They must learn how to hold a paint brush before they can paint a picture; once they know how to paint, they can be creative in what they paint. When the skill of the medium is mastered, the child is ready to create.

THE TEACHER'S ROLE

Considerations

The early childhood curriculum offers many rich avenues for self-expression and creativity. Beyond art and music, there is the ability to think and question, to find more than one answer to a problem. Blocks, climbing equipment, and social relationships offer risk-taking opportunities. Children use themselves as resources as they play outdoor games, experiment with science projects, and participate in dramatic play. Taruna exhibits many creative traits as she attempts to enter into play with two other children. She first asks if she can play, and when met with rejection, she demands to be one of the mommies. Taruna finally offers her doll as a prop and is accepted into the group. Her persistence is exceeded only by her creative problem solving.

Regular creative opportunities give children the necessary experience and skill to be creative. Children need frequent occasions to be creative in order to function in a highly creative manner (Eis-

FIGURE 14.24 When given the opportunity to create, children will gain skill and experience that encourage them to create in all areas of growth.

ner, 1964). When children have a chance to create, their skills in perceiving the world are enhanced.

One of the teacher's most crucial considerations for supporting creative growth is that of *divergent thinking*. To diverge means to take a different line of thought or action, deviating from the normal. Finding ideas that branch out rather than converge and center on one answer is divergent thinking. The creative arts are important if only because they tend to stress this kind of thinking. Where there are no "right" or "wrong" answers, there will undoubtedly be many solutions for problems.

Children and teachers can discuss issues and seek solutions to problems when divergent thinking is encouraged. In a day care center, for instance, children were fighting over the use of the two swings. The children's responses indicate their willingness to take a different line of thought:

Teacher: How do you think we could share the swings?
David: The kids who give me a turn can come to my birthday party.
Sabrina: No. We will have to make a waiting list.
Xenia: Only girls can use the swings; the boys can have all the carts.
Frederico: Buy a new swing set.

Teacher timing and attitudes are also important in stimulating creative development in young children. The early childhood years are probably the most crucial time to encourage creative thinking. "It is here that initial attitudes are established . . . and school can be a fun place where the individual's contribution is welcome and where changes can be sought and made." (Lowenfeld and Brittain, 1975)

Children need plenty of time and a relaxed atmosphere to be creative. They need encouragement and respect for the process and products of their creative nature. The teacher's attitude tells the children that what they do is important, and how they do it makes a difference. Rather than expecting a predetermined right answer, the teacher encourages creativity by valuing the answers the children give even when they appear unusual or illogical.

Curriculum Planning for Creative Growth

In The Class Setting

Teachers set up an environment that promotes creative expression; they choose activities and materials that can be used in many ways. These *open-ended materials* provide a continuing challenge as children use them repeatedly in new and different ways. Clay, playdough, paints, crayons and pens, blocks, water, sand and other sensory materials, and moveable outdoor equipment are good examples of open-ended materials that stimulate creativity. Children are motivated to try new ways to use materials when they are flexible and challenging.

Every classroom has the potential for creative activity. Children use their imagination when blocks become castles, tunnels, corrals, and swamps. Using all their senses to explore a medium helps children discover many approaches to creativity. Teachers enhance imaginative thought when they introduce questions to ponder that are out of the ordinary. "What would you wear if you were twins? What would you eat? Where would you live?" are ways to help children reflect on subject matter in a different light.

Creativity happens out-of-doors also. Large, hollow blocks can become a stairway, and wagons and carts become fire engines, buses, doll carriages, moving vans, or trucks. Their use is limited only by the creativity of the children. Sand, water, and mud provide a place for children to dig, haul, manipulate, and control in any number of ways.

Teachers can apply their own creativity to many routine situations. When looking for a lost mitten, a "hunt" is organized; pretending to be vacuum cleaners, dump trucks, or robots gets the blocks picked up faster.

The dramatic arts offer opportunities for children to express themselves. In order to perform "Goldilocks and The Three Bears," for instance, children will have to create costumes. At music time, children use their creative skills to play drums: tapping, brushing, pounding the drums. Figure 14.25 is a photograph of safe and durable equipment that children can use creatively.

Focus on Skills

The wide range of skills necessary for creative development can be supported throughout the early childhood program. The creative thinker is one who finds many ways to solve a problem, approach a situation, use materials, and interact with others. The teacher's role is one of supporting imaginative use of equipment.

FIGURE 14.25 Creative people use themselves as a resource; children will draw on their own ideas for creating their own activities and play spaces.

To encourage creative thinking, teachers also look at the ways they ask children questions. How can they prompt children to view the unusual and think of the exceptional? How can they encourage divergent thinking? Figure 14.26 illustrates some of the ways teachers can focus on creative skills through the use of questions.

Use of Themes

As teachers plan curriculum around a theme, they keep in mind what creative skills can be developed. Figure 14.27 charts the theme of "Green and Growing Things," and can bring out the child's creative nature.

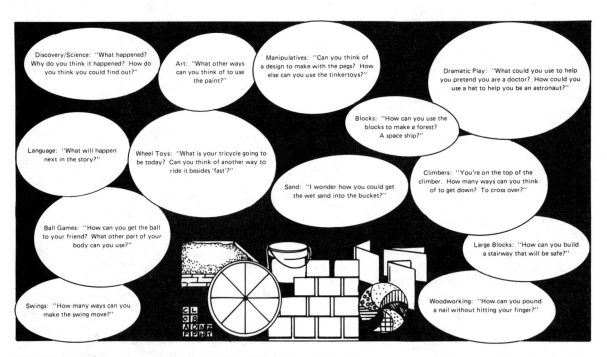

FIGURE 14.26 As teachers focus on the skills of creativity, they can ask children questions to stimulate creative thinking.

OUTDOORS

1. Plant a garden in a corner of the yard, in an old barrel, or in a box flat on a table. Children learn through experimentation why some things grow and others don't. Make space for a compost heap.
2. Add wheelbarrows to the transportation toys.
3. Take a field trip to a farm, at planting time if possible.
4. Add gardening tools to the sand area. With proper supervision, children can see how trowels, hand claws, rakes, and shovels can be used to create new patterns in the sand and mud.

FIGURE 14.27 "Green and Growing Things," a spring science theme, lends itself to creative development.

5. Plan group games that emphasize green and growing things. Older children could run wheelbarrow races, using one child as the wheelbarrow and other as the driver.

INDOORS

1. Leaf rubbings, printing with apples, onions, carrots, potatoes, lemons, oranges, and celery, and painting with pine boughs are ways children can create art with green and growing things.
2. Block accessories might include blue felt forms for lakes, hay for corrals and barns.
3. In the manipulative area, match a photo of familiar plants with a sample of the plant. Add sorting trays with various kinds of seeds to count, feel, mix, and match. Match pictures of eggs, bacon, milk, and cheese with the animals from which they come.
4. In the science area, grow alfalfa sprouts and mung beans. Let children mix them in salads and feed to classroom pets. As the sprouts grow, children can chart the growth. This can lead to charting their own development, comparing it to when they were infants.
5. The dramatic play center can be transformed into a grocery store to emphasize the food we buy to eat, how it helps us, and why good nutrition is important. Other dramatic play units are a florist shop or nursery, stocked with garden gloves, seed packets, peat pots, and sun hats.
6. The language area can be stocked with books about how plants, baby animals, and children grow. In small groups, children can respond to "When I plant a seed . . ." or "When I was a baby I . . . Now I . . ." to stimulate creative expression.
7. Songs and fingerplays can help focus on green and growing things, children's growth, and animals. "The Green Grass Grows All Around" can be sketched by a teacher so that children will have visual cues to each successive verse. A favorite fingerplay, "Way Up in the Apple Tree," can be adapted to a number of fruits and vegetables. When it comes to lemons, children can be encouraged to think of what rhymes with "sour." Children use just their hands to accompany the verse, or they can use their whole bodies.

> Way up in the apple tree
> Two little apples smiled down at me.
> I shook that tree as hard as I could!
> Down came the apples!
> Mmmmmmm, they were good!

FIGURE 14.27 Cont.

FIGURE 14.28 Curriculum planning for creativity can include all of the room and yard, beyond just the arts and music.

Unit 14–3 Checkpoint

Young children are open to the creative process and to creative experiences. The early years are a good time to acquire the skills of flexibility, sensitivity, imagination, risk-taking, resourcefulness, and experience.

The role of the teacher is to plan curriculum that will help develop children's creativity. An atmosphere conducive to creative work is one that supports children's divergent thinking, encourages them to take risks, and provides ways they can use themselves as resources.

Ask yourself:

- What are the creative skills learned in early childhood?

- What is the teacher's role in the development of creativity?

- What classroom area, skill, or unit promotes creative thinking?

SUMMARY

Emotional, social, and creative growth development are at the center of the early childhood curriculum. Planning for these areas involves an understanding of how each develops in the young child and how they are interrelated. Children learn many skills in these three areas as they interact with each other, with adults, and in the environment.

Planning curriculum for emotional, social, and creative growth calls upon teachers to play a supportive role, facilitating children's involvement with the materials and each other. Only then can children discover themselves, explore their relationships, and develop the ability to use their imagination and resources.

Review Questions

1. How do emotional, social, and creative growth relate to each other?

2. How can these three areas affect growth in other developmental areas?

Learning Activities

1. Name five people you consider creative. Match their skills with those we have identified in early childhood. Where are they similar? Different?

2. How does your center promote positive self-concept? What else could be done?

3. Observe a group of four-year-olds at play. How do they decide what roles each one takes? Are they clear in their expectations of what sex roles are appropriate for boys and girls? Is there sex-role stereotyping?

4. Taking turns and sharing equipment and materials is difficult for young children. Cite three examples you have seen where children used their social skills to negotiate a turn. Was teacher intervention necessary?

5. Make behavioral definitions of emotions you think you will see in the children you teach. Observe the children, then check the accuracy of your definitions.

6. Give three examples of children in your center trying to "break mental set." In what area of the classroom did it occur? What were the adults' responses?

7. How do teachers in your setting plan for creativity? What place does such expression take in the priority of the school philosophy?

Bibliography

GENERAL

Brophy, Jere E., and Willis, S.L. *Human Development and Behavior.* New York: St. Martin's Press, 1981.

Day, David E. *Early Childhood Education: A Human Ecological Approach.* Glenview, Ill.: Scott, Foresman and Co., 1983.

Hymes, James L., Jr. *The Child Under Six.* Englewood Cliffs, N.J.: Prentice-Hall, 1963.

Markham, P.M., ed. *Play: Children's Business.* Washington, D.C.: Association for Childhood Education International, 1974.

Shallcross, Doris J., and Sisk, D.A. *The Growing Person.* Englewood Cliffs, N.J.: Prentice-Hall, 1982.

Stone, Joseph, and Church, J. *Childhood and Adolescence.* New York: Random House, 1979.

EMOTIONAL GROWTH

Clemes, Harris, and Bean, Reynold. *How to Raise Children's Self-Esteem.* San Jose, Calif.: Enrich, 1980.

Fraiberg, Selma H. *The Magic Years.* New York: Charles Scribner's Sons, 1959.

Jensen, L.C., and Wells, M.G. *Feelings: Helping Children Understand Emotions.* Provo, Utah: Brigham Young University Press, 1979.

SOCIAL GROWTH

Hurlock, Elizabeth. *Child Development.* New York: McGraw-Hill, 1972.

Rubin, Zick. *Children's Friendships.* Cambridge, Mass.: Harvard University Press, 1980.

Smith, Charles A. *Promoting the Social Development of Young Children.* Palo Alto, Calif.: Mayfield Publishing Co., 1982.

CREATIVE GROWTH

Eisner, Elliot. *Think with Me About Creativity.* Dansville, N.Y.: F.A. Owen Publishing Co., 1964.

Lowenfeld, Victor, and Brittain, W.L. *Creative and Mental Growth.* New York: Macmillan, 1975.

McVickar, Polly. *Imagination: Key to Human Potential.* Washington, D.C.: National Association for the Education of Young Children, 1972.

SECTION VI

ISSUES FOR THE FUTURE

Bettye M. Caldwell

Can you remember your excitement the first time you looked under a microscope at a droplet of your drinking water? Surely it was not possible that all that life, all that movement, all those amoebae and paramecia could be there, moving around in a gracefully patterned cellular ballet! Were we able to put the field of early childhood under a microscope at this point in the eighties, we would react with similar astonishment at the extent to which synchronous activities are taking place in our little droplet of history. From the mid-sixties to the present, the field of early childhood development has impacted modern society and reciprocally has been impacted by modern society, so that neither will ever again be quite the same. It has been a period of intense activity, and all of us who have been part of it can legitimately feel that our efforts will affect children in all areas of the world for decades to come.

And activities of the next two decades will be every bit as exciting as those of the past two. At this point in history, I feel confident in identifying the following four trends as representing major conceptual and programmatic developments in the field of early childhood education.

1. *Extra-home services will become the norm, rather than the exception, for young children.* At this point in history, the first half of the eighties, we have crossed the magic fifty percent mark in terms of enrollment of young children in early childhood programs. Throughout this century, there has been a steady climb in the percentage of children younger than age six—our former traditional age for putting children in formal school programs—who are enrolled in some type of early childhood program. As utilization of such services varies with economic need and educational level of parents, it is difficult to cite any one figure that accurately represents the entire population. However, across all census categories, more than half the children under six participate in some type of early childhood program. About two fifths of the children younger than three are enrolled, which represents a truly dramatic rise over the past 20 years. These increases represent changes in family styles in America— the rising divorce rate, the greater social acceptability of parenthood out of wedlock, the increase in the number of women who choose to or who must, for economic reasons, work outside the home.

How Do We Teach for Tomorrow?

As these increases began to register with demographers, there were many who decried the changes and predicted disaster for the future of our children. These predictions were based partly on the fear that participation in group programs would weaken the ties that children have to their parents and partly on a concern that most of the available programs were of poor quality. Fortunately, we now have information to reassure us that out-of-home care part of the time need not weaken a child's basic tie to her or his parents or stunt cognitive development. Also, we have now developed professional consciousness to the point where program directors and child care givers are acutely aware of their responsibility to offer quality programs that will enhance, not distort, the development of the children in their care. With this reassurance, which comes from both research-based knowledge and practical experience, has come greater social acceptance and increased public awareness of the importance of quality early childhood programs. Within the next ten years, it will become a rarity to hear people speak of age six as the age of beginning school. Far more likely, will they speak of age three, two, or even one.

2. *We will recognize that early childhood services lie along a continuum.* Let me clarify this point. At present, some people make a big point of trying to differentiate among various kinds of early childhood programs. And certainly we have enough names for describing our programs to make it easy to play this game! For example, we speak about early childhood education, preschool education, nursery schools, play schools, day nurseries, cooperative nurseries, day care, child care—and on and on. The public is legitimately confused by our proliferation of terminology. Furthermore, we have subtle ways of implying that some of these services are good for children, whereas others should be avoided. The "outcast" of the field has been day care (or child care, to use the most common synonym). Many professionals, policy makers, and parents often seem to imply that anything called "early childhood education" is good for children and anything called "day care" is potentially harmful. Such attitudes are based on the false impression that services provided under these two labels are drastically different—as, indeed, they might be. However, it is not inevitable that they be different except in the number of hours per day that each service is offered.

Particularly damaging in these implicit attitudes has been the assumption that children enrolled in day care programs are somehow not being reared by their families. No matter how many hours per day or per week a child might be enrolled in an early childhood program (whether labeled education or day care), that child is being primarily reared by its own family, with supplementation from the professionals who staff the early childhood program. The task for policy makers and service providers is to make available in all communities a broad array of services—a continuum of early childhood services—that will match the need for supplementary care found in all types of family settings. It is my confident prediction that, in the future, we will do a better job both of realizing that such a continuum exists and of providing a full array of needed services.

3. *New and better ways of integrating intra- and extra-family services will be devised.* As early childhood programs have moved more toward the long day, and as more parents are themselves fully occupied with work during the school day, it has become increasingly difficult to obtain as much involvement of parents in the children's programs as most educators and care givers would like to have. The old patterns of after-school and evening programs are less successful than used to be the case because more and more parents are tired in the evenings and need that time for additional work in the home or for private time with their children or one another. This has led to a certain degree of pessimism on the part of professionals in early childhood education about the likelihood of achieving a high level of parental commitment to program quality. It can also be frustrating when teachers need to consult with parents about difficult behavior, about parental goals for the children, and about needed support for the early childhood service. But just as societal changes have brought about the increased need for early childhood services, so will the ingenuity and creativity of professionals lead to the development of new types of services adapted to new family realities. If professional early childhood programs are indeed but a supplement to family care, then new ways of creating a collaborative relationship between the family and the early childhood program will be necessary.

4. *Programs for young children will be considered as a routine part of public policy.* At present, young children tend to be considered by our public policy makers as something of an after-thought. We *have* to have public schools for children between the ages of six and 21, so funds are appropriated and programs launched. Fortunately, the need for adequate health care for young children (and their mothers) has sufficiently intruded into the consciousness of most of our citizens that more and more health programs are becoming available for families at all income levels. But we still seem to labor under the false idea that just *anybody* can take care of young children and that, therefore, only minimal standards of quality need be guaranteed for child care programs for very young children. Some people will maintain that no particular level of training is necessary for those who will be care givers and teachers of the very young. After all, they assert, people have been taking care of young children for centuries without any specific training! Now, of course, during those same centuries, we have had countless children victimized by abuse and neglect and by having to grow up in environments in which childhood was not valued. Fortunately such attitudes are changing. More and more new parents are utilizing books and nonprint media to learn more about how children grow and develop, and they are eager to improve their skills in this most important of human tasks. And more of them are becoming advocates for children and are working to ensure that our government does not slight appropriations that affect the availability of quality early childhood programs.

The parents of the children we serve are our most influential advocates and helpers. As we improve in our ability to serve families, to meet the needs of both the children and their parents, we will find the support we need in the public arena to ensure that children of the future will not be overlooked or forgotten. Developing advocacy skills and strengths within the profession of early child development will go a long way toward ensuring that a reasonable portion of our public assets will be reserved for the development and maintenance of quality programs for children and families.

BETTYE CALDWELL directed the Children's Center at Syracuse University, one of the first infant child care programs in America and one that served as a model for similar programs in many other states. She has been active in child development research since the early sixties and has published over 100 articles and edited three books in the field. She also edited the prestigious journal Child Development.

Dr. Caldwell has served on many governmental task forces and review boards, including the 1970 White House Conference on Children and the 1980 White House Conference on Families. She has received a number of public honors for her work with children and families, most notably Woman of the Year in Humanitarian and Community Service in 1976 by the Ladies' Home Journal. *She is a past president of the National Association for the Education of Young Children and has served on the faculties of Northwestern University and the Washington University School of Medicine. Dr. Caldwell is currently the Donaghey Distinguished Professor of Education at the University of Arkansas at Little Rock.*

15

Issues and Trends in Early Childhood Education

Questions for Thought

- What are the major issues facing early childhood educators today?
- What kinds of programs and services should be available for young children and their families?
- What are the crises children face, and what is our role in helping them?
- How is the family structure changing in our society, and how does it affect the children we teach?
- In light of the current educational reform movement, what issues will early childhood teachers face?
- How do we plan for diversity in our school populations?
- How do we teach the child for the twenty-first century?

Outline

INTRODUCTION

Early childhood education has undergone remarkable changes in the past thirty years. It has evolved from being an option for middle-class preschool children to a necessity for millions of families with children from infancy through the primary years. These changes have signaled a new level of professionalism and training for teachers. Such transformations are a reflection of the economic, social, and political climate of the times. Changes in education historically have been linked to societal reform and upheaval. Issues of today and trends for tomorrow grow out of the problems and solutions in the past.

In the 1960s, social action and a war on poverty captured the American interest and spirit. Head Start programs opened around the country and were the symbols of social action of that era. The 1970s brought changes related to economic crisis. Social services were scrutinized to determine their worth and value. The family unit was affected by the job market, the end of the Vietnam War, an energy crisis, inflation, rising divorce rates, and the feminist movement. All of these factors led more women toward work in the marketplace rather than in the home. One of the expansions in public funding at this time was in the services to the handicapped and bilingual populations.

The 1980s have meant further budget cuts, reduced services for children and families, and an altered state of childhood. Computers are being installed at all grade levels. Children are often in group care for most of their waking hours. They are growing up with change, rather than stability, as a constant in their lives. Child abuse has become a national cause for alarm. Obviously, the need for early child care and educational services is here

FIGURE 15.1 How do we prepare our children to live successfully in the future?

today and will be here for the next several decades. To ignore this need is to deny the reality of family life today.

The renaissance in general education that began in the early 1980s will likely affect reforms in early childhood education. As people become aware of the shortcomings of education at higher levels, they will begin seeing the early years as a starting point for improvements. Interest in young children will likely flourish along with reforms at other grade levels. What will be the impact on young children of these two forces—the need for child care and the growing call for excellence in education?

Looking ahead to the twenty-first century, we see a wide range of issues affecting children and society and, hence, all early childhood educators. In this chapter, we look at some current points of discussion and controversy on raising and educating children in America today. Six major questions deserve serious consideration:

1. What programs and services should be available for young children and families?

2. What are the crises children face, and what will we do to help them?

3. How is the family structure changing in our society today, and how will this change affect the children we teach?

4. Given the current educational reform movement, what issues and skills will early childhood teachers need to confront and master?

5. What challenges will teachers face when dealing with diversity in schools, neighborhoods, families?

6. How will we teach children so that they will be able to cope with the demands of the twenty-first century?

PROGRAMS FOR CHILDREN

Extending School Services

Schools are under pressure to provide a longer school day and expanded services for more children. Parents and educators are asking for public programs to provide a wide range of educational and recreational activities for children up to their early teens. Beyond the home and the regular school day, these programs would offer local support for families so that children could learn and live in caring environments.

The public school is seen as the obvious solution to many child care issues. Indeed, it is the largest single program for day care in our country today. The buildings and staff are already in place and community use of schools after hours is a well-established precedent. Using existing school buildings at a time they are not otherwise in use is considered to be a good *stewardship* of community resources. Four particular programs under consideration are: (1) programs for three- and four-year-olds; (2) all-day kindergartens; (3) after-school care for children; and (4) year-round school.

The Controversy

Controversy surrounds all four issues. Should three- and four-year-olds be exposed to formal education? Will children be rushed in their development if they have a longer school day or school year? Will schools be burdened by after-school responsibilities? How will programs be financed? Underlying these questions are concerns that the academic quality of the regular school curriculum might suffer if these extra programs are put into operation and become an added responsibility of the school.

The need for providing care beyond the regular school day is well-documented. An estimated seven million children 13 years and under are without adult care after school while their parents work (Children's Defense Fund, 1984). Many of these are cared for by older siblings who arrive home with a house key around their necks. These *"latch-key children"* are responsible for the safety and well-being of themselves and often of younger brothers and sisters. The social, emotional, even physical effects on these unsupervised children have not been researched extensively at this time, but the need to develop after-school alternatives seems clear nonetheless. Stress, fear, isolation, boredom, even resentment at having to care for others younger than themselves have been cited as some of the negative consequences for children who are left without adults after regular school hours.

Future Directions and the Role of Educators

The answers to the debate over extended school services will depend on how these programs are perceived and put into effect. The major concern of parents and educators is the question of how extra time in school will be spent. If public schools are kept open until early evening for preschool, elementary, and middle-school students, what will be the shape of the program?

Consensus among educators is that a longer school day, school term, or school year does not necessarily mean more "schooling." They envision programs that will provide continuity in children's lives. Taking place at the same setting as their formal education, these programs would provide a balanced day. Most likely the curriculum of after-school care would focus on the physical, social, emotional, and creative aspects of children's devel-

opment, as the academic content of the regular school day concentrates on cognitive and language skills. Program quality will be the key, and supervision by qualified adults is imperative. The critical issue of child care for older children could be resolved if the doors were open before and after school. The time is right for schools to consider ways to merge care and learning.

Providing Day Care

The continuing need for quality day care programs cannot be ignored. The needs of parents who work must be recognized and addressed. Part of the solution can be found in the extension of school services; however, programs for the child under three years of age are still difficult to find and increasingly difficult to afford. Thus, the issue of providing day care is a serious one. In fact, day care today is no longer being talked about in terms of "when" it will happen. The debate today focuses on the "who" and "how" of the needed services to families.

Need for Standards and Accessibility

Day care services lack consistent and appropriate regulations and are scattered throughout the country in a variety of separate agencies. Churches, through programs affiliated with religious groups of all kinds, are probably the largest single day care providers in the country today, with 25,000 churches serving more than two million children (Lindner et al., 1984). Franchise and industry-sponsored day care, family day care homes, family members, and an increasing number of unlicensed facilities provide the bulk of child care services. This hodgepodge of care urgently needs a set of national standards and policies to ensure safe and caring environments for the youngest of children.

Availability of child care services is much too dependent upon the ability to pay. Single-parent families (generally headed by women) and poverty-level families (usually ethnic minorities) often do not have access to child care because of its cost.

Federal cutbacks on social service programs have affected these groups more than any other (Children's Defense Fund, 1984). Middle-income parents also suffer the lack of child care options as costs increase. Child care should be made available (by government, industry, and private agencies) as a voluntary program for those who want and need it.

Future Directions and the Role of Educators

The two issues of extended school services and day care raise questions concerning the institution-alization of children. Is it in the best interests of children to be raised primarily in group care away from their homes? How can we ensure that we are supporting, not undermining, family life and responsibility by providing these services? And, finally, who should be responsible for child care . . . the government? parents? schools? the local community?

Regardless of the politics of funding, we must respond to the wave of demand in the child care area. In our view, the welfare of children should be the concern of everyone. It is our responsibility as citizens, as it is their right and privilege, to care

FIGURE 15.2 The need for quality day care cannot be ignored. (Courtesy of Stride Rite Children's Centers, Cambridge, Mass.)

for children, to broaden their educational opportunities, and to use community resources to the fullest extent.

Going Back to Basics

The rise of the *back-to-basics* movement that began in the mid-1970s is understandable in light of the history of educational reforms. As with so many movements in the past, "back to basics" seems as much grounded in the desire for social, political, and economic reform as in educational philosophy. A review of Chapter 1 will show that these same forces historically have created the necessary climate for change—from the Renaissance to the Reformation to the War on Poverty.

By the end of the 1970s, we experienced a wave of political and economic conservatism, extensive inflation, and high unemployment. A ten-year decline in national test scores of high school students was observed. There was a general but rampant feeling that "Johnny and Jane" could neither read nor write very well, barely able to decipher a menu or fill out a job application. All these became evidence of a failing public school system. Parents became discontent about the nature of education in their schools. Thus, the back-to-basics movement emerged.

Much of the pressure for this movement came from parents who experienced school policies they did not understand. Parents were reacting to some of the educational innovations of the 1960s and early 1970s. These included shortened school days and curricula that confused parents, such as the "new math" and courses in "psychology" or "human sexuality and family life." Letter grades were dropped in favor of teachers' written comments about a student's progress. Children were promoted to the next grade regardless of whether or not they had passed all their coursework. Parents were puzzled; they felt their standards and values were being rejected. In their eyes, the self-directed and open education of the 1960s and 1970s was just another name for inadequate teaching. When their children graduated from high school without basic reading

and writing skills necessary to find and keep a decent job, parents demanded reform.

Issues and Implications

But the back-to-basics movement is more complicated than it appears. There are fringe issues—many with religious and moral overtones—that are relevant to the general question. The return to strict, if not harsh, disciplinary procedures, the restoration of school prayer and dress and behavior codes for students are a few of the concerns that have attached themselves to the cause. In the emotional climate created, the main point is sometimes lost.

The major issue of the back-to-basics movement is the desire for schools to return to teaching the *basic skills.* The main emphasis in such a schoolroom is continual rehearsal of those fundamental skills, usually defined as the classic "3Rs" of reading, 'riting, and 'rithmetic. Learning by rote is common. That often means that art, music, drama, and other subjects of the humanities are curtailed or modified. In some cases, these "extras" are eliminated from the curriculum, so that teaching time is spent practicing the "basic" skills. Supporters of back to basics would institute these methods at every level of education, preschool through high school.

In the early childhood realm, this approach is implemented in classes for children in several ways. Formal reading programs, often with basal readers and regular formalized tests, may be an early and regular part of kindergarten. Memorizing letters and practicing printing may be required in preschool and day care centers. Drills in beginning sounds and flashcards may take precedence over songs and fingerplays in groups.

Clearly, a back-to-basics approach has an impact on the teaching and learning process:

Teaching is affected when:
- The teacher becomes the dominant figure; it is a teacher-centered, teacher-controlled approach.
- The teacher's role is to instruct, to tell how, or to give a lesson.
- The teacher has a prescribed standard to measure and test all student response against.

Children are affected when:
- Intellectual skills are stressed, and there is a lack of emphasis on the whole child.
- Child-centered learning through exploration, choice, and discovery are valued less than teacher-directed instruction.

The learning process is affected when:
- There is a deemphasis on the arts and humanities.
- Testing and measuring for gains made by children is frequent.
- There is less creativity in the teaching and learning/response methods and in the content of the curriculum itself.

Future Directions and the Role of Educators

Many parents and educators on both sides of the argument would agree that there is a need for curriculum reform. The importance of having children learn basic skills is not really in question. The debate begins by first defining exactly what are "basic skills," particularly in the early years, and then deciding how they should be taught. For the teacher who is concerned with total growth and the individual child, a back-to-basics approach could be difficult to implement. In our view, the early childhood educator recognizes that the more child-centered style of teaching has greater meaning to the child than one determined entirely by grown-ups. And the early childhood teacher knows that the full range of children's skills and developmental needs must be addressed for well-rounded and complete growth to occur.

CRISES IN CHILDREN'S LIVES

Endangered Childhood

Children and childhood have changed. Gone are the days when the majority of children arrived home from school to be greeted by Mom in the kitchen, serving milk and homemade cookies. Today's child spends the bulk of time in day care centers or with a neighbor while the parent is at work. Too many arrive at empty homes and spend the next few hours alone or caring for younger siblings. As often as not, the child of today lives with just one parent at best.

Emphasis on Survival

A decade or two ago children seemed to be more protected than they are today; they seemed more innocent. Adults of yesteryear perceived their roles as protectors of children, keeping them at arm's length from life's stresses. Today's parents, on the other hand, are concerned that their children learn to survive, to cope with problems at an early age. They believe the best way to teach children survival skills is to expose them to adult experiences and "reality" early.

FIGURE 15.3 Every child has the right to a full and wondrous childhood.

The impact of social changes in the last twenty years has been hardest felt by the children of the nation. The breakdown of the nuclear family unit, the sexual and feminist revolutions, television, drugs, and worldwide violence have thrust children into adult situations with adult troubles. Dual-parent careers and single working parents, together with the lack of extended families, have meant that children's behavior is not as closely monitored as it once was.

The Television Set

In many homes and other settings, the television set has replaced the adult supervision of the past. Ninety-eight percent of the homes in the United States have televisions, and the average set is on for more than six hours each day (Trelease, 1984). When we know that the average kindergarten graduate has already seen more hours of television than the time it takes to get a bachelor's degree from college (Waters *in* Trelease, 1984), several areas of concern arise regarding the use of television as a child care method.

Television watching is a passive way for children to spend their time. It is a method that encourages children to watch life rather than actively pursue it in vigorous activity. Growing children need to exercise their bodies and perfect their physical

FIGURE 15.4 Adults should monitor children's television viewing.

skills. Too much television detracts from more lively pursuits.

While the content of most television programs is questionable, there is no doubt that children are not discriminating viewers. They will watch most anything they are allowed to watch. Children at home alone have the opportunity to select inappropriate programs. Too many programs portray life issues in unrealistic ways. Solutions by violent means, a disrespect for human life, and disregard for family values are shown as amusing and acceptable ways to cope. The portrayal of life situations in unreal or humorous forms presents children with life views that ignore the real issues of childhood and distort the ways humans deal with reality.

Changing Parent–Child Relations

People are dealing with their children differently than did their parents. They are opening up to their children, telling them of (rather than protecting them from) their own fears and anxieties. Children have been enlisted as coparents in their own upbringing, collaborating with their parents on child-rearing practices, dress codes, and behavior expectations. While this is obviously more democratic and less authoritarian, the results have been that the boundaries between children and adults have become increasingly hazy. It would appear that we are asking young children of today to assume a mantle of maturity before they are capable. We are requiring them to respond to life as adults, not as children. We no longer assure children that the adult is in charge and that their needs will be met. Instead, we ask children to share that burden with us.

Another type of parent has emerged in the 1980s, the creator of the "superbaby" (Langway et al., 1983). These children begin life enrolled in a series of classes by parents who hope to give them as many stimulating experiences as they can absorb. Infant gymnastic workouts, alphabet flash-cards in the nursery, and violin or acting lessons to supplement preschool signal parental expectations for these children. These wonderkids, children of the post–World War II "baby-boom" children (who now are affluent, knowledgeable, and generally over 30), must fulfill every conceivable potential as early as possible. They are being pushed toward success by parents who themselves are more successful than their parents were. "The more, the better" sometimes seems the motto of the day.

The focus for these parents is often on infant academics and superior physical achievement. This raises concerns about the welfare of the child. When the emphasis is on performance and not on unconditional acceptance or feelings, the development of the child may be focused on only one or a few areas of the child's growth. It raises questions as to whether all the basics are being met—social and emotional needs as well as creative, intellectual, and physical ones.

For many children, the result has been a hurried childhood (Elkind, 1982). Parents push their children through the early years, urging them to grow up fast, succeed, achieve. Designer clothes are just the outward trappings these parents use to encourage adult attitudes and behaviors. The loss of childhood seems to have brought with it new problems for children. Clinicians are seeing more children with stress-related problems: headaches, abdominal pains, and even ulcers are occurring in younger and younger children.

Future Directions and the Role of Educators

Children are not equal to adults and are unable to assume the responsibility for their own care. Children need to be nurtured and protected, to have the time of childhood in which to discover themselves and to be guided and directed toward maturity. Children need adults, teachers, and parents who understand this, who respect childhood and children, and who will help them achieve their potential in supportive ways.

Child Abuse and Neglect

The Crisis

Respect for children and childhood is seriously eroded when adults violate the trust of and responsibility for children through neglect and abuse. Social change over the last few decades has put many of our children at risk. The changes in the family unit, unemployment, loss of funding for programs and subsidies for families, and rising divorce rates have put parents under stress and are having a negative effect on children's well-being. When children are cared for improperly, the results are often child neglect and abuse.

A neglected child may be one whose waking hours are mostly unsupervised by adults, in front of the television or simply unconnected with—and unnoticed by—parents or an important caregiver. *Neglect* takes other, more hazardous, forms, how-

ever. When the basic needs of adequate food, clothing, shelter, and health care are unmet, parents are being neglectful. Failure to exercise the care that children need shows an inattention to and lack of concern for children.

Child abuse is the most severe form of disrespect for children. Violence in the form of physical maltreatment and sexual abuse is an improper treatment of children, regardless of their behavior. Abusive language and harsh physical aggression are other forms of child abuse that occur in families and, unfortunately, some settings for child care.

Publicized investigations into sexual abuse of children in day care centers, preschools, and family situations have brought national attention to this hideous violence. Whether or not its increased incidence is due to a change in reporting practices, it is clear that the abuse of children knows no social, racial, or economic barriers. It is happening to children at all levels of the social spectrum.

Standards of Care

For child care workers, the heart of the issue lies in the regulation and licensing of early childhood programs. In light of recent disclosures concerning incidents in centers, we need to take a long, hard look at who is caring for children. In what physical, emotional, and interpersonal environments are our children living? Licensing regulations for schools and teacher certification vary greatly throughout the country. Primarily they ensure only minimum health and safety standards of the physical environment. The great number of unlicensed child care facilities and the quality of children's programs are urgent issues. Governing and regulatory agencies in most states are inadequately staffed and insufficiently budgeted to handle the monitoring of child care settings.

A national call to action to increase public awareness and understanding of child abuse is underway. Standardized licensing procedures, upgrading of the certification of child care workers, and national *accreditation* of all preschools are some of the most frequently mentioned solutions to the problem. Helping parents identify what qualities to

FIGURE 15.5 Social change has put many children at risk.

look for when placing their children in someone else's care is another way to prevent child abuse in centers.

Future Directions and the Role of Educators

Teachers have a role to play. Reporting suspected child abuse is mandated by law in *all* states (Fraser, 1977). Educators must assume the responsibility to inform the proper authorities if they suspect that a child in their care is being abused by adults (see Appendix E for excerpts from the California Penal Code). Figure 15.6 lists the signs a teacher should look for if child abuse is suspected.

In some early childhood programs, teachers and other specialists have started programs for young children that will help them recognize and

---

Child abuse should be suspected if a child:

- Is constantly late, stays away from school for long periods of time, or arrives early and stays late, avoiding going home.
- Is withdrawn, passive, and uncommunicative or aggressive, destructive, and nervous.
- Has unexplained injuries, too many "explained" ones, or has an injury that is inadequately explained.
- Complains of numerous beatings, of someone "doing things," whether or not the parents are home.
- Goes to the bathroom with difficulty; has burns, limps, or bruises, patches of hair missing, bad teeth.
- Wears clothing that is too small, soiled, or inappropriate for the weather, or uses clothing to cover injuries.
- Is dirty, smells, is too thin or constantly tired; exhibits dehydration or malnutrition.
- Is usually fearful of other children or adults.
- Has been fed inappropriate food, drink, or drugs.

FIGURE 15.6 A child who exhibits several of these signs should be investigated as a possible victim of child abuse. (Adapted from Fraser, 1977)

---

avoid abuse. Perhaps most important, teachers must stay in close touch with the parents of all their children. By knowing parents personally and being in contact with them regularly, an early childhood professional may be able to detect early signs of impending problems of both abuse and neglect. The perceptive teacher can then support parents through their difficulties, offering them help by informing them of a parental stress hotline, suggesting strategies to avoid stress and violence, and recommending professional help.

Missing Children

The phenomenon of missing children is another national problem. Each year approximately 1.2 million children disappear from their homes and neighborhoods (Bridgeman, 1984). Some are runaway children; others are kidnap victims, most of whom are snatched from one divorced parent by the other. To help locate missing children, national efforts have focused on a massive fingerprinting campaign to identify those missing. Dramatic presentations on television with case histories and photographs of missing children have contributed to an increased level of public concern. The U.S. Congress established a National Center for Missing and Exploited Children in late 1984. Teachers can help by supporting these steps. And they can ensure that children are not taken from their care unless written permission is given by the parent with whom the child lives.

THE CHANGING FAMILY STRUCTURE

How has the American family structure changed in the last two decades? With the social changes of the 1960s came changes in the ways people looked at themselves and their opportunities. Children raised on Dr. Spock's philosophy of freedom of movement became adults who wanted to express themselves more freely. "Without consciously setting out to do so, American adults have spent the last decade and more trying to adjust the way society works—giving themselves a bit more freedom (to move, to play, to work, to divorce) while devising alternative arrangements for bringing up the kids." (Murphy, 1982) Thus, the family is undergoing serious transformations in the last quarter of this century. Who the family is, how much time children spend with their parents and with other children, and family relationships and attitudes are important issues.

Divorce and Change

Nearly one out of every two marriages ends in divorce these days. That means more and more children are confronted with the trauma that the breakup of a family can bring. Divorce has affected the family structure in far-reaching ways.

Financial Impact

After a divorce, the family usually must survive on one income. Whatever emotional problems children experience as a result of a divorce are compounded by financial woes. In 1982, most of the 11.4 million children under 18 who lived in below-poverty-level families were not living with both parents (Murphy, 1982).

Effects on Parents

Having only one parent to handle the daily struggles of family life alters family patterns. If the single father is busy with food preparation, there is no other parent available to help children with homework, listen to how their school day went, or watch them play. The single mother who is with the toddler in the tub cannot help the first-grader with reading.

To be sure, two-parent families experience similar incidents. However, in a single-parent household, children may find themselves needing to wait more often, perhaps for longer periods of time. And the parent may not get the adult support, or respite from a relentless child, that is so helpful when raising young children.

After divorce, parents are confronted with many pressing issues all at once. Their own emotional needs are often left unmet. Their main contact is no longer at home. Privacy is difficult when young children's needs are so immediate. And these parents get very tired. We know from family therapists that many problems are either created or made worse by fatigue.

Parents must address their own needs for privacy and for socializing in order to be able to share themselves with their children in meaningful and untroubled ways. Single parents must take care to avoid making their children their confidantes. Further, parents need to establish an adult support network of their own. As the family structure changes from a two-parent, nuclear family to that of a single-parent family (with little or no contact with the other parent), the challenges for parents and children alike are tremendous. Growing up without two parents often puts a household in continual difficulty.

Impact on Children

Most children exhibit classic reactions to divorce: shock, depression, denial, anger, low self-esteem and, among younger children, a sense of blame. Some studies show that divorce may have a more negative effect on boys, that the timetable for adjustment for them is twice that for girls, and they may express their concerns more aggressively (Francke, 1983).

In early childhood, children show emotional changes and behavioral reactions to divorce. These responses tend to differ for each age group. Two-year-olds may regress in their speech and toilet training. They may show increased irritability and crying, outbursts of separation anxiety, and may even ask questions about things they already know (*cognitive confusion*). Preschoolers will likely show more sadness and confusion and develop strong fears (*phobias*) of death, loss of both parents, of injury. Early school-age children may become anxious and aggressive or extremely moody and depressed. Often these children act as if they do not need or want *anyone* and, at the same time, are quite possessive of a parent's attention or possessions (Family Service Association of Santa Clara County, 1982).

It is clear that at all ages, children in divorce situations experience some insecurity and possibly even regressive behavior until the family structure becomes more stable. Children sometimes become pawns of angry parents, receptacles of resentment each parent feels for the other.

Future Directions and the Role of Educators

Adults in the school setting can help these children by minimizing the stress for children at school and providing them with a safe, supportive, and constant environment until their lives have adjusted to a new routine at home. Teachers can be good resources for both children and parents in this critical, sensitive time.

Children need help from adults to deal with the loss of a parent and the resulting changes. Teachers can help children of all ages cope with divorce by:

- Being available for some one-to-one time together.

- Answering any and all questions children may ask.

- Sharing openly feelings of sadness, loss, anger, and confusion in an appropriate way so that children feel less alone and feel safe in expressing their own feelings.

- Explain that the child is not to blame whenever the divorce issue arises.

- Provide books that both explain family changes and show different kinds of families.

- Maintain as much of a stable, caregiving role as possible.

For parents, teachers can be sources of information and support, whether by providing books (for adults and children), suggesting participation in parental support groups, or giving specific referrals of family or individual counselors. Teachers are most helpful when they can be available to listen to and confer with parents about their child's behavior, their feelings, and their adjustment to the new situation. Support of the family—whether it involves one parent or both—should be the goal of every early childhood center, especially when divorce is involved.

Work and Change

According to the Bureau of Labor Statistics, 46 percent of mothers with children under three are in the labor force (Collins, 1984). The Congressional Budget Office estimates that by 1990 the majority of American mothers will hold jobs outside the home, including more than half of those with children under six years of age. They further predict that one of four children under 10 years of age will be living in a single-parent household (Collins, 1984). By 1978, nearly 60 percent of all children under 18 were living with neither parent or with one parent only (Murphy, 1982). The nuclear family—two parents with mother at home full time—is fast becoming the exception rather than the rule, more a myth than reality.

How is the change toward more working mothers affecting the family structure? Caretaking arrangements are becoming a major issue and a part of daily life in every socioeconomic group. This affects both the workplace for adults and the school place for children.

Impact on Adults

As adults become more aware of their children's caretaking needs, they begin to look to their employers to provide some kind of support. Child care costs, after all, are becoming a large part of a family's budget. In fact, after housing, food, and taxes, they are the average American family's biggest expense (Kolben *in* Sommers, 1983). Employers must recognize the importance of the child care issue. Dialogue about employer-supported child care, tax credits, flexible working hours, paternity and maternity leaves, job sharing, and cash subsidies by employers encourages employers to get involved in child care at a meaningful level.

Impact on Children

How will the increase in the number of working parents change children's lives? Today's child is likely to be cared for outside the home in an alternative child care arrangement. "Of all American preschoolers with working mothers, 29 percent are taken care of in their own home by a relative or by hired help, 47 percent are taken care of in someone else's home (usually by a nonrelative), and 19 percent are taken care of by the father or mother (at work, or at home when the return of one parent enables the other to depart for a job)." (Murphy, 1982)

Future Directions and the Role of Educators

For children, these arrangements mean that, from early morning until evening, they will be socializing with each other. And, while adults will be available, they may not be interacting with an individual child very often. Therefore, adults must structure adequate private time to ensure that children get to be alone with an adult and to reenergize themselves. They must balance the day so that it is not too peer oriented. Children who are with each other all day may find themselves unwilling or unable to relate significantly to adults, who bring to children their knowledge, affection, and values. Losing such connection is risky, particularly if we value children learning about societal values, rules, and codes of conduct.

Sex-Role Changes

Married, unmarried, or divorced, women with children have entered the work force of America in great numbers. Whether from necessity or choice, women have become part of the labor force and are unlikely to leave it. One result of working has been a change in women's self-images and in their ideas of the roles that men and women play in today's and tomorrow's world.

FIGURE 15.7 Children today spend more time socializing with each other.

Parents as Adults

How people look at themselves and their roles in life is undergoing considerable transformation. Women who are heads of households are likely to deal with their children differently than did those in the old-style, traditional families. They will question how parents and children treat each other, what they do and talk about together, and who is responsible for the children's upbringing. Blended families (families following remarriages that include parents, step parents, children, step children, half-siblings, etc.) will be headed by women and men who have experienced another kind of "parenting," different from the intact nuclear family of the past. These adults will enter society and become parents with the stamp of these experiences upon them.

Children Becoming Parents

One side effect of the changing sex roles and attitudes of the last quarter-century has been the increase in sexual activity among teenagers. There are an estimated 52 births for every 1,000 females under age 20 (Murphy, 1982); this ratio is among the highest in developed, industrialized nations. Among the consequences of teenage births and families are birth defects and low birth weight. Teenage women may not be able to finish school or get a job and may become dependent on welfare. When children are raising children, all are at risk. Moreover, the cycle of teenage pregnancies, like those of child abuse and poverty, is self-perpetuating. Over 80 percent of teenagers with a first child before their fifteenth birthday had mothers who were also parents in their teen years (Murphy, 1982).

Impact on Children

Children will be exposed to and live with models of women, mothers, and adults that are different from those of 30 or more years ago. What the effects will be on children is difficult to predict. Some say that a less stable, more *androgynous* outlook and upbringing may blur children's identity and views of sexuality, causing confusion and *aberrant* behavior. Others claim that children will now have a more realistic outlook. With a wider range of choices in personal life-style and habit, they will ultimately be freer to express themselves fully and authentically. Regardless of personal opinion, the changes in sex roles will influence children's behavior and attitudes about themselves and each other.

Future Directions and the Role of Educators

Early childhood educators have long recognized how important it is for children to understand their world, particularly of family, interpersonal dynamics, and the roles people play in life. Adults have a critical part in helping children develop a realistic and clear view of themselves and the world around them. How a young child perceives the world of people and their roles influences self-concept, future attitudes, and behavior in significant ways.

The role of the teacher is to accept children and families for who they are, to clarify sex roles for children, and to interpret others' behavior to children so that they learn to understand and are able to act for themselves. In our view, teachers fulfill these responsibilities best when they offer choices in class that invite a freedom of response, rather than ones that dictate behavior with restrictions according to sex, dress, age, etc.

The teacher organizes space and develops materials that encourage broad participation. Varying art, dramatic play, and outdoor games with an eye toward including girls and boys will stimulate skill development and interest in all areas. Books chosen to depict men and women in a variety of roles encourage children to do the same, widening their possibilities rather than narrowing their world view.

Throughout the day and with all children, a teacher must be sure that all children know their biological sex. Helping children learn appropriate gender role behavior is the next step in learning. However, present trends appear to point to a future with changed views of such behavior. Already, dress and activity level for young boys and girls have undergone attitude changes: it is acceptable for girls to be athletic and active physically, just as it is appropriate for boys to cook in the kitchen and be active parents. The teacher must balance professional training and experience with the personal viewpoints of both self and parents. In this way, educators can take an authoritative yet even-handed approach to sex-role changes and the changing family structure.

The current generation of Americans is materially the richest in our history. Yet no other generation has experienced so much divorce, so much shifting family structure. No other children have been exposed to such different sex-role models, nor have adult American women and men had so much

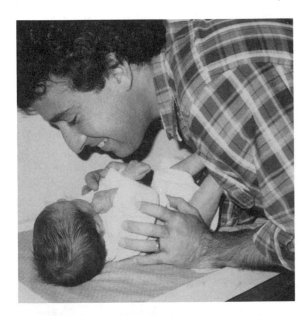

FIGURE 15.8 Changing sex roles will influence future generations.

to question so freely. While we may not know the effects of such changes for some time to come, we are assured that tomorrow's children will be different from those of yesterday in significant ways.

ISSUES FOR EDUCATORS

While every issue discussed in this chapter affects early childhood educators, there are several topics that are of more specific interest to educators. Some of these are:

- Money
- Educational reforms
- Learning the political game
- Teacher burnout

Each one will affect the quality of education for children since it touches the lives of every teacher.

Money

Money is one of the most pressing issues for teachers today. Finding funding sources for pro-

grams has become a problem in the 1980s. Public monies, once relatively plentiful in the past, have been curtailed in recent years. Federal funds in particular are less available now than in the past, and state funding priorities often are for secondary, elementary, and special education rather than for programs for children under five.

Issues and Implications

To improve teaching and provide a high quality of education and care for children, the field of child care and early childhood education must attract superior talent. Business, medicine, law, and also the military attract intelligent young people with good pay and benefits. Teaching has not remained competitive with other professions. One estimate puts average annual teaching salaries in elementary and secondary levels at $12,800 for starting pay and $17,000 after 10 years' experience (Peirce, 1983); early childhood teachers have substantially lower average salaries. According to Census Bureau statistics (1982), the range of monthly salaries for child care workers was between $346 and $2,008, with the average yearly salary $10,155. Considering how many early childhood teachers support themselves and a family, the financial aspects of the field are dismal. Poor wages, difficult working situations, and overall low job status contribute to job dissatisfaction. Should these conditions continue, current qualified staff will undoubtedly leave the field, and students will make other career decisions (Pettygrove et al., 1984).

In the past, teaching was one of the few professional opportunities open to women and minorities; thus, the lower pay was accepted. Now, however, more options are open. Unless education can improve teacher pay, the field itself will neither attract nor keep people of high caliber.

Future Directions and the Role of Educators

Money issues boil down to these questions: How much will teacher and school improvements cost, and what are the possible funding sources? The answer to the first depends on what kinds of improvements are made. If teacher salaries are improved at the entry level, rather than across the board, the overall increase in cost would be gradual. If the school day or term—either preschool or kindergarten/elementary—is lengthened, the costs would be considerable. For the thousands of day care centers already operating fulltime, the issue is more complicated. Raising tuition fees may not be a solution if the result is shutting out families in need. Merit pay and master teacher plans may be workable, depending on the type and extent of each. Caregivers, parents, and communities joining together in efforts to improve teacher salaries may become essential for maintaining any quality at all in the teaching field.

The answer to the second question—where the money comes from—depends, again, on the type and scope of school improvements. Some advocate a return to the post-Sputnik 1960s with massive federal support. Others, remembering that those funds did not solve all our educational problems, advocate more local control through state and community resources. We are inclined to believe that the task of teacher and school improvement is so large that more than one financial source will be needed.

Finally, we think it critical that each beginning teacher enter the field of early childhood education with the understanding of the financial issues facing educators today. No serious improvement in fiscal status will occur without our own support and advocacy. If we feel strongly that our society needs good teachers, we must make our voices heard to have teachers compensated fairly for their work.

Educational Reforms

How committed is society to a high standard of education for our children? How will we recognize and reward excellence in our teachers? The issue of the 1980s is now focusing on merit pay and other educational reforms to answer these thorny questions.

In the spring of 1983, the National Commission on Excellence in Education released a report on American schools. Since that time, other groups have announced findings similar to that of the Commission: American schools are drowning in mediocrity and face a crisis of quality, particularly in public schools. Panels nationwide recommended various educational reforms, most notably merit pay and master teacher plans.

Merit Pay

Since lack of financial incentive is one reason why the brightest college students are not choosing educational careers, it follows that improvements in teaching must involve increases in salary. Many plans call for a *merit pay* system. This is a system that gives pay bonuses for excellent teaching. Performance would be evaluated, and a salary established according to the level of teaching excellence. While the idea of rewarding superior work with additional pay is a logical one, critics argue that it would be easy for administrators to show favoritism, that parents would begin pressuring schools to have their children in master teachers' classes only, and that the teachers themselves would become competitive and divided.

At this date, merit pay systems have begun in individual districts around the country, but not on a large scale nor for a long enough time to accurately assess whether or not these potential problems will occur. For early childhood purposes, we feel that the idea of merit pay has some promise, particularly if paired with a general upgrading of teacher pay scales. In fact, *every* teacher of young children who attempts to maintain continuing excellence in the classroom ought to be recognized for those achievements.

The Master Teacher

Master teacher plans offer teachers promotions, higher salaries, and other benefits. One of the major causes of poor teaching is inadequate teacher training. Often, those studying to become teachers have too little "hands-on" experience. A student teaching semester towards the end of one's academic preparation is often the only regularly supervised experience a teacher ever gets. Master teacher plans might encourage more of these experiences as a regular part of one's work. Young teachers and those less acquainted with new teaching techniques would have the chance to learn from good role models, mentors who work to train other teachers or develop curriculum. Master teachers would receive financial incentives and bonuses for doing so.

The criticisms of these plans are similar to those of merit pay; that is, of favoritism and *divisiveness*. Since we advocate for regular and ongoing teacher performance and training, we feel that both educational reform issues are worthy of attention. Further, the daily challenges of teaching an early childhood classroom take their toll. To keep excellent teachers, we must add to their professional careers by offering new and exciting ways to expand their skills. Learning from—and becoming—a master teacher can be one way to achieve this goal.

Future Directions and the Role of Educators

The educational reform movement of the 1980s that we are experiencing now has focused more on public than private education, and more on secondary or elementary than on early childhood education. Nonetheless, early childhood teachers are called upon to take a stand on these issues. We are *all* affected by the public's attitudes toward education. Further, it is important for us as professionals to set and maintain a high level of standards for our own field. Since early education encompasses programs of such diversity, it will be a challenge of major proportions to establish professional standards for all who work with young children.

Learning the Political Game

With the issues of money and educational reform of such immediate concern, teachers need to understand the forces that affect how these issues are resolved. Teachers will have to educate themselves about the political process. They will need to know the rules and regulations regarding public funding sources. It is important to know how monies are allocated and who to work with in order to

affect the decisions regarding education. By being acquainted with legislation, teachers can rally support for bills that will help children, families, and schools.

Teachers have long kept out of the political process, not unlike many minorities. But they have not been immune from its effects. As teachers, we must become informed in order to increase our power in the political and financial arenas of daily life. Just as we encourage children to help themselves, we must support each other in taking the initiative for our own profession's well-being.

Teacher Burnout

Job *burnout* often results when a person is faced with a demanding work load, uncertain or inadequate rewards, and other pressures that damage work effectiveness. At its most extreme, teacher burnout can drive a good professional out of the field altogether. In other cases, skilled teachers become lackadaisical workers. Rather than searching for excellence and innovative methods or curriculum, they become disgruntled and disillusioned. The teacher approaching burnout has little to give except criticism and low morale. Teacher burnout is an occupational hazard of substantial proportions.

Issues and Implications

Our job is one of human service, of caring for people dependent upon us. It is inherent in the job that child care workers and teachers are vulnerable to the stress of this daily demand. Teachers do not have the luxury of putting an irate parent or upset child "on hold." And too few have the time or money for regular vacations and sabbaticals to recharge professional and personal batteries.

Furthermore, when a teacher begins to deteriorate from job stress and overwork, that individual is not the only one affected. Children, fellow workers, families are all touched when a skilled and dedicated teacher feels powerless and discouraged.

If burnout in the early childhood setting affected only individuals in isolation, it might be far less devastating. But it can multiply like a cancer, affecting the morale of others on the staff and ultimately their collective capacity to give to and nurture young children. The statistics are painfully obvious: staff turnover averages 15 to 30 percent in child care centers, well above other professions. Equally significant, many potential workers are taking a serious second look at child care jobs and passing them up for more lucrative and less stressful positions.

(Jorde, 1982)

Future Directions and the Role of Educators

It is up to all of us as early childhood professionals to work together to give each other support—both moral and financial. Our profession is at once difficult and rewarding. We have the capacity to develop early warning signals of stress and to plan strategies at our work sites to deal effectively with such times. If administrators and teachers regularly communicate, problems that add to burnout will be brought to attention. If the school offers opportunities for job advancement as well as varied kinds of professional involvement, teachers are likely to find their jobs stimulating rather than overly stressful.

We face some serious issues as educators in the 1980s and beyond. Yet there is cause for optimism. As Walter Cronkite put it:

Fortunately, this country does have a marvelous way of suddenly awakening to a problem, realizing its implications, and moving ahead to solve it.

The Seventies was the Decade of the Environment. We became aware that we couldn't

FIGURE 15.9 Early childhood educators support each other and issues they care about. (Courtesy of Noah's Ark Preschool, Richmond, California)

drink some of our water or safely breathe some of our air. Then people began to do something about the problem.

Now that the serious problems of American education have come to the fore, I believe we're going to do something about them.

The Eighties could be the Decade of Education.

(Cronkite, 1983)

DIVERSITY IN SCHOOLS

Multicultural Education

Issues and Implications

America as a "melting pot," where all cultures and ethnic groups blend together smoothly and completely, is a myth. Unfortunately, much of American society historically can be characterized as racist and *ethnocentric* in nature. The gap between our ideals—equal opportunity and freedom to pursue life, liberty, happiness, and self-expression—and daily reality can be narrowed only if we recognize its existence and then set concrete goals and plans to change it.

What is needed is to form a new concept of society and, as educators, of programs for children. It is imperative that we bring an awareness and sensitivity to children concerning the diversity of mankind. Diversity means difference—how we each express our unique cultural, religious, and ethnic heritage. There is strength and positive power in cultural and ethnic diversity. Our goal in early childhood education is to have children appreciate and respect those differences as they are socialized into the larger community beyond their homes.

Education has always been a process of socialization; early childhood education is the transition from the child's first socializing experience to that of mainstream society, as expressed in schools. By knowing a child's family and background, teachers work to make this enormous and important transition smoother and less stressful. And when the goal of the program is to accept children for who they

are (rather than to change their identities), cultural pluralism is respected and celebrated.

We must equip children to live in the United States of the twenty-first century, an era when the white population will become a minority group. Children will need to learn about a variety of cultures and their expressions in people; *cultural pluralism* will mark that century as it has never before. As children maintain identification with their own culture within the broader framework of schools and society, they can better come to tolerate and appreciate a genuine variety of ethnic groups. Society will run smoother and survive with less violence if the cultures of its citizens are respected.

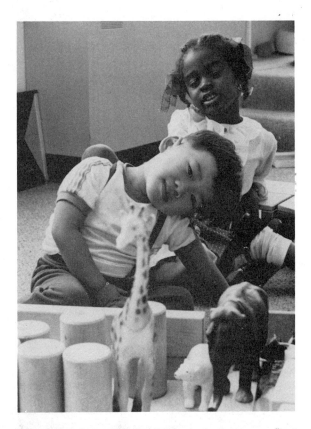

FIGURE 15.10 Early childhood classrooms reflect the cultural diversity that is the cornerstone of modern society. (Courtesy of Stride Rite Children's Centers, Cambridge, Mass.)

Future Directions and the Role of Educators

Curriculum can become rich when based on a commitment to help children learn to know and understand people. Our classrooms are a good place to begin teaching a crosscultural perspective. With the young child, we begin closest to home with concrete experiences (celebrations, songs, books, foods) about people close by: class members, neighbors, all the people children see in their everyday settings. Local celebrations and holidays may be used to bring the black, American Indian, Hispanic, and Asian cultures into the classroom. Parents can help their children share their diverse heritages with one another.

The model of family and school as partners is of particular importance when working toward multicultural education. No one knows better what is meaningful to a child's personal cultural experience than the family. Of course, teachers expand their own information base with educational classes,

FIGURE 15.11 A crosscultural curriculum helps children understand similarities and differences.

books, and materials. However, this is a supplement to a regular dialogue between themselves and parents.

Moreover, teachers must not assume, when faced with a monochromatic group of children, that there is no cultural diversity. Scratch the surface and there are family histories from all parts of the globe. These profiles and the children themselves tell personal family stories that can be the basis of curriculum units or an entire class approach. No one needs to lose ethnic identity in order to be part of another group or society in which they live.

We cannot, however, just pad the curriculum with interesting ethnic celebrations and consider that we have fulfilled the responsibilities of multicultural education. By teaching about our differences we are, in fact, teaching about our similarities as people. The accent does not have to be on food, clothing, song and dance, and language as setting people apart from one another. Rather, the focus can be on how very similar are the components of many cultural and religious celebrations. Eggs, for instance, are a common theme in spring holidays around the world. Gift giving and creating presents for the family can be another theme to cross cultural and religious barriers. Emphasizing commonalities brings depth and interest to the curriculum, not simply a look at something different and therefore less valued.

We want to teach the values of a pluralistic society, but we also want to teach the values our diverse cultures hold in common. No one culture or religion should feel less valuable than any other. As teachers, we must be certain that we respect the values of others and that our own standards are in no way demeaning to the heritage of any child we teach.

Bilingual Education

The 1980s have left unresolved the basic questions concerning bilingual education. The goals and purposes of bilingual education remain little understood by the American population. Disagreements persist over how to define bilingualism, how to determine who needs it, and who is primarily responsible for providing the service. The long-term impact of current bilingual programs remains in dispute.

Issues and Implications

Changing populations and the influx of immigrants from Asia as well as from the Hispanic nations have brought with them the challenges of bilingual education. In the past, immigrants were forced to reject the culture and language of their parents and learn English by immersion. This attitude no longer prevails; instead, bilingual education and respect for heritage are seen as more humane approaches to the situation.

Bilingual programs serve primarily Spanish-speaking students. It is estimated that the number of school-age Spanish-speaking children in the country will increase by 50 percent by the year 2000 (White, 1984). How will this affect the early childhood teacher?

The School Age Child. The questions about bilingualism for the school-age child are different from those for the young child. In elementary school, teachers and children are forced to deal with issues beyond those of receptive and expressive language. Learning graphic language (reading and writing), acquiring concepts in other subject areas through listening, and dealing with the more complex social patterns and interpersonal issues are just a few of these issues. Moreover, the age at which children should be taught a second language is highly controversial. Research shows that children *can* acquire nativelike mastery of a second language if they learn to speak the language before the age of five. Others will argue that a child should learn all the fine points of the first language before being exposed to a second one and that this exposure should not occur prior to the age of six.

Much research is centered on how children achieve second-language competence and performance. We do know that by age five, children know most of the sounds and grammatical structure of their native tongue and appear to learn a second language in a similar way. With a bilingual child,

the level of competence in both languages may be low while gaining mastery in the second language.

The two pieces of legislation that have most influenced the bilingual issue are the 1968 Bilingual Education Act and the 1974 *Lau* v. *Nichols* Supreme Court decision. Since 1968, schools have been required by the aforementioned law to offer special instruction to children without competence in English. And in 1974, the Supreme Court determined that a lack of instruction in one's first language is a violation of children's civil rights.

The result is that children are taught, in public kindergarten and elementary schools, by using both the primary language and English. For instance, children may be taught to read in their primary language first; once they have learned the reading process in their own language, they are then taught to decode in English. One area needing research

FIGURE 15.12 Children acquire a second language when given many opportunities to converse with their peers in play.

and policy direction is what private schools are doing in instructing children without English competence.

The Young Child. In preschools and day care centers, children are still taught in a regular class setting, often with little extra instruction. This means they are learning English through the "immersion method," hearing mostly English at school. Teachers report success with this method, since much of the curriculum is developed for learning by *doing*, not just by listening. Moreover, children hear English throughout the day but may not be required to produce it until they are ready. Finally, children's play for those under five years of age is often carried out without the need for much spoken language. Yet we do not know definitively if this method of language acquisition really serves the non-English speaker well. Early childhood programs—both public and private—need more research to be able to take a clear direction in the area of bilingual education.

Future Directions and the Role of Educators

We need appropriate measures to determine which children need bilingual services. Assessment of the methods for teaching bilingual children should be examined: Is a bilingual program still immersion in English or is it a true two-language experience? Do the same needs apply to all children in the early childhood years?

For the teacher working with young bilingual children, "caretaker language," noted by Krashen (Gingras, 1983), can be useful. This is the language that researchers found was used by adults who deal with young children. Specific features are that the caretaker:

• Does not teach language acquisition as such, but helps children understand the meaning of what is being communicated.

• Deals with the here and now.

• Uses short, simple sentences that increase in complexity as the child matures.

• Uses slightly more complex sentences than children are using.

• Repeats syntactic patterns frequently and slows down by pausing longer when speaking.

(Gingras, 1983)

Social and political forces affecting bilingualism must be addressed as we look at methodology and curriculum. The real world and education cannot be isolated from one another. The impact of poverty and discrimination as a barrier to language acquisition and academic achievement are crucial factors in bilingual education.

Special Education

In 1976, Congress passed the Education for All Handicapped Children Act, which stated that by 1978 all children three to 18 years of age were to have access to public educational facilities. Since then, handicapped and normal youngsters have spent more time together in school because this federal legislation requires that handicapped children be placed in the least restrictive environment possible. That attitude has led to greater acceptance of the handicapped in many other areas of daily life.

Many handicapped children now participate in the full range of programs offered to normal children, from gymnastics to summer camps. The law that required their inclusion also mandated individual education plans (IEP) for each handicapped child. Thus, all handicapped children can have an education that is designed to meet their needs. The results of removing these barriers have been to encourage the handicapped to travel, work, shop, and play in the mainstream of American life.

Public institutions have been forced by the law to include handicapped children in their programs. Three important issues must be addressed.

First, an important question concerns the private sector. Are private schools taking the initiative in enrolling and educating the special child? Early childhood educators in these settings have a responsibility to help others see this issue as critical to the nature of teaching.

Second, teachers must be trained and supported in methods that will integrate the handicapped in school so that quality education is maintained for all children. The teacher cannot be expected to provide for children's special needs alone, without help. At the same time, most activities offered in early childhood programs, especially for children under five years of age, can be made appropriate for children with a variety of handicaps. The key issue here is teacher training and ongoing support.

A final issue is the value of mainstreaming for all children. One of the goals of mainstreaming is to give both nonhandicapped and handicapped children an opportunity to interact with each other and develop more tolerance and acceptance of people with handicapping conditions. Is this happening? If so, what works well? What does not work? Research in this area would enlighten both families and educators as they plan programs in special education.

TEACHING FOR THE TWENTY-FIRST CENTURY

Every day, teachers open their classroom doors to young children by the thousands. As they do so, they are influencing the course of our nation in the next century. If this statement seems overwhelming, consider this: the child who is born in 1985 will be voting in the twenty-first century. We are teaching the children of the future. What is the kind of world our children will face, and what skills will they need to deal with that world?

Computers in School

The computer and other high-technology equipment are definitely part of that world. It is clear that children in school today will need to be exposed to and familiar with computers. Two recent studies, by the Corporation for Public Broadcasting and the Center for Education Statistics, show that schools are using computers, video cassette record-

ers, and public television more today than ever before. Another study estimates that the percentage of elementary schools using computers for instruction is as high as 63 percent and confirms that the gap between wealthy and poor schools in owning computers is narrowing (Toch, 1984).

The computer cannot replace the teacher, for a computer will never be able to calm an upset child, negotiate a dispute for a favorite toy, notice the withdrawn youngster, laugh at a joke, or pet a hamster. Many critics argue that the computer is a smoke screen that diverts us from teaching children critical basic skills. It will always be true that the computer is only as "smart" as the teachers themselves choose it to be. That is, a computer may be able to teach a child a specific skill needed, but only after the teacher has noted what the child needs to learn, how that skill can be best learned by that particular student, and what program will do the job. For these reasons, teachers need not be defensive about the use of computers.

A computer can entice an otherwise reluctant child to engage in the learning process.

Khosrow, for example, had a difficult time in the busy, verbal classroom. English was his sec-

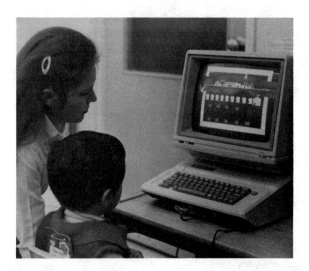

FIGURE 15.13 The computer cannot replace the teacher.

ond language, and the chatty children were overwhelming to him. After two months, he still refused to even take off his hat. When the computer was introduced, Khosrow changed markedly. Here was something that did not use rapidly spoken English or demand that he understand English much at all. It called upon his well-developed fine motor and intellectual skills. He could relax and enjoy himself. The other children noticed his talent and his delight. Soon, he was showing them how to operate and use the system. From then on, Khosrow began to interact in the classroom and with the children more successfully.

The computer and other learning-assistance devices can help a child with linguistic, social, or other problems be successful. Some children have difficulties connecting with a teacher while learning, often because of anxiety regarding performance. This can look like withdrawal and fear, or anger. The teacher breaks that failure pattern when offering the child a nonteacher to learn from. Since teachers' overall goals are to find the best match between the child and the learning process, they will welcome a variety of strategies to maximize success in school. With young children, the reward may be to hear the pleasant song played at the end of a program, to see their thoughts printed out by a machine, or simply to be able to press buttons and watch things happen. Whatever the attraction, computers are here to stay. The teacher of future generations is well-advised to take advantage of

FIGURE 15.14 The computer is here to stay in our early childhood classrooms.

what computers offer. (See Appendix F for what to look for in computer software for young children.)

Fostering Divergent Thinking

Children of the twenty-first century will be faced with a variety of issues and problems, some that we can anticipate now and some we have yet to dream of. How we teach our children now can give them strategies to solve both kinds of problems. One way to prepare today's children for tomorrow is to help them with problem solving and encourage them to think in many ways.

We believe that cognitive memory skills and covergent thinking are important to learn, but that they must be paired with divergent and evaluative thinking. It is important to start early and support this kind of thinking throughout childhood, helping children look at problems from many angles. Creative and varied brainstorming leads to solutions with many perspectives.

If we are to hope that the people of tomorrow will solve their problems in mutually productive ways, we must lead our children to understand that there is more than one way to look at the world, an issue, any situation. Fostering divergent thinking helps children gain this perspective. By finding out early that a point of view is *not* the only one, the child learns to accept and even embrace the notion of people working together to solve their common problems. In a democratic society, the honest expression of views and acceptance of others' rights to the same may be the key to our very survival on this planet.

Teaching Values

Education has never been free of values. Whenever someone chooses to teach something to another person, a choice of what and how to teach it implies what that person values. In early childhood education in particular, teachers and parents know that a neutral education is not possible. Our values reflect what we believe is important, what is accepta-

ble, and what we will not tolerate. Teaching our children our belief system is part of their education.

What is critical for us to realize is that we *are* teaching values. Children learn about themselves, their place in the school setting, and how to get along with others in the same classroom where they discover how to mix colors, memorize a fingerplay, and ride a tricycle.

Teaching values starts with knowing your own belief system and its place in your career. Ask yourself:

- Why am I teaching? Why young children? Why children at all?
- What made me choose early childhood education as my career?
- What do I stand for? Why?
- How did I come to have my beliefs?
- Do I allow others their beliefs?
- How do I state my values to children? To parents?
- How do I keep my values and integrity while allowing myself to grow and change?

The answers to these questions may strike a raw nerve here and there. If so, congratulations for being courageous enough to look at personal values honestly. The teacher who believes in such a process is one who has a gift for every student in class: that of a conviction to values, purpose, and sharing.

> Each generation of Americans has the responsibility to prepare future generations for the world that will confront them. Our forefathers prepared us to cope with the complicated world we live in, and we, as the current adult generations, must fulfill our responsibility for preparing our children for the . . . world of the future. We must heed H.G. Wells' warning that "human history becomes more and more a race between education and catastrophe." Action is required now to ensure that America's people are prepared for the twenty-first century.
>
> (National Science Foundation Commission, 1983)

How do we prepare our children to live successfully in the future? We begin by looking ahead to predict what intellectual, social, and emotional tools our children will need. We embrace the willingness to change while at the same time holding to our beliefs of personal choice, integrity, equality, and opportunity.

SUMMARY

Early childhood educators are facing issues today that challenge the very definition of childhood. How society handles these issues will help determine where we are headed—as teachers, children, families, a nation.

Some of the issues presented here may seem somewhat personal and even political. This is deliberate: as caretakers of the future—our children—we have serious and far-reaching questions that we must ask ourselves *now*. This book is dedicated to the quest for knowledge and action concerning a most important endeavor of the twentieth and twenty-first centuries: teaching young children. We can hardly do anything less than address those topics that are critical to the success of this task and of our profession.

Topics for Discussion

1. Why do you think child care workers have low salaries? How can you work to change these conditions?

2. Is it possible to provide needed day care at the same time as you are given a fair salary and work environment?

3. What can you say to parents who ask what you teach their child? How can you respond to their insistence on teaching children to read and print before kindergarten?

4. What would you do if you suspect a child in your center is being seriously neglected or abused?

5. What can you say to help children handle separation and divorce? How will you deal with *both* parents?

6. How can you articulate your own aspirations for yourself as a professional?

7. How can you provide for and deal with diversity in the classroom? What can you do to support both cultural pluralism and a sense of togetherness and mutual respect?

8. How will children develop acceptance, not intolerance, of multicultural and handicapped children? What can you do to deal with teasing and exclusion of children different from themselves?

9. How will you prepare yourself and your profession for the twenty-first century?

Bibliography

EXTENDING SOCIAL SERVICES

Children's Defense Fund. *Children's Defense Budget*. Washington, D.C.: Children's Defense Fund, 1984.

Lindner, Eileen; Mattis, Mary C.; and Rogers, June R. *When Churches Mind the Children*. Ypsilanti, Mich.: High/Scope Press, 1984.

CRISES IN CHILDREN'S LIVES

Bridgeman, Anne. "Schools Joining National Fight Against Child Abuse." *Education Week*, January 18, 1984, pp. 1, 16.

Elkind, David. *The Hurried Child: Growing Up Too Fast Too Soon*. Reading, Mass.: Addison Wesley, 1982.

Fraser, Brian G. *The Educator and Child Abuse*. Chicago, Ill.: National Committee for Prevention of Child Abuse, 1977.

Langway, Lynn, et al. "Bringing Up Superbaby." *Newsweek*, March 28, 1983, pp. 62–66.

Murphy, Cullen. "Kids Today." *Wilson Quarterly,* Autumn 1982, pp. 61–82.

Packard, Vance. *Our Endangered Children.* Boston: Little, Brown and Co., 1983.

Trelease, Jim. *The Read-Aloud Handbook.* New York: Penguin Books, 1984.

Van de Kamp, John. *Child Abuse Prevention Handbook.* Sacramento, Calif.: Child Prevention Center, 1983.

Waters, H.F. "What TV Does for Kids." *Newsweek,* February 21, 1977, pp. 62–70.

Winn, Marie. *Children Without Childhood.* New York: Penguin Books, 1984.

THE CHANGING FAMILY STRUCTURE

Collins, Glen. "Does Teaching of Infants Have Merit?" *The New York Times,* February 1, 1984.

Collins, Glen. "Employers Offering Seminars to Help the Working Parent." *The New York Times,* June 23, 1983.

Family Service Association of Santa Clara County. "Anticipating Children's Reactions to Separation and Divorce." Santa Clara, Calif.: Family Service Association of Santa Clara County, 1982.

Francke, Linda Bird. *Growing Up Divorced.* New York: Ballantine Books, 1983.

Hunter, Marjorie. "Senate Day Care at Hand." *The New York Times,* December 9, 1983.

Sommers, Carl. "What's New in Corporate Day Care: Consciousness Raising for Executives." *The New York Times,* July 24, 1983.

"When Children Bear Children." *The New York Times,* August 1, 1983.

ISSUES FOR EDUCATORS

Cronkite, Walter. "What to Do About America's Educational Crisis." *American Express Newsletter,* July 1983.

Cummings, Judith. "Los Angeles Weighs Merits of Bonus Pay for the Best Teachers." *The New York Times,* June 28, 1983.

Fiske, Edward B. "Paying the Bill for School Reform." *The New York Times,* November 13, 1983.

Hechinger, Fred M. "The New Strategies for Paying Teachers More." *The New York Times,* June 21, 1983.

Hechinger, Fred M. "Rush of Contradictory Ideas on School Reform." *The New York Times,* August 2, 1983.

Hochman, Victoria. "National Concern: Are Top Teachers Worth Top Dollar?" *Gannet Westchester Newspapers,* August 28, 1983.

Jorde, Paula. *Avoiding Burnout: Strategies for Managing Time, Space, and People in Early Childhood Education.* Washington, D.C.: Acropolis Books, 1982.

Peirce, Neal. "Money Tops List of Hot Education Issues." *San Francisco Chronicle and Examiner,* August 21, 1983.

Pettygrove, Willa; Whitebook, Mary; and Weil, Mary. "Research Report. Beyond Babysitting: Changing the Treatment and Image of Child Caregivers." *Young Children,* July 1984, pp. 14–21.

White, Eileen. "Poll Finds Public Endorsement of School Reforms." *Education Week,* August 31, 1983, pp. 1, 8.

DIVERSITY IN SCHOOLS

Day, David E. *Early Childhood Education: A Human Ecological Approach.* Glenview, Ill.: Scott, Foresman and Co., 1983.

Gingras, Rosario C. "Early Childhood Bilingualism: Some Considerations from Second-Language Acquisition Research." In Spodek, B., and Saracho, O. (eds.), *Understanding the Multicultural Experience in Early Childhood Education.* Washington, D.C.: National Association for the Education of Young Children, 1983.

Morgan, Dorothy, and York, Mary E. "Ideas for Mainstreaming Young Children." *Young Children,* January 1981, pp. 18–25.

Rashid, Hakim M. "Promoting Biculturalism in Young African-American Children." *Young Children,* January 1984, pp. 12–23.

White, Eileen. "Bilingual Education in the 1980s: Basic Questions Remain Unresolved." *Education Week,* February 8, 1984, p. 13.

TEACHING FOR THE TWENTY-FIRST CENTURY

Castillo, Cathy. "Computers in California Schools." *San Francisco Chronicle and Examiner*, April 29, 1984.

"Educating Americans for the Twenty-First Century: Excerpts from the National Science Foundation Commission's Report." *Education Week*, September 14, 1983, pp. 14–18.

"Public TV Still Big in the Classroom." *San Francisco Chronicle and Examiner*, June 13, 1984.

Toch, Thomas. "Number of Computers in Schools Doubles." *Education Week*, April 18, 1984, pp. 1, 14.

SILICON CHIPS AND PLAYDOUGH

Ann Piestrup

A computer can be as nonthreatening as a paintbrush, and in the hands of a child is a new tool for exploring the world. Nursery classrooms are arranged so that children experience the world directly, through molding clay and sand, mixing paints, and piling blocks. Through these experiences, they gradually form concepts about how the world works and how they can affect it.

Nursery school teachers who are well aware of the many ways of guiding children in building concepts through traditional play may think computers are too abstract and complex for young children to use. Yet these same teachers offer picture books to children, without realizing that an interactive graphic computer program can be more like clay and paint than the static images in a book. A child can touch a key and something will happen, touch another key and there is a new effect. The child is challenged to explore and discover in a way never before possible.

Our ideas about what young children can do are changing as we watch children using computers in the nursery school. Preschoolers are plotting computer graphics using X- and Y-coordinates, playing spread-sheet programs like games, and writing programs to create complex visual patterns. Children probably have more abilities than we have credited them with, and the computer is a vehicle for them to show what they can do.

Children will need to be able to think more logically and abstractly to do many of the things important in our technological culture. Using a computer can help them develop these skills through direct experience, starting at a very young age. A homemaker using a microwave oven can program it to prepare a meal, thaw, rotate, and cook food. This requires a different kind of thinking and planning than cooking the same meal on a stove, but using a microwave oven is more removed from direct experience than using a stove. This is just one example of the way work is changing, with a new emphasis on logical thinking skills.

THE VERSATILITY OF A COMPUTER FOR YOUNG CHILDREN

Children can use computers as tools for drawing or creating music, as game machines, or as learning machines. Using a computer will never make jumping rope more fun, but it can add new dimensions to many learning environments. Drawing programs allow children to explore shapes and colors with a control they can not achieve in other media. Children use metric programs to make music, edit it, tinker with it, and play it back. Children have more capability in their minds than in their fingers. Computer programs can help them explore and express their ideas.

Computers used simply as game machines have their place as well. While playing video games, children can develop split-second responses, as well as the ability to focus attention in the face of distractions. Preliminary research indicates that they may also develop refined spatial and temporal skills that help them learn mathematics. Some games, however, are frustrating for young children, because things happen too quickly. Others are frightening or involve only violence. Carefully chosen games can offer real value for children, when they are used in moderation.

It is as learning machines, though, that computers come into their own. Computer programs can offer playful learning environments to introduce concepts, reinforce skills, and allow exploration of any topic of interest to a child. Computer programs can create a world where failure is impossible, success is rewarded with real power, and mastery of knowledge leads to greater challenges. The best learning software for children leads them through a series of experiences that lay a careful foundation of understanding. New concepts based on this foundation are then presented, step by step. The worst software traps children in a boring experience, where the computer, instead of the child, is in control. These programs are no better than electronic flash cards and workbooks, and waste the power of the computer and the child's time.

WHEN CHILD MEETS COMPUTER

How early can children start computing? In my experience, children need to be about three years old to operate a keyboard or a joystick and to understand its relationship to a screen. Most three-year-olds can't read, so they need help getting started with programs that have written instructions. There are programs simple enough for preschool children to use alone, once they understand the purpose of the program and the basics of play.

When a child first has a turn with a new computer program, he or she needs a helper. When first receiving instructions, the child needs to be operating the program, not just watching a demonstration or listening in a group. Children need to learn by doing—with computers as with everything else they touch. For this reason, an adult, perhaps a parent volunteer, needs to sit by the computer and work with each child in turn. The adult should be fluent with the program children are using and should be able to encourage children without interrupting their process of discovery. Children need time to figure things out for themselves, but they need help when they get frustrated.

Computers are becoming part of a child's culture—a culture that traditionally has included things like jump rope rhymes and rules for games like hide and seek. As with other modes of play, children teach each other the basics of computer play, even when they are only three years old. Most children would rather play with a friend at the computer instead of working alone. Information is passed from child to child without adult intervention. Children seem to have the innate ability to give each other just the information needed to continue play, whereas adults often give too many details.

If children can teach each other how to play with computers, what is the role of the teacher? We all know that language and thought are very closely intertwined, and that computers can't talk. Oh yes, some computers can generate speech, and even respond to a few words spoken by a child, but that's not the same thing. Only a human being can reach out and touch a child, understand his or her questions, and relate them to real-life experience. The computer can present a few simple concepts, but it takes a human to talk about the child's world.

Ideally, the computer should be the focal point of an interest center in the classroom, not isolated. If children can approach it freely when they are interested, play with it as long as they are challenged, and walk away from it when they want to, they will probably be operating at their learning edge. Teachers and parents may worry that offering computer experience to very young children might tend to push them too early into an academic environment. The playful software that is available now can offer powerful learning that meets children at their own level. If children are free to use or avoid the computer, they are not being pushed.

YOU MAKE THE DIFFERENCE

You, the teacher, can make your students' first experiences with computers lively, warm, and fascinating. Many children today first meet computers in a dry, technically oriented programming class. You can shape children's attitudes toward computers in a positive way, and thus offer a playful, powerful learning experience.

ANN PIESTRUP is chairman and founder of The Learning Company. She has designed award-winning learning software and has directed software development projects with grant funding from Apple Education Foundation, the National Science Foundation, and the National Institute of Education. Dr. Piestrup has conducted research projects in children's reading and language development. She has also taught preschool through graduate school classes.

Dr. Piestrup has spoken at many conferences, has been a guest on national television shows, including the Phil Donahue Show, *and has written many articles and book chapters, as well as telling the story of The Learning Company's work to* Fortune, Time, Scientific American, *and many other magazines and newspapers. She earned her doctoral and master's degrees in educational psychology at the University of California at Berkeley.*

Glossary

Abberant. Deviating from the usual or natural type; abnormal, atypical.

Accommodation. A concept in Piaget's cognitive theory as one of two processes people use to learn and incorporate new information; the person adjusts what is already known to "accommodate" new learning. Children usually will change their way of thinking into a new "schema," once they see that their usual ways do not take new information into account; they then will add new thought patterns to handle the new knowledge.

Accountability. The quality or state of being answerable to someone or of being responsible for explaining exact conditions; schools often must give a specific account of their actions to a funding agency to assure the group that the funds and operation of the school are being handled properly.

Active Listening. A child guidance technique of reflecting back to the speaker what the listener thinks has been said.

Activity Areas. Similar to learning centers and interest areas; areas in a classroom or yard that are designed and arranged for various activities to take place. An early childhood setting will offer several centers, or stations, for children that are based on both children's interests and what the staff hopes for them to learn in class.

Advocate. One who maintains, defends, or pleads the cause of another; in early childhood terms, an advocate is someone who furthers the principles and issues of the field by speaking to others about such issues.

After-School Care. Programs designed to care for children after the regular academic school day.

Age-Level Characteristics. Those features of children's development and behavior that are most common among a given age group.

Androgynous. Having to do with either sex; associated with both the male and female identity, behavior, etc.

Articulation. The manner in which sounds and words are actually spoken.

Assess. To make an evaluation or determine the importance, disposition, or state of something or someone, such as in evaluating a child's skills, a classroom environment, or a teacher's effectiveness.

Assimilation. A concept in Piaget's cognitive theory as one of two processes people use to learn and incorporate new information; the person takes new information and puts it together with what is already known in order to "assimilate" the new information intellectually, such as when a toddler shakes a toy magnet first, as with all other toys, in order to get to know this new object. Children usually first try to put new experiences into the "schema," or categories, they already know and use.

Autonomy. The state of being able to exist and operate independently, of being self-sufficient rather than dependent upon others.

Baby Biographies. One of the first methods of child study, these narratives were written accounts by parents of what their babies did and said, usually in the form of a diary or log.

Back to Basics. A movement of the 1970s and 1980s prompted by a desire for schools to return to teaching the "basic" skills usually associated with academic learning, such as reading, writing, and arithmetic.

Baseline. A picture of the status of a child, teacher, or environment that serves as the basis for evaluation and later comparison.

Basic Needs. Conditions, described by Abraham Maslow and other humanists, that are necessary for growth; these needs, such as physiological conditions and safety and security, are critical for a person's survival.

Behavior Swings. Shifts from one behavior to another, usually by a sharp change in what one is doing; e.g., from highly active to motionless, or from gregarious to shy.

Behavior Theory. A psychological theory developed in the United States in the twentieth century, which states that all important aspects of behavior and people are learned and can be modified or changed by varying external conditions.

Bilingualism. The acquisition of two languages during the first years of life; using or being able to use two languages.

Brainstorming. The process of thinking that involves bringing up as many ideas as possible about a subject, person, event, etc.

Cephalocaudal. In the direction of head (cephalic) to toe (caudal, of the tail or hind part of the body), as in how children develop physically.

Cerebral Palsy. A disorder that is the result of damage to a certain part of the brain (motor cortex); "CP," as it is commonly called, is a nonprogressive disorder (does not get worse as the child grows older); usually movement dysfunction is paired with some intellectual and perceptual impairment.

Child Abuse. Violence in the form of physical maltreatment, abusive language, and sexual harassment or misuse of children.

Child-Centered Approach. The manner of establishing educational experiences that takes into consideration children's ways of perceiving and learning; manner of organizing a classroom, schedule, and teaching methods with an eye toward the child's viewpoint.

Child Neglect. The act or situation of parents'/adults' inattention to a child's basic health needs of adequate food, clothing, shelter, and health care; child neglect may also include not noticing a child or paying enough attention in general.

Church-Related Schools. Educational programs affiliated with a church or religious organization; they may have a direct relationship with the church by including religious education, by employing church members as teachers, or by being housed in a church building and using the facilities for a fee.

Classical Conditioning. The most common and basic category of learning in behavior theory, involving an association between a stimulus and response so that a reflex response (eye-blinking, salivating, etc.) occurs *whenever* a neutral and new stimulus is activated (a bell for a light, food, etc.); conditioned-response experiments conforming to the pattern of Pavlov's experiment, sometimes known as "stimulus substitution."

Cognition. The act or process of knowing, thinking, and perceiving.

Cognitive Confusion. State of being unsure or forgetful about what is already known, such as becoming perplexed about things or facts already learned.

Cognitive Theory. The psychological theory developed by Jean Piaget and others; the theory focuses on thought processes and how they change with age and experience; this point of view contrasts with the stimulus-response aspects of behavior theory.

Compensatory Education. Education designed to supply what is thought to be lacking or missing in children's experiences or ordinary environments.

Competency-Based Assessment. Evaluation in which a teacher is judged or rated in comparison with a predetermined set of skills, or competencies, related to the job.

Comprehensive. Inclusive, covering completely, such as a program for children that concerns itself with the physical, intellectual, social, emotional, creative, and health needs of the children.

Continuing Education. The commitment of teachers to learning new approaches and ideas and to continuing to challenge themselves to higher levels of learning and competence.

Continuum. Something that is continuous; an uninterrupted, ordered sequence.

Cultural Pluralism. A state or society in which members of diverse ethnic, racial, or cultural groups maintain participation in and development of their traditional culture within the common society.

Custodial. Those tasks relating to guardianship of a child's basic needs for food, clothing, and shelter; they include providing for eating, dressing, toileting, resting, and appropriate protection from physical hardships such as weather, danger, etc.

Day Care Center. A place for care of children for a large portion of their waking day; includes basic care-taking activities of eating, dressing, resting, toileting, as well as playing/learning time.

Decoding. Converting from code into ordinary language; in terms of language development, decoding is the process of making sense out of printed letters or words.

Developmental Tasks. Those functions or work to be done by children at a particular point in their development.

Discipline. Ability to follow an example or to follow rules; the development of self-control or control in general, such as by imposing order on a group. In early childhood terms, discipline means everything adults do and say to influence children's behavior.

Disequilibrium. Loss of balance, or a period of change.

Divergent Thinking. The processes of thought and perception that involve taking a line of thought or action different from what is the norm or common; finding ideas that branch out rather than converge and center on one answer.

Down's Syndrome. A genetic abnormality that results in mongolism, one of the most common and easily identified forms of mental retardation.

Dramatic Play. Also known as imaginative play, this is a common form of spontaneous play in which children use their imagination and fantasy as part of the setting and activity.

Early Childhood Education. Education in the early years of life; the field of study that deals mainly with the learning and experiences of children from infancy through the primary years (up to approximately eight years of age).

Eclectic. Choosing what appears to be best in various doctrines, methods, styles; comprised of elements drawn from various sources.

Educaring. A concept of teaching as both educating and care giving; coined by Magda Gerber in referring to people working with infants and toddlers.

Elaboration. The act of expanding language; developing language by building complex structures from simple ones and adding details.

Emotional Framework. The basic "feeling" structure of a classroom that determines the tone and underlying sensibilities that affect how people feel and behave while in class.

Employer-Sponsored Child Care. Child care supported in some way by the parents' employers. Support may be financial (as an employee benefit or subsidy) or physical (offering on-site care).

Environment. All those conditions that affect children's surroundings and the people in them; the physical, interpersonal, and temporal aspects of an early childhood setting.

Environmental. Forces that are not innate or hereditary aspects of development; in early childhood terms, environmental aspects of growth are all those influences of physical conditions, interpersonal relationships, and world experiences that interact with a person to change the way he or she behaves, feels, and lives.

Ethics. A theory or system of moral principles and standards; what is "right and wrong"; one's values; the principles of conduct governing both an individual teacher and the teaching profession.

Ethnocentric. Having one's race as a central interest, or regarding one's race or cultural group as superior to others.

Expressive Language. Those aspects of language development and skill that deal with expression: pronunciation, vocabulary, and grammar, as well as speaking and articulation.

Extrinsic. Originating from or on the outside; external, not derived from one's essential nature.

Family Day Care. Care for children in a small, home-like setting; usually six or fewer children in a family residence.

Feedback Loop. In terms of evaluation, feedback loop is used to describe the process whereby an evaluator gives information to a teacher, who in turn uses this information to improve teaching skills.

Fine Motor. Having to do with the smaller muscles of the body and the extremities, such as those in the fingers, toes, and face.

Formal Tests. Evaluation instruments that are administered in a conventional, "testlike" atmosphere for use with groups of children, and may or may not be developed commercially.

Genes. The biological elements that transmit hereditary characteristics.

Gifted Children. Children who have unusually high intelligence, as characterized by: learning to read spontaneously; being able to solve problems and communicate at a level far advanced from their chronological age; excellent memory; extensive vocabulary; and unusual approaches to ideas, tasks, people.

Gross Motor. Having to do with the entire body or the large muscles of the body, such as the legs, arms, and trunk.

Growth Needs. Conditions, as described by Abraham Maslow and other humanists, that are important to a person's well-being; these needs, such as love and belonging, self-esteem and respect of others, playfulness, truth, beauty, etc., while not critical to a person's survival, are necessary for growth.

Holistic. A viewpoint that takes into account several conceptions of a child or situation to form a wider, more rounded description; in early childhood terms, this view includes a child's history, present status, relationships with others, and the interrelationships of development to arrive at a picture of the child; in medicine, this view includes dealing with a person's mental and emotional state, relationships, etc., as well as body signs.

Humanist Theory. The psychological theory of Abraham Maslow and others; it involves principles of motivation and wellness, centering on people's needs, goals, and successes.

Hypothesis. A tentative theory or assumption made in order to draw inferences or test conclusions; an interpretation of a practical situation that is then taken as the ground for action.

Inadequacy. The state of being or feeling insufficient, of not being or having "enough"; if feeling discouraged, children will display their feelings of inadequacy by misbehaving.

Individualized Curriculum. A course of study developed and tailored to meet the needs and interests of an individual, rather than those of a group without regard for the individual child.

Inference. A conclusion reached by reasoning from evidence or after gathering information, whether direct or indirect.

Informal Assessment. Evaluation based on methods and instruments that are not administered formally, as in paper-and-pencil tests, but rather are done while the subjects are at work or play in their natural environments.

Initiative. An introductory step; in early childhood terms, the energy, capacity, and will to begin taking action.

Integrated Curriculum. A set of courses designed to form a whole; coordination of the various areas of study, making for continuous and harmonious learning.

Integrated Day. A school schedule with no prescribed time periods for subject matter, but rather an environment organized around various interest centers among which the children choose in organizing their own learning experiences.

Integrated Development. Growth that occurs in a continuous, interrelated manner; a child's progress as a whole, rather than in separate areas.

Interdependence. Dependence on one another, as in the relationship between teachers' experience in the areas of discipline and their competence at knowing and using appropriate language for discipline.

Interdisciplinary Approach. A method of teaching/learning that draws from sources in more than one field of study; e.g., a course in education that uses background from the fields of medicine, psychology, and social work as well as education itself.

Interest Areas. Similar to learning centers and activity areas; one way to design physical space in a classroom or yard, dividing the space into separate centers among which children move about, rather than assigning them desks.

Interpersonal. Relating to, or involving relationships with, other people; those parts of the environment that have to do with the people in a school setting.

Intervene. To enter into a situation between two or more persons or between a person and an object; to interpose oneself into another's affairs, such as when teachers enter into children's interactions when their behavior calls for some action on the part of an adult.

Intrinsic. Belonging to the essential nature of or originating from within a person or body, such as intrinsic motivation, whereby one needs no external reward in order to do something.

Job Burnout. Exhaustion and stress from one's job, characterized by a wearing down of body and attitude.

Kindergarten. A school or class for children four to six years old; in the United States, kindergarten is either the first year of formal, public school or the year of schooling before first grade.

Laboratory Schools. Educational settings whose purposes include experimental study; schools for testing and analysis of educational and/or psychological theory and practice, with an opportunity for experimentation, observation, and practice.

Latchkey Children. Children who are left home after school unattended or supervised by an adult; children who are responsible after school for themselves and perhaps younger siblings while their parents/guardians are not at home, usually working; such children have a "latchkey" (housekey) to let themselves into an empty home.

Laterality. Of or relating to the side, as in children having an awareness of what is situated on, directed toward, or coming from either side of themselves.

Learning Centers. Similar to interest areas and activity areas; hubs or areas in a classroom designed to promote learning; the classroom is arranged in discrete areas for activity, and children move from one area to another rather than stay at an assigned desk or seat.

Limits. The boundaries of acceptable behavior beyond which actions are considered misbehavior and unacceptable conduct; the absolute controls an adult puts on children's behavior.

Linchpin. Something that serves to hold together the elements of a situation.

Mainstreaming. The process of integrating handicapped children into classrooms with the nonhandicapped.

Maturation. The process of growth whereby a body matures regardless of, and relatively independent of, intervention such as exercise, experience, or environment.

Maturation Theory. A set of ideas based on the notion that the sequence of behavior and the emergence of personal characteristics develop more through predetermined growth processes than through learning and interaction with the environment; the theory of growth and development proposed and supported by Dr. Arnold Gesell and associates.

Merit Pay. A system for teachers that gives pay bonuses for excellent teaching.

Misbehavior. Improper behavior or conduct.

Modeling. A part of behavior theory, modeling is a way of learning social behavior that involves observing a model (either real, filmed, or animated) and mimicking its behavior, thus acquiring new behavior.

Negative Reinforcement. Response to a behavior that decreases the likelihood of the behavior recurring; for instance, a teacher's glare might stop a child from whispering at group time, and from then on, the anticipation of such an angry look could reinforce not whispering in the future.

Networking. Making connections with others who can further career and professional opportunities.

Nonpunitive. Methods that do not involve or aim at punishment; for instance, letting a child be hungry later when he refuses to eat at snack time is a nonpunitive method of enforcing the need to snack with the group; hunger is a natural and logical consequence of the child's behavior, rather than a punishment meted out by the teacher (such as scolding or threatening).

Norm. An average or general standard of development or achievement, usually derived from the average or median of a large group; a pattern or trait taken to be typical of the behavior, skills, or interests of a group.

Objectivity. The quality or state of being able to see what is real and realistic, as distinguished from subjective and personal opinion or bias.

Open-ended. Activities or statements that allow a variety of responses, as opposed to those that allow only one response; anything organized to allow for variation.

Open School. A style of education, developed in progressive American schools and in the British infant schools, that is organized to encourage freedom of choice and that does not use predetermined roles and structure as the basis of education; an educational setting whose ultimate goal and base for curriculum is the development of the individual child, rather than of programmed academic experiences.

Operant Conditioning. A category of learning in behavior theory that involves a relation between a stimulus and response. The response is learned, rather than reflexive, and is gradually and carefully developed through reinforcement of the desired behavior as it occurs in response to the stimulus; behavior leading to a reward.

Parent Cooperative. An educational setting organized by parents for their young children, often with parental control and/or support in the operation of the program itself.

Pediatrician. A medical specialist in pediatrics, the branch of medicine dealing with children, their development, care, and diseases.

Peer Interactions. Associations with people of the same age group or with those one considers equals.

Perceptual–Motor Development. The growth of a person's ability to move (motor) and perceive (perceptual) together; perceptual–motor activity involves the body and the mind together, to coordinate movement.

Performance-Based Assessment. Evaluation based on observable, specific information on what a teacher actually does (performance while on the job).

Philosophy. Concepts expressing one's fundamental beliefs; in early childhood educational terms, the beliefs, ideas, and attitudes of our profession.

Phobia. A strong, exaggerated, and illogical fear of an object or class of things, people, etc.; one of several reactions children often have to divorce.

Phonemes. Language sounds; the smallest units of meaningful speech; two examples of phonemes are /a/ (as in hat) and /p/ (as in sip).

Positive Reinforcement. A response to a behavior that increases the likelihood of the behavior being repeated or increased; for instance, if a child gets attention and praise for crawling, it is likely that the crawling will increase—thus, the attention and praise were positive reinforcement for crawling.

Practice Teaching. The period of "internship" that students experience when working in a classroom with supervision, as opposed to having a role as a regular working staff member.

Precedent. Something done or said that serves as an example or rule to authorize or justify other acts of the same or similar kind; an earlier occurrence of something similar.

Precursor. What precedes and indicates the approach of another; predecessor or forerunner.

Prejudices. Ideas and attitudes that are already formed about other people, situations, ideas, etc., before hearing or experiencing full or sufficient information; in teaching terms, those attitudes or biases that may be based less on mature thought and reasoning than on incomplete or nonexistent personal experiences.

Prepared Environment. The physical and interpersonal surroundings of an educational setting that are planned and arranged in advance with the group of children in mind.

Prerequisite. Something necessary or essential to carrying out an objective or performing an activity; when early childhood teachers determine what skills children will need in order to successfully engage in an activity, they are clarifying the prerequisites for that activity.

Professional. One engaged and participating in a profession and accepting the technical and ethical standards of that profession; in early childhood terms, one who has accumulated methods, course work, and teaching experience with young children along with attitudes of competency, flexibility, and continual learning.

Professional Organizations. Those associations developed for the purpose of extending knowledge and teaching/learning opportunities in the field of education.

Proximal to Distal. In the direction from the center of the body (proximal) toward the outer part (distal, far from the center), as in the way children's bodies develop.

Psychodynamic Theory. The psychological theory of Dr. Sigmund Freud and others; it asserts that the individual develops a basic personality core in childhood and that responses stem from personality organization and emotional problems as a result of environmental experiences.

Psychosocial. Those psychological issues that deal with how people relate to others, and the problems that arise on a social level; a modification by Erikson of the psychodynamic theories of Freud with attention to social and environmental problems of life.

Receptive Language. Those aspects of language development and skill that deal with the ability to receive messages: listening, understanding, and responding.

Reinforcers. Rewards in response to a specific behavior, thus increasing the likelihood of that behavior recurring; reinforcers may be either social (praise) or nonsocial (food) in nature, and may or may not be deliberately controlled.

Routines. Regular procedures; habitual, repeated or regular parts of the school day; in early childhood programs, routines are those parts of the program schedule that remain constant, such as indoor time followed by cleanup and snack, regardless of what activities are being offered within those time slots.

Running Record. The narrative form of recording behavior; this kind of descriptive record of one's observations involves writing down all behavior as it occurs.

Self-Actualization. The set of principles set forth by Abraham Maslow for a person's wellness or ability to be the most that a person can be; the state of being that results from having met all the basic and growth needs.

Self-Awareness. An awareness of one's own personality or individuality; in teaching terms, an ability to understand one's self and assess personal strengths and weaknesses.

Self-Concept. A person's view and opinion of self; in young children, the concept of self develops as they interact with the environment (objects, people, etc.); self-concept can be inferred in how children carry themselves, approach situations, use expressive materials such as art, etc.

Self-Correcting. Materials or experiences that are built or arranged so that the person using them can act automatically to correct errors, without needing another person to check or point out mistakes.

Self-Esteem. The value we place upon ourselves; how much we like or dislike who we are; self-respect.

Self-Help. The act of helping or providing for one-self without dependence upon others; in early childhood terms, activities that a child can do alone, without adult assistance.

Sensory. Having to do with the senses or sensation, as in an awareness of the world as it looks, sounds, feels, smells, tastes.

Separation Process. The act and procedure that occurs when parents leave a child at school.

Sequential Learning. Learning based on a method of consecutive steps; an arrangement of concepts or ideas in a succession of related steps so that what is learned results in continuous development.

Seriation. The process of sequencing from beginning to end or in a particular series or succession.

Sex-Role Stereotyping. A standardized mental picture or set of attitudes that represents an over-simplified opinion of people's abilities or behavior according to their sex; overgeneralizing a person's skills or behavior based upon an inequitable standard of sex differences.

Social Cognition. The application of thinking to personal and social behavior; giving meaning to social experience.

Socialization. The process of learning the skills, appropriate behaviors, and expectations of being part of a group, particularly society at large.

Social Mores. Standards of conduct and behavior that are determined by society, as opposed to those established by family or personal preference.

Social Skills. Strategies children learn to enable them to respond appropriately in many environments.

Spatial. Having to do with the nature of space, as in an awareness of the space around a person's body.

Special-Needs Children. Children whose development and/or behavior require help or intervention beyond the scope of the ordinary classroom or adult interactions.

Specific Development. Area of a person's growth and maturation that can be defined distinctly, such as physical, social, emotional, intellectual, and creative growth.

Spontaneous Play. The unplanned, self-selected activity in which a child freely participates.

Stewardship. Responsibility for judicious management of resources; the obligation assumed by an individual or agency to act responsibly in the use of both personal and natural resources.

Stimulus-Response. The kind of psychological learning, first characterized in behavior theory, that makes a connection between a response and a stimulus; that is, the kind of learning that takes place when pairing something that rouses or incites an activity with the activity itself in such a way that the stimulus (such as a bell) will trigger a response (such as salivating).

Support System. A network of people who support each other in their work and advancement.

Surrogate. Substitute, such as a teacher acting in the place of the parent, a school toy taking the place of a blanket from home, a thumb taking the place of a pacifier.

Tactile. Perceptible or able to be learned through the sense of touch.

Teaching Objectives. A set of goals teachers set for themselves as they plan activities for children; these goals remind teachers what they will do in order to help children learn.

Temporal. Having to do with time and time sequence; in the early childhood setting, refers to scheduling and how time is sequenced and spent, both at home and in school.

Traditional Nursery School. The core of early childhood educational theory and practice; program designed for children aged two-and-one-half to five years of age, which may be part- or all-day programs.

Transitions. Changes from one state or activity to another; in early childhood terms, transitions are those times of change in the daily schedule (whether planned or not), such as from being with a parent to being alone in school, from playing with one toy to choosing another, from being outside to inside, etc.

Upward Evaluation. Assessment procedure in which employees evaluate their superiors.

Vicariously. Experienced or realized through the imagination or the participation of another, rather than from doing it oneself, as in learning vicariously about something by listening to a story.

Volatile. Easily aroused; tending to erupt into violent action or explosive speech or behavior.

Word Pictures. Descriptions of children that depict, in words, norms of development; in this text, these are age-level charts that describe common behaviors and characteristics, particularly those that have implications for teaching children (in groups, for curriculum planning, with discipline and guidance).

Appendix A

Word Pictures of the Six-, Seven-, and Eight-Year-Old

Physical/Motor Development
Six-, Seven-, and Eight-Year-Old

- Growth relatively slow.
- Bones growing and solidifying.
- Permanent teeth appearing to replace primary teeth.
- Hungry at short intervals; insatiable taste for sweets; eats especially after school.
- Still enjoys active play—high, boisterous activity, stunts.
- Likes to roughhouse but may not know when to stop and may get hurt.
- Susceptible to fatigue.
- Visual acuity reaches normal.
- Still susceptible to respiratory and communicable diseases.

Language Growth
Six-, Seven-, and Eight-Year-Old

- Enjoys putting language skills to paper.
- Talks *with* adults rather than *to* them.
- Language skills can be very individual; from quite developed to much less so.
- Acquisition of new words begins to taper off a bit toward end of early childhood; focus now on use of concepts.
- Ability to learn new language and concepts still available.

- If English as a second language has been acquired as a preschooler, bilingual capacities nearly complete.

Socio-Emotional Development
Six-Year-Old:

Six is an active, outgoing age in which children are basically self-centered. Own activities and pleasures take precedence over everything else. They have a certain charm because they are not vain and are proud of what they accomplish. Characteristics:

- Wants things done at once and gets upset if adult doesn't drop everything and do their bidding.
- Needs to be the center of things; to be first and to win.
- Seldom modest; assertive, even bossy.
- Prefers children of own age to siblings.
- Pairs up and has "best friend"; will ostracize a third.
- Friendships are erratic; pairs change frequently.
- Movement toward same-sex friends has already begun.
- Begins to differentiate self by putting self in opposition to mother; father often favored parent.

Seven-Year-Old:

Seven is a more serious, less talkative time; children are often more sensitive to how other people react to them. At home they can become more tractable and polite, eager to take on responsibility.

Yet, they can be complaining and pensive. They are often serious students and concerned about the success of their performance.

- Heightened sensitivity to the reactions of others; shame is a common emotion.
- May often leave the scene rather than put self in a position of being the object of criticism or disapproval.
- Often complains about having been treated unfairly and being disliked. (Not surprising, since they are being evaluated constantly by teachers, little league/soccer coaches, and peers.)
- Likes to know where things begin and end and how far you are supposed to go.
- Shows a politeness and consideration for adults.
- Has a good time with friends but also enjoys solitary activities.

Eight-Year-Old:
　　Eights are outgoing, curious, extremely social. Can be judgmental and critical of themselves and others, and demanding in efforts to get more information about themselves. Are becoming more mature in relation to adults. Friends become extremely important at this age and the prime reason for interest and good attendance in school.

- Regaining self-confidence; greater self-awareness; curious about self and others.
- Interactions with adults more productive; can be attentive and responsive to adult communications.
- Particularly concerned about how parents feel about them; discovery that parents aren't perfect and make mistakes causes some ambivalence that makes the relationships complex.
- Noticeable differences between the sexes. Attitude toward opposite sex is one of attraction and hostility—a pattern that will reemerge with adolescence.
- Starts to feel the impact of social status, clothing, appearance differences.

- Usually friendly and cooperative in social relations, though perhaps not as helpful around home as before.
- Wants mature jobs, adultlike activities.
- Friendships are closer and more exacting than before. Reason for relationship may shift from common activities to personality characteristics.
- Less concerned with teacher; more concerned with the group. May gossip among themselves and pass notes.
- Constantly evaluating self; may criticize own art work, sensitive to being a slow reader.

Intellectual Growth
Six-Year-Old:

- Likes to work, yet often does so in spurts and doesn't show persistence.
- Learns a lot, especially in reading and arithmetic.
- Tends to be a know-it-all, free with opinions and advice.
- Will bring home evidence of good schoolwork.

Seven-Year-Old:

- Relatively quiet after the sixes; assimilating wealth of new experiences.
- Consolidating reasoning abilities; sifts and sorts information.
- Where sixes were physical and motor, sevens are increasingly mental; can conceptualize and mentally visualize situations rather than having to act them out.
- Can listen instead of trying to do all the talking.
- Asks for responsibilities, including around the house.
- More persistent and careful in work habits.

Eight-Year-Old:

- Enormous curiosity: nature, man-made, people; eager to observe adult interactions.

- Likes to see new things and go new places; looks forward to vacations and outings away from home.

- Judgmental attitude, in that they appraise what happens to them and the "why" of an event.

- Has gone beyond the here-and-now stage and is interested in other times, children from other countries; begins to be excited about historical events and people.

====== **NOTE** ======

The above word pictures were adapted from the following texts: Hartley, Ruth E., and Robert M. Goldenson. *The Complete Book of Children's Play.* New York: Thomas Y. Crowell Co., 1963; Elkind, David. *A Sympathetic Understanding of the Child: Birth to Sixteen.* Boston: Allyn and Bacon, 1978.

Appendix B
Four Teaching Leadership Styles

Style	Characteristics	Effect on Curriculum Planning	Effect on Teaching Tasks	Effect on Parent/Child Problem Management	Effect on Handling Difficult Situations	Effect on Team Morale	Effect on Staff Training
Autocratic Leadership	Leader makes all decisions, usually without input from team members	Leader does it all	Leader assigns duties on a rotating basis	Leader handles all problems	Team brings problems to leader to solve	Leader has responsibility for maintaining morale	Leader teaches all members how to teach properly
Authoritarian Leadership	Leader allows some ideas from team members, but still makes all major decisions	Leader has own plans, but will vary them if team contributes	Leader assigns duties after considering team members' preferences	Leader usually handles most problems; team members can ask about them	Leader observes team members; takes over when thinks it is needed	Mainly the responsibility of the leader; might bring up for discussion with other team members	Leader shows all team members, giving feedback about what works
Democratic Leadership	Leader encourages full involvement of other team members, both in contributing ideas and in decision making; final approval rests with leader, but leader tries to get the consensus of the group	Leader asks team members for curriculum ideas	Leader invites team members to state preferences and allows them to divide tasks among themselves	Team asks questions; leader handles problems when they arise	Team solves difficulties; leader steps in only if asked	Team is partly responsible for maintaining morale; leader encourages team to discuss	Leader encourages by asking members to evaluate themselves
Permissive Leadership	All team members, including the leader, have equal power to make decisions	All members plan their own curriculum activities	Whoever wants a task assumes responsibility for it	Each team member deals with issues as they arise	Leader is ready to support team, but does not step in	Leader lets morale take care of itself	Team does most on its own; no special guidance is offered by leader

Appendix C
Katz' Teachers' Developmental Stages

A beginning teacher moves from one stage to the next on the way to maturity. At each stage, there are unique issues, concerns, and needs.

Stage	Name	Time Span	Teacher Concerns	Teacher Needs
I	Survival	First year or two of teaching	Questions ability to do this daily; feels inadequate, ill-prepared	Support, guidance, comfort from someone on-site; skill instruction
II	Consolidation	End of first year into third	Begins to focus on individual children and specific problem behaviors	Continued on-site support and consultation; open to other professional resources in related fields
III	Renewal	Third or fourth year	Tired of doing same old thing; ready to explore new developments in the field	Likes to meet other teachers; goes to conferences; joins professional organizations
IV	Maturity	Third to fifth year on	Has come to terms with self as teacher; searches for insight, perspective	Might work on advanced degree; reads widely; participates in teacher conferences

Adapted from Katz, Lilian G., *Talks with Teachers*, Washington, D.C.: National Association for the Education of Young Children, 1977, pp. 7–13.

Appendix D
An Initial Code of Ethics for Early Childhood Educators

<hr>

PREAMBLE

As an educator of young children in their years of greatest vulnerability, I, to the best of intent and ability, shall devote myself to the following commitments and act to support them.

FOR THE CHILD

I shall accord the respect due each child as a human being from birth on.

I shall recognize the unique potentials to be fulfilled within each child.

I shall provide access to differing opinions and views inherent in every person, subject, or thing encountered as the child grows.

I shall recognize the child's right to ask questions about the unknowns that exist in the present so the answers (which may be within the child's capacity to discover) may be forthcoming eventually.

I shall protect and extend the child's physical well-being, emotional stability, mental capacities, and social acceptability.

From Katz, Lilian G., and Ward, Evangeline H., *Ethical Behavior in Early Childhood Education*, Washington, D.C.: National Association for the Education of Young Children, pp. 20–21. Reprinted by permission from The National Association for the Education of Young Children. © 1984 by the National Association for the Education of Young Children, 1834 Connecticut Ave., N.W., Washington, DC 20009.

FOR THE PARENTS AND FAMILY MEMBERS

I shall accord each child's parents and family members respect for the responsibilities they carry.

By no deliberate action on my part will the child be held accountable for the incidental meeting of his or her parents and the attendant lodging of the child's destiny with relatives and siblings.

Recognizing the continuing nature of familial strength as support for the growing child, I shall maintain objectivity with regard to what I perceive as family weaknesses.

Maintaining family value systems and pride in cultural-ethnic choices or variations will supersede any attempts I might inadvertently or otherwise make to impose my values.

Because advocacy on behalf of children always requires that someone cares about or is strongly motivated by a sense of fairness and intervenes on behalf of children in relation to those services and institutions that impinge on their lives, I shall support family strength.

FOR MYSELF AND THE EARLY CHILDHOOD PROFESSION

Admitting my biases is the first evidence of my willingness to become a conscious professional.

Knowing my capacity to continue to learn throughout life, I shall vigorously pursue knowledge about contemporary developments in early education by informal and formal means.

My role with young children demands an awareness of new knowledge that emerges from varied disciplines and the responsibility to use such knowledge.

Recognizing the limitation I bring to knowing intimately the ethical-cultural value systems of the multicultural American way of life, I shall actively seek the understanding and acceptance of the chosen ways of others to assist them educationally in meeting each child's needs for his or her unknown future impact on society.

Working with other adults and parents to maximize my strengths and theirs, both personally and professionally, I shall provide a model to demonstrate to young children how adults can create an improved way of living and learning through planned cooperation.

The encouragement of language development with young children will never exceed the boundaries of propriety or violate the confidence and trust of a child or that child's family.

I shall share my professional skills, information, and talents to enhance early education for young children wherever they are.

I shall cooperate with other persons and organizations to promote programs for children and families that improve their opportunities to utilize and enhance their uniqueness and strength.

I shall ensure that individually different styles of learning are meshed compatibly with individually different styles of teaching to help all people grow and learn well—this applies to adults learning to be teachers as well as to children.

Appendix E

Child Abuse Code

Following are excerpts from the California Penal Code regarding the responsibilities of child care personnel in reporting suspected child abuse.

REPORTING CHILD ABUSE

While *everyone* should report suspected child abuse and neglect, Article 2.5 of the Penal Code provides that it is a crime for certain professionals and laypersons who have a special working relationship or contact with children *not* to report suspected abuse to the proper authorities. Following are excerpts and summaries of sections from this article regarding child abuse reporting:

> . . . any child care custodian, medical practitioner, nonmedical practitioner, or employee of a child protective agency who has knowledge of or observes a child in his or her professional capacity or within the scope of his or her employment whom he or she knows or reasonably suspects has been the victim of child abuse shall report the known or suspected instance of child abuse to a child protective agency immediately or as soon as practically possible by telephone and shall prepare and send a written report thereof within 36 hours of receiving the information concerning the incident. For the purposes of this article, 'reasonable suspicion' means that it is objectively reasonable for a person to entertain such a suspicion, based upon facts that could cause a reasonable person in a like position, drawing when appropriate on his or her training and experience, to suspect child abuse. (Penal Code Section 11166.)

Failure to report by telephone and in writing within 36 hours is a misdemeanor punishable by six months in jail or a $500 fine, or both. (For those required to report who do not do so, there may also be civil liabilities.) Basically, this penalty ensures that those required to do so will report all suspected incidents of child abuse immediately to a child protective agency (the local police authority, sheriff's department, juvenile probation department or the county welfare department).

Those required to report should be aware that mere reporting does not always mean that a civil or criminal proceeding will be initiated. However, all reports are investigated.

Those agencies to whom reports are made are obligated to follow procedures in the reporting law which ensure that all reports of suspected abuse or severe neglect reach the Department of Justice statewide central index.

It is important to note that reporting under the law is an *individual* statutory responsibility, and that no one should in any way interfere with an individual's legal obligation to report. Additionally, no individual required to report is relieved of his or her obligation by depending on another person or a supervisor to report the suspected incident.

Those professionals required to report by Penal Code Sections 11165 and 11166 are:

> *"Child care custodian"* means a teacher, administrative officer, supervisor of child welfare and

From *Child Abuse Prevention Handbook*, Sacramento, Calif.: Office of the Attorney General, State of California, 1983, pp. 19–20.

attendance, or certificated pupil personnel employee of any public or private school; an administrator of a public or private day camp; a licensed day care worker; an administrator of a community care facility licensed to care for children; headstart teacher; a licensing worker or licensing evaluator; public assistance worker; employee of a child care institution including, but not limited to, foster parents, group home personnel and personnel of residential care facilities; a social worker or a probation officer, as well as others.

Employees of community service programs or organizations for abused or neglected children under contract or agreement with a county to provide shelter, care or counseling are also considered "child care custodians." (Welfare and Institutions Code Section 307.5.)

Persons required to report are not liable either in civil damages or for criminal prosecution as a result of making a report. Other persons are not liable either civilly or criminally, unless it can be proven that a false report was made and that the person knew that the report was false. (Penal Code Section 11172.)

When making the telephone report, the following information is to be provided:

name of the child;
whereabouts of the child;
character and extent of injuries and/or molestation, and any other information which led person to suspect child abuse;
age of child; and
address of the child and parents.

WHAT HAPPENS TO THE REPORTS?

Reports are investigated by either the local law enforcement agency or by the county children's protective services agency assigned to handle dependency cases (the welfare department or juvenile probation department). If the investigation reveals evidence of criminal child abuse, the local law enforcement agency has the authority to: take the child into protective custody, file criminal charges against the parent(s) or responsible parties and/or to refer the case to probation, welfare or another service agency (counseling, church, etc.). Ideally, this decision is made after consultation with representatives from other disciplines.

Appendix F

Computer Software: What to Look For

Too many programs available for young children offer only a thin veneer of learning over a slow video game. Of the thousands of programs available, very few were designed by people who understand child development. In evaluating a program to use in your classroom, consider these points:

- Does the program present basic concepts and encourage children to learn basic skills, or does it merely recite a few facts and ask children to repeat them?

- Is the child continually active, or is the computer having all the fun? Some programs display animated graphics that are appealing, but the child is passive, watching the show. Better programs are more interactive.

- Is there a sequence to the program, and enough depth to hold a child's interest? Are difficult topics presented from several perspectives to assure understanding?

- Is the program open-ended, encouraging exploration and invention, or are there only "right" and "wrong" answers? Does the program use a rigid, narrow path that traps the child, or can he or she move freely from one activity to another?

- Is the program internally consistent, easy to use, and intuitive, so that it is fun to use? Many public-domain programs are not designed for easy use. Unfortunately, that is also true of many commercial programs.

How can you know whether a program is worthwhile before you buy it? Try to preview the program, if possible, in a store or resource center. Look for endorsement of the program by the National Educational Association or other groups of educators. Read reviews in magazines like *Family Computing, Popular Computing,* and *Electronic Learning.* Ask other teachers and librarians whose judgment you trust.

Courtesy of Ann Piestrup, The Learning Center, Menlo Park, California.

Index